Co/y 1

23

23

TECHNICAL TRAINING

T15/Co

International
Hospitality Management

International Hospitality Management

Edited by

Richard Teare

and

Michael Olsen

John Wiley & Sons, Inc.
New York · Chichester · Brisbane · Toronto · Singapore

PITMAN PUBLISHING
128 Long Acre, London WC2E 9AN

A Division of Longman Group UK Limited

Published in the United States, Canada, and the Philippines by
JOHN WILEY & SONS, Inc.,
605 Third Avenue, New York, NY 10158

First published in 1992

British Library Cataloguing in Publication Data

A CIP catalogue record for this book can be obtained
from the British Library.

ISBN 0 273 03797 8

Library of Congress Cataloguing in Publication Data
International hospitality management : corporate strategy in practice
/ Richard Teare and Michael D. Olsen, editors.
    p.cm
    ISBN 0-471-57099-0 (Cloth)
    1. Hospitality industry—Management.   I. Teare, Richard.
II. Olsen, Michael D.
TX911.3.M27I54   1992
647.94'068'4—dc20   92-993
                                                            CIP

Typeset, printed and bound in Great Britain.

Contents

Part 4 Corporate systems and analysis

Contributors

Editors

Richard Teare, B.Sc. (Hons), Ph.D., MHCIMA, Cert. Ed.
Richard Teare is Professor and Associate Head of the Department of Food, Hospitality and Retail Management, Bournemouth Polytechnic, and a non-executive director of the National Society for Quality through Teamwork, UK. He is Editor of the *International Journal of Contemporary Hospitality Management* and has edited and contributed to three research-based textbooks on strategic aspects of hospitality management and marketing. He received his Ph.D. in Business Administration from the City University Business School, London, and has held management positions with both national and international hotel companies.

Michael D. Olsen, BA, MBA, Ph.D.
Michael D. Olsen is Professor and Head of the Department of Hotel, Restaurant and Institutional Management at Virginia Polytechnic Institute and State University, USA, where he received his Ph.D. He currently serves as Associate Editor of the *International Journal of Hospitality Management*. His international experience includes service as a Visiting Professor in Australia, China, Finland, France, Hong Kong, Switzerland, the Netherlands, and the United Kingdom. He is the Founding President of the International Academy of Hospitality Research and also President of Michael D. Olsen and Associates.

Contributors

Debra Adams is Senior Lecturer in Accounting in the Department of Food, Hospitality, and Retail Management at Bournemouth Polytechnic, UK. A graduate of Bournemouth Polytechnic, she trained in Accounting with Forte Hotels, holding management accounting positions in the hotels division and in the Ring and Brymer specialist catering division. Her main research interests are in the areas of business analysis and information systems.

A. John Basch is Assistant Professor and Director of the Undergraduate Program in Hospitality Management at Bond University, in Australia. A graduate of the University of Surrey, he received his MBA from the University of Queensland and is currently completing his Ph.D. at Bond University. His research interests focus on problem recognition and strategy formulation in service industries.

Celeste Bottorff is Director, Strategic Planning, Holiday Inn Worldwide, with responsibility for tracking strategic hotel market trends worldwide and leading the strategy formulation process. She has ten years of experience in developing strategies as a consultant with McKinsey & Co., Inc. and with the Fountain Division of Coca-Cola, USA. She has a B.S. in Physics from Purdue University and an MBA from the Darden School at the University of Virginia.

Andrew Bould directed sales teams at Grand Metropolitan and Bass before joining Ladbroke in 1984. He was appointed as Hilton International's Senior Vice President (Sales and Marketing) in 1991, having previously held the position of Vice President (Sales and Marketing) for Europe, Africa, and West Asia.

John T. Bowen is currently Associate Professor of Hospitality Management at Bond University, Australia. He received his Ph.D. from Texas A&M University, and his research interests include business culture, customer satisfaction, service quality and pricing. He has extensive hospitality management experience at unit and corporate level and has taught hospitality and services marketing courses at universities in Europe, North America, Asia, and Australia.

Geoffrey B. Breeze has held a variety of marketing positions with multinational companies, working in more than thirty countries worldwide. Between 1980 and 1985 he was a member of the international management team at Avis Rent-A-Car, from 1983 directing all international marketing operations from New York. He was appointed Vice President (Corporate Marketing) Hilton International in 1988 with responsibility for the company's worldwide marketing activities.

Bernd Chorengel graduated from Hotel School in Germany and joined Hyatt in 1969, rising through various Assistant then General Management positions to Area Vice President roles in Asia-Pacific, Europe, Africa, and the Middle East. He became Executive Vice President in 1982 and President and Chief Executive of Hyatt International Corporation in 1983.

Simon Crawford-Welch received his Ph.D. with a major in strategic management from Virginia Polytechnic Institute and State University. He is currently Assistant Professor of Marketing and Research at the William F. Harrah College of Hotel Administration, University of Nevada at Las Vegas, and Director of Marketing and Research, Lexes Enterprises Inc., USA. He is also Editor of the *Journal of Restaurant and Foodservice Marketing*.

Bonnie M. Farber is Associate Professor at the College of Business, San José State University, USA, and Regional Editor (Americas) of the *International Journal of Contemporary Hospitality Management*. She spent five years as Co-ordinator of Tourism and Hospitality Training Centers for the governments of Puerto Rico and Venezuela. Her Ph.D. from the School of Hotel

Administration, Cornell University, focused on organizational theory applied to the hotel industry.

The Hon. Rocco Forte is a graduate of Oxford University, UK, and a qualified accountant. He is Chief Executive of Forte PLC, one of the world's leading multinational hospitality firms. He was appointed to the main board of Forte PLC in 1973 and became Chief Executive in 1983. He is a board member of the British Tourist Authority and a visiting Professor of the Universities of Strathclyde and Surrey, UK.

Paul R. Gamble, Ph.D., is Professor and Dean of the Faculty of Human Studies and Director of the Surrey European Management School, University of Surrey, UK. He has written widely on many aspects of tourism and hospitality management, specializing in information systems, an area in which he has undertaken consultancy and project work in several countries. His research is focused on organizational decision making, especially related to European enterprises.

Frank M. Go is Director of Tourism and Hospitality Management, at the University of Calgary. His research interests are in transnationalism, managing change and management education. He is a member of the editorial advisory boards of *Leisure, Recreation & Tourism Abstracts*; the *International Journal of Contemporary Hospitality Management*; the *Journal of Hospitality & Leisure Marketing* and co-editor of the *World Travel and Tourism Review Indicators, Trends and Forecasts*.

Philip J. Goulding is Course Leader of the Tourism Management program at Napier Polytechnic of Edinburgh, UK. He received his Masters degree in Tourism from the University of Strathclyde and has wide experience of travel and tourism management in the UK and the Middle East. His research interests focus on tourism market analysis and the international organization of tourism, and his publications include sectoral analyses of the UK's travel and retail leisure industries.

Evert Gummesson is Professor of Services Management at the University of Stockholm, Sweden, where he also received his Ph.D., and is a faculty member of the Swedish School of Economics and Business Administration, Helsinki, Finland. He has been Marketing Manager of the Reader's Digest Swedish subsidiary and a Senior Management Consultant and Director of the Scandinavian Division of the PA Consulting Group.

Lynn O'Rourke Hayes is a writer and travel industry consultant and has held several executive positions in the tourism industry. She is currently spokesperson for the Choice Family Travel Council, an organization created by Choice Hotels International to provide research and education to the industry and consumers on the subject of family travel. A graduate in journalism from Arizona State University, she has written several books and contributes to three industry magazines.

Robert C. Hazard Jr. is Chairman and Chief Executive of Choice Hotels International, which is the world's largest franchise lodging chain with more than 2,400 inns, hotels, suites and resorts. A cum laude graduate of Princeton University's Woodrow Wilson School of International Affairs, he served in the U.S. Air Force and with IBM and American Express. Before joining Choice, he spent seven years as Chief Executive of Best Western International.

Jan Hubrecht is Managing Director of Scott's Hotels Limited, the largest franchisee of Marriott Hotels in the UK. A native of Holland, he graduated from the Hague Hotel School and received his MBA from the Cranfield School of Management, UK. His special interests are concerned with total quality management and motivation, and he is a non-executive director of the National Society for Quality through Teamwork.

Giles A. Jackson is Visiting Lecturer at Victoria University of Technology in Melbourne, Australia, where he has established the Asia-Pacific Trends Database Project. He is completing his Ph.D. on cross-national comparisons of environmental policy in tourism at Virginia Polytechnic Institute and State University, where he was Trends Director. His major research interests are corporate strategy, public administration and policy and regional tourism development.

Peter A. Jones is Professor and Head of the Department of Food, Hospitality and Retail Management, Bournemouth Polytechnic, UK. He was formerly a Lieutenant-Colonel in the British Army Catering Corps, where he gained research experience in information systems and also in corporate strategy as a corporate planner in a branch of the British Ministry of Defence.

Francis A. Kwansa Ph.D. is an Assistant Professor in the Department of Hotel, Restaurant and Institutional Management, Virginia Polytechnic Institute and State University, where he teaches undergraduate courses in hospitality financial management. His research interests are focused on aspects of business failure and bankruptcy and on mergers and acquisitions.

Bryan D. Langton is Chairman and Chief Executive of Holiday Inn Worldwide. He joined Crest Hotels Limited (then part of Bass) in 1971, became Managing Director in 1982 and joined the board of Bass PLC in 1985. He assumed responsibility for all of the Group's hotel and restaurant interests in 1988 and in the same year, he was made a Commander of the British Empire in recognition of his services to the hotel industry.

David Litteljohn holds a senior position in the Department of Hotel and Catering Studies, Napier Polytechnic of Edinburgh, UK, and he is also Associate Editor of the *International Journal of Contemporary Hospitality Management*. He has written extensively in the tourism and hospitality management fields, specializing in the development of international organizations and international marketplaces, market analysis and commentaries on UK hospitality sectors.

Andrew Lockwood is a Lecturer in the Department of Management Studies for Tourism and Hotel Industries, University of Surrey, UK. He has published two books and many articles on aspects of hotel and catering operations. His main research interest is in quality management in the industry, and he has undertaken consultancy and run numerous courses on this subject both in the UK and overseas.

Katherine M. Merna is a graduate student on the Hotel, Restaurant and Institutional Management program at Virginia Polytechnic Institute and State University. She has a Bachelor's degree in human nutrition and foods and ten years' foodservice management experience. She has also co-authored several articles which have been published in American hospitality trade journals.

Eddystone C. Nebel, III, Ph.D., is C. B. Smith Professor, Department of Restaurant, Hotel, and Institutional Management, Purdue University, USA. He was previously Professor & Founding Director of the School of Hotel, Restaurant & Tourism Administration, University of New Orleans. He has recently completed *Lessons from Outstanding General Managers*, a textbook based on extensive field research of American hotel general managers.

Alan C. Parker is a graduate of the University of Surrey, UK. Following a variety of sales and marketing positions, he joined Bass PLC's subsidiary Crest Hotels in 1982 where, most latterly he held the position of Managing Director for mainland Europe. When Bass acquired the international division of Holiday Inn, he became Senior Vice President and Managing Director of the Europe, Middle East and Africa region, becoming a member of the Holiday Inn Worldwide Board in 1990.

Preston D. Probasco received his Ph.D. from the University of Wisconsin specializing in organizational development. He is currently Professor at the College of Business, San José State University, USA, with management consulting interests focused on the formation and growth of new venture firms. His publications range from organizational behavior cases in manufacturing and electronics to experimental social psychological work in venture capital firms.

Michael Riley is Lecturer in Management Studies at the University of Surrey, UK. He received his Ph.D. from the University of Essex and he is the author of several books on hotel labor markets, organizational behavior, careers and vocational training. He has held industry positions in the fields of Food & Beverage Management, Conference Management, and Personnel Management, and his research interests include skill development and management development.

Jeffrey D. Schaffer, Ph.D., is Director of the School of Hotel, Restaurant and Tourism Administration at the University of New Orleans, USA. During a twenty-year career in the lodging industry he held managerial positions with Sonesta Hotels and was Vice President and General Manager of the

Pontchartrain Hotel in New Orleans. He is an active consultant and his work on corporate and competitive strategy has been published in numerous international journals.

Martin Senior is a Researcher with the Hotel and Catering Training Company, London, where he is currently working on a government-funded initiative concerned with employee performance standards. A postgraduate researcher of Bournemouth Polytechnic, he has authored a number of recent publications on aspects of service quality and systems, especially as they relate to the UK roadside lodging sector.

Mark Stephenson is Director of Sales and Marketing, Resort Condominiums International (Australasia) Pty Ltd, whose holiday exchange and travel agency operations are noted for the high level of emphasis placed on customer service. He is a Masters graduate from Cambridge University, UK and gained his marketing experience at two of the UK's largest travel tour operators before moving to Australia with RCI.

Eliza C. Tse is Assistant Professor, Department of Hotel, Restaurant, and Institutional Management, Virginia Polytechnic Institute and State University, USA, where she also received her Ph.D. She has held managerial positions and served as a consultant in both the USA and Hong Kong. Her main research interests are in the areas of strategic management and organizational policy, hospitality research and development activities, cost control and market analysis.

Sandra Watson holds a senior position in the Department of Hotel and Catering Studies, Napier Polytechnic of Edinburgh, UK. She previously held a variety of management posts with hospitality firms in the UK and abroad. Specializing in the human resources field, her research and writing interests focus on management development and the conception and implementation of learning contracts.

Joseph J. West is Chairman of the Department of Hospitality Administration, Florida State University, USA. He received his BS in Hotel Administration from Cornell University, an MS in Systems Management from the University of Southern California, and his Ph.D. in Hotel, Restaurant, and Institutional Management from Virginia Polytechnic Institute and State University.

Brian Wise is Dean of the Faculty of Business, Footscray Campus, Victoria University of Technology, Australia. He received his B.Comm. and B.Ed. degrees from the University of Melbourne and his M.Sc. in Tourism from the University of Strathclyde, UK. He is Fellow of the Australian Society of Travel and Tourism, and of the British Tourism Society among others, and has special interest links with the People's Republic of China and many other Asia-Pacific region institutions.

Jin-Lin Zhao is Research Associate and Ph.D. candidate in the Department of Hotel, Restaurant, and Institutional Management, Virginia Polytechnic Institute and State University, USA. He received his MA degree in Political Science from Indiana University. Prior to this, he was a faculty member of the China Tourism Institute, Beijing, People's Republic of China. His current research is focused on the international strategies of the global hospitality industry.

Preface

In recent years observers of international business will have noted the increasing degree of complexity associated with trading in both domestic and foreign markets, notably as they have become more volatile and the impact of economic, environmental, social, political and technological change has become more difficult to predict. In this context, the aim of the book is to explore the theory and practice of corporate strategy as it applies to the international hospitality industry. In order to do this, the nineteen chapters are divided into four parts. The International Environment (Part 1) and Competitive Strategies (Part 2) address the wider perspective of trading in an international business environment. Corporate Structures and Planning (Part 3) and Corporate Systems and Analysis (Part 4) focus on the interrelationships between hospitality organizations and their markets by examining operational and functional issues relating to effective organizational performance.

Working from established strategic frameworks and models, the academic contributors examine how and why hospitality firms are using particular strategies to achieve their objectives. This is done by analyzing key strategic developments and by reviewing, and commenting on, the effectiveness of systems and methods currently used in international hospitality organizations. Many of the examples are drawn from academic research undertaken by the authors, thereby providing a truly international perspective on the management and development of multinational hospitality companies. The views of industrialists are essential to the study of corporate strategy, hence six shorter chapters containing executive viewpoints on the issues affecting multinational business development provide the practitioner counterbalance. In this respect, we are grateful to the senior executives from Choice Hotels International, Forte PLC, Hilton International, Holiday Inn Worldwide, Hyatt International Corporation and Scott's Hotels Limited who contributed their views. Their insights and willingness to talk about the strategic challenges which major multinationals face in the 1990s reflect the dynamic nature of the international hospitality business.

The book is well suited to the needs of management students on undergraduate and postgraduate courses in the areas of corporate strategy/business policy or strategic management, marketing, organizational behavior, human resource and operations management. The involvement of industrialists strengthens the relationship between theory and practice, making this a valuable resource book for practitioners too.

We would also like to thank Penelope Woolf, Marie-Ann Rijs and Suzanne Dempsey at Pitman Publishing, Claire Thompson at John Wiley, Chris Bessant (the freelance copy-editor), Robert Barnard and Sheila Harrington

(Forte PLC), Catherine Lord (Hilton International), Jane Baxter (Holiday Inn Worldwide – Europe, Middle East and Africa), Nicola Hancock (Hyatt International Corporation) and above all, Rachel and Sandy for their support throughout this project.

Richard Teare and Michael Olsen
August 1992

Part 1

The international environment

The four chapters in Part 1 are concerned with aspects of trading in an international business environment. They share a common perspective in that they demonstrate the close interrelationships between the international hospitality and tourism industries, in so far as each is affected by macro economic policy and global issues which affect the business and natural environments in which they operate.

Chapter 1 opens by defining the nature of the international business environment and this is followed by a detailed review of the environmental influences and competitive forces shaping trends in the international hospitality and tourism industries. These include political, economic, sociocultural, ecological and technological issues. Environmental scanning can be used to determine the impact of these forces and to support strategic decision-making. In order to examine their potential value, the remainder of the chapter is devoted to environment-scanning and impact-analysis techniques and outlines how to devise an integrated system for gathering information and assessing the impact of environmental forces on business activity in the international hospitality industry.

If they are to optimize their performance, international hospitality firms must try to match their strategy and structure to the conditions of the environment in which they operate. Few firms attain the ideal co-alignment, but the danger in achieving an effective balance is that complacency can ensue. To avoid this pitfall, it is necessary to stay ahead of environmental changes so that co-alignment can be continually monitored and adjusted. Chapter 2 aims to illustrate the practical considerations influencing this task by providing a summary of the key environmental issues facing Holiday Inn Worldwide. These are reviewed in relation to the choice of competitive methods which make up the firm's overall development strategy.

As the hospitality industry matures and suppliers become multi/transnational, greater attention should be paid to the international political and regulatory environment. One way of doing this is to analyze the interactions which occur between host governments and hospitality suppliers. This can provide a wider understanding of the dynamics involved in competitive strategy formulation and implementation. Chapter 3 begins with an assessment of economic, social and other key trends in relation to the emergence of international hospitality companies. The authors then identify the main public policy issues by examining tourism policy at both national and international levels.

This analysis provides an appreciation of the impact of public policy on the international hospitality and tourism business and demonstrates the utility of understanding the processes involved.

Entering the 1990s, hospitality corporations in certain parts of the world are streamlining and networking their organizations in order to cope with the levelling out of their investment returns and changes in market structures. Chapter 4 aims to explore the forces driving the ascendancy of the Asia-Pacific region and the measures required to adapt to rapidly evolving regional economies. The chapter begins by illustrating with reference to a policy framework and country study examples, why hospitality and tourism firms need to be sensitive to the critical changes taking place in the Asia-Pacific region. The second part of the chapter outlines the many and varied development dimensions of the region and their implications for international hospitality firms.

Richard Teare

I

Impact analysis and the international environment

Jin-Lin Zhao and
Katherine M. Merna

Businesses today are competing in a world economy for survival, growth, and profitability. The globalization of the hospitality and tourism industry has accelerated under the pressures of advances in technology, communication and transportation, deregulation, elimination of political barriers, sociocultural changes, and global economic development, as well as growing competition in a global economy. A single international firm in the hospitality industry must perform successfully in the world's business environment. A myriad of influences in the external international environment greatly affect the multinational hospitality organization.

This chapter is divided into two sections: the first section presents definitions of the environment and environmental scanning and includes discussion of the environmental influences and competitive forces shaping the trends in the international hospitality and tourism industry; the second section relates to environmental scanning techniques and impact analysis. Environmental scanning and impact analysis is a system that assists the hospitality organization in gathering information and assessing the impact of these environmental forces on the firm's business. Using these tools helps facilitate strategic planning and decision making for the firm. Swift dissemination and analysis of environmental information within the organization enhances the firm's competitive position; allows a quicker response, either defensive or offensive; and strengthens the firm's ability to change and/or control the environmental forces that are a part of the international hospitality environment.

The environment

Definition

Daft (1989) defines the external organizational environment as including 'all elements that exist outside the boundary of the organization and have the potential to affect all or part of the organization.' The hospitality firm does not exist in a vacuum. It exists in an open system in which complexity increases as the firm interacts with and adapts to the environment. Unlike the relatively stable external environment of the hospitality industry in the 1950s and 1960s, the business environment began changing through the 1970s and change accelerated throughout the 1980s and 1990s as many hospitality organizations expanded both domestically and internationally. As hospitality firms expand globally, environmental forces become more complex, dynamic, uncertain and turbulent. Therefore, it has become necessary for hospitality managers to understand the worldwide sociocultural changes, political, economic and technological developments, and ecological considerations which make up the general environment.

The operating environment or task environment relates to competitive forces which affect the hospitality firm. Figure 1.1 shows how external environmental forces in the general and operating environments impact upon the internal organizational environment. A later section of this chapter will provide more detailed definitions and discussion of each of the individual environmental forces depicted in Figure 1.1. Awareness of both general and competitive forces within the business environment of the hospitality industry is an important aspect of environmental scanning.

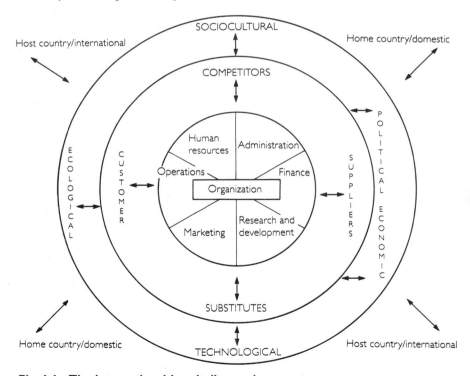

Fig. 1.1 The international hospitality environment
Source: Adapted from Bates (1985).

Research in the area of the environment

Scholars have studied the relationship between organizations and their environments (Thompson, 1967; Child, 1972), the influence of environmental forces on organizational structure and decision making (Burns and Stalker, 1961; Lawrence and Lorsch, 1969), the nature of the environment (Dill, 1958; Child, 1972; Emery and Trist, 1965; Duncan, 1972; Bourgeois 1980), and the relationship between environmental uncertainty and managers' perception (Duncan 1972; Lawrence and Lorsch, 1969). Table 1.1 shows selected authors and their contributions to the concept of environment.

Many scholars believe that when an organization expands outside of its national boundary, its environments become more complex and uncertain (Preble *et al.*, 1989). A multinational firm faces special challenges of unavoidable differences among cultures (Lawrence and Lorsch, 1969). Daft (1989) added the international domain in further defining the structure of the organization's environment.

Table 1.1 Selected research studies on the concept of environment

Author/date	Contribution
Dill (1958)	Divided the environment into general and task environments, and identified the task environment as: customers, suppliers, competitors, and regulatory groups.
Burns and Stalker (1961)	Classified the mechanistic and organic systems; stated that organic system is needed in a very uncertain environment.
Emery and Trist (1965)	Identified four types of environments: placid and randomized, placid clustered, disturbed reactive, and turbulent field.
Lawrence and Lorsch (1969)	Studied the relationship between environment, uncertainty, and managers' perceptions; referred to the various external environmental forces as the outside contingencies that 'can be treated as both constraints and opportunities that influence the internal functions and processes'.
Thompson (1967)	Argued that the complex, differentiated environment requires different organizational structure; strategic managers must adapt to external forces to co-align the organization with the environment.
Duncan (1972)	Typed the environment in two dimensions: simple-complex or static-dynamic.
Miles et al. (1974)	Portrayed four types of managerial perception of the environment and the enactment between organization and environment: domain-defenders, reluctant reactors, anxious analyzers, and enthusiastic prospectors.
Bourgeois (1980)	Classified the environment into objective vs. perceived environment; objective environment was then further divided into general and task environments.

Environmental scanning

Today's businesses must operate in an environment in which change is occurring at an even greater pace than in past decades. Indeed, change can be depended upon as potentially the only constant factor in the hospitality industry. This fact forces managers to scan and monitor the changing business environment and to be capable of assessing its impact upon their business operations.

A definition

Environmental scanning is defined by Byars (1987) as 'the systematic methods used by an organization to monitor and forecast those forces that are external to and not under the direct control of the organization or its industry.' Byars also notes that 'these forces may affect not only the success of particular organizations within the industry, but the industry as a whole,' this statement strongly indicates the importance of international environmental scanning for the identification of trends which may have organization and industry-wide significance.

Many researchers have defined the term 'environmental scanning'. Table 1.2 gives a summary of such definitions to further clarify the concept. Based

Table 1.2 Definitions of environmental scanning

Author/date	Definition
Aguilar (1967)	The process that seeks information about events and relationships in a company's outside environment; the knowledge which would assist top management in its task of charting the company's future course of action.
Thompson (1967)	A process by which the executives assess the trends and events outside organizations.
Preble et al. (1989)	That part of the strategic planning process in which emerging trends, changes, and issues are regularly monitored and evaluated as to their likely impact on business decisions.
Stroup (1988)	Quotes the Daniel Yankelovich Group's definition as 'the study and interpretation of what is happening in society at large today in order to forecast development in the business operating environment of tomorrow'.
Ghoshal (1988)	The activity by which organizations collect information about their environments.
Burack and Mathys (1989)	The systematic search of the main environment and change forces on a regular basis.
Michman (1989)	An early warning system that assembles and analyzes information concerning external forces and events and determines their impact on the strategies of the organization.

on these definitions, it can been seen that environmental scanning is a systematic process to collect information, interpret trends and events, and provide possible courses of action for the hospitality firm.

Research in the area of environmental scanning

The growth and survival of an organization depend on the environment it faces. In today's information-driven economy, firms which have access to correct information pertinent to their environment gain a competitive advantage. Development of more effective ways of providing environmental intelligence to strategic decision makers will assist managers in anticipating and adapting to the environment in their strategic planning. Table 1.3 shows

Table 1.3 Selected research studies on the concept of environmental scanning

Author/date	Contribution
Aguilar (1967)	Argued that information acquisition should be part of the manager's daily routine work; categorized the source of information into personal and impersonal and found that personal information was more important; personal network of communication is endorsed.
Fahey and King (1977)	Proposed a conceptual framework which is composed of three environmental scanning models: irregular, regular, and continuous scanning models.
Klein and Newman (1980)	Proposed the Systematic Procedure for Identifying Relevant Environments (SPIRE) approach in environmental assessment, which provides a direct link between the environmental assessment task and the specific area under strategic planning concern.
Hofer and Haller (1980)	GLOBESCAN – a technique for international environmental analysis and strategic decision making; focuses more on (1) strategy than tactics, (2) global than country-by-country perspective, (3) opportunities rather than risk, (4) operating profitability and cash flow than asset protection and investment recovery, (5) the entirety of the international strategic decision-making process than parts of it.
Diffenbach (1983)	Defined seven types of outcome to firms engaging in organized environmental analysis resulting from payoff, deterrents to formal environmental analysis activities in firms, and managerial implications of interpretation, accuracy, acceptance, and perception.
Jain (1984)	Examined the evolution and state of environmental scanning among corporations; defined four phases in the evolution of environmental scanning in corporations.
Bates (1985)	Proposed the MAPping Model, which suggests three steps are necessary for monitoring the environment: scanning the environment, analyzing the environment, and predicting the environment.
Lenz and Engledow (1986)	Identified organizational roles of environmental analysis units: policy oriented, strategic planning oriented, and function oriented; summarized environmental analysis into five models: industry structure model, cognitive model, organizational field model, ecological and resource dependence model, and era model.

Table 1.4 Studies of environmental scanning in the international environment

Author/ date	US/ foreign firm	Scanning practices	Reliance on internal/ external sources	Forecasting techniques
Keegan (1974)	50 executives in 13 US international corporations	No systematic methods for obtaining information	66% external sources 34% internal sources	N/A
O'Connell and Zimmerman (1979)	50 US and 50 European executives	Both groups focused on technological and economic domains	Greater reliance on internal sources Less reliance on external sources	More formalized interpretation and evaluation for economic and technological domains
Kobrin et al. (1980)	193 US-based multinationals	55% had environmental scanning group reviewing international political and social factors Of these it is reported that they have one or more units with formal responsibility for environmental assessment and evaluation Political and economic aspects deemed most important in the international environment 58% feel that integration of analysis with planning and investments decisions is essential; 33.2% state that it is useful	Greater reliance on internal sources Less reliance on external sources	*Quantitative* 10.9% computerized econometric models 13.5% statistical analysis *Qualitative* 30.1% standardized country checklists 26.4% scenario analysis 16.1% structured qualitative analysis 9.8% Delphi techniques

Study	Sample	Findings	Sources	Analytical methods
Klein and Linneman (1984)	500 foreign firms	95% had corporate planning units; 51% used environmental assessment practices; 41% had formal environmental assessment units	50% internal 50% external	72% used trend extrapolation; Only 29% went further to complete trend impact analysis; 61% scenario analysis; 52% brainstorming
Kennedy (1984)	61 US-based multinationals	74% had formally institutionalized the external environment function with one or more persons and departments; Focus on socioeconomic and political risk assessment and evaluation; Scanning unit most often located in planning departments	N/A	N/A
Lenz and Engledow (1986)	9 US-based and 1 Canadian-based multi-billion dollar corporations	All had a formal environmental scanning structure; 5 units located in corporate planning divisions	Varied used of external and internal sources among firms	No specialization of analytical methods among personnel
Ghoshal (1988)	6 Korean firms	All had a formal environmental scanning unit with 5–20 employees; All units reported to head of planning	56% external sources; 44% internal sources	N/A
Preble et al. (1989)	450 US-based multinationals	48% have at least one employee scanning on the countries in which they operate; 5.3% have environmental scanning unit tied into corporate planning process; Stated that economic (90%) and competitive domains (63%) were most important	61% internal sources; 39% external sources	70% Delphi technique; 52% trend extrapolation; 39% scenarios; 19% computer simulations

some of the major contributions in the study of environmental scanning. As can be seen, a variety of different approaches and systems are available as tools for hospitality managers.

Scanning the international environment

Environmental scanning practices of firms operating in the international arena have been studied by several researchers. Table 1.4 shows the pattern of greater use of international environmental scanning, more formalized and sophisticated methods (i.e. computer use), and greater integration into strategic planning processes, which was suggested by Sethi (1982) in the early 1980s.

Ghoshal (1988) states that 'environmental intelligence is rapidly becoming a major source of competitive advantage in an era of global competition,' while Fayerweather (1981) includes environmental assessment as one of the 'four winning strategies for the international corporation.' Assessing single future trends and changes through environmental monitoring is quite accurate and comprehensive through a growing number of methods. However, its usefulness in practice is constrained because prediction of the effects and impacts of trends are much more difficult to interpret (Utterback, 1982).

The general environment

The general or external environment consists of many forces that exist outside the boundary of the organization. The dimensions of the general environment which are depicted in Figure 1.1 are further defined in Table 1.5. The

Table 1.5 Forces in the general environment

Sociocultural	Economic	Technological	Political	Ecological
Demographics	GNP/income distribution	Communication	Governments	Natural resources
Culture/language	Monetary/fiscal policies and exchange rates	Transportation	Laws and regulations	Environmental maintenance and conservation
Psychographic	Financial and investment markets	Safety and security	Stability and risk	
Social change/public opinion	Taxation and tariffs	Food/nutrition/packaging		
Education	Trade and industrial	Computers and software/robotics/electronics/equipment		
Nationalism	Labor markets	Energy Layout and design/architecture		

combined forces of these specific dimensions in the general environment greatly influence the hospitality industry. The next section will define and give examples of these distinct dimensions.

The political dimension

The political environment includes political systems, regulations, and laws, as well as political stability and risks within a country. Political risk for a firm may be defined as the risk of 'strategic, financial or personnel loss' (Kennedy, 1988) 'arising from political forces or government actions which interfere with, or prevent, foreign business transactions, or change the terms of agreements' (Weston and Sorge, 1972).

The multiplicity of political environments is addressed by Onkvisit and Shaw (1989). They emphasize the increased complexity of the political dimension when the interests of the company, the host country, and the home country do not coincide. They define the political environment as including the following:

- *Foreign politics* – the politics of a local or host country; host country laws.
- *Domestic politics* – politics that exist in the company's home or parent country; home country laws.
- *International politics* – the interaction of the overall environmental factors of two or more countries; international laws.

These three elements of politics must be taken into consideration when analyzing the broader scope of the political environment.

Governments
Political systems, or types of government, are an important environmental consideration for the international hospitality firm. Most industrialized and democratic nations have political parties which devise and operationalize policies that reflect the preferences of the society through parliamentary procedures. Other countries are controlled by monarchies or dictators who may not consider their society's needs. Political stability is not inherent with a specific type of government or degree of economic development, or with capitalism or communism, and therefore awareness of a home or host country's internal and external political environment is necessary in comprehensive environmental scanning.

Laws and regulations
There are important political implications for the hospitality and tourism industry regarding laws and regulations which influence strategic planning decisions. Some countries, for example, seek tourism policies to protect and maintain the current level of tourism development. Regulations and laws can limit market development of tourism through burdensome visa requirements, entry or exit procedures, as well as currency controls. Such administrative

regulations actually create barriers for the development of the hospitality and tourism industry.

Business operations are controlled by politics in the home and host countries. Laws of the firm's home country may restrict the geographic areas in which a business can locate (e.g. Cuba is presently off-limits for US developers). Host country regulations are influenced by local governments and may not, for example, allow the international firm to repatriate their investment and profits fully. Laws of host countries directly influence the financial structure, investments, and even recruitment of personnel for the entering company; joint ventures and strategic alliances are a case in point. Minimum wage, environmental, and pricing legislation are examples of laws which may impose limitations on the international hospitality firm within a host country.

However, not all government regulations and laws are restrictive. For example, to attract foreign investment in the hospitality and tourism industry, and to boost national economies, many countries have passed laws allowing tax incentives such as tax holidays, reductions, exemptions, and accelerated depreciation when developers and investors consider hotel or tourism projects in their country. Additionally, worldwide deregulation in travel will likely result in greater destination travel.

Stability and risk

It is well known that multinational firms face specific events such as political revolution, terrorism, riots, coups, civil war, expropriation, and repatriation in host countries. Therefore, multinational hospitality firms must be aware of inherent political changes and potential risks which may result. Root (1982) classifies these risks as follows:

- *General instability risk*. This refers to the general political fortitude of the host country's government in the long term. Considering the recent global political upheavals, this risk is particularly relevant.
- *Ownership/control risk*. This is directed toward the likelihood that a host government's actions could harm a business through confiscation of property without compensation, or expropriation with forced surrender of property and some compensation.
- *Operation risk*. This includes the possibility that a host country may impose restrictions on a business operation (i.e. its production, marketing, and/or finance).
- *Transfer risk*. A host government can obstruct or restrict the firm's ability to transfer payments, capital, or profits back to the home country.

When a country's political stability is questioned, even a temporary riot can greatly damage tourism. For example, the events of Tiannanmen Square, Beijing, in 1989 hurt the Chinese tourism industry. The bloody suppression of protests in the capital cost China an estimated $1 billion in potential tourist revenues (Anon., 1991a). Repercussions are still being felt today for existing multinational hospitality and tourism firms located in China.

Although the war in the Persian Gulf did not last long, its impact reverberated throughout the global hospitality and tourism industry. Consumer fear due to political disruption typically results in concern for personal safety. When political risks are present, multinational firms must take measures to protect the safety and security of their customers and employees. Lessons are to be learned from events such as the terrorist attack on Pan Am Airline Flight 103 over Lockerbie, Scotland, in 1989.

Political instability may not always have adverse effects. The unification of Europe in 1992 has resulted in dramatic political and economic changes in the former Soviet Union and all of Eastern Europe. The removal of the barriers between East Germany and the rest of the world has set off a chain reaction, with many countries and geographic regions still claiming independence as communism retreats. These political changes will result in the opening of what were once closed societies, and will increase opportunities for hospitality and tourism expansion. The recent release of hostages in the Middle East and other political changes in the region may also offer new opportunities for the industry.

To summarize, multinational hospitality and tourism firms wishing to invest abroad must evaluate the governments, political stability and risks, and laws and regulations which will impact on their firm's businesses, as well as on their suppliers, customers, and competitors, when forming strategic plans for international expansion. The recent political changes in Eastern Europe and the former Soviet Union offer exciting challenges and opportunities to the hospitality industry.

The economic environment

The travel and tourism industry is the world's largest industry and is investing in future growth at a significantly faster rate than other industries (Blalock, 1991). According to the World Travel and Tourism Council (WTTC), the annual gross output of the industry is greater than the GNP of all countries except the United States, the Soviet Union, and Japan. Worldwide, the tourism industry employs 112 million people and produces 5.5 percent of the global GNP (Blalock, 1991). As tourism is such an important part of the global economy, managers must be aware of economic trends which have the potential to affect the industry.

The general economic vitality of a country is an important consideration because an indication of its economic condition will be reflected in such factors as consumer demand and prices. When scanning the economic environment the following factors should be considered:

- *Gross National Product (GNP)* – the total market value of goods and services produced in a country per year and its growth rate.
- *Income distribution* – the level of personal consumer income and the tendency to consume.
- *Foreign exchange rates* – the rate of exchange of one currency for another.

- *Monetary and fiscal policies* and exchange controls. Some countries may limit the amount of money which can be withdrawn from their country as well as impose large payments for international transactions (e.g. joint ventures, entry into country).
- *Financial and investment markets* – individual consumer and corporate interest rates, the availability of credit, the rate of inflation, stock exchanges, etc.
- *Taxation and tariffs* – taxes on individuals, corporations and imported goods imposed by the host country government.
- *Trade/industrial factors* – import/export, measures of activity in commerce, etc. These can serve as indices in determining the state of the economy (e.g. prosperity, depression, recession, recovery).
- *Labor markets* – the level of unemployment, the labor pool, welfare spending, etc.

In many countries, the hospitality and tourism industry plays a very important role in the national economy. Hospitality and tourism are the major foreign currency earners in many countries and areas, such as Hong Kong, Egypt, and Kenya (US Dept. of Commerce, 1989, 1990, 1991).

With the lifting of regulatory restrictions by many industrialized countries, the financial markets of previously separate national capital markets are now integrated into a global financial market. As a result, many capital-rich multinational companies in all industries have taken advantage of interest and exchange rates and expanded through mergers and acquisitions globally. In hotels and restaurants, for example, Bass PLC (United Kingdom) has acquired the US-based Holiday Inn, and New World Holding Company (Hong Kong) has merged with Ramada (US).

As the world economy continues to become more interdependent, increasing amounts of business travel will occur. As can be seen, the global economic environment plays a significant role in the internationalization opportunities for hospitality and tourism firms. Global economic policies and developments play a critical role in the hospitality and tourism industry.

The sociocultural environment

The sociocultural dimension helps to define the attributes of society and aid the hospitality manager in interpreting how his or her business will be affected by social and cultural changes. Of utmost importance is the interpretation of how these changes will influence preferences for products and services as well as consumer demand. Ultimately, trends in the sociocultural dimension will greatly impact upon decisions made by the hospitality organization. The sociocultural dimension consists of several factors:

- *Demographics* – attributes of consumers and the workforce, such as age structure, sex, race, education, language, birth/fertility/death rates, geographic distribution/density, and income levels.

- *Culture* – learned patterns of behavior, feeling and reaction which are shaped by social class, family, subcultures, reference groups (e.g. religion), and lifestyle. Culture influences behavior, expectations, perceptions, values, attitudes, beliefs, preferences, communication, memory, past experience, and both psychological and physiological needs. Culture is subjective, enduring, cumulative, and dynamic (Onkvisit and Shaw, 1989). Inherent differences in languages and word usage are culturally based and are an important consideration in both verbal and written communication.
- *Psychographics*. This is defined as 'a quantitative analysis of consumers' lifestyles, and activities with the purpose of relating these variables to behavior' (Onkvisit and Shaw, 1989). Interests, habits, and opinions along with personality characteristics are used to predict consumer behaviour.
- *Social factors* – relationships, attitudes, values, opinions and beliefs.
- *Education* – the educational level of employees and customers potentially affecting the design and operations of products, facilities, training, and the provision of services.
- *Nationalism* – emphasis on a country's interests before everything else (Cetron and Davies 1989); the strength of patriotism and consumer action relevant to patriotism.

One prominent demographic trend occurring in the United States and in such countries as Japan, Southeast Asia, and Western Europe is the growing elderly population. For example, in the USA the age group of 50 years or older comprises 42.8 per cent of all households, but 76.4 percent of financial assets and 69.5 percent of net worth (Kiplinger and Kiplinger, 1989). This market is an important segment for both leisure travel and dining out because older people generally have a greater amount of disposable income and time.

Concurrently with the increase in the elderly segment of the population, there is also a slowing of population growth in parts of the world. Worldwide population forecasts predict no growth in population through the year 2050 in Germany, the United Kingdom, Denmark, the Netherlands, and Italy because of low fertility rates. Slow population growth is predicted in France, Canada, Japan, Russia and the USA, while rapid population growth is foreseen in China, India, Mexico, Iran, and other nations of Asia, Africa, and Latin America (Kiplinger and Kiplinger, 1989).

These demographic transformations will pose a great challenge to the hospitality and tourism industry in terms of availability of labor. By the year 2000 'one of four Americans will work for the hospitality industries' and 85 percent of the total US labor force will be working in jobs in the service sector (Cetron and Davis, 1989). At the same time there will be a 'severe shortage of entry-level workers aged sixteen to twenty-four years,' an essential element in today's quick-service labor pool, for example. The changing workforce internationally will also be greatly influenced by the number of women entering the labor market. This trend is already being reflected in the increasing numbers of female business travelers.

All these sociocultural changes challenge multinational hospitality companies. What to serve to whom and where, and how to serve customers with different cultural backgrounds are questions for the leaders of the industry to answer. The success of multinational hospitality firms relies on their anticipation and adaptation to these changes and on the creation of the best products and services to meet the customers' needs.

The work environment will also be influenced by increasing cultural diversity. With barriers removed between countries, the blending of societies has already begun to occur. Managers will now face the challenge of leading a diverse assembly of workers with differing cultural backgrounds and perhaps speaking different languages. These changes require our hospitality executives to become cosmopolitans, communicators, negotiators, leaders in cultural change, influencers of organizational culture and work and team cultures (Harris and Moran, 1987).

Recent sociocultural trends, such as greater concern for the environment, demand for value in products and services, increasing cultural diversity, changing eating behaviors, educational levels and patterns in family units, as well as the changing roles of women, have already greatly affected the hospitality and tourism industry. As the global economy is formed, the understanding of sociocultural changes, cultural variance and their effect on customer needs will be moved to the global scale.

The technological dimension

Technology is the utilization of available knowledge and techniques to produce products and services (Daft, 1989). Technological information is doubling approximately every ten years, and many of the technologies which will be used in the year 2000 and beyond have yet to be invented (Anon., 1989a). This could either be a major stumbling block or provide a competitive edge for firms within the hospitality industry. Driving forces for technological advancement in the hospitality industry are directly attributed to consumer demand for convenience and quality. Industry's demands for new technologies are focused towards the attainment of convenience, speed, efficiency, control, and to meet labor shortages.

For the hospitality and tourism industry technological innovation will influence how businesses are operated and it is therefore necessary to recognize advancements in such areas as those listed in Table 1.6. This table also provides a list of recent innovations that have already impacted or will potentially impact on the hospitality industry in the near future.

Foodservice is an important segment of the hospitality industry. The trends which are influencing the development of new food products are largely socioculturally based. For example, greater societal awareness of health, fitness and nutrition needs, demand for convenience and quality of food products, as well as increased consumption of take-out and pre-prepared foods has driven technological advancement in this area and in the creation of artificial foods. Additionally, these same technologies are being used to

Table 1.6   Areas of technological advancement and examples of important innovations for the hospitality and tourism industry

Communication	Computerized reservation systems (CRS) linking airlines, hotels and car rental structures, fax machines, bitnet, tele-net, modems, LANs (local area networks), telephone systems and voice mail, electronic (E-)mail, point-of-sale, touch-screen ordering, computer screen communication programmed in various languages, voice recognition, note-pad/stylus computers, video-conferencing, high-density television (HDTV), interactive television, cellular phones
Transportation	High-speed and magnet levitation trains, Concorde, Airbus, 'smart roads', infrastructures such as the English Channel Tunnel
Safety and security	Electronic key access to hotel rooms, credit-card locks, biometrics (i.e. identification of hand, fingerprint, retina needed for room access), digital keypads, fire protection systems, infrared sensors, closed-circuit television security systems
Food and nutrition	Biotechnology, genetic engineering, seed vaccination technology, pharmacological foods, fat-free foods, non-nutritive sweeteners, artificial foods, research to eliminate use of pesticides
Computers and software/electronic equipment	Computer centers and PCs in hotel rooms, debit or 'smart card' technology, videotext, interactive computer technology, 'smart hotel rooms', integrated property management systems (PMS), information systems, artificial intelligence, decisions support systems, database applications, yield management, increased interface between systems, computerized ticket dispensers
Robotics	Increased use of robotics and automation in airline catering and hospital foodservice, sensor fusion technology
Energy	Management-controlled computer-aided technologies for electricity and water conservation in hotels, customer-controlled in-room consoles to control comfort level, US federally mandated 27.5 m.p.g. for motor vehicles; technology available today to boost this to 45 m.p.g. by the year 2000 (Painton, 1990)
Layout and design	Food courts, kiosks
Equipment	Greater variety multipurpose foodservice equipment, point-of-sale foodservice and hotel technologies, handicap access
Packaging	Controlled and modified atmosphere packaging (CAP and MAP), biosensors, interactive packaging, environmentally friendly and functional packaging, 'edible' cellulose packaging, reusable containers

create an array of convenience food products and advanced packaging materials that will preserve quality and extend shelf life. Packaging technology is expected to play one of the most significant roles in the future of prepared foods, and in many instances packaging will lead the developmental effort of such foods (Anon., 1989d). The greatest challenge which food technology will face in the next several decades will be producing high-quality, low-calorie, fortified foods that will furnish appropriate pleasure and satiation for the consumer (Clydesdale, 1989). Some examples of foods which have reached the consumers recently are fat-free ice creams and other dairy products, McDonald's low-fat McLean Deluxe, and non-nutritive/high-intensity sweeteners, just to name a few.

New food and packaging technologies will greatly impact on the foodservice industry of the future. It therefore becomes necessary for hospitality managers to develop heightened awareness by environmental scanning to forecast how technological changes will ultimately affect the foodservice industry. Environmental scanning will become an imperative, almost obligatory, course of action for the successful hospitality firm.

The challenge to the hospitality industry is fully to realize the power of technological innovations to facilitate and expedite service, and to use them, along with personal service aspects, to provide a superior experience for the consumer and a profitable venture for the hospitality firm.

In the hotel industry, high-tech hotel equipment has been grouped into two categories: (1) systems to maximize profits; and (2) systems to maximize guest service (Zugmier, 1989). The future includes implementation of technological innovations into hotels which will improve guest services and be used as revenue generators.

The introduction of sophisticated new technologies in communication and transportation will facilitate the worldwide development of the hospitality and tourism industry as a result of increased ease of travel across borders. However, the introduction of tele-conferencing could pose a threat to the industry if it becomes a substitute for business travel. Robotics and other technologies may become an answer in the future for labor shortages in the hospitality industry. Taco Bell is well poised in its development of taco-making equipment, which is a completely self-contained process. Multinational hospitality firms have begun to realize the need for improvement of technology in order to obtain and maintain the competitive advantage. Most multinational firms have put great effort into developing new technology within the industry. Many have adapted technology to improve both the guest experience and marketing and operating efficiencies, thereby reducing operating and labor costs.

Lastly, it is important for the hospitality manager to realize the level of technology and technological capabilities within the host country in order to assess the advantages or disadvantages the firm may face.

The ecological dimension

In this dimension, the monitoring of global ecological conditions and issues, and the availability of natural resources, are the central focus. Globally, heightened perception and greater individual understanding have resulted in aggressive activism regarding global environmental policies within both the general population and the corporate business environment. Hooper and Rocca (1991) state that 'virtually all company operations today have environmental implications.'

The creation of a new legal specialty – 'environmental law' – has occurred as a result of the recent ecological enlightenment of society. Fines against polluters have skyrocketed. In 1982, fines were $300,000, and since then they have escalated to $11.7 million in 1989 (Kass, 1989).

Targeted areas for concern in the hospitality industry include recycling, conservation, solid waste management, clean air, waste water management, maintenance of permits, and compliance. Table 1.7 defines categories of ecological concern and recent events which are affecting the industry.

Table 1.7   Areas of concern in the ecological environment and recent events applicable to the hospitality and tourism industry

Recycling	Mandated recycling laws in 38 of US states in 1990, overflowing landfills, advancements in recycling technologies and infrastructures. Research program funded by McDonald's Environmental Defense Fund (EDF) to promote waste reduction research for fast-food industry. Recycling programs have been implemented at McDonald's (McCycle). 'Recycling police' on duty to begin fining offenders in New York City in 1992.
Conservation	Increased awareness of need for energy and water conservation, new development in equipment for conservation. Tourism industry concerned for ecological conservation of biosphere. Conservation methods such as low-flow shower heads, ultra-low flush toilets, compact fluorescent bulbs are used in many hotels worldwide.
Solid waste/source reduction	Study of landfill composition found fast-food garbage to be less than 1% of total landfill (Bernstein, 1989; Anon., 1989b). Taxes, hauling, and tipping costs are cost considerations. Alternatives include recycling, incineration, super microbe 'bioremedy' to break down toxic waste, compacting/minimal landfilling, public education, laws in place banning polystyrene packaging (which accounts for less than 10% of waste problem by weight (Herlong, 1989; King, 1990)).
Air quality	US Clean Air Act imposed higher air pollution and acid-rain emissions standards which will indirectly impact on industry in transportation costs (Malovany, 1990). Regulations restricting tailpipe emissions affect food distributors/trucking companies, builders of drive-thrus, and tourism transportation methods. Chlorofluorocarbons (CFCs) destruction of ozone layer, responsible for greenhouse effect and global warming, will affect ecotourism. Restaurant charbroilers' emission of hydrocarbons have driven California laws to regulate air pollution from cooking as well as vehicles. No-smoking sections in hotels and dining places, some with total no-smoking policies, smoking ban on domestic US airline travel, 40% of business travelers rate no-smoking rooms as a key factor in lodging selection (Anon., 1989c).
Water quality	Growth of toxic algae, due to contaminants from farming, acid rain, industrial byproducts, oil spills and ocean-dumped urban sludge and garbage, is causing harm to sea life and coastal ecosystems (Schechter, 1989).
Pesticides	Consumers have rated pesticides as their number one concern regarding food safety (Trioble, 1989)

Effective management of environmental complexities has become one of the issues on the corporate strategic planning agenda and may well become a key measure of corporate success (Hooper and Rocca, 1991). For example, McDonald's has a recycling project at 450 Northeast stores and is testing trash compactors in units. McCycle USA is a program in which McDonald's will spend $100 million on recycled building materials to use in remodeling or new unit construction (Moore, 1990). Sixty million dollars per year is already spent on recycled paper for tray liners, napkins, carry-out trays, and Happy Meal containers. They have changed specifications for more efficient cardboard packaging, use polystyrene without chlorofluorocarbons, have decreased the thickness of clamshells and the diameter of straws, deliver soda syrup through a truck tank system and have changed to orange juice concentrate instead of individually packaged portions to reduce waste.

The hotel industry is greatly affected in terms of water availability and quality, and it will face difficult issues to alleviate overconsumption and deal with the cost of water and water conservation. Individual hotel room water meters may be used to discourage waste and pass the high costs of water onto the culprit consumers.

The hospitality and tourism industry has been a leader in the development of environmental policies. An international joint venture between Ramada International Hotels and American Express is a commitment to global environmentalism, agreeing to make contributions to the Nature Conservancy, an environmental organization based in Washington, DC (Anon., 1991b). Ramada Renaissance Hotel in Atlanta, Georgia, has also set up an Energy and Environmental Committee with responsibilities to develop and implement environmental improvement programs which include property/community beautification and natural resource (energy and water) conservation.

Globally, hospitality industry environmental issues are an emerging challenge with the expansion of US firms abroad and the high levels of industrial pollution in Eastern Europe. Environmental issues impact greatly upon the eco-tourism segment, which includes travel with the purpose of visiting areas with specific climatic conditions, animal and plant kingdoms, and other natural wonders. When the global ecological balance is disturbed, the impact is widespread with considerable consequences for the tourism industry.

Environmental realities have just begun to strike industries such as hospitality. Revelations of foreboding ecological predictions will force managers to face challenges and implement changes to manage ecological issues pertinent to our industry. Scanning and evaluation of ecological issues will assist the manager in assessing individual responsibility for and liability to environmental damage, in integrating environmental affairs with operations, and in developing policies and professionals to manage environmental issues. Additionally, this will result in the development of proactive industry programs to address the present and future environmental issues to promote positive ecological management.

The operating environment

The operating environment has also been referred to in the literature as the 'task' (Dill, 1958) or 'specific' environment and includes key competitive elements which a firm encounters in the market. The task environment evolved from Dill's definition, which included the customer, competitor, supplier, and regulator, to Porter's five competitive forces: the threat of new entrants, the bargaining power of customers, the bargaining power of suppliers, the threat of substitutes, and competitors (Porter, 1980).

In the international arena, a hospitality firm faces four types of major competitive force:

- *Competitors*. Competition includes both established and new competitors from the home country, host country/countries, and foreign countries both within and outside of the hospitality and tourism industry.
- *Customers*. The challenge is to produce and serve a product that meets the needs, wants, and demands of a multicultural clientele.
- *Suppliers*. Greater opportunities as well as greater restrictions exist in discussion of suppliers. A restrictive situation would be securing food products that meet McDonald's specifications, which is why McDonald's has established food production alternatives globally.
- *Substitutes*. These involve supplying alternative products and services, such as convenience stores and gourmet/deli sections in the supermarket vs. restaurants, tele-conference and camping vs. lodging facilities, and domestic travel vs. international travel.

All these forces could expose threats to and provide opportunities for the international hospitality firm and greatly influence the strategic decisions that are made by a hospitality multinational's management. Formalized competitive analysis integrated into the strategic planning process assists the international hospitality firm in ascertaining its competitors' actions. Analysis of the operating environment allows the firm to identify its own strengths and weaknesses, to seek opportunities, and to beware of threats to its viability.

The environment and the hospitality industry

The concept of the environment and environmental scanning were first introduced to the hospitality industry in the 1980s (Olsen, 1980). Since then, researchers have continued to study the relationships between environment, strategy, structure and performance in the hospitality industry. Table 1.8 summaries the research studies pertinent to the hospitality literature.

Industry executives have also realized the importance of monitoring the environment. Robert Hazard (1989) of Choice International discussed five key trends which are expected to shape the travel industry of the 1990s: consolidation, globalization, segmentation and niche marketing, technological change, and the quest for service. Eric Hilton (1991) of Hilton Hotel Corporation states that change is occurring at a greater pace than ever before. His

Table 1.8 Contributions to the concept of environment in the hospitality industry

Author/date	Contribution
Olsen (1980)	Introduced the concept of environment and environmental scanning into the hospitality body of literature through a review of literature.
Olsen and DeNoble (1981)	Focused on the relationship of environment, lifecycle, and firm technology; discussed impact of environment on strategic planning.
DeNoble and Olsen (1982)	Concluded that foodservice executives have limited view of the environment; managers focus on operations rather than place emphasis on strategic management.
Slattery and Olsen (1984)	Conceptual integration of individual perception, organizational perception, and the environment to the hospitality industry.
DeNoble and Olsen (1986)	Volatility of foodservice industry environment.
Kwansa et al. (1986)	Environmental scanning, trend identification during the period of 1981–5 through content analysis
Pinto and Olsen (1987)	Focused on information needs, sources, and uses by hospitality executives for strategic capital investment decisions.
West and Olsen (1988)	Studied the extent of environmental scanning of hospitality managers and found significant differences in firm peformance in support of scanning activities.
West and Olsen (1989)	Proposed model incorporating environmental scanning into the strategic management process of restaurant firms.
Dev and Olsen (1989)	Suggested that lodging firms must co-align firm strategies with environmental influences to gain competitive advantages.

discussion emphasized the importance of sociocultural/demographic changes and political changes on the global tourism industry, stating that 'the success of hotel and resort companies will be based on how well they anticipate and adapt to changes and create products and services that are best reflective of the varying markets' needs.'

Scanning the hospitality industry environment

Monitoring, analyzing, and anticipating trends in the hospitality industry has been the objective of the Center for Hospitality Research and Service at Virginia Polytechnic Institute and State University. Olsen (1980) stressed the importance for executives in the hospitality companies to gain knowledge about the environment and learn how organizations interact with its frequent changes and complexity.

Several researchers have studied the relationship between environmental scanning, strategy, and performance (West and Olsen, 1988; Dev and Olsen, 1989; West, 1990). The result of those studies indicated that there is a positive relationship between environmental scanning, strategy, and performance. A formalized system of scanning with a broad scope enhanced hospitality firm performance. In sum, to reach an optimal level of performance, a hospitality organization must match its strategies to a dynamic business environment.

A hospitality industry environmental scanning unit

Noticing the complex, uncertain, and changing environment and the low awareness of the broad scope of the environment among industry executives, the Center for Hospitality Research and Service serves to scan and analyze the environment through data collected in its Trends Database. The objective of the database is to identify, classify and monitor trends in the hospitality environment. The system has been in existence for eight years and contains over 12 million bytes of information (equivalent to ten 400-page books) about worldwide hospitality industry trends. The data are accessed and analyzed using content analysis of information computerized in a text-based database program called askSam. The process of the trends analysis is as follows:

1 A selection of industry/trade, academic, and periodical journals, and newspaper sources were selected and verified as the most valuable and accurate sources of information by both academicians and industry executives.
2 A classification scheme was devised and tested by both academicians and industry leaders to define the important areas to monitor.
3 Researchers are responsible for coding and inputting information, using the classification scheme, into the computerized database.
4 Through statistical manipulation, researchers are able to monitor and define trends successfully as well as analyze and forecast into the future.

Information on the environmental forces discussed in Table 1.4 is further classified to define the various segments of the hospitality industry: for example, lodging (budget to casino), foodservice (quick service to fine dining), institutional foodservice, and tourism. The use of keywords helps further classify information into functional areas, such as finance, marketing, administration, research and development, administration, operations, and human resources. This assists in interpreting trends in these domains. The information presented in Tables 1.5 and 1.6 has resulted from ongoing research at the Center for Hospitality Research and Service. This system has served industry executives by providing information in the form of newsletters, trade publications,[1] seminars, and conferences (Olsen *et al.*, 1990) to guide hospitality firms and their executives in strategic planning.

---

1. See the following issues of *Hotel and Motel Management* (1991, vol. 206): no. 2, p. 41; no. 4, p. 35; no. 10, p. 53; no. 12, p. 39; no. 13, p. 33; no. 14, p. 47; no. 16, p. 37; no. 17, p. 31.

Establishing an environmental scanning unit

The importance of building an environmental scanning system within the hospitality organization cannot be disputed. Systematic study of the environment allows managers the advantage of knowledge which can be used to determine trends and their impact on the corporate environment.

The following guidelines are proposed for use in development and implementation of a scanning system within the hospitality firm:

1 A senior administrator should be given responsibility for the environmental scanning program. Sufficient funding should be allocated to support the program.
2 Establish a formal unit which will work cooperatively with the strategic planning staff. The unit is to screen the general environment and coordinate the scanning and forecasting processes.
3 Identify and select key environmental variables which are critical to the firm's external environment.
4 Identify relevant sources of information, such as publications, trade meetings, etc. Establish information network of affiliations through suppliers, distributors, and subsidiaries from which the scanning unit may seek information routinely.
5 Scan, categorize, and code/abstract the information obtained into a computer database system.
6 Identify and evaluate forecasting methods and determine the appropriate method(s) for the firm.
7 Complete trend analysis and trend forecasting. Disseminate information organization-wide as well as integrate forecasts into strategic planning.
8 Monitor and evaluate the environmental scanning process, sources of information, and procedures. Adjust as necessary to maintain maximum functionality.

Information sources for scanning the environment

Information can be obtained from many sources both inside and outside the organization – from within the organization, co-workers, administrators or executives in specific functional areas, and executives with affiliations to foreign operations, to name a few. Information external to the organization can be gathered from the following individual sources: bankers, consultants, academicians, government officials, competitors, distributors, customers, and suppliers. Additionally, databases, electronic collections of journals, newspapers, and other public or private sources of information are available and can be either internally or externally maintained for the hospitality organization to use in its scanning process. Other important sources include:

● The US government, through the Federal Department of Commerce and the Department of Travel and Tourism, offers census information, import and export statistics, and other relevant information. State commerce

departments and other state and federal government agencies have limit-less amounts of information which may be useful. Government publications such as the *US Industrial Outlook* and the *Statistical Abstract of the United States* provide a wealth of material.
- International and host country governments also print many sources of trade, economic and political information.
- Trade associations provide a wealth of information, including magazines and journals, as well as databases.
- Documentary information can be easily found at local libraries. This includes government documents, trade, academic and newspaper publi-cations, and other reports.

Pearce and Robinson (1988) offer a comprehensive bibliography of sources of environmental information and forecasts. By reading reports and publi-cations, consulting with peers, academicians, and other professionals, as well as visiting trade shows, vast amounts of information can be gathered for use by hospitality managers in strategic decision making.

Environmental forecasting techniques

Thus far in this chapter we have identified the key environmental forces and areas which should be included in environmental scanning. The next major step is environmental forecasting – the identification, prediction, and evalu-ation of the trends, threats, and opportunities in both the general and operating environments of the hospitality firm. Table 1.9 defines the process.

According to Lebell and Krasner (1977) there are fundamental limitations in confronting an unknown future: (1) we cannot always be certain of future purposes, objectives, and strategies; (2) we may not even know what ques-tions to ask; and (3) we may not know crucial cause-and-effect relationships. Additionally, there is an inherent fear of forecasting the future, a sort of crystal-ball phobia, because of the risk involved. No one likes to be wrong, but imagine the stagnation of the industry if one did not speculate and take a chance on a new opportunity or avoid a potential threat. Firms with an

Table 1.9 The forecasting process of environmental scanning

Identification	Characterization of the industry's environmental structure Determination of the key individual components of the industry Identification of significant environmental changes
Prediction	Forecasting the magnitude and dimensions of the change Impact assessment on the firm Estimation of critical time frames and duration of impact
Evaluation	Estimation of critical time frame and duration of action Generation of alternative solutions/trade-offs Cost/benefit analysis Development of strategic plan for problem resolution

Source: Adapted from Canter (1977)

Table 1.10 Environmental forecasting techniques

Econometric models	Through computer applications complex simultaneous regression equations are used to relate economic occurrences to areas of corporate activity in a causal model method (Pearce and Robinson, 1988).
Trend analysis and other statistical methods	1. Trend extrapolation – using historical as well as current information, the trends or particular phenomena are tracked. 1a. Trend impact analysis – once trends are tracked, the impact is determined and a set of potential alternative actions is defined. 2. Time-series model – pattern identification of trends through historical, seasonal and cyclical business information. 3. Decomposition, exponential smoothing statistical techniques further refine the analysis.
Delphi technique	Uses expert opinion of individuals with the consensus opinion of the expert panel used as the forecast.
Scenario analysis	Determination of hypothetical situations and the possible courses of action to prevent, facilitate, or solve such situations.
Brainstorming	Members of the group present forecasts based on individual judgment, knowledge and creativity. Final consensus includes plausible ideas and alternative solutions.

environmental scanning structure in place have a system which can provide objective, systematic, logical, and empirical information to assist them in researching accurate and realistic predictions of business conditions as well as generating appropriate business strategies.

There are several methods that can be used in forecasting, both qualitative and quantitative, to delineate and identify trends. These can be seen in Table 1.10. Use of particular methods will depend upon the hospitality organization's needs and resources.

Summary

As hospitality firms expand internationally, they will confront a multitude of uncontrollable forces which should be proactively identified and planned for in the company's planning process. Environmental scanning and analysis is the tool to complete such a task effectively. Integration of the scanning unit into the strategic planning system is necessary to achieve the greatest benefits for the firm.

Environmental scanning will also provide an impetus to hospitality firms to move towards envisioning themselves not just as a US or UK-based firm operating internationally, but as a truly global firm operating in a global industry. Global perspective is a critical quality for managers undertaking environmental scanning and analysis given the dynamics of today's business environment. The challenges of today and tomorrow will require insight into changes in the global environment by proficient business executives. Success will be enjoyed only when these businesses can anticipate and adapt to environmental changes to create products and services to meet the customer's needs.

References

Aguilar, F. J. (1967) *Scanning the Business Environment*, New York: Macmillan.

Anon. (1989a) 'Technology: changing the business forever', *Lodging Hospitality*, vol. 45, no. 2, pp. 26–8.

Anon. (1989b) 'Solid waste: the need for action', *Restaurants USA*, vol. 9, no. 6, p. 27.

Anon. (1989c) 'Travelers want smokeless', *Lodging Hospitality*, vol. 45, no. 10, p. 24.

Anon. (1989d) 'Packaging's effect on the future of the food industry', *Food Engineering*, no. 61, p. 64.

Anon. (1991a) 'World wire: tourism in China rebounds', *The Wall Street Journal*, vol. CCXVII, no. 27, A-10.

Anon. (1991b) 'Joint venture benefits nature conservancy' *Hotel and Motel Management*, vol. 206, no. 8, p. 50.

Bates, C. (1985) 'Mapping the environment: an operational environmental analysis model', *Long Range Planning*, vol. 18, no. 5, pp. 97–107.

Bernstein, B. (1989) 'Digger: fastfood packaging minute part of waste crisis', *Nation's Restaurant News*, vol. 23, no. 10, p. 3.

Blalock, C. (1991) 'Global tourism', *Hotel and Motel Management*, vol. 206, no. 8, pp. 1–40.

Bourgeois, L. (1980) 'Strategy and environment: a conceptual integration', *Academy of Management Review*, vol. 5, no. 1, pp. 25–9.

Burack, E. H., and Mathys, N. J. (1989) 'Environmental scanning improves strategic planning', *Personnel Administrator*, vol. 34, no. 4, pp. 82–7.

Burns, T., and Stalker, G. M. (1961) *The Management of Innovation*, London: Tavistock.

Byars, L. L. (1987) *Strategic Management: Planning and implementation; concepts and cases*, New York: Harper & Row.

Canter, L. (1977) *Environmental Impact Assessment*, New York: McGraw-Hill.

Cetron, M., and Davies, O. (1989) *American Renaissance: Our life at the turn of the 21st century*, New York: St Martin's Press.

Child, J. (1972) 'Organization structure, environment and performance: the role of strategic choice', *Sociology*, vol. 6, pp. 194–206.

Clydesdale, F. M. (1989) 'Present and future of food science and technology in industrialized countries', *Food Technology*, vol. 43, no. 9, pp. 134–46.

Daft, R. L. (1989) *Organizational Theory and Design*, St Paul, Minn.: West Publishing Co.

DeNoble, A. F., and Olsen, M. D. (1982) 'The relationship between the strategic planning process and the service delivery system'; chapter 25 in *The Practice of Hospitality Management*, Pizam, A., Lewis, R. C., and Manning, P. (eds), Westport, Conn.: AVI Publishing Co.

DeNoble, A. F., and Olsen, M. D. (1986) 'The food service industry environment: market volatility analysis', *FIU Hospitality Review*, vol. 4, no. 2, pp. 89–100.

Dev, C. S., and Olsen, M. D. (1989) 'Environmental uncertainty, business strategy, and financial performance: An empirical study of the US lodging industry', *Hospitality Education and Research Journal*, vol. 13, no. 3, pp. 171–86.

Diffenbach, J. (1983) 'Corporate environmental analysis in large US corporations', *Long Range Planning*, vol. 16, no. 3, pp. 107–16.

Dill, W. R. (1958) 'Environment as an influence on management autonomy', *Administrative Science Quarterly*, vol. 2, no. 2, pp. 409–43.

Duncan, R. S. (1972) 'Characteristics of organizational environment and perceived environmental uncertainty', *Administrative Science Quarterly*, vol. 17, pp. 313–27.

Emery, F. E., and Trist, E. L. (1965) 'The causal texture of organizational environments', *Human Relations*, vol. 18, Feb., pp. 21–32.

Fayerweather, J. (1981) 'Four winning strategies for the international corporation', *Journal of Business Strategy*, vol. 2, no. 2, pp. 25–36.

Fahey, L., and King, W. R. (1977) 'Environmental scanning for corporate planning', *Business Horizons*, vol. 20, pp. 61–71.

Ghoshal, S. (1988) 'Environmental scanning in Korean firms: organizational isomorphism in action', *Journal of International Business Studies*, vol. 19, no. 1, pp. 69–86.

Harris, P. R., and Moran, R. T. (1979) *Managing Cultural Differences: High-performance strategies for today's global manager*, Houston, Tex.: Gulf Publishing Co.

Hazard, R. C. (1989) 'The industry of the future', *Lodging Hospitality*, vol. 45, no. 2, p. 42.

Herlong, J. E. (1989) 'Misguided panic over plastics', *Restaurants USA*, vol. 9, no. 7, pp. 22–3.

Hilton, E. (1991) 'Interface 1991', Luncheon Speaker at the 1991 Annual Conference of the Council on Hotel, Restaurant, and Institutional Education (CHRIE), 27 July, Houston, Texas.

Hofer, C. W., and Haller, T. P. (1980) 'GLOBESCAN: a way to better international risk assessment', *Journal of Business Strategy*, vol. 1, no. 2, pp. 41–55.

Hooper, R. L., and Rocca, B. T. (1991) 'Environmental affairs: now on the strategic agenda', *Journal of Business Strategy*, vol. 12, no. 3, pp. 26–30.

Jain, S. C. (1984) 'Environmental scanning in US corporations', *Long Range Planning*, vol. 17, no. 2, pp. 117–28.

Kass, M. (1989) 'R & I exclusive: the 90s – environment', *Restaurants and Institutions*, vol. 99, no. 30, pp. 115–36.

Keegan, W. J. (1974) 'Multinational scanning: a study of the information sources utilized by headquarters executives in multinational companies', *Administrative Science Quarterly*, vol. 19, no. 3, pp. 411–21.

Kennedy, C. R., Jr (1984) 'The external environment–strategic planning interface: US multinational corporate practices in the 1980s', *Journal of International Business Studies*, vol. 15, no. 2, pp. 99–108.

Kennedy, C. R., Jr (1988) 'Political risk management: a portfolio planning model', *Business Horizons*, vol. 31, no. 6, pp. 26–33.

King P. (1990) 'The high cost of garbage wars', *Food Management*, vol. 25, no. 1, pp. 96–115.

Kiplinger, A. H., and Kiplinger, K. A. (1989) *America in the Global Nineties*, Washington, DC: Kiplinger Washington Editors, Inc.

Klein, H. E., and Linneman, R. E. (1984) 'Environmental assessment: an international study of corporate practice', *Journal of Business Strategy*, vol. 5, no. 1, pp. 66–75.

Klein, H., and Newman, W. (1980) 'How to use SPIRE: a systematic procedure for identifying relevant environments for strategic planning', *Journal of Business Strategy*, vol. 1, no. 1, pp. 32–45.

Kobrin, S. J., Basek, J., Blank, S., and LaPalombara, J. (1980) 'The assessment and evaluation of non-economic environments by American firms: a preliminary report', *Journal of International Business Studies*, vol. 11, no. 1, pp. 32–47.

Kwansa, F., Dev., C., Ishak, N. K., Meyer, M. K., Olsen, M. D., Robichaud, R., Saleem, N., and West, J. J. (1986) 'An analysis of major trends and their impact potential affecting the hospitality industry as identified by the method of content analysis', in *Proceedings of the Annual Conference of the Council on Hotel, Restaurant and Institutional Education*, pp. 168–93.

Lawrence, P. R., and Lorsch, J. W. (1969) *Organization and Environment*, Homewood, Ill.: Irwin.

Lebell, D., and Krasner, O. J. (1977) 'Selecting environmental forecasting techniques from business planning requirements', *Academy of Management Review*, vol. 2, no. 3, pp. 373–83.

Lenz, R. T., and Engledow, J. L. (1986) 'Environmental analysis units and strategic decision-making: a field study of selected "leading-edge" corporations', *Strategic Management Journal*, vol. 7, pp. 68–89.

Malovany, D. (1990) 'Keeping baking's image clean', *Bakery Production and Marketing*, vol. 25, no. 2, pp. 58–74.

McCarthy, E. J., and Perreault, W. D. (1987) *Basic Marketing: A managerial approach*, 9th edn, Homewood, Ill.: Irwin.

Michman, R. D. (1989) 'Why forecast for the long term?', *Journal of Business Strategy*, vol. 10, no. 5, pp. 36–40.

Miles, R., Snow C., and Pfeffer, J. (1974) 'Organization-environment: concepts and issues', *Industrial Relations*, vol. 13, pp. 244–64.

Moore, Martha T. (1990) 'McDonald's to build on recyclables', *USA Today*, Section B, 18 April, p. 1.

O'Connell, J. O., and Zimmerman, J. W. (1979) 'Scanning the international environment', *California Management Review*, vol. 22, no. 2, pp. 15–23.

Olsen, M. D. (1980) 'The importance of the environment to the food service and lodging manager', *Journal of Hospitality Education*, Winter, pp. 35–45

Olsen, M. D., Crawford-Welch, S., and Tse, E. Y. (1990) 'The global hospitality industry of the 1990s: A position statement', Presented at the 2nd Conference of the *Journal of Contemporary Hospitality Management*, Dorset, England.

Olsen, M. D., and DeNoble, A. (1981) 'Strategic planning in dynamic times', *Cornell Hotel and Restaurant Administration Quarterly*, vol. 21, no. 4, pp. 75–80.

Onkvisit, S., and Shaw, J. J. (1989) *International Marketing: Analysis and strategy*, Columbus, Ohio: Merrill Publishing Co.

Painton, P. (1990) 'Planet-saving report card', *Time*, vol. 135, no. 17, p. 83.

Pearce, J. A., and Robinson, R. B. (1988) *Strategic Management: Strategy formulation and implementation*, 3rd edn, Homewood, Ill.: Irwin.

Pinto, E. S., and Olsen, M. D. (1987) 'The information needs of finance executives in the hospitality industry', *Hospitality Education and Research Journal*, vol. 11, no. 2, pp. 181–90.

Porter, M. E. (1980) *Competitive Strategy: Techniques for analyzing industries and competitors*, New York: The Free Press.

Preble, J. F., Rau, P. A., and Reichel, A. (1989) 'The environmental scanning practices of multinational firms: an assessment', *International Journal of Management*, vol. 6, no. 1, pp. 18–28.

Root, F. R. (1982) *Foreign Market Entry Strategies*, New York: AMACOM.

Schechter, M. (1989) 'The poisoning of the Earth...', *Food Management*, vol. 24, no. 1, pp. 110–13.

Sethi, N. K. (1982) 'Strategic planning system for multinational companies', *Long Range Planning*, vol. 15, no. 3, pp. 80–9.

Slattery, P., and Olsen, M. D. (1984) 'Hospitality organisations and their environment', *International Journal of Hospitality Management*, vol. 3, pp. 55–61.

Stroup, M. A. (1988) 'Environmental scanning at Monsanto', *Planning Review*, vol. 16, no. 4, pp. 24–39.

Thompson, J. D. (1967) *Organizations in Action*, New York: McGraw-Hill.

Trioble, E. (1989) 'In search of meaning', *Food Management*, vol. 24, no. 9, p. 53.

US Department of Commerce (1989) *Foreign Economic Trends and Their Implications for the United States*, International Trade Administration, FET 88, no. 48 (May).

US Department of Commerce (1990) *Foreign Economic Trends and Their Implications for the United States*, International Trade Administration, FET 90, no. 34 (March).

US Department of Commerce (1991) *Foreign Economic Trends and Their Implications for the United States*, International Trade Administration, FET 91, no. 14 (Feb.).

Utterback, J. M. (1982) 'Technological forecasting and strategy: environmental analysis and forecasting', in *Readings in the Management of Innovation*, Michael L. Tushman and William L. Moore (eds), London: Pitman.

West, J. J. (1990) 'Strategy, environmental scanning and firm performance: an integration of content and process in the foodservice industry', *Hospitality Research Journal*, vol. 14, no. 1, pp. 87–100.

West, J. J., and Olsen, M. D. (1988) 'Environmental scanning and its effect upon firm performance: an exploratory study of the foodservice industry', *Hospitality Education and Research Journal*, vol. 12, no. 2, pp. 127–36.

West, J. J., and Olsen, M. D. (1989) 'Environmental scanning, industry structure and strategy-making: concepts and research in the hospitality industry, *International Journal of Hospitality Managaement*, vol. 8, no. 4, pp. 283–98.

Weston, F., and Sorge, B. (1972) *International Financial Management*, Homewood, Ill.: Irwin.

Zugmier, G. (1989) 'Ring in the New Year with systems integration', *Lodging*, vol. 14, no. 5, p. 54.

2

The strategy, structure, environment co-alignment

Bryan Langton and Celeste Bottorff
with Michael Olsen

The challenge of matching a firm's strategy and structure to the conditions of the environment in order to achieve optimum performance is a daunting task. Few firms achieve the ideal co-alignment, but many manage to come close. Once a balance is obtained they must avoid the natural feeling of complacency that often occurs when an objective is achieved. They must discipline themselves to engage continuously in the constant struggle to stay ahead of environmental changes so that they can continue to achieve this co-alignment. Holiday Inn Worldwide (HIW) is no different from any other multinational firm in this regard. Since the Bass acquisition of the Holiday Inn core brand, the firm has been restructuring itself to enable it to meet the needs of a business environment that is becoming increasingly hostile. In this chapter a summary of the key environmental issues facing this global lodging giant will be identified along with the choice of competitive methods making up the firm's overall strategy.

Environmental events

The broad environment of today's global lodging firm can be broken into five categories: economic, technological, sociocultural, political, and ecological. In addition to this broad classification structure, the more immediate or task environment can be subdivided into the areas of finance, marketing, human resources, administration, operations, and research and development. The key events in these environmental categories which HIW see as influencing their strategy and structure are presented below.

Broad environmental events

While it is generally agreed that there is a global recession going on, this does not take away from the fact that business expansion continues to drive growth. This growth in business will continue to stimulate the lodging business in various regions of the world, but this will be tempered with the difficulties associated with obtaining capital. The availability of needed funds to support growth in this industry has diminished considerably as a result of declining global real-estate values, lower inflation, and competition for funds to support the move to market economies in the East. Important to this issue are the stability of the governments in need of capital, the policies they develop to permit investment, and the ease with which capital can be moved in and out across a country's borders. This phenomenon will no doubt hasten the consolidation of the industry as only the financially strong will be able to exist in this climate.

Technology will continue to make a difference to the way the industry grows. The deregulation of national telecommunications systems worldwide will enhance opportunities for marketing hotel rooms. This deregulation will have to be accompanied by continued growth and development of smart logic systems which will be used to assist managers in improving the pricing of their product to meet the needs of the increasingly demanding customer. Developments in technology will continue to change the way hotels are managed and how customers choose the hotels they will stay in.

The critical event in the sociocultural domain will be the continued, and in some cases increased, reliance upon employees whose native language is different from the one in the nation they are working in. This issue of language and cultural diversity will place increased burdens on managements as they try to compete in the hostile environment. The diversity will be compounded if the industry continues to employ technology to meet its needs, for not only will typical language problems be present, but these will be made more complex by the language of technology which almost inevitably accompanies this type of innovation. All this implies that firms will become increasingly responsible for the education (especially the literacy) of their employees. Employees of this type also tend to be high risk as their basic health may not be the best and thus they will also demand from the employer more responsibility for their care.

From the customers' perspective, the sociocultural domain will reflect less patience with service deficiencies. Their expectations are much higher and prone to comparison as never before. With these higher standards and a more complex labor force problem, multinational chains will be hard pressed to develop strategies that can deliver on service expectations consistently from day to day and from country to country.

The political domain impacts business investment opportunities based upon the degree of risk associated with the stability of a nation. Stability is tied to the ability of government officials to maintain economic growth and consistency in governing. If governments are able to offer a safe harbor for investments, then these will occur at a cost of capital which is realistic. If stability is in question, then firms are forced to utilize capitalization rates which have risk hurdles that often prohibit the investment. Beyond stability comes the question of trade barriers. Growth in lodging investment will be contingent upon the ease with which firms can do business in various countries around the globe. Governments will have to address the issue of trade barriers, including not only investment but also travel. Issues regarding the exchange of currency, visas, and taxes on entry and exit are important political variables that must be considered in the development of hotels globally.

The environment has become an important focus for the hospitality industry. While much concern has been generated about the role the industry plays in producing solid waste and waste water, the issue tends to be one which is addressed at the local legislative level as opposed to on a global basis. Thus, as yet, few universal policy statements or guidelines have been developed by firms because they are primarily interested in, and monitor, what will occur locally.

As can be seen, the broad-based environment contains many important issues which will have significant impact upon the lodging industry. While these issues are being addressed by firms, they cannot afford to ignore the events occurring in the more immediate or task environment. These often have more direct impact upon the way business is done for their repercussions are more immediate and observable.

Task environment events

The principal activity occurring in the environmental category of marketing is the increased expenditures in marketing by all firms. This increase has been brought on by a combination of the global recession exacerbated by the Gulf War and the maturation of the industry demand curve itself. It is important to recognize that, if this increase in expenditures continues, it will make it increasingly difficult for firms with limited funds and expertise to mount large-scale and effective marketing and advertising programs. Only firms with strong financial backing will be able to afford, and thus realize, the benefits of more effective methods of target marketing and subsequent pricing strategies designed to reach these markets.

In the areas of finance, the industry throughout the 1980s has been plagued by short-term financing strategies to finance long-term projects such as hotels and resorts. This type of thinking has resulted in too many short-term decisions. Until firms take a more realistic approach and decide to match financing with project duration, conditions in the industry will not improve and only the financially strong will be able to weather it out in the long run.

The shrinking and more culturally diverse labor pool was referenced earlier in the discussion of sociocultural changes, but it will impact more directly on the costs associated with the management of human resources. The cost of health care for this more high-risk group, along with the costs associated with providing them with appropriate education and training, will likely put continued upward pressure on labor costs.

In the task environment category of operations the emphasis will be on new product development, both in the room and in the food and beverage operations. From new food items to mattresses which last twice as long, firms will be directing efforts on a more continuous basis to searching for or developing new products to meet the needs of their target markets. In addition to new products, firms will also be in search of new business processes or systems (such as yield management) to make them more competitive. There is a cost to this type of development process and so it will likely be those firms that have deep pockets that will be able to lead the industry in this regard.

Given these events in the broad and task environments, it is up to management to design an organization and strategy to address these issues. Matching environment, strategy, and structure is what HIW is attempting to do, and this will be highlighted in the sections that follow.

Obtaining the match

To steer its way effectively through these environmental forces HIW has attempted to create a strategy that will utilize a variety of competitive methods to capitalize upon its financial strength and vast distribution system. While it will still take some time to implement each method fully, it is felt that the methods which will be most effective for them include: product differentiation, high value for money, superior execution of the basics, utilization of economies of scale, and superior management of the distribution processes that bring in customers.

These primary competitive methods suggest that the overall strategy for HIW will be to continue to work on improving quality while utilizing the strengths associated with the economies of scale that such a large firm possesses. This financial strength will also permit it to compete effectively on price while investing in technology that will help it differentiate its product and make it the leader in systems and processes designed to improve the use of information in business decisions and management.

As can be seen, these competitive methods do reflect in part the events in the environment. The method of pricing the product to provide the highest quality at the appropriate price point for the target market clearly reflects the growing demands by the consumer in this regard. The use of technology will bring about better ways to market the product through improved management of the channels of distribution. This mirrors the industry's growing emphasis on marketing and advertising. Improved management of the basics reflects the overall need to strengthen quality in the light of consumers' higher expectations.

Given that these methods reflect conditions in the environment, how has HIW adjusted its structure to match its overall strategy? First, the move from Memphis to Atlanta resulted in a significant change in the overall culture of the firm. With fresh minds and ideas being hired, the company now has a new, more aggressive culture that will enable it to meet the needs of the 1990s. The organization chart, compensation system and benefit package have been designed to support this new breed of talent.

As HIW implements this strategy globally, it will rely upon a matrix organization which will maintain primary strength and control of policy for finance, marketing and human resources at the head office level. There will be a field counterpart to these head office functions organized according to geographic region (Europe, Middle East and Africa, and Asia and the Americas). Additionally, there will be organizational units for franchised and company-managed hotels. This structure, it is believed, will allow HIW to react to changing regional and local market conditions swiftly while still permitting it to achieve a new improved image for its hotels.

Planning will reflect more input from the regions, and changes in strategy resulting from this will be subject to more competition among organizational divisions for capital and management attention. This means that plans will have to fit a more comprehensive model which will look at groups of decisions or deals as opposed to piecemeal evaluation of new opportunities as has occurred in the past.

Timing of the match

It is too early to know whether or not HIW will accomplish the successful implementation of its strategy, for the match between strategy, structure, and environment is not a matter of decree by planners and top-level executives. Nor is it a matter of perfect precision. The match takes time to develop and often management must accept less of a match than it likes, primarily because it is difficult to control events in the environment. In this case the match may take longer to achieve, for it will be difficult to synthezise new personnel, ideas, and needs in a competitive and mature environment. The job of all the executives, no matter what level of the organization, will be to help bring about the match as quickly as possible. Time will tell whether or not its choice of competitive methods will make up the right strategy, but for now HIW feels that it is on the right track.

3

The international hospitality industry and public policy

Frank M. Go, Philip Goulding,
and David Litteljohn

As the twenty-first century approaches, business environments can best be characterized by change, complexity, constraints, and conflicts; some authors go further to mention chaos as an important environmental feature (Peters, 1987, p. xi; Makridakis, 1990, p. 89).

Traditionally, many managers have been trained and educated to give their primary focus to ensuring the efficiency of their organizations. This has often meant that the target for their attention has been the internal functions of the organization. However, environmental turbulence requires that managers and planners within the hospitality industry be in a position to interpret developments for the operations of their organizations quickly and accurately.

This requirement is met when managers see that their organization's development and success lie within the markets and societies that it services. A prime point in arriving at this understanding is to appreciate the concept of business environments. Essentially this ensures that attention is given to those factors which, although important, lie outside the narrow confines of an organization's operations.

Slattery and Olsen (1984) have classified this in the following manner:

- The general environment, consisting of a set of conditions such as technology, law, politics, economy, demography, ecology, culture, time, and society. These are the conditions that apply to all organizations.
- The specific environment, which for hospitality organizations includes potential customers, suppliers, competitors, and regulatory groups.

When relating this type of analysis much attention is usually given to the specific industrial environment under consideration. Within the general environment such aspects as demography are studied in some depth. While not ignored, however, political factors are often given only very general treatment in many instances; and while elements of political risk are seen to impact on hospitality investment, particularly as organizations move out of the relative political stability of advanced industrial societies, these risks are considered on a one-by-one basis and are not given the depth of analysis that other factors receive.

Even recently Vern Terpstra (1985) opined that economic factors were of prime importance as they conditioned a nation's differential in terms of industrial and commercial output. In contrast, he stated: 'The political map of the world does not change rapidly. Our present wall maps will probably be good for the year 2000.' However, part of the turbulence referred to above may be attributed to the very real political changes that have taken place since 1989 in Eastern Europe and the former Soviet Union, and the realigning of trading relationships, both globally (in the General Agreement on Tariffs and Trade) and regionally (in the Americas and Europe, for example).

Changing trading arrangements and new political alliances that may adjust notions of national sovereignty, including the nature of regulating the business environment within its own borders, mean that hospitality decision makers will need to consider the political context in more detail than has hitherto been the case. This political setting is further emphasized by movements from many sides that organizations pay more attention to the impact of their operations on the environment – here the reference extends to the pollution, energy, and natural resource sustainability aspects of hospitality activity.

In surveying these changes and considering their implications for their organizations, managers will have to distinguish between strong and weak movements. They are interested in identifying trends which are essentially increases or declines lasting long enough to bring about a structural change or transformation of some activity or institution (Martel, 1986). These contrast to cyclical, temporary changes which leave untouched the basic conditions of society and its institutions, notwithstanding their impact over the short term.

What follows is an overview of these external environments which act as a catalyst for setting up new frameworks for understanding the business environment. This is termed the *public policy impact chain*. It has been developed bearing in mind the current emphasis on internationalization within hospitality. The emerging issues (Ritchie, 1991) that follow may be seen as significant factors that influence the other elements in the public policy impact chain, national goals and strategies, and tourism policy, with the tourism sector and the hotel industry at the end of the chain.

The first part of this chapter will assess major demographic, social, economic, technological, and political trends; later the emergence of international hospitality companies will be established. The second part of the chapter will evaluate the main types of public policy issue that are likely to be encountered, through an examination of tourism policy at the international level and, in turn, within the national policy context. Thereafter an appreciation of the utility in understanding the process of the public policy impact chain may be gained.

The role of government

Within the context of government business relations, the role of government can be seen to embrace a number of different factors: 'governments everywhere are major economic agents acting as legitimizer, planner, regulator, economic developer, supplier of various scarce goods, customer and competitor' (Boddewyn, 1975).

Thus governments are major influences in setting the nature of the economic climate through monetary and fiscal policies. In addition they will have industrial strategies which may include elements of competition policy and regional aid programs. Governments may supply scarce goods in the nature of capital towards investment projects, assistance for workforce training, and more intangible elements such as law and order. They may provide customers for an organization if, for instance, they buy services produced by the organization, while in other situations they may be in direct competition with it, if it operates businesses of a similar nature.

Traditionally, firms have often been considered to have a narrower outlook than governments in relation to their environments. For example, governments will have to consider areas of social policy, while commercial organizations will concentrate on more limited commercial goals. The exact make-up of the relationship that exists between any organization and a government will depend on the type of company and its history, the nature, economic health, and strategic importance of the industrial sectors within which the company operates, together with the political and ideological disposition of the government. Current trends in the world economy may, however, be seen to be changing the nature of this relationship.

In the first place, there is the element of scale which multinationals inject into the balance of power in their relationships with host governments. It was often considered that the independence of governments was brought into question by powerful large businesses whose interests span several countries; this was particularly felt when the host countries were relatively small, but can also be a concern in larger economies. Recently, movements in economies which have seen convergence in policies affecting business aid and regulation, and monetary and fiscal aims have impacted on the nature of government business relations, with businesses sometimes having to make considerable changes in their relations with the bodies which have a direct effect on their operations in the spheres mentioned above.

In the second place, there is the convergence in operating practices that multinationals themselves may bring to their organizations. Thus it has recently been reported that a number of multinational companies are taking a more proactive, even visionary, stance towards environmental issues, often adopting energy-saving and pollution control measures ahead of current legislation (International Institute of Management Development, 1991).

Overview of trends

Demographic environment

Demographics, defined here as the study of human population trends, are of interest to hospitality industry decision makers from two very different perspectives:

- On the demand side, demographic trend analysis can be a key tool for researching future consumer markets, particularly where organizational scale and spheres of operation necessitate both a macro and long-term approach to demand forecasting.
- On the supply side, the labor-intensive nature of the international hospitality industry should determine how the industry assesses the impacts of demographic trends on its labor market. The International Hotel Association, for example, sees human resource issues resulting from long-term demographic trends as a primary concern for hoteliers into the third millennium (Dix, 1990).

The issues arising from demographic change are as complex in their own right as their impacts for corporate hospitality organizations. However, instead of viewing such changes as potentially threatening or destabilizing, a proactive approach by industry decision makers sees them as an opportunity for organizational evaluation.

At this point, it is worth considering the global demographic scenario, in terms of both its headline trends and its important undercurrents. The former impact particularly on international growth and social cohesion, and accordingly focus governments' attention on such issues as these within matters of national policy formulation. The undercurrents, meanwhile, may be of more specific interest to companies by virtue of their strategic impact implications.

Aggregate population growth

- The world's population will rise from the current 5.1 billion to 6 billion by the year 2000, and to a safe estimate of 8 billion people by 2025. Such increases are based on headline population growth rates having peaked at 2.5 percent per annum in the 1960s and having declined to around 2.0 percent by the start of the 1990s. Ninety percent of this growth will be in the developing countries, whose collective share of world population will increase from approximately three-quarters to five-sixths. Indeed, the European Community (1991 membership) will have fewer inhabitants than the Moslem countries in the Middle East (Godet and Barre, 1988) by 2000.
- Europe's aggregate population growth rate declined from just over 1 percent per annum in the 1960s to just under 0.75 percent by 1990 (Rogaly, 1991). A few countries with moderately high fertility rates (Turkey, Poland, and Romania, for example) compensate those in much of the rest

of the continent with near zero growth or net population decline. With rates of fertility at significantly less than the net reproduction rate of 2.1 children, late twentieth-century Europe has accumulated a problem of inherent population shrinkage. Reversal of this state of affairs will require a generation of increasing family size to restore growth.

Thus, the headline trend is a fundamental shift in the geographical spread of the world's population. Of specific strategic importance, however, is that the hospitality and tourism industries of the developed world can expect to face shortages in those labor markets on which they have traditionally largely drawn. Where the industry's medium-term growth forecasts are generally optimistic, as in the UK and the USA (BTA, USTTA), the issues of servicing the industry's labor needs to sustain such growth become acute.

Immigration has often played a vital role in supplying the developed world's hospitality industry labor market thus far, and to some extent this can be expected to continue in the 1990s. However, a combination of stricter First World immigration policies (led by a common post-1992 European Community approach) and the continued need to sustain the economic growth of these advanced nations (despite a reduced productive human resource base) means that labor-intensive industries will be forced to address recruitment, retention, and productivity issues on a more systematic basis. In short, if the economically advanced countries' indigenous work forces experience zero or negative growth, advances in productivity or corporate expansion will be activated only at a significantly higher scale of investment in training and capital resources.

The developing world faces a reverse pressure – the creation of jobs to meet the needs of the young unemployed and underemployed, currently estimated to measure 500 million (Kurent, 1991, p. 78) and growing. This exposes the second major feature of the demographic scenario.

Fundamental shifts in the population age structure

- The consequence of long-term declining fertility rates in the developed world is an aging population. Coupled with advances in real purchasing power, savings propensities, housing standards, medical science, public health, and social welfare, the conditions for increased life expectancy have been carefully fostered in all advanced societies. In the United Kingdom, the 65 and over age group now constitutes 12.5 percent of the population, as against 9.2 percent in 1950. By 2025 they will represent nearly 16 percent (Rogaly, 1991). Similar patterns are evidenced in nearly every industrialized society. The 'old old' (75-plus years) will likewise constitute a larger sector of the aging populations as average life expectancy continues its upward trend.

- In most of the developing world, on the other hand, the more recent fertility peak combined with declining net mortality rates is responsible for a more youthful population profile. Despite declining rates of childbearing in many faster developing countries such as Brazil, Mexico, and

Indonesia, the total number of births each year continues to increase and will do so until such time as their national rates of fertility fall to the net reproduction rate. According to UN medium variant estimates, the watershed will not be reached in South Asia, Latin America, and Africa until at least the year 2020.

Kurent (1991, p. 178) characterized this emerging demographic scenario as 'a First World Bust and a Third World Boom' in which the number of young people in the Third World is projected to rise from 665 million to 900 million with a proportionate decline in the young population of the developed countries.

Demographic trends thus create their own economic, social, and political dynamics. For national and international policy makers the issues range from immigration to social welfare provision to birth control to investment and employment creation. Where commercial organizations operate across international boundaries, they are inevitably affected to a greater or lesser extent by aspects of policy making which stem from population pressure. In many cases, a firm's operations may form an important part of a country's industrial or regional development policy. Indeed, many authors have analyzed the relationship between host, governments and tourism multinationals (Dunning and McQueen, 1981; Sinclair and Sutcliffe, 1988; etc.) and the economic cost/benefit arguments of developing an international hospitality sector (Jenkins and Henry 1982; Dieke, 1989).

For the hospitality decision maker, however, the demographic undercurrents may well be of greater concern, in either domestic or international contexts. Unlike manufacturing organizations, hospitality service operators do not have the strategic option of transferring production to more cost-effective, productive or skilled locations abroad. Rather they must adapt to national circumstances. In the demographic context this means managing change proactively.

This analysis has attempted to provide a global overview of demographic trends and their public policy implications as they impact on the hospitality industry. The overriding human resource issue, as defined by Ritchie (1991), is the 'continuing and growing need to increase the supply of personnel and to enhance their professionalism.' The dynamics of demographic change may be characterized as an increasing human resource mismatch between developed and developing regions of the world, in which labor and skills shortages and surpluses coexist within an organization's global operating environment. In order to address Ritchie's thesis, hospitality decision makers must first address the demographic realities which, according to Dix (1990), may be the catalyst required to prompt the industry to develop a strategic response to human resources.

Social trends

The main focus arising from the process of population change was seen in terms of its human resource implications. The wider processes of social change merely add to the complexity of issues confronting hospitality decision makers. The following paragraphs aim to highlight a few of the issues, and consider their implications in terms of emerging market characteristics.

The decline of childbirth, the deferred age of marriage, and rising divorce rates in industrialized countries are leading to smaller average households and a population characterized by a higher average life expectancy. Medical advances will enable people to live longer, healthier lives as new drugs and types of surgery will help control and counter the effects of diseases and push back the frontiers of aging. The Baby Boom generation has applied the concept of preventive medicine, and a generally healthier lifestyle will help assure a healthier old age for many consumers. The combination of demographic and social trends have two main implications for the hospitality industry:

- Smaller average household size tends to equate with greater mobility and more discretionary income and time to devote to travel activities.
- As a result of the increase in life expectancy, a larger share of travelers will consist of older consumers, many of whom have a secured income and fewer family responsibilities and are physically more active (Shafer, 1989, p. 3).

At the same time, the preferences of the 'mature' market concerning the type of travel experience desired is likely to change. Adjusting the hotel product to changing social structures and special needs will become increasingly important. So far, attention in industrialized nations has focused largely on the pressures the growing group of elderly will place on pensions and health care. But in fact the changes to come will range from where seniors will live to where they will eat, and what foods they will consume – a market with enormous opportunity for the hotel industry. Developers are beginning to investigate the relatively new, but rapidly expanding market for senior citizen housing: private retirement centres, including the lifecare centre concepts, have excellent growth potential well into the twenty-first century. This is particularly so in those societies where traditional family and community bonds are weakest.

Sociocultural determinants, especially the higher levels of education and cultural values, are having a pronounced effect on consumer lifestyles in industrialized countries. As a counter-reaction to global homogenization in the marketplace, many individuals and groups make a conscious effort to strengthen and sustain their cultural identity. As a result, a paradoxical situation seems to be emerging 'in which cultural diversity is thriving in a sea of homogenization' (Ritchie, 1991). Moreover, the media have accelerated the confrontation between social traditions and consumer behavior.

The once accepted authority of family, religion, and political institutions is being replaced by emancipation, a concern for ecology, and a growing interest in well-being, health, and lifelong learning. The tourism industry will be the potential beneficiary of these trends in increasingly diverse lifestyles if it manages to adapt to 'demographic shifts [that] are occurring which will dramatically transform the level and nature of tourism' (Ritchie, 1991).

For the hospitality industry, some of the more significant social changes have included the following:

- Young professionals constitute a major travel market in developed countries where existing attitudes have made the two-income household the norm. Typically in the 25–44 age group, this segment tends to be better educated and more widely traveled than previous generations, and they place a high priority on travel as a means of broadening personal experience. This category of traveler is affluent, status conscious and brand loyal, though time constraints will tend to shorten trip duration and increase trip frequencies.
- The growing older section of the population includes a significant segment with retirement savings and relatively high disposable incomes for leisure travel. This 'grey market' segment is also healthier and more mobile than previous generations, and better educated. According to the US Bureau of Labor Statistics, for example, the median income for US households headed by individuals aged 55–64 is about 8 percent above the average national level of discretionary income. With both time and income available, older Americans are more inclined to travel than ever, and also tend to stay in the better class of accommodation when they do so.
- The family vacation remains a vital element in leisure travel, and the peak summer months, despite attempts by many destinations to spread the peak, remain of central importance. Vacations tend to be more activity oriented, however, and as major markets such as the USA amend their educational patterns toward longer school years, the nature of this market may also change (Go and Welch, 1991, p. 11).

Economic and trading environments

Economic development since the Second World War has raised living standards in most industrialized countries to unprecedented levels and provided the impetus for the growth of tourism. The explosive growth of tourism during the post-war era is partially the result of the economic growth triggered by the rise of the service sector, which in turn has been the product of several interrelated processes (Gershuny and Miles, 1983). First, the increasing geographical specialization that characterized the industrial era had the effect not only of stimulating trade, but also of generating new opportunities for employment and investment in the service sector. Second, the market for many basic manufactured goods had become saturated, leaving consumers free to spend a larger proportion of their incomes on leisure and personal services. Finally, a large number of jobs were created in the public sector of industrial economies where gross domestic product (GDP) from services has reached more than 60 percent (Price and Blair, 1989, p. 12).

Travel growth is inextricably linked to GDP growth in general, and growth of per capita income in particular. In this regard, the speed with which Japan caught up with and overtook European countries (see Table 3.1) is striking:

Table 3.1 **Average annual growth rates of real per capita income (%)**

	1960–69	1970–79	1980–84
Total OECD	3.9	2.2	1.1
Japan	9.1	3.2	3.0
Total developing countries	3.1	3.1	0.0
Africa	2.2	0.8	−2.5
Asia	3.6	3.8	2.3
Latin America	2.6	2.9	−2.6

Source: *Tourism Policy and International tourism in OECD Member Countries,* Paris, OECD.

its per capita income increased by 152 percent during the twenty years, compared to 67 percent for North America and 58 percent for Europe.

The swift rise of Japan to second place in terms of gross national product among industrial powers, the advent of the unified European market, and 'free trade' between the USA and Canada and potentially Mexico has resulted in what Ohmae (1986) refers to as the 'Triad', comprised of three main trading blocs: Europe, Japan, and North America. The emergence of the Triad has led to increasing tensions and may result in protectionist trade barriers. Since international trade and tourism are intertwined and the growth of international tourism depends primarily on the free movement of people, there is a need to reduce barriers to international travel, including restrictions on passports, visas, currency controls, and travel allowances. Edgell (1990, p. 55) notes that more than a hundred countries have some form of travel allowance restriction, which can only be removed through multilateral negotiations between the governments of nation states. Since its inception in 1947, the General Agreement on Tariffs and Trade (GATT) has engaged in seven Rounds of Negotiation. The GATT was due to conclude its Uruguay Round in December 1990 with the controversial question of the desirability of including trade in services within the scope of the Agreement or in a separate agreement to be known as GATS, the General Agreement on Trade in Services (Cobbs, 1991, p. 213).

The extended Uruguay Round continues to focus the world's public and corporate policy makers' attention on securing stability and opportunity in international trading relations. Discernable movements are occurring toward greater regional economic cooperation between nation states to the extent that evolving trade blocs are viewed in terms of potential geopolitical realignments. The EC debate over 'deepening' its process of economic, social, and political integration in preference to 'broadening' its membership base must be considered in the context of its synergic gains. Cecchini *et al.* (1988) noted the EC12 expect to reap an additional growth of 5 percent of their combined GNP from the 1992 process of market integration.

The Association of South East Asian Nations (ASEAN) is increasingly reflecting a convergence of external trade, investment, social and environmental policy among its member states, in international fora. An example is ASEAN's common voice on the Trade Related Investment Measures (TRIMs) policy proposals in the GATT negotiations. The recent interest in North American regional trade cooperation is producing shock waves throughout the Americas, where moribund or malfunctioning regional associations (the Andean Pact, Central American Common Market, and Caricom) are beginning to redefine their mutual economic interests. The proposed Mercosur grouping in the Southern Cone of South America aims to be a functioning common market by the mid-1990s. Table 3.2 provides a general outline of developments in major regional economic groupings.

Citing the lessons of the effective integration of the world's financial markets, Julius (1990) noted three outcomes for public policy of the process of general economic or market integration:

- National policy is less able to influence either the market structure or the behavior of its market participants, leading to a loss of national policy autonomy over trade, investment, and economic issues.
- A powerful internal dynamic is created for policy convergence across national boundaries (corporate tax rates across OECD countries, EC VAT harmonization, etc.).
- Pressures for systematic stability in the process of market integration could, in theory, drive regulation to the lowest common denominator (e.g. financial, environmental, health and safety, or social policy controls).

Despite the significance of the GATT negotiations, Ostry (1990, p. 10) suggests that the present phase of accelerating world integration may be less dominated by increasing trade linkages than by foreign direct investment and technology flows.

Within this framework the transnational corporation and government become the main actors (Dicken, 1986) that will shape the international economic environment of the coming decades. The rise in influence of the transnational corporation has been explained earlier. The access which transnational corporations have to technology, financial resources, and marketing expertise provides them with a substantial competitive advantage. Although few transnational corporations, and arguably none in hospitality, currently operate on a truly global scale, many are accelerating their involvement in the global market through corporate alliances with key players.

The rise of the transnational corporation has led to the emergence of a requirement for a common global return on investment which influences investment decisions around the world in all industries. As a consequence, the tourism industry is increasingly being pressured into competition with other industries for investment funding. Given the growing high cost of capital for the development of tourism infrastructure, the present environment favors the transnational corporation because of its adequate resources, management talent, and financing (Ritchie, 1991, p. 155).

There is a caution in the acceleration of the global deployment of transnational tourism corporations. Perhaps most significant is the emergence of the

Table 3.2 International organization of regional economic groupings

Organization (and date of establishment)	Membership	Sphere of operation/aims	Developments
OECD Organization for Economic Cooperation and Development (1961–OEEC)	24 advanced industrial nations comprising the 'Triad', Australia/ New Zealand, and other Western European States	Not a customs union or trade bloc as such, rather a forum for cooperation in economic, social, and environmental policy formulation in member states; fosters common outlooks toward creating stable economic conditions in OECD members and in their policy toward other nations Measures economic performance in member states and across a wide range of industries including tourism; encourages common policies in measurement of tourism	Active semi-autonomous bodies, including conference of Ministers of Transport Increasing involvement in service industries policy and in evaluation and forecasting of economic performance
EC European Community (1957 Treaty of Rome; 1987 Single European Act)	12 European states; Extensive preferential trade and economic development agreements with 51 African, Caribbean and Pacific (ACP) states through Lomé agreements, latterly extending to tourism development Trade agreements with Maghreb states, Turkey, and Cyprus 1991 agreement with 7 EFTA states to create tariff-free 'European Economic Area'	Economic integration through removal of all internal barriers to movement of goods and services; harmonization of economic and social policy	Pressures for increasing convergence in social, judicial, defence, and foreign policy Pressures for wider membership; formal applications lodged by several nations; possible membership of 20+ nations by early 21st century

EFTA European Free Trade Association (1960)	7 European nations (4 Nordic, 3 Alpine): Norway, Sweden, Finland, Iceland, Austria, Switzerland, Liechtenstein	Economic cooperation through dismantling of common internal tariffs and other trade barriers	Since 1984 Development of EFTA–EC agenda for abolishing trade barriers; 1991 EFTA–EC agreement to create a European Economic Area Most EFTA members committed to EC membership in short to medium term
Caricom Caribbean Community and Common Market (1973)	13 member states (UK Commonwealth Caribbean countries) plus 3 observers (Dominican Republic, Haiti, Surinam)	Economic cooperation; coordination of foreign policy; provision of common services and cooperation in areas such as education, health, cultural issues, communications	Some success in developing common policies towards external trade relations, civil aviation, shipping Intense inter-island competition in tourism development
ASEAN Association of South East Asian Nations (1967)	Malaysia, Singapore, Thailand, Indonesia, Philippines, Brunei (fast-developing economies exhibiting high annual rates of GDP growth since 1980s)	Acceleration of economic growth, social progress, and cultural development; collaboration and mutual assistance in matters of common interest, e.g. air traffic control, tourism (1992 is ASEAN Tourism Year)	Increasingly representing a unified voice in international trade fora Significant dismantling of service sector trade and inward investment barriers since 1980s
Andean Pact	Bolivia, Colombia, Ecuador, Peru, Venezuela	Economic cooperation through dismantling trade barriers, collaboration in matters of common regional infrastructure and development issues, and common voice in external trade negotiations	Largely ineffective in promoting regional economic integration or advancement. Recent moves to revive the grouping in response to free trade agreements in North America and within the Southern cone

(continued)

Table 3.2 (continued)

Organization (and date of establishment)	Membership	Sphere of operation/aims	Developments
ECOWAS Economic Community of West African States	Nigeria, Ghana, Gambia, Sierra Leone, Liberia, Côte d'Ivoire, Senegal, Togo, Benin, Mali, Niger, Burkino Faso, Guinea, Guinea-Bissau, Cape Verde, Mauritania (16 members)	Promotion of cooperation and development in trade, industry, agriculture, transport, social and cultural affairs, communications, energy and finance	Some moves toward dismantling barriers to freer movement of people, e.g. visa liberalization. Common policies toward regional transport networking, air traffic control, signage etc. Very limited market development inhibits effectiveness
SADCC Southern African Development Coordination Conference (1979)	Angola, Botswana, Lesotho, Malawi, Mozambique, Namibia, Swaziland, Tanzania, Zambia, Zimbabwe	To reduce dependence on South Africa; harmonization of development plans; tourism and transport included among several sectoral commissions, though tourism given low priority in project funding	Real progress severely impeded by civil unrest in several member states throughout the 1980s. More optimistic outlook for the 1990s with changes in South Africa mapping the route to closer economic ties and opening up of market access in the region

'stateless' corporation which is not bound by the laws and regulations of any one country. In order to avoid serious problems, both real and perceived, especially at the destination level, policy makers must think through the potential implications that the transnationals could have on tourism in their countries (Go and Ritchie, 1990). More specifically, 'The widening gap between the North/South (developed/developing) nations continues to cause frictions and to be a constant source of concern for harmonious tourism development.' (Ritchie, 1991.)

The expanding involvement of less developed countries (LDCs) in tourism has caused intensification of interregional travel. However, despite the highest growth rate of arrivals, LDCs have the worst earnings record. On a worldwide basis, tourism receipts, both domestic and international, amount to 9.3 percent of world gross national product, but to only 5 percent in the Third World. The abundance of low-cost labor in many LDCs coupled with their novelty appeal means that Third World tourism destinations are often in keen competition, and it may follow that some should develop indigenous tourism (Gunn, 1988, p. 273) and manage their relationship with transnational corporations from a stronger base.

At the same time it is becoming more important for transnational corporations to learn about project development in the regional tourism planning context because of the rising sentiment that the tourism industry is too important to local communities to be left in the hands of 'outsider' professionals (McNulty and Wafer, 1990, p. 293). The growing desire for local participation on the part of the host community would suggest that transnational hotel corporations should examine their options to become more sensitive to cultural assets and the potential for involvement of local entrepreneurs. Consequently, the time may have come when the international tourism industry must proceed on a new assumption: namely, that it will be welcome only when it is willing to respect the host community. It follows that TNCs, in their own interest, should become more sensitive to matters regarding the host environment in which they operate.

Furthermore, it can be noted that the trend to market economies and shrinking government budgets is creating strong pressures for privatization and deregulation of tourism facilities and services – nowhere more so than in Eastern Europe, where the cracking of the Iron Curtain has resulted in ideas, goods, and services flowing more freely between East and West. Formerly centrally planned economies will be increasingly plugged into the global economy. With the Soviet Union and Eastern European countries opening their doors to foreign trade, Western-based MNCs are establishing toeholds in key industries like transportation, telecommunications, and tourism. For example, the Warsaw Marriott represents the first joint venture to be signed with a Polish company after sanctions were lifted in 1987. The hotel employs 900 local Polish workers and is helping to bring much-needed foreign investment as well as state-of-the-art hospitality training and service to the fledgling free-market economy.

Technological environment

Technological advances, especially in transportation, have influenced the development of the physical means through which passengers and goods are moved. However, scientific discoveries in sectors other than transportation are currently auto-feeding themselves and drag, at an accelerating speed, a series of chain reactions. The sectors where innovations are occurring that are particularly relevant to tourism development include telecommunications, computers and video equipment, natural sciences and medicine, and automation/robotics (Shafer, 1989).

As discussed earlier, innovations in telecommunications are laying the foundation for an international information highway system that will eventually wire the world into a more or less integrated communications network. Developments in telecommunications are vital to the service sector (Price and Blair, 1989, p. 114) because they have the potential to change the way people work, learn and shop, and the way they are entertained and cared for, in terms of social, legal, medical, and travel services.

Much debate has centered on whether tele-conferencing capabilities will improve to an extent where they will offer a substitute product for business travel, or whether tele-conferencing will serve as a supplementary product to face-to-face meetings because of the ongoing need for human interaction. At present no specific patterns have emerged to answer these questions. In general, technological advances have been affirmatively beneficial to the development of leisure activities in society, especially with respect to home entertainment. Broadcasting technology has contributed to tourism by encouraging greater awareness of place. Czinkota *et al.* (1989, p. 632) view international (tele)communications as the great 'equalizer' of the future, because it involves the transmission of news and information about lifestyles, products, and ideas.

The trend toward higher levels of automation will increase as mechanical and information technologies are combined and computer and micro-processors become smaller, more powerful, and less expensive (Makridakis, 1990, p. 269). The new breed of factory worker in Japan may be a robot by the year 2000. Industrial robots are steadily getting better and cheaper, and the number of such robots in developed nations is growing rapidly, Weil (1982) estimated that by 1990 there would be 70,000 robots in use in Japan, 60,000 in the USA, and 25,000 in Sweden and the UK, followed closely by France.

The elimination of many manual factory jobs may take place in the 1990s. Office and service jobs, on the other hand, will increase but only for those who are prepared to increase their technical knowledge. Automation in the form of robots, supercopiers, and information networks are anticipated to replace, during the 1990s, many of the low-skilled and semi-skilled jobs prevalent in the advanced economy of the 1980s.

The impact of computer reservations systems (CRS) on the world's international hospitality and tourism industries has been immense. In less than a decade their role has metamorphosed from simply facilitating market access for a firm's product information to that of providing an integrated market distribution system in strategic alliance with complementary travel services. The level of competitive advantage thus conferred on a participating organization increases commensurate with the scale of change in the role and size of the CRS. The magnitude of their importance has been defined in terms of their constituting an industry in their own right which will significantly alter the pattern of international tourism in the 1990s (Collier, 1989).

Increasing technology has both positive and negative implications for the international hospitality industry. The positive aspects of technological advances include enhancement of performance and effectiveness in production and service delivery systems. Also, as automation increases, more free time should be available to workers in such automated industries, accelerating the trend towards more leisure activities such as sports, entertainment, and vacation travel (Makridakis, 1990).

Potentially negative aspects include the replacement of skilled and semi-skilled workers in the labor force and the application of inappropriate technology in developing countries. Thus, 'technological advances are giving rise to both opportunities and pressures for improved productivity, human resource development and restructuring of the tourism industry' (Ritchie, 1991).

Political environment

Arguably the most visible aspect of contemporary change influencing the public policy impact chain is the international political environment, in which 'growing dissatisfaction with current governing systems and processes may lead to a new framework for tourism' (Ritchie, 1991). Political transformation in Eastern Europe and the former Soviet Union since 1989, along with reforms in other parts of the world, emphasize the opportunities as well as the threats of destabilization resulting from this fluid environment.

Political emancipation, if accompanied by economic liberalization, can provide new market opportunities for trade in goods and services to the benefit of the international hospitality enterprise, as recently witnessed in Hungary, Czechoslovakia, and Poland, where many international hotel groups and fast-food operators have begun to seize the opportunities for foreign direct investment. Conversely, weakening political control may deter investors wary of the ethnic forces unleashed in, for example, Yugoslavia and the Caucasus.

The main political shift of the 1980s was the liberalization in international trade, the deregulation of markets and the desire to open up the international economy as never before. Indeed, the shift to market-driven economies is bringing about a global restructuring in which market forces rather than ideology are used to guide decisions and develop policy. This trend will likely continue during the 1990s insofar as in Europe, for example, the fabric of the single European market will finally be implemented among the nineteen nations of the European Community and the European Free Trade Area.

Similarly, many countries in Europe and potentially also in Asia are emerging from central planning towards market-oriented economies, which again will help stimulate international and domestic travel (Go and Welch, 1991, pp. 112–13). In China, economic liberalization is viewed from abroad as the pathway towards political liberalization that will ultimately open a domestic market of 1.1 billion people. In India, meanwhile, a long tradition of state intervention in economic affairs appears to be giving way to economic liberalization.

For the foreseeable future the international political environment will continue to be shaped by the direction of trade among the most influential political blocs. The nascent trading bloc forming in North America (the Free Trade Agreement between the USA, Canada, and potentially Mexico) and the convergence of Europe towards a massive domestic market of some 330 million inhabitants from 1993 will give rise to important implications for tourism planning, development, marketing and management of destinations and facilities. In other parts of the world too, the process of regional political convergence is perceivable via the mechanisms of economic cooperation. The Association of South East Asian Nations (ASEAN) is a clear case in point. Its primary aim of accelerating economic growth among its members has passed the test. Increasingly now, ASEAN's intergovernmental focus is towards collaboration and mutual assistance in matters of common interest: 1992, for example, is ASEAN Tourism Year.

North/South relationships offer tourism growth potential due to the improvement of transportation access, but only to the extent that destination areas in developing nations are perceived to be safe. In this regard the health and security of tourists is a concern that could become a major deterrent to tourism travel from North to South as well as within the North itself.

Some countries such as Iran, North Korea, Myanmar, and Albania have opted for protracted periods of political isolation over and above relationships with other nations or full participation in the international community. Conversely, the process of developing an international tourism industry, albeit under controlled circumstances, is an avenue some governments take to emerge from political isolation, as demonstrated by Vietnam, Laos, and Cuba. But just as isolation of the nation state may have a significant effect on tourism development in many countries, so too can terrorism. Cetron and Davies (1989, p. 114) anticipate that terrorism will be a continuing threat because it is an economical and effective means to carry the message of the disenfranchised to a global audience. Terrorist activities and regional conflicts such as the 1991 Gulf War have proven major impediments to the development and prosperity of tourism.

Another serious impediment to the sustainable development of tourism has been the uncoordinated approach some countries follow with regard to tourism policy (OECD, 1990, p. 13). Tourism enterprises have greatly contributed to the economic development of countries in the European Community, but can only continue to do so if mechanisms and means (both financial and organizational) are designed and implemented to link commercial tourist industry and government interests to address some of the vital issues that threaten a viable future for tourism. These include, amongst others, the risk of a breakdown of air traffic in Europe, North America, and some parts of East Asia, and of road traffic in Europe; and extensive damage to the Mediterranean, North Sea, and Baltic Sea coasts.

A knowledge of how to assess geopolitical developments and the role of international tourism within the global political environment are then clearly useful weapons in the hospitality decision maker's armory.

Internationalization of the hotel industry

National hotel industries are often best characterized by the label of fragmentation. Essentially this holds that ownership in the industry is very dispersed; the number of corporate players is small and their importance is slight when compared to the large number of independently owned businesses. In many instances this may still be the case, but there are important trends in the industry which contradict this simplified view. This brief section aims to provide an indication of the increasing number of international players in the field, and put the internationalization of hospitality companies within a context of the policy debate of the impact of multinational companies.

Growth of international hotel companies

The growth of international tourism described above has been parallelled by the development of international hotel companies. Although their growth has been recorded at a general level, to date little systematic analysis has been published. For an indication of the scale of international hotel holdings, Kleinwort Benson (1990, 1991) provide an excellent starting point. For more background and analysis see Litteljohn and Roper (1991).

International hotel operations began in the late 1940s. It was the American-branded organizations which first saw the potential of catering for international traveling markets, although inevitably they placed a heavy emphasis on their American parentage in the style of their operations and management. Companies that grew at this time include Hilton International, Inter-Continental and Sheraton. In general, they dealt with a fairly narrow upmarket brand, often appealing to national characteristics – Hilton International stated that they were creating 'little Americas' in different parts of the world. They catered for an exclusive travel market, but could often be associated with business travel markets (partly reflecting the dominant power of the USA in world economic matters during the period from the late 1940s to the 1960s). Often growth was achieved through the medium of management contracts, which allowed low capital involvement in their foreign holdings by the hotel operators.

During the subsequent period – from the middle 1960s to the end of the 1970s – there was considerable expansion of international hotel operations: by 1978 there were a total of 1,025 hotels with 270,646 rooms operated by 81 companies (Dunning and McQueen, 1982). By this time American companies operating internationally numbered 22 and accounted for 56 percent of the total internationally held rooms. Often the growth during this period centered on the successful operators of the previous period entering new geographical markets by adopting the same type of operating and management strategies that they had employed earlier: for example, there was a great increase in the presence of American hotel chains in the oil-rich Arab countries.

However, this period also witnessed an increasing diversity in company involvement. In the first place, new companies arrived on the scene. Some were North American, others were French- and UK-domiciled companies, which by 1978 respectively accounted for 13 and 12 percent of internationally held rooms. Another interesting trend was the fact that North America itself, previously the home of international hotel companies, now began to play host, as some foreign companies began to expand into US locations – sometimes with poor results, as when Howard Johnson was taken over by a UK company, only to be sold on a few years later to Marriott, after a very poor trading record.

Changes in the international hotel industry since 1980 have continued apace. This change can be characterized as having elements which were different in type, as well as different in extent, from those of earlier periods.

During the period 1978 to 1989, for example, the largest ten international hotel groups in 1978 had increased their foreign hotel holdings by 93 percent (Litteljohn and Roper, 1991). New international hotel companies also emerged: for example, entrants came from the newly industrializing nations of the Pacific Rim.

Ownership patterns also saw major changes. Holiday Inns were acquired by the UK brewer Bass, and Inter-Continental was sold twice during the period, latterly becoming a joint venture between a Japanese building company and SAS, the Scandinavian airline. Thus acquisition, rather than merely representing growth along traditional lines, became a more pronounced strategy. Headline takeovers were supplemented by the acquisition of smaller national chains by companies eager to penetrate new markets.

Thus the period also saw a change in the previously minimal role of foreign direct investment as a means of expansion. Acquisition meant that borrowings had to be raised. In summary, therefore, the period can be characterized as having a much broader range of motivations where companies were both pushed and pulled into mounting an internationalization strategy.

Along with more attention being paid to the financial elements of operations, the period was further characterized by a greater awareness of marketing factors. On the one hand, more varied levels of market provision were being offered by different companies. It was also the case that some companies adopted market segmentation policies which were implemented on an international basis. Whereas the international business hotel had been the model for much previous expansion, lower market segments such as low-spend budget hotel accommodation provided by Travelodge (Forte, UK) and

Formule 1 (Accor, France) were now more prominent, if only on a European basis.

The policy debate on multinational development

No short account can do full justice to the debate in much of the literature which centers on the impacts of multi or transnational companies. Part of the debate addresses the policy issue of their economic and social impacts within host economies. Another component looks at the consequences of multinationals within the narrower confines of particular industries, placing an immediate emphasis on the effects on the locally owned competitors. These two aspects are by no means exclusive, and they will often be analyzed at the same time. In essence the question which the analysis attempts to answer is the extent to which government should either encourage or regulate the development of multinational enterprises.

Thus much of the literature deals with the impact of these organizations in less developed economies (see, for example, Jenkins, 1987), although it will be noted in the preceding analysis that a more recent aspect of internationalization within the hotel industry is the emergence of Western multinationals expanding within other Western countries.

Analysis that favors the development of multinationals will stress the positive impact of foreign direct investment within a local economy, together with the benefits of companies with greater access to resources of capital, skill, and information than local ones. Counterclaims will be made that the economic impact of foreign firms is far from advantageous, particularly if the long term is judged. In the first place, their economic benefits will be diluted due to several factors, including their repatriation of profits and employment of non-local management. In the longer run, it could also be argued that their presence may hinder the growth of local firms in their market area, and encourage policies – such as pricing – which may favor the company, but not necessarily the host country.

As has been shown in various studies (see, for example, Dunning and McQueen, 1981), one very important industry-specific factor for tourism and hotels is the social impact of the industry on local host economies. In addition to the economic and physical effects of their activity, multinationals may often have significant social consequences, particularly when entering areas which have comparatively low levels of affluence and social traditions and cultures considerably different from those of the visitors they hope to attract.

These factors, together with economic, political, and other environments, will guide and inform the nature of the debate in the public policy chain.

International hospitality and the public policy chain

The international policy context of tourism

In the past 25 years tourism has arguably had more effect on economic and social development internationally than any other trade.

Regional distribution of tourism has hardly changed. With twenty industrialized countries accounting for two-thirds of total visitor movements, the OECD member states represent the wealthy world with an estimated population of 700 million and a dominating position in world travel.

Tourism does not occur randomly, but is instead influenced by geographical and economic variables. In particular, populations which possess discretionary income and time migrate from time to time to destinations that offer change: beneficial climates, and natural and artificial tourism amenities. Often these are located in middle latitudes, and this migration is sometimes referred to as the North–South phenomenon of tourism. It has caused multinational agencies such as the Organization of Economic Cooperation and Development, the European Community and the Organization of American States (OAS) to become involved in tourism-related issues and policy formulation at regional and international levels. In recent years, international tourism platforms at which policy issues have been debated, have included the following:

- The International Symposium on Tourism and the Next Decade convened in Washington, DC, in 1979. This addressed the global power and influence of tourism and identified the need for tourism policy formulation at the international level.
- The World Tourism Conference held in Manila in 1980 and sponsored by the World Tourism Organization. The conference examined the responsibility of nation states for the development and enhancement of tourism as more than a purely economic activity of nations and people (WTO, 1981, p. 117). The conference objective of the Manila Declaration was to recognize the social, cultural, and educational aspects of tourism and identify principles that should be incorporated into international tourism policy.
- The First Global Conference: Tourism – A Vital Force for Peace convened in Vancouver in 1988. Funders and developers of tourism projects were encouraged to support development which is consistent with the social fabric of the host community and which reinforces local values and culture and the sustained vitality of the natural environment, while providing equitable economic benefits to the local community.
- The Inter-Parliamentary Conference on tourism convened in the Hague, the Netherlands, in 1989. This urged parliaments, governments, and other tourism-related private and public organizations, associations and institutions responsible for tourism activities, together with tourism professionals and tourists themselves, to draw constant inspiration from its principles.
- The First International Assembly of Tourism Policy Experts convened in Washington, DC, in 1990. This identified priority issues affecting world tourism, anticipated future trends, and made recommendations on improving the industry internationally.

Thus international tourism has become a significant field for policy makers because a number of political, economic, and social factors influence government actions and regulations that affect tourism. These include bans on travel, immigration control, and terrorism prevention measures. Even the 1975 Helsinki Accord recognizes rights of migration, thereby acknowledging the policy link between politics and tourism.

The influence of intergovernmental and non-governmental organizations is becoming more pronounced in the emerging international environment (Edgell, 1990). Issues which confront policy makers may at first appear largely irrelevant to hospitality industry practitioners. However, hospitality managers need a thorough understanding of the policy formulation process to understand the actions of all the tourism players on the board, and the obstacles that affect companies involved in travel. Among the barriers affecting businesses are travel allowance restrictions and duty-free allowances. Furthermore, transportation impediments and restrictions that discourage the establishment of businesses by foreigners in a host society may also create significant deterrents (Ascher and Edgell, 1986; Edgell, 1988).

Thus, the role of international parastatal organizations and trade associations is increasingly associated with lobbying within the international public policy framework. Figure 3.1 identifies some of the major players and indicates their relative importance in international hospitality and tourism policy formulation, according to the criteria of their level of membership and their general level of influence.

Negative and positive sociocultural aspects of tourism are increasingly viewed as significant issues that businesses must address. Tourism may have detrimental social impacts on host communities as regards their local culture. For example, a local community may distort festivals and ceremonies to please international visitors. A carefully planned, well-organized tourist destination can benefit residents optimally if they are prepared for and understand their new social context. As observed earlier, the hospitality industry must strive to develop as a socially responsible industry, and adopt a proactive approach rather than responding to pressures as they arise.

Thus the dynamic nature of tourism requires an ongoing process of environmental scanning and analysis, in order for hospitality firms to match their strategies and structure to the changes brought about by the public policy impact chain (see Figure 3.2).

The public policy chain

The interfacing within a multi-unit hospitality firm and other organizations in the worldwide tourism network requires the development of a global perspective. However, competition in the hotel industry, even for the largest global conglomerate, occurs mainly on the local level. Furthermore, according to some economic theorists, hospitality firms and airlines, like steel factories, are part of the basic sector generating economic activity, and often create exports, which in turn create employment in non-basic sectors of the economy like education, retail trade, and government. Many communities therefore recognize the value of attracting a hotel, leisure, or conference project to enhance an area's economy. Conversely, the destination area's

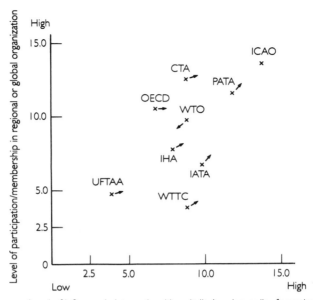

Fig. 3.1 Mapping the position of international hospitality/tourism organizations in regional or global public policy formation

Note: Level of participation/membership rating is based on number of members in the organization proportionate to full potential membership. Level of influence rating is based on the international influence of the organization within its particular sphere(s) of activity/interest. Direction of arrow indicates trend in terms of membership and influence.

This map is indicative only as judgments are, by nature, subjective. In addition, bearing in mind their political contexts, their direction may change.

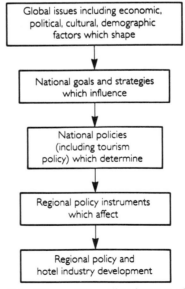

Fig. 3.2 The public policy impact chain
Based on Austin (1990, p. 77)

growth and stability typically influence the performance of a hotel project. In turn, the ability to create and carry out improvement strategies that link quality-of-life and economic development objectives depends, in part, on public policy.

Like business strategies, national strategies are shaped by global issues: economic, political, cultural, and demographic variables which have been discussed earlier in this chapter. These global issues create constraints and opportunities based on which government policy makers formulate the national strategy. National strategy and tourism policy will vary among nation states and be more explicit and clear in some than in others. Regardless of the level of economic development, the needs and economic and social objectives of a host destination area or country are dynamic: shifts in policy are constantly influenced by a series of external and internal factors, including economic, political, and environmental issues. Table 3.3 indicates major policy issues for the 1990s which have been chosen to illustrate the wide range of factors which can influence the policy chain.

National strategy and tourism policy

International tourism can play an important role in the economic development of a country, and assist the nation state to achieve its national goals.

Tourism development in many countries has been based on the neo-mercantilism of maximizing trade surplus to achieve a variety of domestic

Table 3.3 Policy issues for the 1990s

- Protection of wildlife and natural resources
- Pollution control
- International transport and deregulation
- Tourists' responsibility
- Underwater, polar and space frontier controls
- International currency fluctuations
- Fossil fuel impacts
- Energy costs and availability
- Destination land inflation
- Industry consolidation and competition
- Travel facilitation
- Consumer protection
- Historic and cultural preservation
- Criminal prosecution of tourists
- Global telecommunications and reservations
- International standards for the safety of travellers
- Terrorism
- Global transmittable diseases
- Foreign investment initiatives
- International visa waiver programs
- Community empowerment and local control
- Annual paid vacation/work week regulations
- Geographic and cultural literacy
- Rights of disadvantaged and handicapped travellers
- Consolidations, mergers and acquisitions

Note: The above list represents only a select number of recurring themes that have policy implications for tourism development.

Source: Tourism Policy Forum Brief, vol. 1, no. 2 (1989), p. 3. The George Washington University, Washington D.C.

goals, such as the accumulation of investment capital or the enhancement of employment (Czinkota *et al.*, 1989, p. 27). Theoretically, any country can be involved in the development of international tourism, but each country is likely to have certain advantages in some type of production and disadvantages in others.

Historically, trade has been one of the most important motives for relations between countries. Tourism can contribute to furthering relationships between countries and social relationships between individuals. Richter (1989, p. 2) views tourism as a highly political phenomenon, the implications of which appear to be only rarely perceived and almost nowhere fully understood. Tourist flows in general might be seen (pp. 4–5) as a crude but reliable barometer of international relations among tourist-generating and receiving countries. Richter suggests how the politics of tourism affect international relations, public administration, and public policy making. Some examples she cites of how the governments of nation states have used tourism as a tool to manipulate political means and ends include the following:

- The judicious blend of capitalistic profit and socialist political advantage sought by the People's Republic of China, Cuba, and Vietnam from encouraging Western tourism, directed at both long-term economic prospects and the immediate political goodwill and publicity the new hospitality may provide.
- The use of tourism as a means of improving their international press notices by authoritarian nations like the Philippines under Marcos. For example, the Philippine tourism slogan, 'Where Asia wears a smile', was a promotion specifically designed to defuse criticisms of martial law and allay the fear of political visitors as to their security.
- The use of international tourism as a political weapon by one nation against another nation. For example, the United States sought to boycott the 1980 Moscow Summer Olympics with the intent to deny the Soviet Union respectability and prestige in response to the latter's invasion of Afghanistan.

Shifts in the economic and political power of nation states are occurring more rapidly in contemporary history than in previous times, as witnessed, for instance, by the economic rise of Japan. Countries must seek to be competitive, perhaps by applying scale economies and/or niche strategies. If they do not, a loss in competitive advantage may result in unemployment for the innovator country and its immediate followers.

With trade becoming more global and vital in improving people's lifestyle the world over, good international relations between countries will remain essential. Developing nations continue to question the value of liberalizing trade in services, seeking to narrow the scope of the negotiations and put forward an agenda which includes preferential market access, restrictive business practices, transfer of technology rules and priority sectors. This reflects a view that the development of the domestic services sector should be accomplished through traditional infant industry models rather than through foreign presence (Zall, 1989, p. 3).

Tourism is part of international trade in services and may be used in the economic advancement of developed and developing countries and to enhance competitive advantages in the global market. O'Brien (1988, pp. 10–12), for example, demonstrates how the competitiveness of the US travel industry is inextricably tied to global market trends. Furthermore, she illustrates the impact of tourism on the American economy and the importance of strategies to maintain a leadership position and create new business opportunities. Given the confluence of communications, transportation, and economic forces, and especially the role of TNCs in greatly accelerating the international product life cycle and international shifts in production (Terpstra, 1985, p. 10), competition, rather than protectionism, is more likely to produce economic success.

Mowlana and Smith (1990) furthered the concept of tourism infrastructure as part of the information structure of a country. When combining their concept with the notion that tourism is an economic activity of considerable proportions it becomes evident that there is a need (Edgell, 1985, p. 8) for greater policy awareness among government leaders of tourism as an integral force in economic cooperation between nation states.

In general, public policies are designed to expand tourism, whether in the relatively infant stage (Spain in the early 1950s) or in the more mature stage (the UK in the 1980s). Specifically, governments promote tourism: (1) to earn foreign exchange, (2) to increase national income and employment, and (3) to achieve regional development of backward areas (de Kadt, 1979, p. 20). However, due to tourism's pronounced spatial impacts, seasonal distribution, and determinate life cycles, some form of interventionism is often necessary (Williams and Shaw, 1988, p. 230; Jenkins and Henry, 1982, p. 502). As noted earlier, specific functions of governments, in both developed and developing countries, normally involve coordination, planning, legislation, regulation, entrepreneurial ventures, and tourism-industry stimulation. The degree of emphasis given to these principal roles varies from destination to destination, but is usually directly related to the importance accorded tourism by four main types of country in which: (1) tourism is limited and likely to remain so; (2) tourism has limited possibilities; (3) tourism is existing and has the potential to become an important contributor to the national economy; and (4) tourism development is highly advanced and the main problem is how to maintain it (Wolfson, 1964).

Building and maintaining success in tourism (Kaiser and Helber, 1978, p. 15) depends to a large extent on the ways in which the industry is organized in a country. Its impacts depend to a significant extent on a country's political-economic structure. For example, the first objective of tourism policies in Eastern Europe, prior to the fall of the communist regimes in 1989, was to ensure the provision of appropriate recreational facilities for the citizens of the state; foreign exchange was only a secondary objective (de Kadt, 1979, p. 19).

By combining the level of economic development and the level of tourism development it is possible to construct a matrix which depicts on the vertical axis a country's economic development level: industrialized, emerging, or developing; and on the horizontal axis the level of tourism development: discovery stage, local initiative stage, or institutionalization stage. The stage of economic development in a region, and the stage of tourism development it is in, will to a significant degree determine the structure of the regional tourism industry and its strategic conduct (see Table 3.4).

Furthermore, the structure of the regional economy is also important in conditioning the economic impact of tourism on the region and by extension its hotel industry. In order to be successful, hotel development should be viewed within the regional development context. Within this framework the hotel developer should generally ask three questions: (1) Is there a possibility of integrating tourism into an existing settlement and is the scale of the development such that it can be absorbed by the existing economy? (2) Is the tourist industry able (Williams and Shaw, 1988, p. 9) to utilize local resources and might there be a tendency for marketing to pass into the hands of outsiders? (3) What are the barriers that impact on services trade in tourism?

Most governments play a significant role in restricting trade in services by erecting financial and legal barriers which reduce tourist flows. Restrictions tend to be most severe in the Americas and have contributed to the decline in tourism market share *vis-à-vis* East Asia and the Pacific where international travel has recently grown greatly. Focusing on the American situation, Edgell

Table 3.4 The level of a country's economic versus touristic development

Economic development level	Touristic development stage		
	Stage 1 Limited and likely to remain so	*Stage 2* Limited possibilities	*Stage 3* Potential to become an important contributor to the national economy
Industrialized, e.g. Western Europe, North America, Japan			
Emerging, e.g. NICs, Central and Eastern Europe			
Developing, e.g. Africa, South Asia, Middle East			

Source: Based on van Doorn (1989).

(1985) cites several factors that impact negatively on services trade in tourism:

- Government attention is focused more on promotion of inbound tourist business rather than on a more general approach that deals with the reduction and removal of travel restrictions.
- Government has not fully assessed the tourism impact of its laws and regulations.
- Government policies concerning international relations – political, economic, monetary, financial – often conflict with and override tourism policy.
- An increasing variety of international organizations deal with aspects of international travel and tourism. For the most part, these organizations deal with problems in piecemeal fashion and not with tourism as an integrated activity. Thus, greater coordination and cooperation among these organizations would improve their effectiveness.
- There is a lack of general, internationally accepted rules and principles for dealing with new problems as they arise, and there is no mechanism for dispute settlement.

The dynamic nature of tourism requires an ongoing process of defining policy and its applications, in order that the benefits from tourism can be maximized. For example, the deregulation of air transport, the Channel Tunnel between the UK and France, and the anticipated rail link connecting Paris and Cologne via Brussels should further what van Doren (1981) has coined 'an era of "post-mobility adjustment".'

The main features of regulations affecting transnational companies include: (1) controls on entry, establishment, and ownership; (2) nationality requirements; (3) policies bearing on the operations and competitive opportunities of foreign affiliates; (4) economic regulations affecting the scope of foreign participation; (5) incentives and performance requirements (UNCTC, 1988, p. 473).

Before advancing to the planning stage, it would be wise for hotel firms to investigate the attitude of the host country toward inbound tourism and TNCs as this varies from place to place. The needs of a host society and the resulting objectives it sets may change over time, as has recently been illustrated by government efforts in Mexico to open Mexican markets, cut red tape, and relax restrictions on foreign investment (Go et al., 1990, p. 300).

Government attitude toward TNCs is a significant criterion on the TNC rating scale for screening national environments (Go et al., 1990, p. 301). However, the attitude toward TNCs goes beyond the national level to local and regional governments, which must in turn consider the consequences their policies may have on tourism in general and TNCs in particular.

Conclusion

In summary, public policy is the force which drives all aspects of tourism on both the supply and the demand side. Public policy formulation and implementation are essential elements of tourism. They provide the decision maker with parameters in the decision-making process, and effective public policy fosters private sector initiative (Edgell, 1990, p. 95).

The role of tourism in the national economy varies from country to country, as does the involvement of government. Though there are areas where government interests do not coincide with those of the private sector – for example, as regards the raising of taxes – there are opportunities where their interests do coincide, such as in the desire to attract visitors and ensure a profitable tourism trade (which can afford to pay taxes and create employment). In order to achieve goals that are complementary or of mutual interest, the public and private sectors should cooperate to harmonize their respective policies and strategies. Public–private sector cooperation is especially relevant in the tourism area because parts of the activity involve to a lesser or greater extent many other ministries and local and regional governments.

Another reason for closer public–private sector cooperation is that tourism is becoming a major policy issue at the international level. This trend is primarily driven by the international expansion activity of transnational corporations like hotels and by international organizations like the European Commission, whose decisions impact on member states. Among the main issues that have ramifications for the regional level are: ensuring there is sufficient transport for travelers to fill a region's available hotel accommodation; minimizing tourism activities that cause the degradation of the natural environment; and improving manpower planning and hotel industry involvement in educational institutions supplying the hotel industry. All of these areas offer scope for greater cooperation between the private and public sectors.

Often the public sector is recognized as relating to national governments. The foregoing analysis has, however, emphasized that trends within hospitality will increasingly require decision makers to interpret developments from international perspectives. This requirement is driven by two different, though related trends. First, there is the phenomenon of international hospitality markets where both customers and the companies that serve them are international. Second, there is the development of supranational trading blocs and specialist organizations which will have growing influence in shaping general attitudes towards commercial development and specific industry regulations.

The environment is therefore distinctly different from that of the past, and will require decision makers to ensure that they are proactive in the new institutional public policy frameworks, rather than merely reactive to public policy decisions once these have been made.

References

Ascher, Bernard, and Edgell, David (1986) 'Barriers to international travel', *Travel and Tourism Analyst*, October, pp. 3–11.

Austin, James E. (1990) *Managing in Developing Countries*, New York: The Free Press.

Bodewynn, J. J. (1975) 'Multinational business government relations: six principles for effectiveness', in P. M. Boarman and H. Schollhammer (eds) *Multinational Corporations and Government*, New York: Praeger.

Cecchini, P., Catinat, M., and Jacquemin, A. (1988) *The European Challenge: 1992, the benefits of a single market*, Aldershot: Wildwood House.

Cetron, Marvin, and Davies, Owen (1989) *American Renaissance: Our life at the turn of the 21st century*, New York: St Martin's Press.

Cobbs, Louise (1991) 'Air transportation services and the GATT', *Travel and Tourism Revue*, pp. 213–14.

Collier, David (1989) 'Expansion and development of CRS', *Tourism Management*, vol. 0, no. 0, pp. 86–8.

Czinkota, Michael R., Rivoli, Pietra, and Ronkainen, Ilkka A. (1989) *International Business*, Chicago, Ill.: Dryden Press.

de Kadt, Emanuel (1979) *Tourism: Passport to development*, New York: Oxford University Press.

Dicken, Peter (1986) *Global Shift: Industrial change in a turbulent world*, London: Harper & Row.

Dieke, Peter U. C. (1989) 'Fundamentals of tourism development, a Third World perspective', *Hospitality Education and Research Journal*, vol. 13, no. 2, pp. 7–22.

Dix, John (1990) 'Population changes: problem or opportunity?', *Hospitality*.

Dunning, John H., and McQueen, M. (1981) *Transnational Corporations in International Tourism*, New York: United Nations Center for Transnational Corporations.

Dunning, John H., and McQueen, M. (1982) 'Multinational Corporations in the Hotel Industry', *Annals of Tourism Research*, vol. 9, pp. 69–90.

Edgell, David L., Sr (1985) *International Trade in Tourism: A manual for managers and executives*, Washington, DC: US Department of Commerce, US Travel and Tourism Administration.

Edgell, David L., Sr (1990) *International Tourism Policy*, New York: Van Nostrand Reinholt.

Gershuny, J., and Miles, I. (1983) *The New Services Economy*, London: Frances Pinter.

Go, Frank, and Welch, Peter (1991) *Competitive Strategies for the International Hotel Industry*, London: Economist Intelligence Unit, Special Report no. 1180, March.

Go, Frank, Sung Soo Pyo, Muzaffer Uysal and Mihalik, Brian J. (1990)' Decision criteria for transnational hotel expansion', *Tourism Management*, vol. 11, no. 4, pp. 297–304.

Godet, Michael, and Barre, Remi (1988) 'Into the next decade: major trends and uncertainties of the 1990s', *Futures*, vol. 20, no. 4, pp. 410–23.

Gunn, Clare A. (1988) *Tourism Planning*, 2nd edn, New York: Taylor & Francis.

International Institute of Management Development, as quoted in 'Multinational management strategies – multinational green lights', *Multinational Business*, Spring 1991.

Jenkins, C. L., and Henry, B. M. (1982) 'Government involvement in tourism in developing countries', *Annals of Tourism Research*, vol. 9, no. 4, pp. 499–521.

Jenkins, Rhys (1987) *Transnational Corporations and Uneven Development: The internationalization of capital and the Third World*, London: Methuen.

Julius, De Anne (1990) *Global Companies and Public Policy: The growing challenge of direct foreign investment*, London: Royal Institute of International Affairs/Chatham House.

Kaiser, Charles, Jr, and Helber, Larry E. (1978) *Tourism Planning and Development*, Boston, Mass.: CBI Publishing Co.

Kleinwort Benson (1990) *UK Hotels PLC – The Decade Review*, London: Kleinwort Benson Securities.

Kleinwort Benson (1991) *The Decade Review, Quoted Hotel Companies: The world markets*, London: Kleinwort Benson Securities.

Kurent, Heather P. (1991) 'Tourism in the 1990s: threats and opportunities', *World Travel and Tourism Review*, pp. 78–82.

Litteljohn, David, and Roper, Angela (1991) 'Changes in international hotel companies' strategies', in R. Teare and A. Boer (eds) *Strategic Hospitality Management*, London: Cassell.

McNulty, Robert, and Wafer, Patricia (1990) 'Tourism management: transnational corporations and tourism issues', *Tourism Management*, vol. 11, no. 4, pp. 291–5.

Makridakis, S. G. (1990) *Forecasting, Planning and Strategy for the 21st Century*, New York: Free Press.

Martel, Leon (1986) *Mastering Change*, New York: New American Library.

Mowlana, Hamid, and Smith, Ginger (1990) 'Tourism, telecommunications and transnational banking: framework for policy analysis', *Tourism Management*, vol. 11, no. 4, pp. 312–24.

OECD (1990) *Tourism Policy and International Tourism in OECD Member Countries*, Paris: Organization for Economic Cooperation and Development.

Ostry, Sylvia (1990) 'Governments and corporations in a shrinking world: trade and innovation policies in the United States, Europe and Japan', *Columbia Journal of World Business*, vol. 25, nos. 1 and 2, pp. 10–16.

Peters, Tom (1987) *Thriving on Chaos: Handbook for a management revolution*, New York: Alfred A. Knopf.

Price, D. G., and Blair, A. M. (1989) *The Changing Geography of the Service Sector*, London: Belhaven Press.

Richter, Linda K. (1989) *The Politics of Tourism in Asia*, Honolulu: University of Hawaii Press.

Ritchie, J. R. Brent (1991) 'Global tourism policy issues: an agenda for the 1990s', *World Travel and Tourism Review*, pp. 149–58.

Rogaly, Joe (1991) 'Shrinking Europe', *Financial Times*, 24 September 1991, London.

Shafer, Elwood L. (1989) 'Future encounters with science and technology', *Journal of Travel Research*, vol. 27, no. 4, pp. 2–7.

Sinclair, Thea and Sutcliffe, Charles (1988) 'The economic effects on destination areas of foreign involvement in the tourism industry: a Spanish application' in Goodall and Ashworth, (eds) *Marketing in the Tourism Industry*, London: Croom Helm.

Slattery, Paul, and Olsen, Michael (1984) 'Hospitality organizations and their environment', *International Journal of Hospitality Management*, vol. 3, no. 2, pp. 55–61.

Terpstra, Vern (1985) 'The changing environment of international marketing', *International Marketing Review*, vol. 2, no. 3, pp. 7–16.

UNCTC (1988) *Transnational Corporations in World Development: Trends and Prospects*, New York: UN Centre on Transnational Corporations.

van Doorn, Jozef W. M. (1989) 'A critical assessment of socio-cultural impact studies of tourism in the Third World', in *Towards Appropriate Tourism: The case of developing countries*, Tej Vir Singh, H. Leo Theuns, and Frank M. Go (eds), Frankfurt: Peter Land.

van Doren, Carlton S. (1981) 'Outdoor recreation trends in the 1980s: implications for society', *Journal for Travel Research*, vol. 19, no. 3.

Weil, Robert (ed.) (1982) *The OMNI Future Almanac*, New York: World Almanac Publications.

Williams, Alan M., and Shaw, Gareth (1988) *Tourism and Economic Development: Western European experiences*, London: Belhaven Press.

Wolfson, M. (1964) 'Government's role in tourism development', *Development Digest*, vol. 5, pp. 50–6.

Zall, Milton (1989) 'Public international law trends in tourism: current developments', *Tourism Policy Forum Brief*, vol. 1, no. 3, pp. 1–4.

4

Corporate diplomacy in the Asia-Pacific era

Giles A. Jackson
and Brian Wise

During the 1980s, the dynamic Asian economies (DAEs) outperformed Organization for Economic Cooperation and Development (OECD) countries whose market economies account for 72 percent of the world's GNP (Barsony, 1991). The Asia-Pacific is now both a strong tourism destination and a strong tourism generator. However, rapid and chaotic tourism development is undermining this region's attractiveness as an aspirational, quality travel experience. The Asia-Pacific may well degenerate into a huge mass market with severe sociocultural, environmental, and economic consequences unless action is taken by corporations at their boundaries with states and communities.

The first section of this chapter uses a micropolicy framework and country case studies to explain crisis tendencies resulting from the Asia-Pacific's economic ascendancy. The sheer complexity and volatility of development conditions means that the conventional drive for more sophisticated products can no longer be relied upon as a recipe for success. It is now in the self-interest of hospitality and tourism corporations to adapt to new and often conflicting development expectations by expanding their role from service providers to participants in overall development. This will help negate the adverse effects of crisis tendencies that are beyond their control and increase the chances for more sustainable development. Diplomatic approaches are discussed as an appropriate means for fulfilling this new corporate role.

Asia-Pacific ascendancy

'Asia-Pacific ascendancy' is an economic description of the rapid rates of growth achieved by a handful of countries in this vast region (Japan, Hong Kong, Singapore, South Korea, Malaysia, the Philippines, Thailand, and Taiwan). The idea of regional ascendancy includes the expectation that other countries will be able to replicate successfully the economic experience of these countries. This expectation is reflected in the fact that there are now nine economic classes formally represented in this region vying for international attention. One of these classes, the Association of South East Asian Nations (ASEAN) spans 2,000 miles from north to south and 3,000 miles from east to west, with a population base of 280 million.

These Asian countries industrialized in the 1960s and 1970s and were able to overcome the problems of dependence on the First World. Countries such as Singapore and South Korea did this through a shift in economic policy which emphasized incentives to exporters rather than protection of domestic production (Gilbert, 1985).

In the last 30 years the Asia-Pacific region has expanded from less than a quarter of North America's and one-tenth of the world's production to equal North America's and represent a quarter to a fifth of the world's production (Barsony, 1991). Hong Kong, Singapore, Korea, and Taiwan collectively generated $220 billion in merchandise exports in 1988. Table 4.1 shows shifts in relative economic weight, merchandise imports, and exports of manufactured goods between DAEs (Hong Kong, Singapore, South Korea, Taiwan, and Thailand) and selected OECD countries. The table shows on the one hand how DAEs have raised their international economic profile, and on the other how tied they are to OECD markets. The convergence of productivity and incomes in DAEs toward OECD figures occurred during a period of non-inflationary growth in the OECD area, combined with a favorable trading

Table 4.1 The USA, Japan, Germany, and the dynamic Asian economies: shifts in relative economic weight 1965–1989

	1965	1975	1985	1989
Real gross domestic product as a % of total				
USA	65.2	58.3	56.0	55.0
Japan	14.2	21.0	23.3	23.9
Germany	18.5	17.5	15.7	15.1
DAE's	2.1	3.3	4.9	6.0
	100%	100%	100%	100%
Merchandise imports				
USA	41.2	37.2	45.2	38.8
Japan	14.5	20.7	16.4	16.0
Germany	34.0	29.2	21.7	22.2
DAE's	10.3	12.9	16.7	23.0
	100%	100%	100%	100%
Exports of manufactured goods				
USA	41.8	32.1	26.5	25.4
Japan	17.0	23.3	28.2	24.0
Germany	37.4	37.1	28.3	29.8
DAE's	3.8	7.6	17.0	20.8
	100%	100%	100%	100%

Source: Reprinted from The OECD Observer.

environment which led to increases in demand for DAE exports (Barsony, 1991).

Barsony (1991) suggests that this catching-up process is based on several factors that DAEs have in common:

- Successful policy responses to external conditions, giving them flexibility.
- Domestic policies which emphasize savings.
- Efficient investment, including incentives for exports and substitution of imports by domestic production.
- Significant investment in education, training, and public and private science and technology programs.
- Modern transportation and communications infrastructure.

Although the rapid growth of these economies has been attributed to internal changes in policy, there have been important external changes that have provided the context for these policy changes to work. The first is the fact that these countries industrialized during the rapid world economic growth of the 1960s and 1970s. The second major factor is changes in the structure of global capital markets.

The term 'capital market' generally refers to the arena where investment funds are channeled to productive areas of the economy. 'Global' capital markets were created by deregulation in the 1970s and 1980s. This gave businesses, savers, and borrowers much wider investment choices in the productive areas of many economies. The DAEs have attempted to sustain their growth rates by importing capital to fill domestic resource gaps and reduce balance of payments problems. Meanwhile, Western investment firms have been penetrating newly deregulated financial markets in Asia to exploit opportunities with skills acquired in their home markets (Ziegler, 1990). There is speculation that DAEs will have to rely increasingly on trading partners and transnational companies to maintain their international profile.

A critical stage in development

DAEs are reaching a critical stage in their development, where state intervention is needed to keep their momentum going, in part because the world recession has affected demand for their exports. The latest trend in restructuring has created some uncertainty since it is difficult to assess whether states are intervening in the right place at the right time or creating more obstacles and neglecting markets when state action is required.

The benefits from economic restructuring are limited by external conditions in capital markets, where there has been a steady decrease globally in the proportion of stock owned by individuals and an increase in stock owned by institutional and corporate interests (Ziegler, 1990). These interests are sensing risks from social, cultural, and political tensions in the Asia-Pacific. They are also seeking ways to overcome narrowing profit margins resulting from the global debt crisis of the 1980s. One way out has been to trade on their own account and to seek short-term moves in interest rates and currencies. The result is that the Asia-Pacific, as well as the rest of the world, is facing problems in selling securities and raising capital.

The Asia-Pacific region has enjoyed low costs of production and a low overall debt–service ratio (Euromonitor, 1987). In 1986 this was 12.3 percent versus 43.5 percent in the West. However, cost advantages are realized from access to OECD markets (OECD countries accounted for nearly 70 percent of DAE merchandise exports in 1987). The Asia-Pacific region is now facing access problems, fueled by capital market conditions and the emergence of trading fortresses such as Europe and North America. Countries within the Asia-Pacific region have attempted to combine forces (as shown, for example, by agreements between Japan and South Korea), but these tend to be jeopardized by stormy past relationships.

Internal problems

In the long term there will be a growing interest from Asia-Pacific nations in industries which are able to contribute significantly to stability, regional unity, and self-reliance. Tourism may well fulfil these criteria. But the degree to which these long-term benefits materialize will depend largely on the perceptions that transnational companies and institutional investors have of investment conditions in the region. Investment criteria no longer revolves around cost advantages, but depends also on how well institutions in these countries maintain a stable and ordered society in face of massive population growth, technological advances, urbanization, and pressures from the nternational political economy.

On the other hand, there are also strong incentives for powerful interests to maintain the status quo. Gilbert (1985) points out that in some of the newly industrializing countries (including DAEs) it is these companies rather than local enterprise that have produced the exports. These companies tend to prefer autocratic governments, weak trade unions, tight government budgets, and low spending on social services. DAE cities such as Seoul fit this mould. Seoul may not suffer from the squalor of many Third World cities, and may have a strong education system, but health care and water supplies are poor, and available space is very limited.

Weiss (1989) has argued that Asia is in its second stage of development in which 'she is discovering the problems born of success as she seeks to consolidate her economic gains.' This section, which focuses on problems in twelve countries, shows the kinds of barriers being faced in the region. Future paths of development and their implications for tourism can be determined only by close monitoring of conditions in each country and of relationships between countries.

Australia

Australia is currently in severe recession. Thousands of small shareholders have suffered after the collapse of high-profile empires and the chain reaction falls of other investment groups. Unemployment is the highest since the 1930s, at around 10 percent. The government has a relatively weak opposition and is not facing the critical issues of the country (Adams *et al.*, 1991).

Although tourism in Australia is worth $6 billion a year, its major problems are its long-haul status and transportation infrastructure. Another problem is management of the tourism industry – there are 22 national bodies and no clear directions for the future.

Japan

Japan is seeking integration into the international community. Whether investors can take advantage of the world's second largest economy will depend on Japan's preference either to create a Yen bloc or to build stronger relations further afield (Adams *et al.*, 1991).

However, Japan has recently experienced tight financial conditions and the labor shortage crisis is growing. There has been a 330 percent increase in bankruptcy rates in real estate over last year. In July 1991 alone there were 875 business failures. On the other hand, conditions are better than ever for foreign investment as confidence in the economy improves. Corporate investment is expected to rise by 7 percent in 1991 (Business International, 1991a).

China

China is in the midst of a dramatic transformation, struggling with questions that have been troubling the country for two hundred years. The most basic is how to reconcile modern China with three thousand years of tradition, and how modern China should relate to the outside world (Adams *et al.*, 1991).

On the positive side, China's political upheavals have had little effect on the economy. Living standards have improved dramatically over the past ten years. Despite the Tiannanmen Square incident, there are enormous opportunities for tourism development and the China Travel Service has recognized these. The government has allowed independent Chinese-run travel companies to operate.

However, the inefficient state sector remains intact and has not given tourism the freedom it needs to flourish (Chui, 1991). This is the same for economic reforms in general, and the government is uncertain how to proceed. What is certain is that change is irreversible. The post-Tiannanmen lull will be temporary – more dramatic changes are in store when Deng Xiaoping dies (Adams *et al.*, 1991).

South Korea

Per capita income in South Korea is now over $5,000 and the country's growth rate is one of the highest in the world. In 1990 1.5 million South Koreans travelled abroad. However, domestic travel has been less buoyant because of unsettling political reforms and the threat of North Korea collapsing, with the prospect of thousands of North Koreans heading for the South (Adams *et al.*, 1991).

Hong Kong

Despite doing more trade than all of China, Hong Kong is not set to become a driving force of South East Asia. Residents are emigrating at the rate of 1,200 per week. Prices are up, growth is down. Relations with the international community are at a low, and fraud and corruption are on the increase. Rows over major projects such as the international airport have damaged confidence. A steady decline is expected beyond 2000 (Adams *et al.*, 1991).

Despite these trends, according to the Hong Kong Tourist Association (HKTA) the number of available rooms will rise 17 percent to more than 33,000 rooms by the end of 1991. A further 3,000 rooms will be built in 1992. Overcapacity has not affected developers (Goldstein, 1991).

Malaysia

The Malaysian economy grew around 10 percent in 1990. The Prime Minister calls for the economy to grow by another 100 percent by the year 2020. He is seeking to raise the country's profile further in the region (Adams *et al.*, 1991). In Malaysia, as in many other countries in this region, the state has a tight rein on development.

The Philippines

The economy of the Philippines remains much the same as it was when the Marcos regime was swept from power. Meanwhile the volcano Mount Pinatubo has been devastating. The official 1991 economic growth projection has been scaled back from 1.5–3.5 percent. This region is politically very unstable at present (Adams *et al.*, 1991).

Vietnam

Economic reforms allow private enterprise and foreign investment, but they have had limited success because Vietnam remains diplomatically and economically isolated. Vietnam is attempting market-oriented policies while political changes are very cautious after events in Eastern Europe. The result is extremely volatile conditions (Adams *et al.*, 1991). Countries like Singapore have banned ventures with Vietnam. Nevertheless, behind the scenes investments are flourishing, the attraction being lower labor costs in Vietnam. Currently, New World Group and SAS are negotiating developments (Business International, 1991b).

Taiwan

The vision of an 'alternative China' is emerging in Taiwan after political changes. This may help Taiwan recover from a tourism receipt slump in the long run. Receipts slumped from US$2.7 billion in 1989 to US$1.8 billion in 1990. Chaotic traffic conditions and pollution played a part. Occupancy levels in hotels are expected to decline to 55 percent this year. Experts predict that the island will eventually be reincorporated into China after political reconciliation. This will probably increase Taiwanese travel to China beyond one million people a year (Adams *et al.*, 1991).

Thailand

This country is basically stable, the last coups having little effect in the country. Tourism and investment led to a boom in the 1980s. The downside of tourism is that Thailand faces the worst AIDS crisis in Asia (Adams *et al.*, 1991). Still, tourism development continues as it did in the 1980s, with hotel room supply set to double to 40,000 in Bangkok alone in 1992. Meanwhile, tour operators are shifting emphasis to northern cities and resort islands. There appears to be no environment planning policy and this will have severe negative effects on tourism in a decade's time.

India

Until both economic and political reins are loosened, India's great potential will remain unrealized. The positive side is that in this post-cold war era India is seeking deeper cooperation with the USA, Britain, France, Germany, and Japan (Adams *et al.*, 1991).

The proposal in the new industrial policy is to allow foreign companies to hold shareholdings of up to 51 percent in subsidiaries in 34 selected industries. However, the incentive structure is such that overseas companies must use India as a base for exports. Overseas companies are more interested in India's huge domestic market. Many industries will be hit hard in the 1990s by the controls being placed on imports. These curbs are part of the effort to control the balance of payments problem (*International Reports*, 1991). The result of this situation is that corporations with established joint ventures with Indian companies or subsidiaries are entering into alliances with third-party companies or business groups, e.g. Hewlett-Packard India with HCL, and Digital Equipment Corporation with Modi-Olivetti (*International Reports*, 1991).

Indonesia

Indonesia is the dominant power in the six-nation ASEAN. It has a population of 175 million, abundant natural resources, and unique physical environments. The economy is doing well and Indonesia is seeking a greater role on the world stage (Adams *et al.*, 1991). The country earned US$1.89

billion from tourism in 1990, and tourism is being targeted by the government for employment creation. 'Visit Indonesia Year' is expected to increase tourism beyond 2.5 million persons in 1993. There is interest in setting up more educational training centers for tourism (Schwartz, 1991).

Summary

Growth figures have tended to disguise some of the traumatic aspects of Asia-Pacific development. From an economic, social, technological, and political standpoint the region is diverse and dynamic. There has been a great variety of development experiences which reflect unique histories. The logic of economic competitive advantage should be tempered with knowledge of these realities to reveal possible uncertainties. Economic development is only one aspect of the development process and, given non-economic conditions, the 'Asia-Pacific ascendancy' is not an inevitability.

Table 4.2 summarizes three types of crisis that may emerge to different degrees and at different times in this region. This is not a predictive model but serves to classify possible long-term crisis tendencies. Hospitality and tourism corporations must recognize the form and implications of these crisis

Table 4.2 Potential crisis tendencies in the Asia-Pacific region

Economic crisis	The economic system fails to provide the extent and quality of consumable values demanded. The economic crisis (especially the inequitable distribution of wealth) leads to tensions aggravated by tourism, which relies on local labor to service affluent markets.
Administrative crisis	Government actions become more and more visible as it plays a more prominent role. More demands are then placed on government, but these cannot be fulfilled by existing institutions. The implications for tourism are that civic responsibilities may increasingly be shifted onto the shoulders of corporations (e.g. new forms of taxation).
Legitimation crisis	Asia-Pacific nations have economic growth and stability as a priority. A legitimation crisis occurs when, in the process of protecting economic growth, the state is seen as unfair and the mass loyalty that it needs dips below a threshold level. This has important implications for tourism because if tendencies toward a legitimation crisis occur, communities are likely to view corporations with the same suspicion as they do the state.
Sociocultural crisis	Irreplaceable traditions and meanings are eroded by the market mechanism, achievement ideology, and commercialization. These in turn are being undermined by taxes and other measures that the state enacts to meet the demands of its expanded role. Hospitality and tourism developments are frequently developed at the boundaries of tradition and modernity. Prospects for tourism growth are good, but so are prospects for tourism contributing to this crisis.

Source: Adapted from Jürgen Habermas's (1973) classification of crisis tendencies in advanced capitalist societies.

tendencies and create buffers to circumvent, reduce, or confront them when they occur. The remainder of this chapter focuses at a micro level, articulating the many development dimensions of the region and the implications for a future corporate role.

The development context and tourism

The investment and export orientation of the DAEs prioritizes productivity growth over employment growth. With some exceptions (such as Hawaii), tourism has been seen mainly as a service to the needs of the industrial economy rather than as a core industry. Tourism, with its emphasis on employment growth and its high closure rates, does not fit the high-productivity mold. However, given massive increases in tourism demand and investment (which according to the Pacific Asia Travel Association is estimated to be $130 billion a year), and the crisis tendencies discussed above, perspectives on tourism are likely to change. This section discusses changes in supply since the 1970s.

Since the 1960s hotel companies have established themselves in gateway cities, and more recently in secondary cities, where there are opportunities for joint ventures and where credible relationships with financial institutions exist, such as Chiang Mai and Chiang Rai in Thailand, Osaka and Kobe in Japan, and Hanoi and Ho Chi Minh in Vietnam.

In the Asia-Pacific region the major players consist of eleven principal hotel groups, six European hotel groups, three US-inspired Asian hotel management companies, and some aggressive Asian newcomers (such as Shangri-La, the Tokyo Group, and New World Hotels International). Airline subsidiary hotel companies have also proliferated (Hunt, 1990).

The DAEs have recognized the importance of establishing a strong position in the international air traffic network by becoming capable of servicing any market. Japan is a case in point. The three major carriers, ANA, JAS, and JAL, have been expanding their international routes after the abolition of the Airline Constitution in 1985. Due to airline capacity constraints, they have had to form joint ventures with foreign carriers. For example, ANA works with the Malaysian airline system, the Scandinavian airline system, Austrian airlines, and Sabena. In addition, more international flights are being scheduled from more airports in Japan, such as Sapporo (Westlake, 1991).

This type of mainstream hotel and airline development continues unabated in the region. For example, Holiday Inns plans to double the 13,500 rooms it owns in the next five years. Accor has eleven properties under construction. Shangri-La International plans to increase inventory by 5,000 rooms by 1993. Regent, Mandarin, CJ International, and Peninsula are also planning expansion. Hotel chains are forced to look outside major cities for growth. Meanwhile, tourism arrivals have increased 59.7 percent over the last ten years. By 2000 the region is expected to account for 40 percent of all flights, with 72 million arrivals. According to the Pacific Asia Travel Association (PATA), tourism will continue to grow by 6–7 percent in the 1990s.

Diversification of tourism products and services

A large variety of developments have emerged. Apart from the mainstream hotel developments described above, new products range from multi-million dollar projects to small island niche resorts to hostel and educational development.

Technological advances will be a significant catalyst for new kinds of development to meet the competitive challenge. The travel industry is being rationalized worldwide as the impacts of technological advancement are felt. Recent advances in aircraft technology have led to the re-accreditation of medium-bodied, twin-engined aircraft to allow extended over-water operations. According to Le Page (1991), this has adversely affected the marketing clout of tourism products in major urban centers by allowing more frequent flights into smaller centers.

Rationalization continues in the international travel industry. In this competitive battle, the aviation industry continues to polarize. This stems from political changes and the trend toward bigness in carriers simply to match the competition. In the long term the movement is towards the elimination of arbitrary boundaries and restrictions, with the strongest country group and carrier either economically or operationally calling the tune. Boeing is planning high-speed aircraft for commercial operation by 2005 which are capable of 2,500 km/h. They expect transpacific traffic to be 300,000 seats a day, reaching 600,000 by 2015.

Technology also favors the development of luxury, self-contained resorts which cater to the growing demand for 'safe adventure' and closer experience of the environment. Flexibility in resort location has been facilitated by the development of cost-effective water treatment plants and cheap electric power from improved generators. This will have very significant consequences for tourism because it allows diversification away from coastlines into sensitive microenvironments which cannot be duplicated. Some resorts have also attempted to harness gas-thermal power resources in cost-effective ways for resorts of 100 room capacity and upwards (Le Page, 1991).

Newer resorts are also adopting construction techniques which are consistent with the environment and which are more flexible. Standard bricks and mortar approaches are giving way to natural woods, open planning, and low upkeep décor.

Farm holidays, cultural, educational, and sporting holiday products have a better chance of surviving now that electronic booking methods have been improved and networking is available at low cost.

Destinations are becoming relevant for a greater number of markets and purposes of visit due to advances in technology. For example, consumer perceptions of Australia are now expanding beyond Ayers Rock and Sydney Opera House due to advances in technology such as scuba diving equipment and medicine, off-road and over-water transport, and self-contained wilderness resorts. According to Le Page (1991), some niche tourism providers are 'thinking beyond the limits' and seeing technology as creating more possibilities for more authentic experiences.

Tourists themselves are also thinking beyond the limits as technology is unlocking possibilities. Electronic still-cameras are being developed, allowing images to be sent home immediately in digital form. Optical amplifiers using earth element Erbium will introduce inexpensive long-distance communications and will dramatically increase the amount and variety of information that can be sent across networks. This will allow the precise transmission of voice, data, and video signals. The first applications will probably be in cable and telecommunications networks of companies such as AT&T around 1996. The implication of this is that remote destinations such as Palau in the Pacific will become more relevant as a potential residential site. With companies like Matsushita spending $2.4 billion annually on research and development, these advances are set to continue.

As consumers have gradually come to accept or demand more control in their travel decisions, some more progressive companies have moved from basing products and services on consumer demands to basing entire companies on customer/market input. One example is Boeing, which created 220 design-build teams blending experts with customer input right from inception. These are the companies which will respond the fastest to changing times.

One example of how all of the above factors may come together is the planned Desaru resort project located at the southeastern tip of the Malay Peninsula. The first phase of this project will include nine hotels, 4,030 units of vacation homes, four golf courses, three country clubs, tennis courts, beach parks, equestrian facilities, 300 acres of entertainment facilities with theme parks, and a marina and harbor. But as we shall see, these kinds of mega developments may fail due to short-term thinking and breakdowns in relationships.

The diversity of developments has been fueled by changes in market demands. Travel writers talk of a new age of travel in which people move away from the traditional tourist sights which can be appreciated in books to experiences which broaden the mind and are good for the body. These may involve adventure (as long as safety standards are met) and education. One example of this is the phenomenal growth in Bungi-Jumping, which was developed on a commercial basis in New Zealand and was then introduced in New Zealand, and now in Europe. There are now many activities suiting the needs and budgets of a more segmented market.

One of the major growth markets being targeted by Asia-Pacific destinations and travel companies is Japan. According to the Japanese Travel Bureau, the Japanese travel market is worth US$134 billion. This is growing due to a steady increase in personal consumption levels, the availability of longer holidays and eight long weekends in the year. The emerging markets are: diversified and personalized travel, off-season holidays, more resort trips, special interest charters, sports and recreation, skiing and marine sports, couple travel, company-sponsored educational tours, and language study. Sensing these types of development, companies such as Sheraton are shifting emphasis from corporate to personal spending in many locations. The cheaper, longer, more experiential travel experience will increase in different forms in Asia just as it did in the West. Hospitality and tourism corporations are gearing themselves up for this.

These examples are part of a general diversification of the standard development formulas of the 1970s and early 1980s. Mass tourism operators are diversifying the range of options in their packages in order to adapt. It is encouraging that more sophisticated products are being developed. However, sophistication is not a luxury but a basic requirement. The need for a balanced understanding of other interrelated factors will be discussed in the following section.

The emerging development context

Diplomacy has been defined as 'tact' (*Webster's*, 1982, p. 131). In the corporate context this means a careful balancing of many sometimes obscure factors which nevertheless will have a bearing on long-term success. The central argument is that although the global transition toward the market economy has provided more opportunities in tourism and emphasized the importance of marketing the right product, this is a basic requirement and not a recipe for success. The shift toward the market economy has in itself created a false sense of security and has encouraged the view that things will stabilize after a short period of adjustment. However, current ethnic, social, technological, political, and economic conditions indicate that the centrally planned–market economy dichotomy is dangerously simplistic.

What corporations must now do is learn to balance the specialized skills encouraged by technology with a generalized knowledge of the development contexts in which they will be working. In doing so they will be more likely to maintain a competitive edge while coping with uncertainty. The emerging development context can be described as having five streams: (1) more complex success factors; (2) the question of control; (3) the question of implementation; (4) pressure from international organizations; and (5) pressure from local communities. These are discussed below.

More complex success factors

Despite the possibilities technology can offer, problems arise when it is assumed that a new product type is a strong enough basis for a successful project. At the outset there is a tendency to describe tourism market needs on the basis of available products around the world. This is a dangerous assumption but one that might explain short-sighted attempts by some corporations to out-do others by providing bigger, more elaborate, more expensive, and higher profile developments.

One of the major trends in this region is to build on a large scale because larger-scale projects are perceived as being more successful. This is also one way for developers to attract larger investment groups. Because of the magnitude of such proposals, the development process is often staged with further financial or operational partners being sought further down the road. This can become very complex. For example, the A$15 million wilderness resort that has opened in Alice Springs, Australia, involves several partners. It is being developed by Kings Canyon Nominees Pty Ltd with a joint venture between the Aboriginal and Torres Strait Islander Commercial Development Corporation, the Centrecorp Aboriginal Investment Corporation, and Australian Frontier Holidays. Building on a large scale is also more likely to attract large clients. This is an important consideration given the fact that firms like IBM, BASF, and Mitsubishi have travel budgets in excess of US$100 million per year.

One result of these developments is a growing concern with the integrity of the joint venture. The joint venture is based on trust, and herein lies the uncertainty. In the future, tourism corporations will have no option but to be more cautious in their alliances with other firms and not jump on the joint venture bandwagon. Corporations involved in tourism developments will also have to be more and more cautious now that capital markets have been liberalized. Deregulation increases the possibilities and probabilities of 'discretion' and corruption. The recent BCCI scandal involving millions of dollars is the tip of a black iceberg which is likely to keep growing in the current debt-ridden financial environment.

Corporations involved in tourism can no longer isolate themselves from the social and political environment around them. In manufacturing, the Asia-Pacific region has been attractive due to relatively low wages, prices, and costs. Most of the many tourism projects that fail use the same criteria. This is an insufficient basis for the tourism investment decision. This is because the consumer is there at the point of production, and his or her view of many additional factors (such as accessibility, product reliability and ability to fulfill promises, service and hospitality, atmosphere, as well as political conditions and other uncontrollable risks) strongly influences the long-term viability of tourism projects.

There are some other factors that are only just being recognized as having a bearing on success. These include satisfaction with the project on the part of local communities, which inevitably influence how efficiently tourism projects operate on a day-to-day basis, especially when it comes to service standards and other personnel issues. The perceptions that tourists (for business and pleasure purposes) may have of different countries, as shaped by social and political risk factors, are also critical. Media messages are especially powerful when consumers have no experience with which to compare them.

Tourism is also linked to the health of other industrial sectors. The kinds of infrastructure provided in countries affect tourism development potential. The health of manufacturing sectors may determine how much interest governments have in tourism as a contributor to the balance of payments, and how much business tourism can benefit from.

A most significant change is in the new emphasis travelers are placing on understanding host cultures, whether the motivation is negotiating a better business deal or learning new cultures, ideas, and values. This is likely to continue as the media encourages curiosity by injecting windows of the world into people's everyday lives. More pressure will be felt by corporations in the form of less repeat business if destinations are misrepresented in promotional material. The likelihood of this is greater for corporations which are not in tune with their environment.

The question of control
Now that the DAEs have gained ground in the international arena, they are looking at tourism not only to service this position but to style development so as to reinforce their international status. An example of this is the aforementioned Desaru project in Malaysia. Developments like this on a large scale create an image of a mass market on the horizon, along with its debilitating effects. The fulfillment of this image is not hard to believe, given expected demographic changes. For example, of the projected world population of 10 billion by 2060, 56 percent is predicted to be Asian. The population rise that has taken 100,000 years to happen will happen again in 70 years. This has major implications for tourism infrastructure, which is already running beyond capacity (*PATA Travel News* 1991). In Asia, traveling populations are channeled almost exclusively through the air transport system. Table 4.3 illustrates the dependency of Asian destinations on air travel.

The negative effects of tourism are shown in a great many destinations in the region. This is because most countries have let tourism developments take their own course. A prime example of this is in Hawaii. In 1988 GNP rose 4 percent in real terms as a direct result of visitor spending. Tourism has surpassed the military and pineapple farming as major industries in the state. From an economic standpoint Hawaii has been successful, but from other standpoints it has not. According to the Center for Responsible Tourism (NACCRT, 1991), local populations have been displaced and exhibit high levels of unemployment and various social problems, notably drug trafficking.

Table 4.3 Tourist arrivals in Asia by air, 1989 (%)

Hawaii	100
Australia	100
Indonesia	100
India	100
Japan	100
Taiwan	99
South Korea	95
Hong Kong	80
Singapore	80
Thailand	76

Source: PATA Travel News (1991).

Out of the liberalization of technology and capital and consumer markets discussed earlier in this chapter is emerging a concern for the environment and for resource and land use to support millions living on the brink of survival. This will eventually lead to more comprehensive development policies and policy implementation in areas where there are incentives for foreign investment in infrastructure. Tourism will continue to develop as a service to the industrial base.

Enlightened countries will see that tourism is an alternative to stripping a country's asset base because, if managed properly, it can help a country progress economically (by reducing the regional disparities and the rural migration problem) without serious degradation to the environment. The enlightened countries will be those that shift their focus from the individual tourism business level to viewing tourism as a large-scale entity with potential for change in many forms. Current restructuring of DAEs suggests that the climate is right for more control of tourism development. More countries will be employing experts and assessing impacts of tourism in order to make sure it is sustainable and to attract corporations which favor sustainability.

The question of implementation
In less dynamic Asian economies (LDAEs) with air access and underdeveloped infrastructure, tourism is a revenue generator even if industrialization is first priority. There are two options for development in these countries. Either (1) they can pursue productivity growth at all costs, or (2) they can pursue it within predetermined limits on the basis of lessons learned from the problems DAEs are experiencing.

The route taken by these countries may well depend on whether policy makers can agree on objectives and on the means to achieve them. The most progressive of the LDAEs will be the ones which control both regional tourism development and urban industrialization for the mutual benefit of both. One way of doing this is to avoid the temptation of attracting all possible markets. Papua New Guinea is a good example: tourism operators who have survived over the years have provided a product that appeals to the higher-spending traveler and have avoided attracting large numbers of budget travelers.

However, the control imperative has not been met well in the past, even where incentives exist. Bali represents an excellent example of how tourism, despite overall government planning, has taken its own course. Whilst tourism enclaves such as Nusa Dua have been planned, the rapid growth of major resort hotels within its confines, and the resultant increase in tourism, have placed intolerable demands upon infrastructure development, including airports, residential development of roads, water, and sewerage for local residents, and the future development of older neighbouring resort areas such as Kuta.

Similarly, in Bangkok the rapid development of hotels, condominiums, and office and other buildings has placed enormous stress upon the ability to provide matching infrastructure such as roads, water, and other basic services.

The result is that a once gracious city with wide roads and canals is grinding to a halt.

Savignac (1991) summed up the problem of hitherto poorly planned tourism when he stated that for too long the normal project cycle for many tourist resorts has involved discovery of a pristine natural site, development in an unplanned fashion, and measurement of success in terms of tourist operations and large numbers of tourists. This success has been accompanied by internal migration of labor, the growth of shanty towns and unplanned human settlements, degradation of the environment, and inadequate infrastructure to meet the demands of the new tourist and local populations. This leads to the decay of the resort or, in the examples given above, of the cities.

Thus whilst a specific resort or tourist enclave may be well planned and developed, unless the full ramifications of residential and infrastructure requirements for both the tourist and the supporting local population are taken into account, tourism development may not be sustainable into the future. The challenge, therefore, to planners of mega-projects such as Desaru, the dimensions of which were referred to earlier in this chapter, is to ensure that any project is sustainable and sensitive. The question is how to achieve total planning, including all aspects from airport facilities to the needs and preservation of the host community.

Tong (1991) emphasizes that recent developments are increasingly being designed to complement, not contrast with, the environment. The Chungman resort in Cheju, Korea, Nusa Dua in Bali, Indonesia, and in the future Desaru in Malaysia, are cited as resorts sensitive to the environment and local culture. The author, an architect, does not touch upon problems of development or infrastructure that arise external to the resort itself.

The question of who is responsible for infrastructure is debatable. Traditionally, infrastructure has been viewed as the responsibility of governments rather than developers of the hotel and associated superstructure. The future, however, is likely to result in an increasing contribution both from a consultative and financial viewpoint between the private and public sectors. Unfortunately, when a developing country decides to seek initial development in tourism, it is often not in a strong position to demand assistance from the private sector but instead has to offer various incentives.

In Asian countries such as Laos, Cambodia, and Vietnam, which are desperate to develop their economies, sensitive and environmentally planned tourism is likely to be regarded as less significant when there are so few tourists coming. While planners in these countries have a unique opportunity to learn from the mistakes made elsewhere, once borders open fully to destinations such as these, the pressure of demand will represent an immediate threat to the presentation of precious heritage and cultures.

Nevertheless, there is an undercurrent of hope as some countries become more aware of some of the negative effects of development. The natural environment is a case in point. In Singapore the government is responding to increased government awareness of environmental matters and shows a new emphasis on quality-of-life issues. The Philippines have embarked on a

25-year restoration strategy with a master plan involving the Asian Development Bank and other organizations. Malaysia has initiated a tropical forest action plan. Indonesia now has 320 conservation reserves, with a further 185 areas proposed. The government has made mandatory the application of environmental impact analyses to prospective projects. Thailand is embarking on a forestry master plan. According to Collins *et al.* (1991): 'During the past few years there have been changes in public opinion which are rapidly leading to new emphasis in the planning and management of forest lands.'

At this early stage it is difficult to assess how committed some of these initiatives are. What is certain is the enormous interest being generated. In Australia the Australian Tourism Commission has made the environment a priority area. PATA is pioneering a study on tourism and the reef and rainforests. The problem yet to be overcome is the plethora of environment legislation enacted in a complex web of fragmented regulations, agencies, and policies which discourage development even when development proposals meet guidelines. In many cases there exists no single environment initiative such as a companies code. In Australia there are 50 separate acts. It is hoped that pressures of recession in Australia and elsewhere will encourage rationalization.

The poor record of environmental and regional planning coupled with severe capacity problems and the extraordinary population growth projections for the region are strong motivators for taking preventative action. But whether this action will be taken on a scale that makes a difference is an unanswered question at this point.

Pressure from international organizations

Pressures from international organizations are not just confined to corporations and developers, but are exerted by a large proportion of the traveling public in tourism-generating countries through the media. The major concerns of these countries are wide ranging, from the environment to equality and human rights, and legislation to control development. For example, certain groups such as the Center for Responsible Tourism are advocating a global moratorium on tourism development that should be ratified at the UN Environment Conference in 1992. There are increasing concerns over the futility of devastating the environment for land use and personal gain through production. This message is brought home by realities such as the 800–900 year period required for a cleared rainforest to regenerate.

Similarly, in 1990 the International Air Transport Association (IATA) resolved that 'the airline industry has a public responsibility to minimize, within technological and economic constraints – the effects of its operations on the environment' (Meredith, 1991). More recently, lobbies such as the Travel and Tourism Council have been raising the profile of tourism and making connections between sustainable development and corporate growth.

These concerns, which are increasingly being voiced by writers such as Suzuki, will inevitably lead to increasing restrictions in the form of community controls and government legislation. Whether this will have any significant impact will depend on the local community's appreciation and understanding of the value of their assets.

Pressure from local communities
This pressure is connected with that of changing regional policies as more emphasis is placed on providing employment to local peoples. It has led to a great many problems, since many local communities have their own defined sociopolitical systems which do not fit either into Western ways of seeing things or even into the policy mechanisms of their own countries. In many countries small tourism developments can have far-reaching implications for community life.

Tourism is an opportunity for progression. Nevertheless, many communities are more aware of the negative effects of tourism development and of their stronger position as a result of changing market demands, expressed in terms of increasing interest in their way of life. They have seen the subtle effects of corporate development, such as when opportunities for employment create inequalities in income and affect the 'sense of community', and the blatant effects of corporate development, such as violation of respected fishing and land rights once development has begun.

In the long term, communities may realize just how valuable less developed regions of the world are to people from developed environments and will exercise their power when development proposals are made. One concrete example of this is to make corporations responsible for some of the local infrastructure costs. The uncertainty of all this is in enforcement. Governments bypass certain procedures in the wake of political pressures. Procedures often contain plenty of discretion.

In the long term, norms must be established for development, and there is a role for proactive corporations to help structure these norms in a framework of respect and to set an example to the industry at large. New Zealand has developed three such principles to guide development. These principles represent an array of preferences about how people should live with other people, whether these peoples are residents or tourists. The first principle is to accept responsibility for the environment and to set guidelines on carrying capacity and resource use. The second principle is partnership and participation in environmental issues. This refers to public/private sector participation, administration by government level, and conservation. The third and final principle is sustainability, and achieving this may involve incentives, price increases, and limits on visitor numbers (Plimmer, 1991).

Although progress is being made in New Zealand, we have seen similar projects elsewhere, and in many cases there is nothing new or startling about the strategies proposed. One example is the plan drawn up by New South Wales Tourism Commission, which contained the usual elements of environment planning, government support, marketing, transport, training, and wages and employment. Until more substantive and well thought-out programs are developed, political and interest-group support will be difficult to build in developed countries.

The future boils down to the question of control. This does not mean control in the conventional uni-directional sense, but control through proper coordination. The objective should be unity of purpose. For this to emerge in typically fragmented development situations, the people involved must be able to look at an overall 'environmental complex.' This concept is not new – it was discussed by scholars such as Parker-Follet in the 1930s. It basically amounts to looking at all the interacting elements to find a solution, and realizing that the process of adjustment changes the things to be adjusted, meaning that problems cannot be solved in any final sense.

Diplomacy will be critical on the part of corporations because, regardless of their power position, control imposed externally does not work. It denigrates standards and degrades the value of the tourism experience. Coordination must be established in the early stages, it must be continuous, and it must involve direct contact with all interests involved. Coordination must become a self-generating process, and this is likely to happen when the actors involved realize that unity does not mean sacrifice. It is now possible to get every interest bound consciously in the process because corporations in hospitality and tourism now have the power to create events rather than just react to them.

Conclusion: toward corporate diplomacy

Standard approaches to development in which blueprint tourism products are divorced from their immediate environments will no longer be viable in this part of the world. Of course, the old standard approaches will be dominant for some time since they externalize many of the realities of the region and make planning and financing easier. But, as this chapter has shown, enlightened corporations will see that it is in their own self-interest to pursue a more diplomatic approach in which more parties benefit in the long run. The argument is simple but powerful – get into the mindset of the local host community and the product user. Many corporations have made the transition from isolating themselves to complying with local needs. Now they must take a more participatory and proactive role in defining and helping to reach these needs.

Corporations now have a responsibility to apply their knowledge of what works and what does not to new situations. This requires considerable tact. Although development principles such as those discussed above are useful, they do not help the corporation in making the transition to the diplomatic mindset. Corporate diplomacy is not something that can be read from a manual and implemented as a corporate-wide program. It is something more fundamental to the corporate mission and *raison d'être*. It runs against the grain of tourism development as we know it. Pergat (1991) stated this conventional wisdom succinctly: 'Tourism has its own theory. Not the theory of supply and demand. Rather the theory of abundance ... that there is more than enough to go around and if there isn't ... we'll pretend.'

In order to understand how new formulas for decision making may be resolved, refer to the Thompson–Tuden matrix (Figure 4.1) in which degrees of agreement on objectives and knowledge of how to attain them are related to each other (Thompson and Tuden, 1959). This can perhaps be applied to both the public and private sectors. Hospitality corporations have generally agreed on the objectives of their strategies and on the means to achieve them. Now the balance of power is changing and corporations will find themselves in more situations that involve more external interests. In this situation, accepted formulas cannot be used to compute solutions.

If corporations simplify their environment to make it more manageable, but at the expense of their understanding of it, they will agree neither on objectives nor on the means to achieve those objectives. In this situation, according to the creators of the matrix, the players will probably decide not to face the issues at hand. Corporations will not cope well with pressures from international organizations and communities, and with social, political, and economic factors. Relations will be unstable and will lack trust. This will immediately affect day-to-day operations and long-term viability.

Corporations should be searching and experimenting in pursuit of new knowledge when they agree on objectives but not on knowledge. Similarly, they should be prepared to bargain and compromise over various objectives when they have the requisite knowledge of countries in which they operate, as might be the case in well-known markets in countries undergoing rapid change. Corporations are likely to be faced with these types of situation in the immediate future. Although the means–ends dichotomy in the above matrix is somewhat simplistic, it does help bridge the concepts of politics and business, which have previously been kept in separate black boxes. These associations are urgently required if we are to progress in our understanding and improvement of tourism development.

OBJECTIVES

		Disagreed	Agreed
KNOWLEDGE	Agreed	Bargaining and compromise	Computation programmed decision
	Disagreed	Immobilization	Search, experimentation

Fig. 4.1 Thompson–Tuden matrix

Source: From *The New Politics of the Budgetary Process* by Aaron Wildavsky. Copyright © 1988 by Aaron Wildavsky. Reprinted by permission of HarperCollins Publishers.

References

Adams, R. *et al.* (1991) 'A plain man's guide to a complicated world', *Daily Telegraph Magazine*, 3 August, pp. 19–48.

Barsony, A. (1991) 'Co-operation with the dynamic Asian economies', *OECD Observer*, pp. 14–19.

Business International (1991a) 'Executive watchlist', *Business Asia*, 26 August, p. 300.

Business International (1991b) 'Hong Kong, Singapore Investors Eye Indochina', *Business Asia*, 26 August, p. 298.

Chui, J. (1991) 'Tourism in China', *Proceedings of first Annual Asia-Pacific Hospitality and Tourism Trends Seminar*, Victoria University of Technology, June.

Collins, N. M., Sayer, Jeffrey A., and Whitmore, Timothy C. (1991) *The Conservation Atlas of Tropical Forests: Asia and the Pacific*, New York: Simon & Schuster.

Euromonitor (1987) *Asian Economic Handbook*, London: Euromonitor Publications.

Gilbert, A. (1985) *An Unequal World*, Basingstoke: Macmillan.

Goldstein, C. (1991) 'Balmy weather ahead', *Far East Asian Economic Review*, 11 April, p. 43.

Habermas, J. (1973) *Legitimation Crisis*, trans. by Thomas McCarthy, Boston, Mass.: Beacon.

Hunt, J. (1990) 'Hotels in Asia', *EIU Travel and Tourism Analyst*, no. 4, pp. 16–36.

LePage, S. (1991) 'Technological trends', *Proceedings of First Asia-Pacific Hospitality and Tourism Trends Seminar*, Victoria University of Technology, June.

International Reports (1991) 'India', vol. XLII, no. 32, p. 20.

Meridith, J. D. A. (1991) 'Air transport and the environment: threat or opportunity?', *Proceedings of 40th PATA Annual Conference on Tourism and the Environment*, 9–13 April.

NACCRT (1991) *Tourism: Cultural diversity and adversity*, California: Center for Responsible Tourism.

PATA Travel News (1991) May.

Pergat, V. (1991) 'Transportation–aviation trends', *Proceedings of First International Asia-Pacific Hospitality and Tourism Trends Seminar*, Victoria University of Technology, June.

Plimmer, W. N. (1991) 'Tourism and the environment: the New Zealand experience', *Proceedings of 40th PATA Conference on Tourism and the Environment*, 9–13 April.

Savignac, A. E. (1991) 'Enrich the environment', *Proceedings of 1991 PATA Annual Conference*, p. 263.

Schwartz, A. (1991) 'Pause for new growth', *Far East Asian Economic Review*, 18 April, p. 13.

Thompson, James D., and Tuden, Arthur (1959) 'Strategies, structures and processes of organizational decision', J. D. Thompson *et al.* (eds) *Comparative Studies in Administration*, Pittsburgh, Pa.: University of Pittsburg Press.

Tong, G. M. B. (1991) 'Architectural planning and environment sensitivity trends in resort development', *Integrated Resort Development in Asia*.

Webster's New World Compact School and Office Dictionary (1982) New York: Simon & Schuster, p. 131.

Weiss, J. (1989) *The Asian Century*, New York/Oxford: Facts on File.

Westlake, M. (1991) 'Spreading their wings', *Far East Asian Economic Review*, 31 January, p. 36.

Wildavsky, A. (1988) *The New Politics of the Budgetary Process*, Boston: HarperCollins.

Ziegler, D. (1990) 'Capital market survey', *The Economist*, 21 July, pp. 5–28.

Part 2

Competitive strategies

The five chapters in Part 2 are concerned with aspects of competitive positioning associated with international expansion. Chapters 5, 6 and 7 focus on international marketing issues and in particular, the two principal brand-development options of multibrand (Chapter 5) and single or 'core' brand extension (Chapter 7). Chapters 8 and 9 take a wider view of international expansion by appraising the development methods and business structures adopted by hospitality firms. Chapter 8 concentrates on how North American companies have handled overseas expansion and Chapter 9 focuses on the organizational development needs which arise from expansion.

The global recession, the Gulf War and industry over-building, among other factors, have in recent years made survival difficult for international hotel operators. One of the key decisions facing the executives who have to deal with these issues is whether they would be able to compete more effectively by strengthening a single or 'core' brand or by adopting a multibrand development strategy. Choice International Hotels has chosen the multibrand approach and in Chapter 5, some of the reasons for this decision are discussed along with the events in the environment which influenced this direction.

The intention of Chapter 6 is to assess the impact of international development, or 'internationalization', on the worldwide hospitality industry from the marketing perspective. Past and present trends in international hospitality marketing are discussed and analyzed in relation to their apparent effectiveness in creating consumer awareness, recognition and purchase. Following this, a framework is developed for the purposes of categorizing international hospitality marketing strategies, thus enabling specific observations to be made concerning the future of international strategic hospitality marketing.

Holiday Inn Worldwide is currently implementing a global expansion program by extending the 'core brand' characteristics and features of the original Holiday Inn at the higher and lower ends of the mid-priced lodging market. This means that the Holiday Inn brands are closely positioned in the mid-priced lodging market under one internationally recognized identity with each hotel type offering an appropriate level of service and facilities for a particular sector of the market. Chapter 7 examines how Holiday Inn Worldwide is using its brand extension strategy to sustain rapid development in Europe.

Whereas some firms replicate successful brand concepts in order to expand overseas, others achieve their development ambitions in other ways. In Chapter 8, the authors review the different development methods employed by hospitality firms when entering international hospitality markets. Specifically, the global strategies of a sample of major North American chains are compared and analyzed in order to identify how they have achieved competitive positions in foreign countries.

Chapter 9 begins by identifying the relative merits of business structures such as direct ownership, joint ventures, franchising and management contracting which are used by hospitality firms to achieve expansion. The implications of this analysis are focused on the human resource needs relating to the maintenance of organizational direction and the achievement of performance standards. Toward the end of the chapter the implications for organizational change associated with expansion are emphasized by using two case studies to illustrate the emerging issues for international management development. This analysis provides an effective link between the external factors affecting international expansion and the internal, structural issues which organizations must address. These are the focal concerns of Part 3.

Richard Teare

5

Going global – acting local: the challenge of Choice International

Robert C. Hazard, Chairman and Chief Executive, and
Lynn O'Rourke Hayes, Assistant to the President,
Choice Hotels International
with Michael Olsen

Choice Hotels International, with headquarters in the Washington D.C. area, is the world's largest franchise hotel company. The organization markets nearly 2,800 hotels in 26 countries under the Comfort, Quality, Clarion, Sleep, Rodeway, Econo Lodge and Friendship brands. The parent firm, New York stock exchange-traded Manor Care, is a large owner and operator of nursing homes throughout the United States.

According to Choice Chairman and Chief Executive Officer, Robert C. Hazard Jr, his company will be the global lodging leader by the year 2000, with 10,000 hotels flying the Choice flag in all the right international locations. The intention of this chapter is to explain decisions influencing this goal and the corporate strategies for the future.

Large multinational lodging firms have been faced with numerous important strategic decisions in the last few years. They have never been more critical than at present. The global recession, Gulf War, and industry overbuilding have made survival, let alone prosperity, difficult. While many firms, such as Swissotel, Kempinski, Meridien, Hyatt and Regency have focused their resources upon a single core brand, firms such as Choice have developed a multibrand strategy. In fact, Choice was the first company to introduce product segmentation into the lodging industry in 1981. Since then, many other hotel companies have followed their lead.

Multibrand versus single brand

With seven brands, Choice feels it is well positioned across all segments of the hospitality industry. These seven brands are tied together by one reservations system.

The multibrand strategy is designed to put as many Choice guests into a specific marketing area as possible. Choice feels that this tactic permits all hotels in the market to benefit. If a caller to the reservations system cannot get the hotel he or she desires in an area, they will be directed to another Choice brand nearby. While some may argue that putting too many hotels of the same firm within a specific market area contributes to a cannibalization of business, Choice executives believe the opposite is true and have substantial evidence to support the argument.

The multibrand strategy developed by Choice has proved very successful in the United States and is well underway in the overseas markets. There are ten reservations centers serving 26 countries to support this development strategy.

Global factors affecting growth

While expanding globally is an important strategic objective for Choice, the environment poses many challenges and obstacles for the industry as a whole. Principal among them is the recession. Among its implications has been a cutback in both business and leisure travel. While this represents an impediment for the industry, it signals an opportunity for most Choice brands. Travelers are slicing out frills and excesses and looking for easily accessible lodging choices that represent value and dependability around the globe. Choice is well positioned to capture its fair share of this increasing market. This is not a short-term phenomenon, but rather a major structural change in the industry which will continue to shape the types of products and services offered by multinational lodging firms for many years to come. Additionally, this recession may also have a negative impact upon business growth in the newly liberated nations of the Eastern bloc. Thus the opportunities for growth in the hotel industry in these developing nations will suffer a setback. Similarly, while business growth in Asia may be somewhat more vigorous the recession will result in fewer opportunities compared to the growth years of the 1980s.

Technology continues to surface as an important ingredient in the strategy of many hospitality firms. The term in this context refers to the development of communication, marketing, and management support systems which allow firms to be more competitive in targeting and selling to the customer. In this context, Choice seeks to be the leader in reservations technology. They believe they have a competitive advantage not shared by others on a global basis. Choice has expended considerable capital in creating state-of-the-art reservations systems and they intend to remain at the forefront.

It is also recognized that there are product attributes which must be built into rooms to accommodate the changing communications needs of today's peripatetic business traveler. In-room connections for computers with modems are an example of those features which are being incorporated into the Choice brands which are dubbed 'the hotel room of the future' as they will feature high-tech amenities at an economy price.

The socio-cultural dimension which Choice feels will have the most impact upon their growth is the increasingly diverse workforce. This is especially true in Europe where workers from poorer Eastern bloc countries will migrate to the Western nations in search of employment. It is expected to be evermore difficult to integrate them into the workforce due to issues that are largely nationalistic. Further, this employee group as a whole is not accustomed to providing high levels of service due to a lack of training and industry-specific education.

Choice executives believe they will have an edge in the global lodging game because of their international marketing expertise. In the United States, the company has focused its efforts on attracting individual market segments – seniors, families, government/military travelers – in part through the effective use of television advertising. The award-winning 'celebrity in a suitcase' campaigns, which feature market-responsive individuals popping from a suitcase with a specific message, have dramatically increased market share for the company in the USA. Early results indicate a similar success in other parts of the world. A major effort is made to channel business through the highly effective computerized reservations systems which serves travelers from every point on the globe. In addition, Choice will continue to seek out strategic alliances with business partners in other parts of the world. The combined strengths of selected travel industry partners will further boost Choice's position within the lodging industry.

The lack of capital worldwide for financing hotel development is not a newly discovered environmental threat. It is almost impossible to find the right terms for new construction or refurbishing. While in some cases, franchisees may be able to enjoy better opportunities, due to close ties locally, it is still difficult for them to find the funds needed. It cannot be expected that this problem will abate soon.

Management of an evolving workforce will provide new challenges for business leaders. Language, work ethics and cultural and sexual differences will be among the issues human resource professionals will address. As more parents work, while caring for small children and their own aging parents, flexible work schedules will be essential to keep the most valuable and highly-trained employees in their jobs. Health care and benefit packages will be more complicated and costly. Training and retraining will be necessary as new technologies present themselves. Meanwhile, the overall costs of business management will necessitate the reduction of the labor force. Labor-lean hotels, like Sleep Inns, that rely on technology without sacrificing hospitality, will prevail.

Competitive methods

The future for Choice lies in the effective implementation of their global development strategy. Product segmentation is an important vehicle to achieve this growth. This primary strategic method will be necessary in the context of an industry which is becoming increasingly consolidated. The master franchise concept will allow any individual or firm to develop hotels within a specified regional area. This will permit Choice to have greater control over the product and its day-to-day quality but still permit a decentralized global structure. Franchisees will be able to respond to local competitive and cultural pressures with the backing of an international leader. What is important in this type of structure is that the brand identification remains pure so that product consistency can anchor the global marketing efforts.

There are important differences in the structures of franchise versus other types of hotel companies. Whereas non-franchise oriented organizations seek to achieve control through a system of hierarchical management relationships, franchise organizations maintain control through agreements which detail the quality specifications that must be maintained in order to preserve the franchise integrity. This approach leaves the decision as to what organizational structure is best to implement strategy up to the franchisee organization. Thus, Choice can remain a very lean organization devoted to improving services both to the franchisee and the traveling public.

6

Competitive marketing strategies in the international hospitality industry

Simon Crawford-Welch

In the 1990s hospitality will truly evolve into an international business. For example, hotel and restaurant chain operators are already scrambling to set up shop throughout exotic Pacific Rim locations and in the relatively untouched markets of the People's Republic of China and the Soviet Union. It has been estimated that hundreds of millions of US dollars are being pumped into international sites (Rusth and Lefever, 1988). Correspondingly, the focus on international competition has intensified over the past year. Sharp (1990) notes:

> We've heard for years about the coming global competitive environment. But in just the last few months, we've seen the most substantial changes in 40 years – changes that will lead to nearly unrestrained competition. We've seen border barriers in Eastern Europe repealed by 'people power' and markets being integrated, deregulated, and expanded in North America, Europe, and along the Pacific Rim. Corporations around the world are manoeuvering for market position through takeovers, mergers, and alliances. There's been more consolidation in the last two years than in the past 50. (p. 99)

There can be little doubt that corporate mergers and acquisitions have had a large impact on the international hotel industry. For example, US and Japanese companies, together with European-based operators such as Forte, Ladbroke, and Accor, will each control between 100,000 and 200,000 rooms around the world during the 1990s.

International hospitality investment worldwide is soaring. At least 100 new overseas properties were opened by US lodging chains between 1986 and 1989. In the restaurant segment, about 70 US chains have international outlets. Foreign investment in the American hospitality industry also continues to increase with companies such as Miyako Hotels (Japan), Swissotel Ltd (Switzerland), Forte (UK) and Accor (France) either building or acquiring properties in the USA. The situation is similar throughout the world with many hospitality corporations investing heavily in foreign markets: Ladbroke with their Hilton International chain, Queens Moat Houses in Holland, Forte throughout continental Europe, Four Seasons in Japan, Best Western in Japan, and Days Inns in Europe, to name but a few.

The complexion of the entire global hospitality marketplace is being changed significantly by the coalition of nations into multinational market groups. Examples include Europe 1992; the Arab Common Market; the Pacific Rim Association of South East Asian Nations; the USA free-trade agreements with Canada and Mexico; and the Latin American Andean Common Market.

The hospitality industry is becoming a global industry, an industry which ranks second to none in terms of size and global influence. Global tourism, for example, is a $2 trillion industry and employs over 100 million workers. In 1989 there were a record 403 million international tourists worldwide who spent $208 billion (World Travel Organization, 1990). American travel to foreign destinations, which has not yet reached maturity, is expected to grow at least twice as fast as domestic tourism by the end of the century (Ayala, 1991). The world is becoming one global marketplace.

Despite this unprecedented growth in internationalization throughout the hospitality industry, Thomas Staed of Oceans Eleven Resorts argues that we have not yet scratched the surface of internationalization and that there is a huge, untapped market in Japan and Europe. Unfortunately, the growth in internationalization has not been accompanied by a parallel growth in the sophistication of hospitality marketing strategies. Given that internationalization will only increase throughout the hospitality industry, it is timely and appropriate to investigate the implications of internationalization for the functional strategy of hospitality marketing. To date, there has been only limited research in this area (e.g. Makens and Edgell, 1990; Crawford-Welch, 1991b, 1991c).

The purpose of this chapter is to offer some insights into the implications of internationalization and changing competitive conditions in the global hospitality industry for the formulation, implementation, and content of hospitality marketing strategies. Specifically, this chapter will (1) outline and discuss the growth and nature of internationalization in the worldwide hospitality industry; (2) compare and contrast the various approaches to hospitality marketing that major corporations have adopted in the international arena; and (3) make specific recommendations concerning the formulation, implementation, and content of marketing strategies in the international hospitality industry.

The internationalization of the hospitality industry

Internationalization is rampant in both the lodging and restaurant industries. In the lodging industry, for example, between 1986 and 1989, new overseas properties opened by US hotel chains included Hyatt's Australian flagship, the 580 room Hyatt in Melbourne; the 600 room Grand Hyatt Hong Kong; three new Hilton International properties in Japan totaling 1,777 rooms; Sheraton's Damai Beach Resort hotel in Malaysia; the 1,008 room Sheraton Hua Ting in Shanghai; and the Westin Plaza and Westin Stamford in Singapore (Rusth and Lefever, 1988). Westin Hotels and Resorts in particular have major plans for international expansion.

John Aoki, Chairman of Westin Hotels and Resorts, announced in late 1990 plans to double the size of the organization within the next ten years. Westin now operates 64 hotels comprising more than 35,000 rooms in 10 countries. In 1982 those tallies were 55 properties, 26,686 rooms, and 13 countries. The current plans call for at least six properties per year. Westin's plan is to locate properties in gateway cities around the world. The company is looking for hotel deals in Europe, Asia, South America, Australia, New Zealand, the Middle East, Canada, Mexico, and the USA.

Best Western International is another chain pursuing major international expansion strategies. Chief Executive Officer, Ron Evans, states: 'I truly believe the world is getting smaller, that globalization is more than just a trendy word. The lodging chains of the future will be those that are world players ... The national player is going to be more and more disadvantaged' (Goss, 1989, p. 65).

Best Western already stakes claim to being the biggest hotel chain – based on number of properties – in North America (with more than 1,900 properties in the USA, Canada, and Caribbean nations), as well as in Europe (including Israel, 880 member hotels) and Australia and New Zealand (500 members). The company's next step will be to tackle several new markets through affiliation with an additional 550 properties in approximately 13 countries by 1993. In Japan, for example, Best Western hopes to sign on 50 affiliates over the next five years. Other affiliates they wish to sign include 60 members in China, 55 affiliates in the former Soviet Union and other Eastern European countries (of which 15 are slated for Hungary), 75 in South America, 50 divided between India, Pakistan, and Nepal, about 30 in Africa, some 20 in the Middle East, and 25 in Greece and Turkey (Goss, 1989).

The restaurant industry is no exception to the emphasis on internationalization, with Pacific Rim markets being regarded as potentially very lucrative. Hardee's, Arby's, and Dairy Queen made their first appearance in Taiwan in 1987. White Castle, Red Lobster, and Taco Time have entered Japan, and McDonald's has opened units in Seoul. Kentucky Fried Chicken, after signing an agreement with the Chinese government, has opened its first unit in Beijing. McDonald's and Pizza Hut are well established in the former Soviet Union (Rusth and Lefever, 1989).

Given this momentum toward internationalization throughout the hospitality industry, it is appropriate to outline briefly how hospitality organizations have traditionally marketed their products in the international arena. Such an exercise will allow us to determine whether 'traditional' marketing strategies are appropriate in today's hospitality environment.

Historic trends in hospitality marketing

Historic trends in hospitality marketing can best be described within the accepted framework provided by the traditional 4 Ps (product, place, price, promotion). The most pervasive historical trends in each of these four categories will be briefly described.

1. Product

An emphasis on standardization
The 1970s saw the international hospitality industry passing through a period of intense standardization whereby the provision of a single standard product, operated almost independent of unique locational influences, was the norm: for example, the standardized Holiday Inn. The emphasis was clearly on the provision and marketing of a single concept/brand.

2. Place/channels of distribution

An emphasis on direct channels of distribution (DCDs)
DCDs are channels which both produce and distribute the product, usually simultaneously. Examples include: ownership, e.g. Holiday Inn in the 1970s; management contracts, e.g. Hilton; and franchising, e.g. Motel 6.

An emphasis on franchising
US-based international chains have historically expanded into other countries through one or more of the following traditional franchising methods: master license (as is the case with Days Inns in Europe); direct license, branch or subsidiary operation; or joint venture (Go and Christensen, 1989).

3. Price

An emphasis on cost pricing techniques and discounting
Such an approach was, at best, myopic in nature. The emphasis on discounting has placed the hospitality industry in the midst of what can only be termed a profitless prosperity syndrome. Contrary to popular belief, a 10 percent decrease in price is not made up for by a 10 percent increase in volume. The equivalent volume required (equivalent volume = existing volume multiplied by existing contribution divided by discounted contribution) to make up for a 10 percent decrease in price is a 15 percent increase in volume.

An emphasis on differentiation through discounting
Using discounting as a means of differentiating is indicative of the lack of success of hospitality organizations. Each hospitality product should stand for a unique combination or package of goods and services. If branding and

positioning strategies have been successfully implemented there should be no reason to engage in discounting as a means of differentiation within a product class. It is the author's view that discounting has been primarily brought about by a lack of comprehensive and market-oriented segmentation and differentiation strategies. It is detrimental to the industry as a whole in the long run and is no long-term solution to declining occupancies.

4. Promotion

An emphasis on traditional marketing practices
Little or no attention was paid toward the practices of non-traditional marketing, such as internal marketing, relationship marketing, and micro-marketing.

An emphasis on an ethnocentric approach to international operations
This approach involved the domestic hospitality organization seeking sales extension of its domestic products into foreign markets. This was the orientation that organizations like the Holiday Corporation used in the 1970s when attempting to go international. In effect, tourists were 'cocooned' in a type of environmental bubble – regardless of the country in which the Holiday Inn was located, it was strikingly similar to a Holiday Inn that could be found anywhere in the United States. Such an approach assumes the existence of a mass market and tends to ignore the fundamental cultural, social, perceptual, and economic differences in a country.

An emphasis on mass marketing
The marketing approach adopted in the 1970s was a mass-marketing one whereby consumers were generally treated as a homogeneous mass with similar needs and desires.

It is apparent from the description of historic trends in hospitality marketing that the 'traditional' methods of marketing are no longer appropriate in what has become an extremely volatile, complex, and dynamic operating environment at the international level. Future trends will impact dramatically upon hospitality marketing and cause the industry to react accordingly. Although not exhaustive, the following section discusses what the author believes to be the major future trends in hospitality marketing.

Future trends in hospitality marketing

Warren and Ostergren (1990) succinctly summarize the major trend in international hospitality marketing in the 1990s when they state:

> Marketing will be the key to success in the 90's. Lip service and slogans will no longer substitute for a real understanding of the market place. No longer can we merely respond to market demands. Instead, we must anticipate them by reading market conditions better and faster than before.

As with historic marketing trends, future marketing trends in the international hospitality industry can best be described using the framework provided by the traditional 4 Ps (product, place, price, promotion).

1. Product

There are several strategic trends that will impact upon the nature of the international hospitality product of the 1990s. These include the following.

A greater emphasis on customization
Today's consumer is becoming more sophisticated and there are an increasing number of sophisticated consumers. Existing industry forces such as increased competitive intensity, more substitutes, and low brand-switching costs are resulting in increased levels of customization.

A greater emphasis on product portfolio marketing and product line extension
The 1990s will see an increase in the development of several different lodging and restaurant brands operated by one single organization: for example, Choice Hotels International and General Mills. There are three reasons for this development. First, by diversifying their provision, hospitality corporations can effectively diversify away unsystematic risk. Second, the development of a product portfolio offers hospitality firms the opportunity to grow in saturated marketplaces like the United States. Third, it is often cheaper and financially more astute to build new concepts than to renovate existing inventory (Olsen *et al.*, 1989).

2. Place/channels of distribution

In a recent panel discussion on the internationalization issue, Radisson Hotels President John Norlander stated that globalization will mean that US operators will have to examine their marketing practices and determine new distribution methods. He noted that US companies are not adept in marketing their product abroad.

The major trend impacting on future distribution channels in the international hospitality industry is the move toward indirect channels of distribution (ICDs).

An emphasis on ICDs
ICDs are channels which only distribute the product, as opposed to direct channels of distribution which both produce and distribute the product, usually simultaneously. Examples include consortiums, e.g. Best Western; affiliations, e.g. Movenpick Hotels International of Switzerland, SAS International Hotels of Oslo, and Radisson Hotels of the USA; representative firms, e.g. Utell International; and tour operators and travel agents.

3. Price

An emphasis on customer pricing
Pricing in the international hospitality industry of the 1990s will move away from the traditional cost-oriented and myopic methods toward more customer-oriented techniques such as price/value pricing, expectation pricing, and psychological pricing.

An emphasis on yield management techniques
Yield management is essentially an old concept, modified, enhanced, and integrated into modern computerized reservation systems. It focuses on revenue optimization, utilizing selling conditions and manipulations across different market segments. It is simply a new generation tool used to enhance the present systems analytical methods for market condition analysis and profit equation monitoring capabilities (DeVeau, 1989, p. 1). Undoubtedly, the system has the potential to make the pricing decision far more market oriented than the largely cost-oriented techniques that are currently practiced in the industry. International hospitality corporations will benefit tremendously since they already possess massive reservation systems which lend themselves perfectly to the yield management philosophy.

4. Promotion

An emphasis on a regiocentric and geocentric orientation to marketing
An international hospitality organization guided by this orientation is generally referred to as a global company (Cateora, 1990). A hospitality organization employing such an orientation strives for efficiencies of scale by developing a standardized product, of dependable quality, to be sold at a reasonable price to a global market: that is, the same country market set throughout the world. Important to the global marketing concept is the premise that world markets are being driven toward a converging commonality, seeking in much the same ways to satisfy their needs and desires (Levitt, 1983). Thus they constitute significant market segments with similar demands for the same product the world over. This does not mean that hospitality firms of the future will have a single product and a single marketing strategy which is implemented without modification the world over, as was the case in the 1970s. Rather, it means that hospitality firms will have to adopt an effective benefit segmentation strategy (as opposed to traditional descriptive forms of segmentation) which is capable of dividing the world into different market segments according to benefits sought regardless of country of origin.

An emphasis on micro-marketing
In the hospitality industry of the 1990s and beyond there will be no such

thing as a mass market. Mass marketing is a vestige of the past:

> The mass market has split into ever-multiplying, ever-changing sets of mini-markets that demand a continually expanding range of options, models, types, sizes, colors, and customizations. (Toffler, 1980, p. 248)

> The 1980's [is] a decade of unprecedented diversity.... advertisers are forced to direct products to perhaps a million clusters of people who are themselves far more individualistic and who have a wide range of choices in today's world. The multi-option society is a new ball-game, and advertisers know that they must win consumers market by market. (Ries and Trout, 1986, pp. 231–2)

This demassification means that hospitality organizations are having to become increasingly sophisticated and precise in the simultaneous segmenting and targeting of multiple markets. The future of hospitality marketing will not be mass marketing but micro-marketing. Micro-marketing involves (1) staying close to the customer; (2) heavy customization; (3) use of targeted and new media; (4) use of non-media; (5) use of relationship marketing; and (6) use of middle-men for distribution purposes.

A greater emphasis on green marketing
The environment is a growing concern for hospitality organizations and their promotion efforts. Hospitality organizations of the twenty-first century will have to have credible solid waste minimization programs while promoting a competitive product and simultaneously positioning the corporation and its waste program as part of an overall organizational image of environmental responsibility (Cummings, 1991).

A greater emphasis on non-traditional marketing
Non-traditional marketing consists of internal marketing and relationship marketing. Internal marketing simply involves viewing employees as internal customers, viewing the jobs as internal products, and then endeavouring to offer internal products that satisfy the needs and wants of those internal customers while addressing the objectives of the organization. Relationship marketing is marketing to protect the customer base. It sees the customer as an asset. Its function is to attract, maintain, and enhance customer relationships (Lewis and Chambers, 1989).

Given these projected trends it is suggested that hospitality corporations should adopt, dependent upon their individual environmental conditions, one of three possible international marketing strategies. These three strategies are theoretically founded in the Miles and Snow (1978) strategic typology.

International hospitality marketing strategies for the twenty-first century

The word 'strategy' derives its meaning from the ancient Greek word *strategos* meaning the art of the general. While there is some variation in the conceptual definitions of strategy, most conform to a definition of strategy as the process of continuously adapting to the changes in a firm's environment, and the means through which an organization establishes and re-establishes its fundamental set of relationships with its environment.

Miles and Snow (1978) suggest that there are three generic competitive strategies. These are (1) a prospector-like strategy; (2) an analyzer-like strategy; and (3) a defender-like strategy. Figure 6.1 shows the Miles and Snow generic strategic typology. The key underlying dimension of the strategic typology, as can be seen in the figure, is the rate of change at which an organization adjusts its products or markets. Miles and Snow also note the existence of a fourth strategic type known as a reactor-like strategy, which by definition is such an unstable form of decision pattern and is so inconsistent in its relations with its operating environment that it is not a strategy in the strictest sense of the word.

A prospector-like strategy is usually pursued by organizations which operate in complex and dynamic conditions and have to be innovative to survive. Prospectors are constantly looking for new markets by engaging in high levels of environmental scanning.

A defender-like strategy is generally pursued by organizations that operate in a stable environment. The emphasis is on becoming as efficient as possible while protecting a specific segment of the market. The emphasis is on a tight administrative structure aimed at maintaining tight control in order to achieve the high levels of efficiency required.

An analyzer-like strategy is a mixture of defender and prospector-type strategies in that it attempts to minimize risk while maximizing the opportunity for profit. It seeks to find new product markets while maintaining a stable customer base. One way of doing this is through the adoption of a market-follower strategy: that is, by imitation. Adopting such a strategy means that the initial adopter takes on the majority of the risk associated with a new product or market.

Hospitality organizations operating in the international arena must decide which of these three competitive strategies is feasible and most effective given the specific circumstances in which they operate. Figure 6.2 outlines the three possible strategic departures that hospitality corporations may choose to pursue.

Defender-like strategic marketing departures

Hospitality firms may pursue a defender-like marketing strategy in one way or by some combination of several ways.

Fig. 6.1 The Miles and Snow (1978) strategic typology

Low	Continuum of adjustment strategies	High
Defender-like strategic marketing departures	**Analyzer-like strategic marketing departures**	**Prospector-like strategic marketing departures**
• Price competitive • Cost control • Quality control • Low inventories • Standardization • Segment focus • Operational efficiency	• Do-it-yourself customization • Membership base • Application of technology • Managing supply and demand	• High value added • Innovative • Consumer research • Product development • Market leader • Customization • Opportunity seeker • High environmental scanning

Fig. 6.2 Strategic marketing departures

First, they may target members of a customer segment whose determinant features in choosing a hospitality product are price related. In other words, members of the target market must emphasize price as a determinant attribute in their purchase decision-making process. The target market must be willing to make trade-offs between the products/services it purchases and the cost of these products and services. Examples of firms pursuing this strategy in the international hospitality industry include Forte with its Little Chef Lodges, Accor with its Formule 1 concept in the lodging industry, and McDonald's and Wimpy's in the restaurant industry. The marketing strategy of these firms must be to use price and price/value as a means of positioning their respective organizations and of differentiating their products through effective promotion.

Second, a defender-like marketing strategy will emphasize operational efficiency through standardization. A belief in this approach is the theoretical backbone of the proliferation of brands currently emerging throughout the international hospitality industry. It is marketing's role to set customer expectations by promising a predetermined package of goods and services, and then to deliver this package. Since any hospitality purchase has a certain amount of risk associated with it in the eyes of the consumer, the more effective the firm is at promising and delivering a standardized product, the lower the risk associated with that purchase in the mind of the consumer. Examples of applying this logic to the marketing of hospitality products in the international arena can be seen in the marketing strategies of several international hospitality corporations, such as Choice Hotels International, Trusthouse Forte, and Accor.

Third, because a defender-like strategy emphasizes both cost and quality control, the marketing strategy should focus on making tangible the often intangible characteristics of quality and price/value. This is no easy task. The construct of quality is subjective and is dependent upon the meeting of individual customer expectations by the hospitality facility. Marketing's role, in this case, is to convince potential customers, through a strategy of subjective positioning, that it offers the necessary benefits such as quality, comfort, security, and price/value at a level capable of meeting customer expectations. Successful examples of this marketing theme are Super 8 Motels with its 'Spend a night, not a fortune' campaign, which attempted to make tangible a high price/value relationship; Burger King with its 'Have it your way' and 'Sometimes you gotta break the rules' campaigns, which both go some way to making tangible their willingness to customize their products to individuals' needs and wants; and Marriott's 'Marriott does it right' and 'Marriott people know how' campaigns, which both attempted to make tangible Marriott's knowledge and ability to perform according to customer expectations.

Prospector-like strategic marketing departures

There are several ways in which hospitality organizations can pursue a prospector-like marketing strategy in the international arena.

One method is to enhance service through higher value added per employee. Service enhancement can be effectively achieved and can be charged for at a higher-than-average rate if employees have a high degree of value added. This requires extensive training and may at first appear unrelated to any marketing strategy. However, nothing could be further from the truth. In a situation where the emphasis is on creating high value added per employee, marketing has a vital role to play through the pursuit of a strategy of internal marketing.

Internal marketing is defined as applying the philosophies and practices of marketing to people who serve the external customers so that the best possible people can be employed and retained, and so that they will do the best possible work. The emphasis in internal marketing is on the employee as the customer and the job as the product (Lewis and Chambers, 1989). Four Seasons Hotels actively pursues a strategy of internal marketing by creating the appropriate organizational culture and climate for a customer service orientation. This has resulted in the employee turnover rate at Four Seasons being less than half the industry average (Sharpe, 1990). A prospector-like marketing strategy also requires a heavy emphasis on environmental scanning activities and on consumer research activities so that the organization can adapt to changing consumer demands faster than the competition.

There can be little doubt that the environment in which international marketing decisions are made is far more complex than the environment in which domestic decisions are made. Studies have indicated that the hospitality environment is uncertain, unstable, and highly volatile (Crawford-Welch, 1991a; Olsen, 1980; DeNoble and Olsen, 1984; Dev, 1988). Due to this high level of complexity, hospitality organizations must actively engage in the practice of environmental scanning. The latter simply answers the question 'What is going on out there in the environment that is going to impact on our business?' by constantly gathering, analyzing, and interpreting data and information gathered from an organization's political, economic, sociocultural, technological, ecological, and competitive operating domains. An excellent example of adopting a prospector-like marketing strategy through engaging in the practice of environmental scanning can be seen in the United States with the small but successful Fresco restaurant chain, which has actively sought to attract a long unnoticed and rarely encouraged market. This market is the solo diner and is no small niche when one considers that (1) 77 million adults in the USA are unmarried, divorced, or widowed; (2) 300 million business trips are taken annually, temporarily transforming even happily married travelers into singles; (3) the number of women who travel on business alone is increasing; and (4) more and more singles of both sexes are choosing to vacation alone. The Fresco chain has now actively designed its marketing to attract this largely untapped market.

Marriott offers perhaps what is the best modern-day example of the benefits of pursuing the research element of a prospector-like marketing strategy. The Marriott corporation invested considerable capital and time in conducting consumer research for their 'Courtyard by Marriott' concept. They used a powerful statistical technique known as conjoint analysis, which, if used correctly, is capable of determining the trade-offs that customers are willing to make in their purchase of a product. Whereas the average industry occupancy rate in the United States is approximately 63 percent, the Courtyard by Marriott brand is running at about 20 percent above this level. While there are undoubtedly several contributing factors to this brand's success, there can be little doubt that the use of trade-off analysis and a strong research orientation by the company as a whole is a significant contributing factor. As more and more hospitality companies enter the international arena, this kind of a priori market research will surely be both a wise and a necessary investment.

Analyzer-like strategic marketing departures

An analyzer-like marketing strategy is perhaps the most complex to follow since it requires that the hospitality organization simultaneously adopt elements of both a defender-like and a prospector-like marketing strategy. There are several marketing strategies that are analyzer-like in nature, including, but not limited to, do-it-yourself customization, development of a membership base, and the selective application of technology. Each will be discussed in turn.

'Do-it-yourself' customization is an attempt by hospitality organizations to reduce service costs by involving the customers in the service production process. An excellent example of this approach can be found in the restaurant industry with the salad bar craze which simultaneously reduced labor costs and increased customer satisfaction, and in the lodging industry with in-room video checkout facilities. This type of customization does not operate in an organizational vacuum, however. Marketing strategies must be formulated and implemented to support this transfer of service delivery to the customer. Marketing must accomplish three things in this instance. First, it must make the customer *aware* that he or she has the option of customizing the product.

Second, marketing must inform the customer *how to* take advantage of this option. Third, it must create enough consumer *interest* to encourage them to use the product. This three-step process requires the organization to promise a benefit such as fast and efficient checkout or a salad consisting of one's own choice of vegetables, to set customer expectations accordingly, and to deliver the promised benefit in a manner that either meets or exceeds customer expectations. As an increasing number of US theme restaurants enter Europe, their marketing strategy will have to follow this three-step process to educate the European public in their respective restaurant themes. TGI Fridays pursued such a strategy when it entered the United Kingdom since British diners were at first unfamiliar with the interactive nature of the TGI Fridays brand.

A second element of adopting an analyzer-like marketing strategy is the development of a membership base which reduces the high cost of initiating sales to new customers (as would be the case in a prospector-like marketing strategy), while simultaneously improving services to, and concentrating on, existing customers (as would be the case with a defender-like marketing strategy). The various forms of frequent-stay programs being pursued in the industry are an attempt, albeit somewhat lackluster, to adopt such a strategy. Again, marketing must perform an informative role to create demand for these programs.

Service can be enhanced (a prospector-like strategy) and costs can be reduced (a defender-like strategy) through the selective application of technology. Heskett (1986) notes that greater opportunities for more significant gains from the future combination of people and technology exist in the service industries than in manufacturing. Nowhere is this more true than in the area of hospitality marketing. As we move toward the twenty-first century and an international hospitality industry, marketing will become a highly computerized activity and the competitive edge will not come from having information, as it did in the 1970s; rather it will come from how that information is used. Database marketing will become the rule. This selective application of technology will reduce costs significantly. For example, in 1973 it cost $7.13 to access 1,000 bits of information; 1,000 bits equals about 20 words of data – about enough to record a consumer's name, address, and purchase. Today, it costs about a penny to do the same thing (Rapp and Collins, 1989). In addition, this technology will enhance service by enabling hospitality corporations to use their internal databases to promote additional sales, cross-promote, explore new channels of distribution, test new products, add new revenue streams, start new ventures, and build lifetime customer loyalty.

A fourth way of pursuing an analyzer-like marketing strategy is to manage supply and demand effectively. Examples of this include off-season packages at reduced rates. Heskett (1986) notes that there are two primary benefits from this management of supply and demand: 'First, capacity is reserved for them [customers], allowing for advance planning and lower costs (unless the capacity goes unused). Second, because of advance planning, the level of service provided often meets standards set for it, at least by the service firm' (p. 63).

The US lodging industry is currently experimenting with managing demand using a technique borrowed from the airline industry whereby reservations made a specified period in advance are discounted accordingly. This system is a step above the cost-oriented pricing techniques usually practiced in the hospitality industry. In the next few years, with the synergistic integration of massive computerized reservation systems at the international level, this kind of demand management will become more effective and efficient and will be commonplace.

While by no means offering an exhaustive account, an attempt has been made here to discuss historic and future trends in hospitality marketing at the international level and to offer specific recommendations concerning three possible strategic marketing departures which international hospitality organizations may adopt as they attempt to cater to the increasingly sophisticated demands of international consumers. There is no formula for selecting one strategic departure over another. Rather, the appropriateness of each departure will depend on the unique competitive conditions facing individual hospitality corporations.

References

Ayala, H. (1991) 'International hotel ventures: back to the future', *Cornell Hotel and Restaurant Administration Quarterly*.

Cateora, P. R. (1990) *International Marketing*, Homewood, Ill.: Irwin.

Crawford-Welch, S. (1991a) 'An empirical examination of mature service environments and high performance strategies within those environments', doctoral dissertation, Department of Hotel, Restaurant, and Institutional Management, Virginia Polytechnic Institute and State University.

Crawford-Welch, S. (1991b) 'Marketing hospitality into the 21st century', *International Journal of Contemporary Hospitality Management*, vol. 3, no. 3, pp. 21–7.

Crawford-Welch, S. (1991c) 'International marketing and competition in European markets', *International Journal of Contemporary Hospitality Management*, vol. 3, no. 4.

Cummings, L. E. (1991) 'Solid waste minimization and the foodservice marketing mix', *Journal of Restaurant and Foodservice Marketing* (forthcoming).

DeNoble, A. F., and Olsen, M. D. (1984) 'The food service industry environment: a market volatility analysis', *Florida International Review*, vol. 4, no. 2, pp. 89–100.

Dev, C. (1988) 'Environmental uncertainty, business strategy, and financial performance: a study of the lodging industry', doctoral dissertation, Department of Hotel, Restaurant, and Institutional management, Virginia Polytechnic Institute and State University.

Go, F., and Christensen, J. (1989) 'Going global', *Cornell Hotel and Restaurant Administration Quarterly*.

Goss, W. (1989) 'Best Western stakes out global position', *ASTA Agency Management*.

Heskett, J. L. (1986) *Managing in the Service Economy*, Boston, Mass.: Harvard Business School Press.

Levitt, T. A. (1983) 'The globalization of world markets', *Harvard Business Review*.

Lewis, R. C., and Chambers, R. E. (1989) *Marketing Leadership in Hospitality: Foundations and practices*, New York: Van Nostrand Reinhold.

Makens, J. C., and Edgell, D. L. (1990) 'Internationalizing your hotel's welcome mat', *Cornell Hotel and Restaurant Administration Quarterly*.

Miles, R. E., and Snow, C. C. (1978) *Organizational Strategy, Structure and Process*, New York: McGraw-Hill

Olsen, M. D. (1980) 'The importance of the environment to the food service and lodging manager', *Journal of Hospitality Education*.

Olsen, M. D., Damonte, T., and Jackson, G. A.(1989) 'Segmentation in the lodging industry: is it doomed to failure?', *American Hotel and Motel Association Newsletter*, September.

Rapp, S., and Collins, T. (1989) *Maxi-Marketing: The new direction in advertising, promotion and marketing strategy*, New York: New American Library.

Ries, A., and Trout, J. (1986) *Marketing Warfare*, Vt.: Plume Books.

Rusth, D. B., and Lefever, M. M. (1988) 'International profit planning', *Cornell Hotel and Restaurant Administration Quarterly*.

Sharpe, J. L. (1990) 'Directions for the '90's: lessons from Japan', *Cornell Hotel and Restaurant Administration Quarterly*.

Toffler, A. (1980) *The Third Wave*, New York: William Morrow.

Warren, P., and Ostergren, N. W. (1990) 'Marketing your hotel: challenges of the '90's', *Cornell Hotel and Restaurant Administration Quarterly*.

7

A brand extension strategy for Holiday Inn Worldwide development

Alan C. Parker
with Richard Teare

Holiday Inn Worldwide, owned and operated by UK brewers Bass PLC, is the largest and among the most well-established hotel chains in the world, operating more than 1,600 hotels with over 320,000 bedrooms in 51 countries. Its successful development is, in part, attributable to reputation for quality and consistency enjoyed by the Holiday Inn brand name. In order to capitalize on this, HIW are currently implementing a global expansion program by extending the 'core brand' characteristics and features of the original Holiday Inn hotel style to both superior and economy hotel concepts, thereby enhancing the appeal of Holiday Inn at the higher and lower ends of the mid-priced lodging market. Accordingly, this chapter aims to examine the Holiday Inn Worldwide approach to implementing a brand extension strategy, with particular reference to current and future development issues in Europe.

Past, present, and future moves to maintain Holiday Inn brand prominence

The Holiday Inn network was founded in 1952 when the first hotel was opened in Memphis, Tennessee. It had 120 guest rooms, each with a private bathroom, air conditioning, and a telephone, and children under twelve years old could stay free in the room with their parents. Amenities included a swimming pool and free parking, and the total concept was considered revolutionary at the time. Rapid development followed the introduction of franchising in 1954, and by 1964 Holiday Inns of America Inc. were operating 500 hotels.

A strategically important development occurred in 1965, with the introduction of the Holidex reservation system, now the world's largest privately owned computerized hotel communication system. It links Holiday Inn hotels worldwide with 24 Holiday Inn international reservation offices, more than 60 corporate Holidex terminals, and over 240,000 airline terminals, affiliated to other major systems including Sabre, Galileo, and Amadeus. This enables the Holidex system to handle more than 70,000 reservations each day and a total of over 30 million bookings annually. In 1969 a corporate name change to Holiday Inn Inc. was made to reflect the nature of international expansion, and in 1970 the 'Holiday Inn University' was opened to provide specialized management training.

In May 1988 a significant change of ownership occurred when Bass PLC completed the acquisition of the Holiday Inn trademark and assets outside the United States, Canada, and Mexico. This purchase established Bass, a multinational UK-based company, with operations in more than 80 countries employing upwards of 90,000 people, as a major player in the international hotel business. The strategy formulated by Bass was to expand its hotel interests on a worldwide basis, diversifying from core business activities in beer manufacturing, wholesaling and retailing.

The acquisition was seen to offer an attractive long-term diversification route because the company had successfully managed hotels in the past. Bass had previously operated the UK-based Crest Hotels group, and this experience influenced the process of strategic decision making regarding directions for growth and the identification of the most appropriate acquisition strategy: namely, to develop an international hotel operation based on an internationally recognized hotel brand. Additionally, as Bass already had appropriate expertise, the risks normally associated with venturing into an unfamiliar area of business were greatly reduced.

Bass achieved its objective very quickly through the step-by-step acquisition of the complete Holiday Inn business. The acquisition in May 1989 of Commonwealth Hospitality, a Canadian franchise operation, consisting of some 35 hotels in Canada, was followed by the purchase in February 1990 of the Holiday Inn business in North America. In total, Bass had spent more than $3 billion to purchase the world's largest hotel system, which they renamed Holiday Inn Worldwide (HIW).

When the acquisition phase had been completed, Bass formulated a development objective designed to rejuvenate the Holiday Inn brand on a global basis, with fresh management, new initiatives, increased marketing activity, central cost rationalization, improved franchise relations, continual updating of the Holidex 2000 reservations system, and a single-minded focus on the brand and its extension possibilities. In conjunction with these initiatives, an expansion plan was announced which included the opening of more than 60 new properties worldwide, totaling more than 13,000 guest rooms by 1992, with a large number of additional projects under construction.

This rapid pace of develoment is scheduled to continue until the mid-1990s, during which time Bass will invest US$1 billion in the global HIW hotel business. The investment is part of an overall strategy, which is to ensure the continued development of the Holiday Inn brand throughout the world via the existing portfolio of hotel types and the development of new product concepts.

Extending the Holiday Inn 'core brand'

The original Holiday Inn hotel concept or 'core brand' gained international recognition for setting and achieving consistently high standards in product design and service. Early innovations pioneered by Holiday Inn were remote-controlled television and direct dial telephones, and in the 1990s a uniquely sophisticated satellite communication network provides instantaneous information transfer between North America and Europe. Standard features include spacious guest rooms with large beds, private bathrooms, and a minimum 16-hour room service. Every hotel has a variety of meeting and conference rooms, and most offer a range of leisure facilities as well as the convenience of free car parking.

At present, there are four types of Holiday Inn hotel and two Holiday Inn resorts, all of which feature attributes which are characteristic of the 'core brand' identity. These are:

- The Holiday Inn Crowne Plaza, which is a superior hotel offering a range of amenities and facilities designed specifically for the upper-middle market. Holiday Inn Crowne Plaza hotels are located mainly in major city centres, and in 1991 there were around 50 of these hotels worldwide, offering more than 16,000 rooms. By the end of 1995, the number will have increased to more than 100.
- The original 'core brand' Holiday Inn concept.
- The Holiday Inn Garden Court hotel is a newer type of Holiday Inn, introduced specifically for the European market in 1990. Typically offering 100 guest rooms, they are designed to appeal to price-conscious business and leisure travellers who nonetheless expect contemporary lodging and service standards. These hotels feature the standard Holiday Inn bedroom design together with a compact public area, small meeting rooms, a fitness area and an informal restaurant and bar. It is anticipated that there will be over 100 Holiday Inn Garden Court hotels in Europe by 1995.
- The latest extension to the Holiday Inn brand portfolio is the Holiday Inn Express, designed specifically for the rapidly growing upper-economy segment of the middle market in North America. There are plans to open more than 250 of these hotels in the USA by the mid-1990s. Holiday Inn Express hotels offer among other features a buffet-style breakfast and a lobby equipped with a large-screen television. Small meeting rooms and fax facilities are also available.
- Two further brand extensions were announced in October 1991 to coincide with the launch of HIW's resorts strategy. Holiday Inn SunSpree Resorts (USA only) are positioned as full-activity hotels in preferred leisure destinations. They provide a comfortable, casual, affordable, family-oriented environment for the middle-market traveler. Holiday Inn

Crowne Plaza Resorts will be 'marquee' properties, delivering a full-service resort experience. Located in prime resort destinations, they will feature a variety of restaurants, shops, fitness and leisure facilities, and many other family-oriented services.

The HIW brand extension strategy ensures that the Holiday Inn brands are closely positioned in the mid-priced lodging market – which has the best growth potential – under one internationally recognized identity. Each hotel type offers an appropriate and consistent level of service and facilities for a particular sector of the market. It also enables HIW to operate quality hotels in three distinct mid-market categories ranging from economy to superior, and thereby providing a competitive edge in the most crowded sector of the lodging market, where HIW aims to be the dominant presence. To achieve the planned expansion and to make the most of all opportunities globally, HIW intends to augment the existing hotel types as and when the need arises

Over a two-year period starting from mid-1991, HIW allocated US$17.5 million in additional support for the brand. This supplements the amount which both company-managed hotels and franchisees contribute to developing the Holiday Inn network themselves, and the extra support will be used to maximize global strength and to promote the brand on a world-wide basis. However, this is not at the expense of local marketing, which will be specifically geared to suit the local marketplace and implemented by the regional offices in Atlanta, Brussels, and Hong Kong.

HIW's hotels are grouped into three regions, which in order of size are: the Americas; Europe, Middle East and Africa (EMEA); and Asia-Pacific. In the context of the wide-ranging changes which have taken place and are continuing in Europe, the EMEA region is undergoing a phenomenal rate of growth. This is exemplified by development plans for the UK (where an increase from 20 to more than 50 hotels is planned by mid-decade) and in Mediterranean countries such as Spain, Portugal, and Italy. The EMEA region is also actively involved in hotel developments in Eastern Europe, notably in eastern Germany, Russia, Hungary, Czechoslovakia, and Poland. The European arena effectively illustrates the flexibility which HIW's brand extension strategy provides in addressing current and future development issues.

Using the brand extension strategy to expand in Europe

In late 1990 the EMEA region announced ambitious expansion plans for the 1990s involving the construction of many new hotels at locations throughout Europe. At the time, the portfolio consisted of 105 hotels located in 25 countries with more than 20,000 bedrooms and over 4,000 employees. HIW is continuing its rapid expansion in the EMEA region, aiming to increase the number of its hotels there from the mid-1991 number of 123, offering 24,000 guest rooms in 26 countries, to over 200 by the mid-1990s. In March 1991 alone, eight Holiday Inn hotels opened in Europe – six in the UK and two in Italy – and an additional 24 new hotels, providing over 4,000 guest rooms, are scheduled to open by 1993. Overall, this is believed to be the largest committed expansion program of hotels under construction by any hotel group operating in Europe. In order to identify some of the challenges of this program, the following illustrations are used to outline some of the foreseeable priorities and opportunities for HIW's European operations.

The foremost priority of the HIW board for the EMEA region is to ensure continued growth and improvement in profitability for company-managed and franchised hotels. Since the acquisition of the business, substantial progress has been made in this respect and efforts continue, as this is not viewed as a short-term objective. Having achieved higher profit margins through higher occupancies and sales, the second priority is to achieve increased distribution by expanding the total number of Holiday Inn hotels in Europe. This is being implemented using the HIW brand extension strategy in which the Garden Court concept features strongly, as it is well suited to the economy end of the European middle market. As capital building costs are relatively low and labor-intensive elements relatively limited, these hotels are an attractive investment for existing and potential franchisees. In mid-1991 twelve of these were operating successfully and a larger number were under construction. The EMEA region also plans to increase the number of its core brand Holiday Inns and Crowne Plaza hotels.

As Europe represents a culturally, industrially, and politically diverse marketplace, EMEA recognizes and is sensitive to the fact that each new hotel location has to be viewed on its own merits. The differences, for instance, between Dijon in France and Warrington in the UK, which were among the first places where Holiday Inn Garden Court hotels were opened, are quite pronounced and it would have been unrealistic to assume that market conditions were similar in each place. So it is important carefully to identify the nature, characteristics, and dynamics of demand in every locality prior to development. Although the basic parameters of the Holiday Inn product provide a standardized framework, a high degree of sensitivity to the market is necessary to ensure that customers are able to recognize the Holiday Inn style and standards in geographically and culturally diverse locations. Additionally, HIW aims to perfect its approach to brand packaging in the areas of product quality, service skills, and marketing expertise so that the appropriate Holiday Inn type can be identified for any given market position and location throughout Europe.

Prevailing market and general economic conditions in Western Europe do have an impact on the business, although this is difficult to quantify, as the extent of the effect varies between countries within the region. Consequently, EMEA's policy on development is to maintain a wide geographical distribution, thereby reducing the vulnerability associated with operating on a national basis and helping to minimize the impact of exchange rate movements. Exchange rates in some parts of the region are unpredictable and changes can take place very rapidly, as happened when the Polish currency became freely convertible early in 1990. For these reasons it is desirable to take a long-term view of the key factors that are likely to affect economic prospects in any given country, although short-term economic trends often provide good indicators of business opportunities. For instance, the fact that the building industry in the UK entered an acute recession in the early 1990s meant that conditions were favorable for acquiring and developing hotel sites in conjunction with construction companies.

The implications of reform and economic change for hotel development in Eastern Europe are much more complex, as they extend as far as dealing with logistical and other infrastructure-related problems. For example, the Holiday Inn in Warsaw is a 300 bedroom hotel which operates with over 700 staff. This staffing ratio is far in excess of the norms which apply in Western Europe, but it is required for the present level of productivity. The difficulties began at the construction stage with the procurement of fixtures and fittings which had to be imported. Prior to the opening it was necessary to set up a supply network in order to provide food and other supplies of the appropriate quality. This meant that it was necessary to import some perishable items, although a growing number of local suppliers are now meeting the required standards. By encouraging local suppliers, EMEA was able to identify much more closely with the local community, especially as the suppliers preferred to trade in dollars.

To achieve EMEA's rapid rate of expansion (100 new hotels over a five-year period) and at the same time continue to enhance profitability, it will be necessary to focus attention continually on a number of important human resource issues. This aspect of EMEA's strategic planning is probably the most challenging one for the period ahead. The economic reality now and in the future is that both consumers and providers of hotel services expect a better return from the business transaction. Customers are more demanding of the quality and diversity of services and facilities, especially as the competitive environment continually shapes their perception of what constitutes value for money. Equally, staff expect better pay and conditions of service as their lifestyle and standard-of-living expectations are influenced by societal patterns and trends. These sources of expectation have in common the need to devise systems and methods which will facilitate improvements in productivity.

The enabling mechanism for productivity improvement is a well-motivated workforce. This means that the employee expects the employer to provide opportunities to grow and develop, to be trained and to be promoted within the organization. This perspective fits the EMEA strategy for human resources, which foresees fewer people working differently, earning more profit per capital and getting better paid for doing so. It does, however, raise a number of questions about how such a strategy might be implemented. Changing technology provides part of the answer, allied with new concepts such as the Holiday Inn Garden Court, which typically provides 100 bedrooms serviced by approximately 30 full-time equivalent employees, thereby reducing the operational level of dependence on human resources.

The recruitment challenges for EMEA's Eastern European operations are far less severe. This can be illustrated by the experience of a rival international hotel company which received 25,000 job applications from a single advertisement for hotel staff placed in a Moscow newspaper early in 1990. This is an extreme example, but taking Western Europe as a whole, the issues are reasonably well understood. Demographically, there is a shrinking labor market for hotels to recruit from, although the timing of EMEA's expansion in Europe coincides with a dramatic change in the trading relationships between East and West, providing good prospects for hotel development.

Protecting brand universality: a commitment to quality and consistency

The key to EMEA's progress in Europe is the recognition of and reputation for quality and consistency which the Holiday Inn trademark affords. To safeguard these attributes, which provide HIW with a universally marketable brand, two procedures are used to scrutinize operating standards. First of all, operating standards are clearly and precisely defined in relation to specifications for hotel design and construction as well as for operating and service. In practice this means that a hotel which has not been constructed or converted in accordance with the specified standards would not be allowed to trade as a Holiday Inn hotel. The design specifications include detailed reference to every facet of the operation, ranging from the size of the guest room to the adequacy of life and fire safety systems. Inevitably, it is therefore HIW policy to restrict contract and license agreements to those who clearly understand precisely what is involved in constructing and operating hotels to Holiday Inn standards.

This necessitates the use of a comprehensive quality audit system in which every Holiday Inn participates by undergoing an independent quality audit inspection twice a year as a minimum requirement. If problems are reported, the hotel fails the inspection and typically will undergo scrutiny three times over a six-month period. At the same time, a program to correct the deficiency will be drawn up in consultation with the owner and a timetable for implementation agreed. If the work has not been carried out to the satisfaction of the quality audit team by the agreed date, then the hotel will face termination from the Holiday Inn system. This is an important safeguard as Holiday Inn operating standards are paramount: if substandard hotels are allowed to continue operating, it ultimately jeopardizes the market share of others.

The quality audit program is continually refined so as to improve the effectiveness of the assessment process. For example, a refinement announced in October 1991 provides an overall assessment score for any given hotel, allowing for the measurement of improvement over time. Arguably, protecting the brand in this way assumes greater importance for HIW than for Accor, EMEA's main competitor in continental Europe, as the latter's portfolio of brands are not visibly linked with one another. Conversely, HIW are actively extending the brand so that one universal trademark is offered with variations across the mid-market spectrum.

Announcing a series of corporate initiatives in April 1991, HIW aimed to demonstrate a fresh commitment to brand development by creating a Quality division and by reorganizing its Franchise division so as to meet the needs of its franchisees more effectively. HIW's corporate restructuring also aims to maximize shareholder value, make customer service improvements and focus resources on its core businesses of franchising, owning, and managing hotels. The refocusing is to be achieved by selling non-strategic businesses involved in purchasing, financing and conference planning. Highlights of the restructuring exercise include the following:

- The creation of HIW's first stand-alone Quality division, to demonstrate its commitment to improving continuously the quality of its hotels.
- The reorganization of the Franchise division in response to comments and suggestions from franchisees. A team of franchise service managers (replacing the district director field operation) have been empowered to solve issues quickly, by drawing on company-wide resources.
- Establishment of a Company Managed Hotels division as a strategic business unit, with the resources necessary to lead the system by example.
- Streamlining of the Marketing division to meet the changing needs of the company and its customers. Specifically, marketing now focuses on building the brand through worldwide advertising and public relations programs, expanding intermediary sales programs and developing country Hotel Marketing Associations (HMAs).

Since completing their acquisition of the Holiday Inn business in 1990, Bass have brought an ambitious global perspective to the business and created an effective brand portfolio suited to the diversity of the international marketplace. Survival, growth, and prosperity in the 1990s will depend heavily on the ability to deliver superior product quality, consistency, and value for money. Far from being a mature brand, Holiday Inn is still capable of sustaining extension and growth in response to the changing demands of business and leisure travelers worldwide.

8

Development strategies for international hospitality markets

Eliza C. Tse and
Joseph J. West

In the past twenty years, advances in transportation and communication technologies have significantly enhanced the ability of businesses to deliver their products and services beyond the traditional boundaries of domestic markets. With the growing importance of international competition, the idea of formal global strategy has emerged as a popular concept not only among managers of multinational corporations but also among researchers and students in the field of international management. Today, an industry or firm is considered to be global if there is some competitive advantage to be gained by integrating activities on a worldwide basis (Porter, 1986a), or if the firm's competitive position in one national market is significantly affected by its competitive position in other national markets (Hout *et al.*, 1982).

In recent years the trend toward multinational operations has extended beyond manufacturing industries to include many service industries as well. The hospitality industry is one of the service industries which has recently become involved in exporting products and services beyond national boundaries (Miller, 1989). As the industry approaches the maturity stage of its life cycle, many firms are discovering that their future survival and growth depend upon their successfully competing in the international arena. Because long-term survival and performance are dependent upon the firm's ability to adapt successfully to the demands of the competitive environment, an intimate knowledge and understanding of international opportunities and threats by key organization members has become extremely important to the management of the strategic process.

This chapter will address the different developmental methods employed by hospitality firms when entering international hospitality markets. For example, while some firms replicate successful domestic concepts overseas, others gain footholds through acquisition of existing firms in various countries. Specifically, the global strategies of a sample of major North American chains will be compared and analyzed in order to identify how they have achieved competitive positions in foreign countries. These industry examples will be used to elaborate relevant theoretical frameworks.

Multi-domestic versus global competition

When considering the concept of internationalization of hospitality firms with its resulting requirement for formal global strategies, it is important to distinguish between the two basic types of international competition: multi-domestic and global. These two competitive positions may be viewed as being opposite ends of a continuum. According to Leontiades (1985), there are four generic strategies for firms engaged in international competition: global high share; global niche; national high share; and national niche. The basic distinction here is between those strategies with global geographic scope and strategies limited to a particular national environment (see Figure 8.1). As will be suggested later in this chapter, the hospitality industry is becoming more globally competitive even though its roots have been mostly domestic. The challenge is for hospitality executives to make the transition from domestic and multi-domestic to global strategists.

According to Porter (1986b), the following is a taxonomy of patterns of international competition which clarify this difference:

Multi-domestic competition has the following characteristics:

- The competition in each country is essentially independent of competition in other countries.
- Products/services are present in many countries, but competition is on a country-by-country basis.
- The firm enjoys a competitive advantage from a one time transfer of know-how from its home base to foreign countries.
- The firm manages its international activities like a portfolio, each operation enjoying a high degree of autonomy.
- International strategy becomes a series of domestic strategies which are really 'country-centered'.

MARKET SHARE OBJECTIVE

	High	Low
Global	Global high share strategy	Global niche strategy
National	National high share strategy	National niche strategy

(SCOPE)

Fig. 8.1 Generic international competitive strategies

Source: From *Multinational Corporate Strategy*, by J. Leontiades, Lexington, Mass, Lexington Books. Reprinted with permission of Lexington Books.

At the other end of the continuum, global competition possesses the following characteristics:

- The firm's competitive position in one country is significantly influenced by its position in other countries.
- The firm must integrate its activities on a worldwide basis to capture the linkages among countries.

As may be seen a global strategy is a strategy in which a firm seeks to gain competitive advantage from its international presence through structures which concentrate configuration or coordination among dispersed activities. Considering these characteristics and the firm strategies identified later in this chapter it can be suggested that from an international perspective, the hospitality industry has begun to move from a multi-domestic orientation to a global perspective. With this evolution comes the need for hospitality executives to develop an understanding of global management issues and strategies.

Different perspectives of globalization

Globalization is based on a convergence in world tastes and product preferences. Levitt (1983) identifies technology as the force which is driving the world toward a 'converging commonality' and the homogenization of world markets. Technology, with its revolution in communications and travel, is breaking down the notion of 'foreignness' as people become familiar with the customs and products of various countries. Furthermore, consumers' needs for products and services have continued to converge between countries as business practices and marketing systems have grown more similar (as, for example, with chain operation). Brand reputation and consistent performance have become important competitive weapons worldwide.

Differences among authors writing on the topic of global strategy are not limited to concepts and perspectives. Their prescriptions on how to manage globally have also been very different, often contradictory, as may be seen from the following examination of four leading researchers. Levitt (1983) has argued that effective global strategy is the successful practice of just one activity: product standardization. According to him, the core of global strategy is the ability to develop a standardized product to be produced and sold the same way throughout the world. However, according to Hout (1982), effective global strategy requires the approach not of a hedgehog, who knows only one trick, but that of a fox, who knows many. Exploiting economies of scale through global volume, taking pre-emptive positions through quick and large investments, as well as managing interdependently to achieve synergies among different activities are some of the more important competitive moves that winning global strategists must master. Hamel and Prahalad's (1985) prescription for a global strategy contradicts Levitt even more. Instead of a single standardized product, they recommend a broad product portfolio, with many product varieties, which allow technologies and distribution channels to be shared. Cross-subsidization among products and markets, as well as the development of strong worldwide distribution systems are competitive moves that the authors suggest are necessary if a firm is going to be successful in the chess game of global strategy. Kogut's (1985) global strategists win through flexibility and arbitrage. They create options in order to turn the uncertainties of an increasingly volatile global economy to their advantage. Multiple sourcing, shifting production among various venues in order to benefit from changing factor costs and exchange rates, as well as the practice of arbitrage to exploit imperfections in financial and information markets are some of the hallmarks of superior global strategy.

Critical issues of globalization

Many of the strategic issues confronting a company competing internationally are much the same as those facing firms competing domestically. However, there are some strategic issues which are unique to international competition requiring companies desiring to compete internationally to change their strategic orientation. For a company entering the global arena, there is a need for management to revise their perceptual maps of competitors and markets. Global competition requires that a section of the organization takes the widest possible view of the firm's environmental threats and opportunities (Leontiades, 1986). The initiative for this must come from an international headquarters, which is probably the only part of the organization with the necessary scope of geographic information and authority. Areas of global thinking for international headquarter's top management consideration and action include the following:

● *Corporate intelligence and information gathering*. The collection and interpretation of market and competitor information should be one of the first areas to be globalized. The environment of the various countries in which the firm competes or desires to compete should be closely monitored and evaluated for economic and political stability.
● *Assessing capabilities*. Fundamentally, strategy formulation for the international corporation is no different from that for any firm. The basic requirements are a sound assessment of the capabilities of the firm and perceptive determination about how those capabilities may be employed effectively within the operating environment. These capabilities include the firm's resource strengths of technical/managerial skill as well as the availability of capital, labor, and raw materials. In a global strategy mode the transmission of managerial skills is more complex than that of technological skills – more difficult to acquire and transmit. As for capital, a firm must have the capability of utilizing a variety of sources including alternatives such as licensing and joint ventures. Generally speaking, global marketing systems, including distribution channels, advertising structure, and brand names, have been one of the great strengths of international corporations (Fayerweather, 1981).

- *Strategic choice*. This results from management's response to external pressures, such as customer demands for uniform worldwide treatment which drives the need for internationally uniform standards of quality and pricing in an attempt to capture customer loyalty. The strategic move toward global structure greatly increases the resources required to stay current in international market opportunities and competitive threats. This pressure is evident by the widespread move toward the formation of international joint ventures, acquisitions, mergers, and collaborative agreements.
- *Economies of global scale and scope*. These entail the ability of the firm to provide worldwide service for global customers, and to transfer experience to operations in various parts of the world.
- *Calculation of costs and payoffs*. This is the ability to discern what costs are likely to be incurred in global expansion as well as the returns likely to be achieved.
- *Importance of control by the firm*. Regardless of the degree of ownership by the parent company, a wide range of decisions impacting on subsidiary international operations are either potentially or actually influenced by host governments, including but not limited to decisions on investments, repatriation of funds, and employment of expatriates.
- *Organization structure*. The strategy a firm chooses is dependent upon the environment in which it seeks to compete. The environment/strategy milieu forces the firm to choose among various organizational structures designed to implement the chosen strategy. The primary structural issue facing a firm entering the global arena is the necessity of determining the combination of coordinating mechanisms necessary to achieve the desired multinational integration with minimum interference in the discretion and freedom of nationally based operating units (Porter, 1986a). The two structural issues likely to be of greatest significance are:

(a) how management functions are to be configured worldwide. Configuration options range from concentrated (performing an activity in one location and serving all locations) all the way to dispersed (performing every activity within each national market). Having an international strategy has often been characterized as a choice between worldwide standardization and local tailoring. However, a firm may standardize (concentrate) some activities and tailor (disperse) others to individual nations, regions, etc. It is not an all or nothing proposition.

(b) the degree to which similar activities are to be coordinated in the different countries. Options range from very little to very high coordination activity. In moving toward globalization coordination, a variety of methods and mechanisms such as strategic planning systems, international policies, management reward systems, information systems, etc. are essential (Leontiades, 1986). The firm's upper management must recognize that a significant cost of globalization is friction and antagonism within the organization. When a firm becomes a global competitor a new balance between its managers at the various hierarchical levels and geographic locations is extremely important.

These two issues along with their various components exert a significant impact upon the strategy formulation process in the multinational firm. These strategic implications must be considered in the strategy formulation process because of the existence of unique problems facing the firm's management in their attempt to adapt to local conditions and ways of doing business in foreign countries. As may be seen by examining these issues, in order for management to compete successfully utilizing a globalized strategy, they must embrace a global view. They must spend their valuable resources of time and effort monitoring world events and patterns and analyzing the potential impact they are likely to have. Therefore the demands exerted on the global competitor by these issues during the strategy formulation process require a far more complex look at the world and the marketplace than is required of firms only competing domestically.

A multinational firm has three sets of tools for developing and retaining its competitive advantage. It can exploit differences in the input and output markets among the many countries in which it operates. The firm can also benefit from scale economies in its various activities. Or it can exploit synergies and economies of scope which may be available due to the diversity of its activities and organization (Porter, 1986b). The primary strategic task facing global firms is to use all three of the sources of competitive advantage appropriately to optimize efficiency and learning while simultaneously minimizing risk in a worldwide business. The key to a successful global strategy is to manage the interactions between these goals and means.

Motivations for international expansion by hospitality chains

In the 1990s hotel-chain expansion will be in both directions, with many foreign-based chains purchasing American-based chains while other American chains continue expanding aggressively abroad. Within the decade, it is predicted that most American-based hotel chains will be foreign owned. The foreign hotel firms now operating in the United States include Four Seasons (Canada), Meridien and Novotel (France), Forte (Britain), and Accor, a French management company currently operating the Sofitel, Novotel, Mercure, and Ibis chains. Some of these non-United States firms have been taking advantage of the strength of their national currency against the United States dollar and purchasing hotels in the United States where the assets are actually less expensive than in their home country.

Due to both leisure and business-related travel increasing worldwide, there appear to be more opportunities for US hotel chains to provide lodging facilities in the diverse markets abroad. With 409 million people traveling internationally each year, global marketing has become a critical factor in a chain's success (Miller, 1989). In the next decade there will be a quantum increase in the number of hotels planned within the United States and built outside of its borders. According to a study by Hotels and Restaurants International, between 1970 and 1985 the number of rooms affiliated to the top twenty multinational chains increased by 149 percent (from 576,000 to 1.43 million). Any area in the world is a possible site for expansion, especially those markets which demonstrate political and economic stability. Key areas of expansion have included Europe, the Pacific Rim, and South America (Wolff, 1988). For instance, the stable economies of the five Scandinavian nations – Denmark, Sweden, Finland, Norway, and Iceland – coupled with increasing demands by business travelers and tourist groups for upscale accommodations, are promoting significant hotel development throughout Scandinavia (Conte, 1987). These global chains will deliver international marketing, reservations, and sales capability to a worldwide network of hotels. National and regional chains will begin to affiliate in order to establish an international brand name identity and operate in the international marketplace.

Competitive pressures and economies of scale will continue to encourage the internationalization of hotel chains in the foreseeable future. Megachains, resulting from regional expansion as well as mergers and acquisitions, will spread the segmentation concepts emerging in the United States and Europe around the globe and produce a gradual homogenization of the worldwide lodging industry (Martin, 1988). However, the success of international hotel development will continue to depend on the flexible adaptation of domestic concepts abroad, taking into account the significant cultural, geographical, and political differences among countries. The following are some primary forces in the hospitality industry providing the motivation for international expansion:

- *The need to increase levels of growth and profits.* The US hotel and restaurant industries are maturing, limiting unit growth. It is becoming very difficult to locate and acquire prime locations since many United States chains have penetrated most of their potential market areas. Similar scenarios exist in the rest of the Western world where green-site development opportunities are few.
- *Increasing levels of international business travel and tourism to the Far East.* Asian and Pacific countries have become attractive locations for many multinational chains with the exception of Singapore and Malaysia (excess rooms) and the Philippines (political instability). The two countries in the region which are experiencing the most rapid hotel development are China and Japan. Conversely, many Japanese chains are investing heavily in United States properties, especially in Hawaii (Watkins, 1989).
- *Development of brand loyalty.* With the steady increase in international travel and trade, a tactic employed by chains is to follow their clients to international destinations. In this way, the chain attempts to develop and exploit brand loyalty through familiarity, consistent service, and international reservation systems. Many executives think that international

operations serve as an image enhancer which increases name recognition. Thus the awareness created by firms' global presence strengthens their market position for international travelers. However, there are companies presently competing in the US market which are pressured to expand internationally in order to create well-known names as more Americans travel abroad (Bell, 1989).

- *Protection from fluctuating economies.* International operations can provide a hedge against recession by exploiting differences in the business cycle timing.

The high cost and substantial risk associated with luxury hotel properties create a barrier of entry which limits the number of feasible sites in any one country. Therefore, until recently, the international market has been almost exclusively limited to upscale and mid-range properties. Now, economy chains are evaluating foreign areas for expansion opportunities. For instance, visitor arrivals in the United Kingdom increased by 13 percent in 1987, driving up room and occupancy rates as well as profits at the nation's hotels. However, despite growing demand, hotel development in the UK is very slow. Meanwhile, limited-service budget hotels throughout the country comprise the United Kingdom's most rapidly growing lodging segment.

There are emerging opportunities in Western Europe under the unified European Community's single market which begins in 1992, in Pacific Rim countries due to the rising popularity of Western culture, as well as in a fast-opening Eastern Europe. For example, in the United Kingdom and German markets alone, well over $35 billion is spent annually on travel, compared with slightly more than $30 billion expended by United States travelers. Executives of many chains indicate that they plan to double the number of their properties in the near future as attractive incentives for development are provided by developing countries whose governments recognize the value of tourism to their economies. In some cases, governments serve as intermediaries or even as investors. At the same time as developing governments are liberalizing their trade and foreign investment policies, telecommunications provide instantaneous transmission and processing of information and capital around the globe. Capital moves swiftly across borders because these technological changes have reduced the transaction costs associated with global arbitrage.

This recent globalization of capital markets has radically altered the way lodging and other real-estate properties are financed. Traditionally, funding came from local lending institutions. Today, the global integration of capital markets has widened the gap between real properties and their sources. Since the early 1970s, the industrialized nations of the world have steadily lifted the regulatory restrictions on international capital flows. Additionally, capital controls and restrictions on foreign participation in domestic financial markets were also being lifted. As a result, Middle Eastern capital in the late 1970s, British and Canadian investment capital in the mid-to-late 1970s, and Japanese capital in the 1980s fueled the growth of international real-estate investment. Today, the majority of debt and equity capital for hotel invest-ments originates principally from six geographical regions: Asia, Europe, Canada, the Middle East, Japan, and India. This globalization of financial markets may represent the final outcome of the gradual process of separating the funding source from the hotel property (Tsui, 1989).

These as well as other motivating forces have quickened the pace of inter-national expansion throughout the globe, resulting in the rapid evolution of the hospitality industry to truly international stature. As a result, many types of strategy are employed by firms to assist them in achieving their inter-national growth objectives. The next section will discuss a number of the most popular strategies currently being followed by the major hospitality chains.

Development strategies and ownership structures

When we examine the development activities of the majority of large multi-national hospitality firms, the overall strategy which seems to be most popular can be described as one of concentrated growth. According to Pearce and Harvey (1990), a concentrated growth strategy implies that a firm will direct its resources to the profitable growth of a single product, in a single market, with a single dominant technology. A pure concentrated growth strategy requires the firm continually to seek forms of product improvement, increasing and intensifying promotional activity, and expanding distribution channels. The pricing strategy utilized is one of penetration, which suggests that the firm must fully exploit its expertise as it pursues a strategic advantage in a highly competitive environment.

The development strategy fashioned by the executives of a hotel chain must reflect its objectives in pursuing international expansion. For instance, if the motive is to follow their business clients to international destinations or to capitalize on fast-gowing metropolitan markets, they will probably focus solely on major international cities. If their objective is to maximize exposure, they may establish a presence in secondary markets as well as major business centers. There are several forms of concentrated strategy practiced in the hospitality industry (Olsen *et al.*, 1991) which reflect the unique nature of the industry's almost pure competitive status. These forms are: strategic alli-ance, franchising, market segmentation, management contracts, joint ven-tures, and acquisition (see Tables 8.1 and 8.2).

Strategic alliances

There are many forms of strategic alliance, ranging from the most simple where different firms are tied together by a common reservation and marketing system, to a complex form where not only hotels but also other firms such as travel agencies join the alliance in a move toward vertical inte-gration. The strength of using the strategic alliance as a vehicle of growth is that it can quickly take advantage of the brand recognition aspect of several

Table 8.1   Strategy types

Strategy type	Hospitality examples
● **Strategic alliance** Firms are tied together by a common reservation and marketing system	Best Western and Corsort organizations
In a more complex form of alliance, it not only brings hotel firms together, it also brings in the other hospitality-related firms, such as travel agencies, as a form of vertical integration	Radisson Hotel Company has affiliated with Movenpick (Swiss), SAS (Scandinavian), Park Lane (Hong Kong), Commonwealth Hospitality of Canada Leisure (Australia) to promote the growth of its product worldwide
	Logis et Auberges – the third largest consortium – brings together 4,658 small inns throughout France
● **Franchising** The franchise method can be implemented as simply as one firm with one unit licensed from a franchisor or can be as complex as master regional francisees where one firm would have the right to expand a brand throughout an area or region of the world	McDonald's has over 2,400 units outside the United States Kentucky Fried Chicken has over 2,700 overseas and some smaller chains Holiday Inn Worldwide has close to 200 hotels, Best Western has over 1,500, and Quality has over 130
	Choice International has used the master regional franchisee concept to expand internationally Days Inn has also used this type of arrangement with the establishment of partnerships in India
● **Market segmentation** A variety of concepts developed by one chain to capture all segments of markets	Choice international with 4 concepts: Clarion, Quality, Comfort, and Sleep Inn
● **Management contract** In this type of strategy, a firm with an established reputation for being an excellent manager will grow by contracting to manage properties for an owner and the name of the managing company is how that property is identified	Hyatt International, Hilton International, Marriott, SARA, Nikko, Holiday Inn Worldwide, Forte, ARA
● **Joint venture** This development of local as well as global partners has brought together such firms as SAS and Saison of Japan as they plan to develop their intercontinental chain throughout the world. This strategy has usually taken the form of a large real-estate developer/holder combining with a hospitality/travel-related firm	Omni purchased by World International and Wharf Holdings, and the Pritzker family of Chicago and William Hunt Holdings of Hong Kong have purchased the Southern Pacific Hotel Corporation of Australia
● **Acquisition** This requires a large amount of capital to finance growth of any significance	Norfolk Capital (UK), Queens Moat (UK), and Regent (Hong Kong) acquired other hospitality organizations

Table 8.2 Hospitality industry examples

● **Strategic alliances**

Best Western

Greatest no. of hotels overseas.

More than 1,500 properties in Europe, Israel, South America, the South Pacific, and Mexico.

Plans to have 2,000 more international properties by 1992.

The company is banking on the familiarity of the travelers at home with Best Western logo. It is creating a giant, worldwide system based on familiarity. Best Western is the largest group representing primarily mid-market hotels.

Omni hotels

Plans to double the size of the company over the next two years, especially focusing on markets that are destinations for US travelers. The chain aims to establish a network through the marketing relationship. Omni is a marketing-driven company.

● **Franchising**

Choice International

Plans to expand segmentation abroad through all 4 brands: Sleep Inns, Comfort Inns, Quality, and Clarions.

104 hotels in international markets, all are franchised.

Strategy for international system: allow regional flavor and character in the individual properties, retain the local cultural tradition and architectural styles.

These properties meet American standards of cleanliness and efficiency.

Expects to expand in Europe and the Pacific, South America, Japan, and Turkey; later in Australia, Italy, and the Caribbean.

Plans to double the number of its European properties by 1993, then check out opportunities in Eastern Europe.

The most important area for growth for the company is the Asian Pacific, where it will try to negotiate a master-franchise agreement.

Choice is introducing segmentation and the limited service concept to the lodging industry in a systematic fashion.

By 1993 Quality will increase its properties outside the United States from the current 106 to 240.

It is targeting countries where Americans travel so there is a strong base of business to deliver.

Choice's overseas offices are staffed by 'foreign management' for better understanding of cultural, political, and economic climates.

Park Inns

Pursues expansion via franchising and through management and architectural services.

Radisson

Properties abroad operate under franchise agreements or affiliation accords. 49 in operation, with 14 more in process of completion. The international Radissons operate in five market segments: Plaza Hotels, Suite Hotels, Hotels, Inns, and Resorts. Radisson properties now span Canada, Mexico, Europe, the Middle East, the Far East, Asia-Pacific, and Australia.

Radisson's strategy is to team up with partners who know their areas of the world better: its partner in Europe and the Far East is Movenpick Hotels International; in Australia, Argus Hotels; in Canada, Commonwealth Hospitality Ltd; in Mexico, Paraiso Hotels; in Hong Kong, Park Lane Hotels International.

Through a series of varied deals, ranging from Radisson taking a strong equity position to being sole franchisee, the partnership offers the best of technology and local input. Radisson has the technology and advanced automation; the partners know their cultures.

Table 8.2 (continued)

Sheraton
130 properties in Europe, Asia, Pacific, Latin America, and Canada. 24 of these are franchised and the rest are managed by Sheraton.
Days Inns
Uses master-licensing agreements which offer experience, proven managerial capabilities, and financial strengths.

● **Management contracts**
Hyatt International Corporation
50 hotels outside USA; Asia-Pacific has 29 hotels in Asia-Pacific; will reach 37 hotels in Australia by 1990.
3 types of hotel abroad: the city center/business hotels, destination resorts, and Park Hyatt Hotels (residential hotels).
Future plans include Latin America, Eastern Europe, and former Soviet Union. 1992 provides potential for growth.
Hilton International
In Australia and in French West Indies, Monte Carlo, and London. By 1991 will have additional properties in elite cities, business centers, and resort destinations.
Holiday Inn Worldwide
35 hotels in the Asia-Pacific region: 16 franchised, the rest managed by the company. 94 hotels in Europe–Middle East–Africa market, 28 company managed and 66 franchised. Garden Court hotels will enter the overseas marketplace; these properties are smaller than conventional HI.
Marriott
15 international hotels. 5-year international expansion strategy for overseas properties. Plans include hotels in key European cities and other business centers. There will be concentrated focus on Europe up to 1992 with its full-service hotel product. Europe as a unified market is an important target for development. Hotels mainly city centered, then airport locations. Courtyard hotels will tap the moderate segment.
Ramada
Divides International into five regions: Asia-Pacific, Europe Central, Europe West, Canada, and Latin America. Locally based management teams established to oversee each region. Manages 60 of its 109 international properties.
Continues to be a hotel-management company, and sometimes a franchise company, taking equity positions in most of the hotels it manages.
Continues its expansion in the Asia-Pacific region and Europe, also targets Eastern European countries and former Soviet Union for future development.
Ramada Inc. devised an overseas expansion plan that targeted Canada, Europe, the Middle East, the Pacific Rim, and the Latin America/Caribbean Basin, in that order. Ramada has established regional offices around the world.
By 1993 Ramada plans to build 85 properties outside the USA.
Hospitality International Inc.
A franchisor with 300 properties in the USA and Canada. Plans are to develop 50 more hotels outside USA. Expansion into international markets is a natural progression in the business.
Loews Representation International (LRI)
Largest group representing moderate to deluxe hotels.

To capitalize on both American and European tourist markets, two British consortia linked up with two American groups in 1988: London-based Inter-Hotel joined Los Angeles-based Jarvinen; London-based Prestige joined Small Luxury Hotels (SLH), which focused on upscale market.

multinational firms. Marketing costs can be spread over a larger base, making the effort more efficient and effective through the gains of scale economies. Many of the problems of labor and management expertise are minimized by this growth strategy, as are the problems associated with multicultural differences so often encountered when firms seek to expand into new areas of the world.

Strategic alliances are not only for large corporations. In a world increasingly dominated by global hotel chains, one way independent operations and small national chains survive is by joining a consortium or 'lodging' association with marketing and referral clout (Martin, 1988). Independent properties are experiencing slow, steady sales growth while most chain-affiliated hotel sales are growing rapidly. This will eventually lead to a dominant market share for the chain-affiliated hotels. However, if a shakeout occurs internationally, it should affect the low-room rate independents more severely than the luxury independents, which should be able to retain their share of the market. It appears that there is a trend for consortia and related groups (e.g. Associated Luxury Hotels in the United States and Expotel in London) to target the growing international meetings market, in which it is difficult for independent properties to compete effectively.

Franchising

This form of growth is well understood and utilized by executives in the hospitality industry. Development through franchising is a popular arrangement and continues to be one of the most preferred growth vehicles for international expansion. In Europe, where high building costs encourage property conversions in preference to new construction, franchising provides flexibility in the adaptation of chain concepts such as Holiday Inns to existing structures. The franchise strategy can be as simple as a small firm with one unit being licensed from a franchisor, or it can be as complex as a master regional franchise where one firm has the right to expand a particular brand throughout a region of the world. The major strategic problem faced by the franchiser is the selection of the franchisee. A second concern is the nature of the relationship between the franchisor and the host government. Because of different laws and customs, franchise agreements should be written by a local counsel since they are subject to local laws.

Market segmentation

The development of a variety of hotel products by one chain, a strategy currently employed with varying success by US-based chains due to market saturation, is currently gaining popularity worldwide as these firms expand internationally. However, the translation of segment concepts requires careful consideration due to local tastes. An example is the operation of the hotel restaurant. Hotel restaurants contribute much more to the property's total revenue outside of the United States, which forces some firms which do not normally operate restaurants on premise to alter their concept. For example, Comfort Inn in Europe have restaurants, unlike their US counterparts. Guest expectations also vary widely across countries: for example, European guests frequently expect service amenities additional to those supplied by US hotels in their domestic market. Understanding these differences helps to guide hotel planners toward the most profitable allocation of resources in designing physical facilities and their operations.

Management contracts

One of the quickest forms of strategic expansion has been through the use of management contracts. If the objective is to accelerate growth and minimize risk, given the fact that the hotel company is relatively unfamiliar with the culture and politics of the countries in which it desires to develop its properties, management contracts are attractive vehicles of expansion. Rather than hotel equity ownership, the chain provides technical advice, pre-opening assistance, marketing support, and management services in return for a fee. This policy is consistent with the current tendency of hotel chains in the United States to manage, not own, their domestic properties. In this strategy, a firm with an established reputation as an excellent management company will expand by contracting to manage properties for an owner with the property identified by the name of the managing company. The management contract has outstanding appeal because it generally requires little or no capital investment by the management company, allowing the financial risk to be shouldered by the owner or developer of the property. Occasionally, as a condition of the contract, the management firm will take an equity interest in the business, although most attempt to avoid having to do so. Some management firms also engage in the development of a property and then sell their share once the property is completed and operating. However, they negotiate long-term management contracts for the operation of the facility as a condition of the sale.

Joint venture

Another popular growth vehicle for hotel firms with substantial financial resources is the joint venture. The joint venture strategy is usually employed by a large real-estate developer/holder and a hospitality/travel-related firm. These investors are global in orientation with a long-term strategy of holding assets for long-term appreciation. It should be recognized that this strategy is vastly different from the others discussed. The previous strategies concentrated upon low capital investment by the dominant firms, with the capital risk taken by smaller groups of independent businesspeople. The joint venture strategy is usually employed only by large investment groups with an interest in capital appreciation. This is the most difficult form of growth strategy with the highest level of risk.

Acquisition

Growth through acquisition has become the least desirable strategy for expansion due to the large amounts of capital required to acquire assets of any significance. In utilizing this strategy, firms are often forced to pay the market price or higher for the acquired firm's assets.

As can be seen from a close analysis of these strategy types, they reflect the growth posture desired by most firms. This growth is concentrated on the development of a brand or group of brands worldwide in an attempt to obtain a competitive edge in the fight for market share by taking advantage of scale and scope economies. The majority of firms appear to be trying to minimize risks by avoiding asset investment on a multinational scale. Only those involved in joint ventures and acquisitions have been willing to take this type of risk. These strategies tend to reflect a coordination profile among units in all nations that is relatively high. This is the case because the essence of franchising and management contracting is the maintenance of high uniform standards, which is accomplished only through strict adherence to the overall corporate strategic service concept. This adherence to standards is especially important when the motivation for international expansion is to follow business clients to international destinations, since they will expect the same level of quality that they experienced at other locations. It can be concluded from these strategies that the globalization of the hospitality industry is no longer a trend but a fact of competitive life.

The future of hospitality industry globalization

Having established the fact that hospitality is rapidly becoming a global industry, the next question is: what are the issues likely to be faced by managers in the near future? The answer to this question must reflect global economics and stability and travel patterns. While an in-depth analysis of each of these trends is beyond the scope of this chapter, highlighting some of the issues is important to our understanding of how the strategy types identified above will be affected by events in the future.

Global economics has changed considerably since 1989 and early 1990. As the world moves toward a free-market economy, it can be expected that nations which have begun to make the transition to a free market will likely experience the need for more hospitality facilities as their economies grow. The growth of the hospitality industry in these countries will depend upon how stable and well planned overall domestic growth is. Economic growth will depend upon available sources of capital. As discussed earlier, the capital sources for the industry seem to be concentrated in Japan, Hong Kong, Singapore, and the United Kingdom. However, there is some evidence which suggests that these sources of funds are beginning to find it difficult to keep up with the historic pace of investment. Where will the new sources of capital originate if the present ones dry up? It may be that franchising and strategic alliances which are dependent upon the strength of the small independent entrepreneurs will dominate expansion as it becomes more difficult for large firms to finance ambitious growth plans.

The present labor shortage in the Western democracies will remain a critical factor for the next decade and beyond as the demographics of the Western nations follow similar patterns. This labor shortage will not be totally compensated for by immigration from Third World nations since they are beginning to experience economic growth and opportunity and will be able to employ more of their population. The emergence of Asian nations such as South Korea, Singapore, Hong Kong, Taiwan, and more recently India suggests that these nations will be better able to provide more jobs for their citizens, thus leaving less incentive for them to seek employment in other parts of the world. The labor problem will make it more difficult for hospitality organizations to maintain the level of service and standards that they presently seek.

Information technology which has helped spread the revolution toward free markets will make those newly created markets more competitive. The technology exists today which could result in mega-reservation systems designed to control the capacity of all types of hospitality firms, from hotels to restaurants to destination attractions. This will result in the evolution of a worldwide standard for the provision of goods and services, increasing the competitive nature of the industry and making competitive advantage even more difficult to attain. While one of the answers to heightened competition has been the establishment of multiple brands or concepts by hospitality organizations, with an emerging worldwide standard it is likely that the better informed traveler will be less inclined to be brand loyal if the standards of a particular brand are not maintained worldwide. There is already evidence of this in the United States, which has seen a proliferation of segments in the past decade. It appears to be the case that the actual life cycle of a brand is continuing to decline as new products draw customers away with competitive pricing. Caution is in order when considering brand proliferation and multiple-market products as an effective strategy for global growth.

Travel patterns reflecting economic growth as well as leisure activity are evident. The primary limitation to hotel expansion in many countries is the capacity of the infrastructure designed to service it. The evidence today suggests that there are not enough airline seats going to particular destinations, nor is there the necessary capacity at airports to handle any increases in arrivals and departures. So while future travel patterns are somewhat easy to predict, it is difficult to ascertain whether the infrastructure will be capable of meeting the needs.

The future of the hospitality industry globally is exciting and full of challenges. The success of any firm will depend upon its ability to choose and implement an appropriate strategy in the context of a competitive and changing environment. Tomorrow's strategic manager must possess an acute understanding of global economics and politics. Managers will be expected to function in a multicultural environment, addressing the needs of both the employee and the customer. Today's successful domestic strategic manager must evolve quickly into a global hospitality manager in order to survive.

References

Bell, D. (1989) 'US chains leave home', *Lodging Hospitality*, vol. 45, no. 5, p. 46.

Conte, M. C. (1987) 'Scandinavia provides stable base', *Hotel and Motel Management*, vol. 202, p. 28.

Fayerweather, J. (1981) 'Four winning strategies for the international corporation', *Journal of Business Strategy*, vol. 2, no. 2, pp. 25–36.

Ghoshal, S. (1987) 'Global strategy: an organizing framework', *Strategic Management Journal*, vol. 8, no. 5, pp. 425–40.

Hamel, G., and Prahalad, C. K. (1985) 'Do you really have a global strategy?', *Harvard Business Review*, vol. 63, no. 4, pp. 139–48.

Hout, T., Porter, M. E., and Rudden, E. (1982) 'How global companies win out', *Harvard Business Review*, vol. 60, no. 5, pp. 98–108.

Kogut, B. (1985) 'Designing global strategies: profiting from operational flexibility', *Sloan Management Review*, vol. 27, no. 1, pp. 27–38.

Leontiades, J. (1985) *Multinational Corporate Strategy*, Lexington, Mass.: Lexington Books.

Leontiades, J. (1986) 'Going global: global strategies vs. national strategies', *Long Range Planning*, vol. 19, no. 6, pp. 96–104.

Levitt, T. (1983) 'The globalization of markets', *Harvard Business Review*, vol. 61, no. 3, pp. 92–102.

Martin, F. (1988) 'Global consortia report 1.1 million rooms, 7% growth', *Hotels and Restaurants International*, pp. 60–4.

Miller, G. (1989) 'US chains expanding abroad', *Hotel and Resort Industry*, pp. 42–8.

Olsen, M. D., Crawford-Welch, S. and Tse, E. (1991) 'The global hospitality industry of the 1990s', in Teare, R., and Boer, A. (eds) *Strategic Hospitality Management*, London: Cassell.

Pearce J. A., and Harvey, J. W. (1990) 'Concentrated growth strategies', *Academy of Management Executive*, vol. 4, no. 1, pp. 61–8.

Porter, M. E. (1986a) 'Competition in global industries: a conceptual framework', in Porter, M. (ed.) *Competition in Global Industries*, Boston, Mass.: Harvard Business School Press.

Porter, M. E. (1986b) 'Changing patterns of international competition', *California Management Review*, vol. 28, no. 2, pp. 9–40.

Swerdlow, S., and Chasel, (1990) 'Issues and problems encountered by food service operators when franchising internationally: a preliminary survey of corporate decision making', *Proceedings of the Fourth Conference of the Society of Franchising*, January.

Tsui, J. F. (1989) 'Lodging finance goes global', *Lodging Hospitality*, vol. 45, no. 7, p. 78.

Watkins, E. (1989) 'Here comes the invasion', *Lodging Hospitality*, vol. 45, no. 5, pp. 38–41.

Wolff, C. (1988) 'Chain execs upbeat on global growth', *Hotel and Motel Management*, 25 September, vol. 203, pp. 50, 55–6.

9

Multi- and transnational firms: the impact of expansion on corporate structures

Sandra Watson and
David Litteljohn

This chapter deals with organizational growth within the hospitality industry. In particular, it directs attention to growth in an international, rather than a purely national, arena. By bringing together industry and organizational characteristics, the needs of multinational management within a human resource framework are analyzed and their implications discussed.

While strategic variables are discussed and related to the management of multinational companies, the focus here is not on the structure and strategy debate (Chandler, 1962); the emphasis is more on the maintenance of organizational direction and the achievement of performance standards.

Characteristics of hospitality growth

Hospitality organizations differ from many other types of activity when they expand: as hospitality units need to be located at the point of consumption, any single hotel can only grow so far at one location. Once it exceeds a given number of rooms, restaurants, and bars, it may run the risk of becoming uneconomic. Expansion decisions usually make geographic diversification imperative. Geographic expansion implies a degree of risk taking as the organization will not have previous experience of operating within the new location.

The risks involved in expanding into different localities may be minimized by a number of strategies:

- Choosing similar types of location, such as city centers or resort locations. This type of strategy is designed to minimize differences within the business environment.

- Choosing to cater to the same market segment(s). Because market requirements are similar across the whole of the segment, the company will already have a high degree of knowledge.
- Standardizing operations to as great an extent as possible – replicating the service offered to the customer and the in-house systems used to supply this service.
- Creating corporate economies of scale in such areas as purchasing, finance, and central reservation systems.
- Providing services which could not be contemplated when operating only a few units. This includes developing a branding presence and liaising with major travel business organizations such as airlines and car rental firms to offer joint services.
- Purchasing an existing operation which is already trading and which may afford the acquisitor some of the above advantages while also gaining management with local expertise.

Thus it can be seen that expansion does not simply mean a replication of existing systems. In the first place, locational characteristics will differ, supply and demand conditions will alter between different units, and management at these locations will have to ensure that policies are interpreted in the best interests of the parent organization.

In the second place, the growth of the organization means that new decisions will have to be made relating to the processes that the organization is to carry out and their distribution within the organization. Given the multisite nature of the industry, this involves a strategic decision as to the extent to which certain decisions are made at the center and others are pushed down to lower levels, whether this be the general manager of the individual hotel or some intermediary stage, such as the regional level.

The hotel and catering industry possesses a large number of production and support functions which must be provided to ensure that customers are provided with an acceptable level of service (see Table 9.1). As an organization grows, it is necessary to consider the extent to which it should meet all these functions from its own resources. Some areas may be released from its day-to-day responsibility: for example, a hotel group may decide to lease rather than own property. These are common questions for companies in any sphere of industry and will involve an examination of the precise nature of the business the company is in and the extent of its core activities.

Another key question that a multisite group needs to address, as we have seen, is the extent to which decisions on the operation of its activities are centralized or dispersed within the organization. Relating to Slattery and Clark's typology (Table 9.1), the growing hospitality operation will be able to appraise its operations in three distinct spheres:

- That work which is associated with the buildings in which operations are conducted. The relevant expertise here is that of property management, which will involve finding sites, building development and maintenance, property valuations, and disposals.

Table 9.1 Typology of corporate activities

Hotel and catering tradition	Business orientation	Ancillary and support functions	
Operations or line management	Accounting and finance	Architecture and property	Leisure-linked promotions
Food and beverage (catering)	Marketing and sales	Buildings and maintenance	Stores and supplies
Housekeeping	Personnel and training	Computing	Security
	Audit and control	Public relations	Purchasing, fire, and safety
	Research and planning	Technical services	Reception/ telephone/ cleaning
		Engineering and maintenance	

Source: Reprinted with permission from Slattery, P. and Clark, A., 'Major variables in the corporate structure of hotel groups', International Journal of Hospitality Management, vol. 7, no. 2, pp.117–30. Copyright 1988, Pergamon Press Ltd.

- That skill which is involved in providing service at a particular level in the most efficient and effective manner possible. This is essentially a specialist activity which involves the skill of using people, materials, and property through the medium of management skills. Clear guidance will be needed from an organization's center in relation to the objectives that have to be achieved, although the manner in which they are met will be a matter for organizational discretion.
- That level of organizational expertise which looks at the strategic evolution of the company and which plans and implements major changes in direction and operation within the company. The strengths required to do this type of work essentially revolve around decision-making skills at a strategic level.

The decisions with which the organization is faced are, therefore, many and complex. The degree of communication and coordination which arises in a multisite organization is probably higher than in similar-sized organizations for which geographical growth in their production base is not so important. Within this environment the role of management is vital. This reflects not only the labor-intensive nature of hospitality operations, but also the need to ensure that management is able and willing to undertake the tasks involved in running a successful organization. Depending on the operation systems and management methods chosen, there could be a need to ensure that there are specialists at the center with a sensitivity to units over a range of locations. Alternatively, there may be a need to develop generalists within the operating units who can implement a range of specialist functions themselves, whilst also ensuring coordination with the center of the organization and other individual units.

In ensuring that all these functions are performed, it can readily be seen that human resource management (HRM) plays a crucial role. While the policies adopted for operation of the company will have implications for HRM activities, it could also be claimed that the expansion strategies employed by an organization are in many cases contingent on the aptitudes and development potential of existing management. Thus HRM activities play both a contingent and a supportive role in the company's growth strategy.

Operating in an international arena

There are now a considerable number of hospitality organizations working multinationally (see, for example, Litteljohn and Roper, 1991; Litteljohn *et al.*, 1991; Kleinwort Benson, 1991). Hotel group expansion in international markets has undergone several phases (Litteljohn and Roper, 1991), and while levels of company penetration are still relatively low in many national markets, international companies have become important leaders in many international industry sectors.

The sources quoted above treat multinational operations as encompassing those businesses which have operations based in more than one country. Structurally, a hotel multinational is no different from its national counterpart. Both will be multisite, although the former will have operations in at least two different nations. In addition it cannot be claimed that multinational management practices are different in kind from those associated with purely national companies. Similar financial, marketing, and operating issues will have to be faced by both types of organization.

Essentially, international operation injects greater elements of variability and complexity into organizational activities. Environments become more variable because locational differences in terms of economic, social/cultural, demographic, and legal factors become greater than they would if the company restricted its activities to a single country. In addition, competitive forces in different locations may vary greatly. Operations will become more complex because not only may each location possess differences in culture and other factors, but the way in which these factors, interact and the strategies which the company should use will vary.

Thus it is important that hospitality organizations both recognize the diversity of their operational environments and provide mechanisms which allow units to operate as effectively as possible. This is not to claim that functions should be entirely decentralized; many successful operations over the period 1965–85 came from the development of rigorously enforced standardization, for example. However, when operational environments differ greatly (as they will in the international sphere), it is unlikely that standardization *alone* will play such an important logistical role, or that its maintenance will be delivered as simply as may be the case within a purely national arena.

Multinational operations therefore differ in the degree to which problems must be diagnosed and the manner in which they should be addressed. It is not that they are different in kind from uni-national operations; rather, companies will have to differ in the degree to which they respond to the variations in their international locations (Buckley, 1984). It is this difference in emphasis which we seek to address here.

Hospitality organization

In discussing hospitality organizations in the USA, Olsen (1989) concentrated his analysis of organizational structure on three particular factors: formalization, centralization, and complexity. They seem to form a useful base for further analysis in this context. The parameters can be explained as follows:

- *Formalization* – the degree to which an organization is prescriptive in anticipating problems and providing advice and solutions to these problems (often through the medium of operating manuals).
- *Centralization* – the extent procedures are centralized as opposed to allowing delegation to unit level.
- *Complexity* – the degree of specialization that exists within an organization as measured through the number of specialized staff or sub-units devoted to discrete, well-defined tasks and responsibilities.

Why should firms go international?

Given the greater risk that may be involved in international expansion, there may be some question as to the motivation for embarking on such a strategy. Essentially, the company perceives the potential benefits to be larger than the costs associated with the risk. Many different explanations have been put forward as to why firms go international. Albaum *et al.* (1989) put forward several strategic reasons which explain firms' internationalization decisions (see Table 9.2). As classified by these authors, it will be noted that the reasons may spring from factors which are internal to the firm, or from external factors in the business environment. In addition, motivations are distinguished by whether they are proactive to the situation, i.e. involve an aspect of planning and anticipation within the company, or whether the organization is reacting to perceived changes in its industry environment. The distinction may be simplified by arranging the classification into those tactics which are offensive on the one hand and defensive on the other. Thus it will be seen that these approaches, whether offensive or defensive, may depend on management direction and ability, and emphasize a need for clear policies to develop middle and senior management.

Within the general decision to expand multinationally the company should ensure that all elements of strategy have been considered in respect of international operations. Using Porter's (1980) categorization of strategic

Table 9.2 Reasons for internationalizing operations

	Proactive	Reactive
Internal	● Managerial urge ● Growth and profit goals ● Economies of scale ● Offer a unique product ● Extension of services	● Risk diversification
External	● Foreign market opportunities ● Encouragement through change agents ● Shaping the competition	● Small or declining home market ● Following the competition

Source: Based on Albaum et al. (1989).

factors, the complexity of developing international networks can be further accentuated.

● *Product line.* This concerns the degree to which the tangible and intangible elements of the hotel service can be kept standard. Will room and service standards be provided on the same basis given differences in, for example, climate, custom, and staffing conditions?
● *Target markets.* As a firm internationalizes, it will consider carefully the markets that it wishes to appeal to. Do the national markets exist on an international basis, or will the plans have to be modified in the new localities to suit different economic and cultural conditions?
● *Marketing.* Will marketing functions remain the same or will they change as a company internationalizes to allow the organization to capitalize on international and local target markets?
● *Sales.* This involves the extent to which policies on selling and sales service have to be changed to ensure that the best mix of occupancies is achieved.
● *Distribution.* The company will have to decide on the nature of its policies in regard both to the type of location within countries that it seeks (e.g. major city center, resort, travel associated) and to its relationships with other sales agents, such as tour operators and travel agents.
● *Purchasing.* This concerns the extent to which purchasing will be coordinated on a centralized or regionalized basis, or whether all purchasing decisions will be made at a local level.
● *Research and development.* Again this is tied into the centralization/decentralization debate. These decisions may involve the development and refinement of new hotel services, the development of new menus, and the use of new technology.
● *Finance and control.* These are very important variables. The financing issue has already been mentioned, and decisions on methods of entry will have important implications for the company's relationships with sources of

capital, financial rate of return (performance) and other strategic variables. The control aspect relates not only to the financial controls that the company institutes, but to its whole quality control approach. This will include financial control but for service industry operations is best seen in the wider context of ensuring that overall market and operating standards meet the expectations of the company and its customers.

● *Labor*. The need to develop an international approach to the selection, recruitment, retention, and development of management and other employees will be of great importance in implementing corporate strategy and ensuring that performance standards are met.

(We have not taken into account Porter's 'manufacturing' variable, which is not seen as significantly material to this analysis.)

The analysis once again stresses the need to treat the management resource with great care. The way in which the company decides to operate will have a significant effect on the recruitment, selection, training, and development of managers.

Contextualizing the nature of international operations

To explain further the nature of international operations there follows an appraisal of the complexity of foreign environments. Figure 9.1 shows four broad areas to be considered: organizational, legal, financial, and cultural factors. These will influence both the organizational structure and also the approach taken to managing operations within this context.

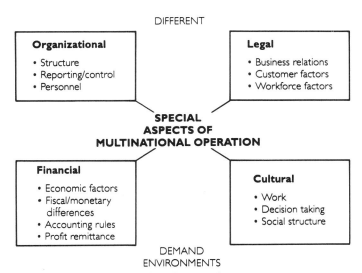

Fig. 9.1 The context of international operations

Source: Litteljohn, D., Beattie, R., and Watson, S. (1991) 'Corporate ownership in Europe and its impact on management development', International Association of Hospitality Management Conference, April.

Organizational factors

These are the issues that revolve around the way in which the company structure is designed in terms of decision taking and communication. In addition, staffing and management factors should be considered. Most decisions will be based on the same principles that will apply to a nationally based firm, although the international aspect may add some special elements.

First, consider the form of expansion. A company may develop wholly through raising its own finance or it may expand through franchise and/or management contracts. The international aspect relates to the lack of knowledge that may exist in relation to foreign locations. For example, it may be difficult to plan an investment strategy well if the company has no knowledge of sources of capital and management talent in the country. The company will also wish to consider whether to set up a wholly owned subsidiary, or whether it should involve local partners and/or shareholders.

Second, whatever the method of ownership chosen, the company will also have to consider the reporting and organization structure that allows both the best form of control from the center and the necessary flexibility at local level. A company could organize its hotels into country or regional (i.e. involving several countries) groupings. This choice can become more complicated if the parent company establishes more than one brand of hotels on an international basis. The decision at this stage will revolve around the advantages and disadvantages of having a single line of control and communication for all units, as compared to the need for hotels to be placed in brand divisions. One solution to the problem lies in the matrix structure where there is a dual chain of command: one link will reflect the geographical spread of the organization and the other will reflect the type of branding policy operated.

J. A. Lee (1966) indicates that the organization of multinational companies should meet these requirements by considering organization in two different dimensions: horizontal and vertical. Horizontally because it must allow units to work effectively within the opportunities and constraints of their individual locations. Vertically because it will have to design management systems which can support and control properties over a number of different locations and cultures.

A third important factor that a multinational company will have to take into account is the recruitment and development of its workforce. It is likely that it will require a number of staff who are internationally mobile; they will need to be sensitive to the problems of operating in different cultures (see below) and must be given the financial and other support systems necessary to adapt to change successfully. On the other hand, the company will have to ensure that it also treats locally based staff acceptably.

Legal factors

A multinational company will have to adapt to the different laws that operate in various countries. As adapting to the legal environment may be a very involved process, only some indicative examples are given below.

Laws concerning building regulation and customer registration spring immediately to mind. Yet there are a host of other factors which will need careful examination. In relation to the early stages of project development, legal requirements on company formation and land or property ownership are crucially important. The situation with regard to permissions for serving meals and drink will have to be obtained. The company will have to ensure that local employment legislation is followed. Particularly relevant labor law within a European context would be European employment legislation and the implications of the Social Charter.

Relevant to laws governing company formation and operation would be the laws which apply to franchising and management contracts; it would not be wise to assume that they will be identical to those in the home country.

Financial factors

As the number of countries a company covers increases, so will the number of currencies that it will have to manage. This may make for difficulties in pricing policies, especially if the problem of moving exchange rates is considered.

In addition, it is more than likely that a number of other differences in the financial environment will affect operations. The cost of finance (i.e. the interest rate on loans) is an important variable. Government policy regarding sales tax, employee taxation, and profits (including profit remittance to the home country) will have to be considered. Another important variable is the way in which profit is calculated – the acceptable accounting conventions. For example, in some countries (including the USA) properties are depreciated; in the UK property appreciation is allowed.

Cultural factors

The third variable to be given attention is the cultural variations which might exist at different locations. Again this is a very wide topic and only a few examples are given here to indicate the nature of the challenge. Culture refers to 'the whole set of social norms and responses that condition a population's behavior.' It is the 'acquired and inculcated ... set of rules and behavior patterns that an individual learns but does not inherit at birth' (Robock and Simmonds, 1989). The point to note is that approaches by management should take into account these differences in behavior. Perhaps the most obvious factor will relate to language differences. Yet this is only one of many characteristics which may manifest themselves in a number of ways. These could include:

● Attitudes to work and achievement. To what extent are individuals motivated by wealth and achievement?

- Patterns of decision taking. Who takes decisions: is it an individual, family, employer, religious adviser or someone else?
- Social structure. Are there barriers to mobility between social, economic, or ethnic groups, and how rigid are they?

Some societies are more alike than others and good management will always see the similarities and build on them. However, it should not be assumed that recognizing the full range of cultural differences is a simple matter: 'it takes a great deal of discipline to force the mind to see things that one's own culture ignores or places in low value' (Robock and Simmonds, 1989).

Human resource management and international growth

In order that HRM is integrated into corporate growth strategies within the hospitality industry, there is a requirement that both internal and external influences on the approach adopted are identified and analyzed. The following commentary focuses on strategic choices for HRM and their implications for organizations in terms of international management development.

Discussion concerns key strategic variables which can be seen to include: networking of management on both a horizontal and vertical basis; the bipolarization of the knowledge base; the mobility of managers; and differing working practices, including cultural issues. These variables can seem to exert a greater influence as organizations develop internationally.

Networking can be seen to play a more important role as a company develops globally in order that expertise can be shared and that isolation does not occur in periphery units.

Bipolarization which can occur at a national level as an organization develops leaner and flatter structures can become more intense as an organization grows. Not only can this occur on a horizontal basis, but it can also appear on a vertical basis.

The degree of geographical growth will impact on the extent to which mobility of managers and working practices in different cultures will require to be addressed. Attention will need to be given to all of these key variables when deciding on the strategic approach to HRM.

The role that human resource management plays in the growth of international hospitality organizations cannot be overstated. On the one hand, HRM will influence the extent to which an organization can expand, while on the other, the approach taken to HRM will be influenced by the growth strategies employed by an organization. The extent to which an organization can take a proactive rather than a reactive approach to internationalization will depend not only on the financial resources available, but also on the skills and abilities of top management, particularly in the area of environmental scanning and business trend analysis.

The mechanisms utilized to develop managers will have to change as an organization changes from a national to an international orientation. For instance, management development may have operated successfully on a centralized basis, but as growth occurs there may be a requirement to decentralize this function, in order that individual managers can fully take account of the external factors on local operations. The traditional lack of involvement of HRM specialists at a strategic level of hospitality organizations (Worsfold and Jameson, 1991) has resulted in this being a reactionary process, rather than management development being planned as an integral component of the growth strategy. However, some organizations, such as Intercontinental Hotels, are now beginning to address this issue.

Perlmutter (1969) developed a model to analyze strategies which the authors have amended slightly in order to provide a framework for HRM strategies (see Table 9.3). In utilizing this framework it must be understood that this model is neither static nor comprehensive in nature. The approach taken will depend on the size of the company, the degree of internationalization, the organizational structure, and the long-term strategies of the business.

Ethnocentric strategy

This is where an organization employs the same strategies and practices in all countries in which it operates. This approach results in a high degree of decision making and authority at the central personnel office. Normally managers are recruited and developed in the home country for key positions anywhere in the world. A slightly different approach which can be taken with this strategy is when an organization shapes the HRM function in all units into

Table 9.3 Human resource management strategies

	Ethnocentric	Polycentric	Geocentric
Definition	The same strategies and practices are employed in all countries	Human resource management is decentralized on a country-by-country basis	Human resource management is managed on a global basis
Characteristics	A high degree of authority and decision making at head office	Authority and decision making devolved to take account of local environments	Harmonizes the overall management of human resources, while at the same time responding to local environmental factors
Management development	Managers are recruited and developed in the company's home country, for anywhere in the world	Local managers are trained and developed for key positions within own country	Allows for the development of the best person within the company as a whole

one mold, by socializing all personnel to the corporate style in attitude and behavior. This approach to HRM can be seen to operate in Walt Disney with all senior managers involved in the Eurodisney development having to undergo socialization into the Disney approach prior to working in France.

Some of the implications of adopting an ethnocentric approach to human resource management include the desirability and costs of long-term managerial mobility. Managers may be quite happy to be located internationally for a limited time span in their career. Organizations will require to make this an attractive option to ensure that there is a sufficient supply of suitable managers to meet their needs. This may result in a high level of cost, including suitable remuneration and support services for the 'corps' internationally mobile managers. This could contrast with unit or nationally based management, and it may be important that a two-tier structure of managers does not emerge where those who are internationally mobile are seen as forming an elite group working under different rules from their less mobile colleagues.

The ethnocentric strategy implies that a high degree of attention is paid to cultural issues in the development of managers to ensure that the company culture infiltrates throughout the organization and that managers are made aware of local cultural issues affecting their operations.

Polycentric strategy

This approach decentralizes the human resource management function on a country-by-country basis in order that the function is aligned to take into account the local external environment and its impact on the operation. It is employed by Gardner Merchant, the contract catering arm of the UK hospitality company, Forte. Management development focuses on the training and development of local managers for key positions within their own country. Although this ensures that external factors are more likely to be considered in the operation of these units, this approach may result in limited career opportunities being available. There could also be problems relating to management loyalty to the organization if local issues conflict with organizational philosophy. This conflict of interests may also appear between localities, manifesting itself as rivalry and making assimilation of expertise across the organization difficult.

Geocentric strategy

This can be seen to exist when human resources are managed on a 'global' basis, to ease intra-unit mobility by harmonizing the overall enterprise management of human resources, while at the same time responding to local environmental factors. Marriott Hotels and Holiday Inns can currently be seen to employ this approach. Management development focuses on the development of the best people from anywhere in the world for key positions. Attention is paid to the development of international managers who have generalist knowledge on operating within this extremely diverse market.

International cultural aspects become a major feature of the organization in order that managers can operate effectively, but again the costs can be high and elitism could become an internal issue.

The approach taken to HRM is hardly ever static; as an organization grows there may be developments within the systems and a move from one of the approaches identified to another.

Another important aspect to highlight at this stage is the relationship between central and peripheral units (Hedlund and Aman, 1986). The power which a periphery unit exerts over a central office may distort the approach taken to human resource management. For example, an organization may adopt an ethnocentric approach, but if the foreign subsidiary units operate independently, a polycentric approach may be the de facto policy. This can be taken a stage further, when an organization undergoes 'internationalization of the second degree' (Hedlund and Aman, 1986). This is where a peripheral unit exerts more influence over other local units than the head office, and again there is a move towards polycentricity. Thus a regional office in Europe may have more influence on the approach taken to training for managers than the head office in the USA.

Management development

Increasing internationalization of business and the forces pushing towards unification of Western Europe have resulted in a questioning of the principles involved in the building of managerial and operational teams, for principles will now have to take into account organizational features which differ from those of national organizations. In addition, there is the problem of dealing with multicultural executive teams. Research carried out at Ashbridge Management College (Barham and Devine, 1991) suggests that leading international organizations are looking for new management development strategies and models to develop an international focus. Management development is a key feature of HRM which has been given much attention recently. Discussion of its role has gained impetus from current trends in organizational restructuring, resulting in the reduction of numbers of middle managers.

Management development can be defined as the process by which an organization ensures that it has effective management to meet its present and future needs. The process is complex as it comprises both formal and informal learning relating to the business needs of the organization and to individual managers' overall aspirations: 'Management development ... is concerned with developing the whole person' (Torrington and Hall, 1991).

Management development is often regarded as peripheral to the business, but success in an environment where there are rapid market changes, increasing mergers and acquisitions, foreign competition, and saturation of domestic markets will require organizations to pay more attention to international development and the kind of managers required to deal with these changes.

Strategically, companies will have to adopt a global approach to planning management development in order to equip managers with the skill and expertise which they require to succeed within this environment. The problem here is that, even on a continental basis, countries cannot be viewed as homogeneous. Country-specific environments are made complex by different factors which need careful analysis. At an operational level, managers will require to be able to view their operations within the broad portfolio of the organization as a whole, but at the same time to be aware of the impact of the local environment on their work and operations.

As competition within the international hospitality industry increases, the organizational structures are altering. Organizations are beginning to develop flatter and leaner structures to allow more effective operating systems to be utilized. These structures would have been more difficult to implement without the support of effective and efficient computerized systems.

This trend in organizational structure can be seen in companies such as Forte Hotels and Intercontinental Hotels which have removed a layer of middle management at the unit operational level. The implication of this change for individual managers is that there may be a bipolarization of the knowledge base between top and middle managers. This may result in those who have the ability and the desire to advance being promoted, while those who do not possess these qualities remain at lower managerial or supervisory positions. The opportunities for advancement will be reduced at an earlier stage in a manager's career, leading to higher competition for fewer jobs. This places the onus for management development on the individual manager, who will have to take on more responsibility for his or her own self-development.

Organizations will have to play an increasing role in the provision of development opportunities on a continuous basis. This will enable individual learning, either on or off the job, to be transformed into organizational learning.

It will be up to individual managers to select training and development opportunities which meet their long-term aspirations and organizational needs. It may be necessary for organizations to offer wider and more flexible management development programs in order that these needs can be realized. This may require more attention to be paid to the recognition and certification of experiential learning (Go, 1990), and to networking between organizations and/or educational establishments to provide courses and development opportunities which are outside the scope and expertise of one organization.

Management development programs have traditionally focused on developing leadership qualities. The issue in the future will be how to develop the qualities which not only best suit the organization but are appropriate to the needs of the individual managers. These will need to reflect the different conditions in the various locations which may require managers to adapt their leadership styles to suit local needs when dealing with a multicultural workforce. Mentoring and coaching have traditionally been used in organizations such as Holiday Inns and Intercontinental Hotels which operate in an international context. However, these are likely to take on a more supportive role as more focus is placed on developing managers who can cope in a rapidly changing, competitive environment. Many international companies are beginning to address the need to ensure that individual managers become aware of those factors which influence their business in both the short and long term. Holiday Inns encourage this through their Organizational Development program, which allows for participation in the development of strategic business direction and the drawing up of individual business plans. This ensures that managers are not only strategically aware but also sensitive to local environments.

Hospitality companies have shown a movement toward customer awareness and orientation. McDonald's and Disney (Peters, 1988) epitomize this focus on service on an international scale, and many other organizations are striving to achieve it, as can be seen by the predominance of customer care training programs within hospitality organizations. However, the organizational structure must allow for customer care by ensuring that individuals are given authority to be able to meet customers' needs.

Organizations may have to delegate the authority to 'front line' employees to enable them to deal with customers' queries and complaints without having to clear decisions with management and lose the 'moment of truth' (Carlson, 1989). This decentralized approach will have implications for management development. Management styles will have to be tailored to suit this independent employee, and this may require training being given so that management is able to empower employee commitment to organizational goals and objectives. Cultural awareness is a key characteristic of international managers, particularly in the context of decentralized authority within operating units.

Hospitality firms are beginning to address the need to develop forms of cultural training for managers. In the European context there has been an increase in the number of linguistic courses available to management staff. However, this is only a beginning and it will be necessary for organizations to identify fuller cultural training programs which will enable managers to operate effectively in a foreign environment. Hilton International (Meeting the Transfer Challenge) and Grand Metropolitan (Managing Internationally) are examples of companies who have developed programs to meet these needs. Cultural training should avoid a manager's frame of reference becoming too parochial (Thurley, 1990) and role conflicts developing between local cultural pressures and those of the parent organization. However, cultural training may also heighten role conflict by alerting the hospitality manager to the cultural implications of company decisions (Cullen, 1981). It is important, therefore, that both the long- and short-term objectives of cultural training are clearly identified, and that these are disseminated to managers participating in the training.

In the international hospitality industry, managers will require to be truly global. Some commentators have noticed that in order to achieve this, education, experience and international mobility will be important, so that cultural differences and their impacts on organizations can be assessed. However, the managers are having to operate in a less stable social context. Social changes occurring in the Western world today are aggravating the issue of managerial mobility: for example, the increase in the number of dual-career families. In France 70 percent of females under the age of 35 are in dual-career families (Lavin, 1991). This complicates the issue of mobility, for gone are the days when the decision was predominantly the prerogative of the male breadwinner. Additionally, more choice is demanded in all aspects of life. Career progression may no longer hold the position of importance it previously enjoyed, especially if standards in other aspects of life are likely to decline as a result. Managers will be analyzing the total package of benefits being offered by the organization and are likely to be in a position to demand more as the skilled international manager becomes a scarce resource.

This, in turn, will influence the approach taken to support services for international hospitality managers. Companies will have to develop better family-orientated policies rather than focusing on compensation and benefits only for the international manager. For example, subsidized housing, educational grants, and longer leave may be support services offered to tomorrow's international hospitality manager.

The relocation of managers will have to be planned, and compensation given which is adequate both in monetary and in other terms. Orientation counseling at a family level may have to be considered in order that the individual manager can be relocated as effectively as possible. 'Multinationals which do consider the family situation in the selection decision experience significantly lower expatriate failure rates' (Scullion, 1991).

Managers within the hospitality industry have traditionally functioned in a multicultural environment due to the high level of cross-cultural representatives in the workforce. This trend will increase as more organizations penetrate the international market and more managers will have to learn to cope with changes in attitude to work and different behavioral aspects of working lives. These complexities not only will be geographical but will vary within locations by class and age factors. Moreover, the level of employee involvement in decision making in many continental European countries such as Germany and France is far higher than in the UK. These factors may require companies to alter management styles to fit new environments. For example, management by objectives has proved to be effective in the UK and USA, but not in France or Portugal (Boella, 1992). Adaptability in new situations is a requirement of the international hospitality manager.

It can be seen from the preceding discussion that the development of international hospitality managers requires the organization not only to address these issues at a strategic level, but also to integrate them into their growth strategies in order that competitive advantage can be attained by the organization. However, not only is the organization required to take cognizance of the human resource management issues; it must also focus attention on the implications associated with the adoption of different operating structures utilized to achieve international growth. The following discussion highlights variables in a range of operational structures, indicating the implications for HRM.

Major variables in operational structures

In deciding on the nature of its core business and the manner in which it wishes to operate its portfolio of units, a company is likely to assess the appropriateness of the three main methods of operation: direct ownership of resources, management contracts or franchising. While there will be overlapping factors amongst the three methods, and while a company is unlikely to operate any of these methods to the exclusion of another, each will have their own particular attributes.

Direct ownership

This may be termed asset-based management. Under this strategy the company retains full ownership of all three levels of the business. All questions of strategy may, therefore, be resolved within one organization. On the other hand, the organization will have to contain a high level of expertise, to ensure the best possible use of resources. Performance criteria will be closely monitored as the company will have heavy capital requirements in funding any expansion.

The company will also maintain full responsibility for all human resource management functions. This will give considerable flexibility in selection and recruitment at all management levels and allow flexibility in promoting in-house talent.

All other strategic factors will be wholly within the control of the parent organization. Of course, this strategy assumes that capital and personnel are easily available; if they are not in adequate supply, a company may either have to slow down its expansion plans or consider alternative methods of enlargement. If resources are available, the company may opt to acquire another company. If this is the case, there may be considerable difficulty in assimilating the personnel and culture of the new operations.

In joint ventures the company will enter into a specific agreement with another organization in order to implement a particular set of aims. The alliance may be one of equal partners, or one where one party is stronger than another because of the resources or expertise it possesses. An immediate problem, as with an acquisition, will be one of welding two different types of corporate culture together. In addition, one of the companies may feel that its competitive advantage is being diluted as its proprietary knowledge is passed to a wider audience. Thus there may be problems with research and development functions, as well as with organizational control.

In relation to labor issues, the joint venture mechanism will mean that, if the new company is wholly independent, it may lack a large enough employee base to ensure that it can nurture sufficient talent within the organization. This problem can be minimized if, for example, one of the partners is given complete operational and strategic control. Thus Intercontinental is owned jointly by Seibu Saison and Scandinavian Air Systems, but SAS has the day-to-day control over hotels.

An interesting development on the normal form of management organization under direct ownership occurs in Queens Moat Houses PLC. This company decentralizes important elements of its operation under its Incentive Management Scheme. This arrangement occurs only where the company has a good knowledge of managers and judges them effective in running a hotel. The company and the manager will jointly assess the profitability of the business for a year in the future and the manager is made liable for the 'incentive fee', which is the budgeted profit in 13 four-weekly installments. The manager is liable for all purchasing, the employment of staff, and the standard of the hotel services as well as the fabric of the property. The hotel must conform to the company standards and has to take part in all company advertising and promotion schemes. Special arrangements are made between the two parties for projects which require substantial amounts of capital. These arrangements allow the top executives to concentrate their efforts on the strategic development of the company to a greater extent than if they adopted the traditional owner/operator form of business.

Management contracting and franchising both allow a decoupling of the ownership of assets and the operational and strategic levels of hospitality operations.

Management contracting

In this case the property owners contract for a company to run the hotel. The operating company provides the property's owners with a saving in risk and an increase in potential income. The operating company may or may not be large, and may or may not have a strong brand image in the marketplace. In any event it will gain the contract, often competitively, because it can offer the owning company a distinctly advantageous set of arrangements.

The contract period may be long or short. Nowadays many contracts will run for twenty years with further extension clauses. In some countries there may be a legal maximum for the length of the contract – in West Germany the longest period for such a contract is thirty years.

The operating company will negotiate a management fee to be paid over the length of the contract. The fee may be computed in a number of different ways. Usually remuneration will be calculated through a mix of a share of turnover (e.g. 3 percent) and a share of trading profit (e.g. 10 percent). Variations may be combined with accelerated fees when profits exceed a predetermined level. Similarly, there may be special arrangements for low levels of turnover and profits.

Under the traditional pattern of a property owner seeking operating company, the split between strategy and operation is large and it is possible that the development company will take on considerable responsibility in the initial decision on where to locate the hotel. Apart from this decision all operational and strategic decisions will be left in the hands of the operating company, though it would be simplistic not to imagine that there may be some friction between the two parties, particularly over financial aspects inherent in the contract. For instance, the operating company may feel extensive refurbishment of the property is necessary for it to maintain its market appeal. The property owner, however, may need considerable persuasion to agree that this eventuality was fully covered in the terms of the original contract.

The divorce between ownership and operation may not be complete. Operating companies are increasingly taking substantial equity positions in the basic property assets, by which they show their commitment to the project. In another variant of the traditional form of property owner seeking suitable operator, some North American operations, for example Marriott, took the initiative by themselves developing properties in locations they wanted, and selling the properties on, while retaining the operating contract. These sale and lease back arrangements allow the operating company to increase the scope of the decisions that it may take. In addition, it increases the risk element in property development, as Marriott experienced when facing the recession of the early 1990s. The company suffered financial hardships and had to make considerable labor savings in its development and estates departments.

The management contracting option allows growth at a much faster rate than would be the case with an asset-owning company. While the company must have negotiating and legal skills to ensure that it can gain and regulate contracts to its satisfaction, it does not need to have the extent of property-owning skills that would be the case in an asset-led company. It may therefore be in a better position to develop other aspects of hotel keeping such as marketing, sales, and so on. Once a certain size is attained, and assuming a regular turnover of contracts, the company will have to ensure a flexibility in management structure to allow for moves. In additions, management themselves may be expected to possess a degree of flexibility to allow them to undertake a range of specialist functions on transfer.

Franchising

Franchising, or more accurately business format franchising, has proved an important strategy for hotel and restaurant operations in North America. In the UK, while the system has seen some success in the eating-out market – more particularly in the fast-food sector – it has not been taken up greatly by hotels. It is currently being developed only within the hotel sector, though projections for European expansion appear relatively optimistic.

The system requires the provision of a whole business service formula. The major prerequisite is a marketable product or service which has a high market acceptability. There are a range of other important business services that the franchiser should provide. In the first place, there will be the business methods, carefully explained through a range of operating manuals. In addition, there will be training and development of key staff and personnel. The parent will also provide marketing and advertising expertise, and may also supply assistance in setting the business up – from site selection to funding advice.

This method of operation has many significant characteristics. By keeping the financial and operating arms separate, like management contracting, corporate energy can be directed at strategic growth and performance factors. The company may also be able to tap into resources that it otherwise could not gain access to, sites in suitable locations being a particular example.

The parent franchisor will have a significant development input in the development of basic training manuals and ensuring that they are up to date. In addition, it will have to ensure that its franchisees are trained and developed in the systems provided. The parent franchisor will, of course, have to provide the specialist marketing and finance services, as well as investing in franchise recruitment and selection, but the amount of development that it will have to provide for the total number of managers within the system will be relatively small as it will only have to provide for the managers that it employs directly; all other positions are technically the responsibility of the franchisees.

It can be seen from the preceding analysis that, as a company grows internationally, the management characteristics become more complex and there is no standard approach which can be taken to meet these needs. The approach taken by two companies operating within the international hospitality industry are described below. These case studies provide illustrations of how some of the main issues identified in this chapter are being tackled in order to compete effectively in this environment.

Company A

This is a large international company with extensive hotel holdings. In addition, the company operates in other sectors of hospitality such as contract catering. This analysis focuses on the approach taken within the hotel sectors only. The company's international hotel holdings cover several countries, although they are biased towards two countries.

It is a feature of this company that most of its units are owned and managed directly. Traditionally, expansion has been achieved by the acquisition of existing hotels and by new building. Little has been made of alternative approaches such as joint ventures; however, this position is beginning to alter with planned joint ventures overseas.

Organizational structure and communications

Foreign operations are managed either directly from headquarters or through subsidiary companies which have a close relationship with the center. However, the company is currently reappraising its organizational structure in order to maintain and increase levels of profitability. This involves a restructuring across the whole range of the company's activities. A major feature of this exercise has been the establishment of strategic business units. These have been defined in terms of hotel brands and allow for clear strategic direction. However, the situation with the overseas division is slightly different in that no clear branding policy has been introduced. This is due to the range and diversity of both locations and types of hotel. However, for international operations, geographical subsidiaries have been developed which have resulted in a number of different approaches being adopted to meet organizational objectives. Within individual units, flatter and leaner structures have been a recent focus with the removal of a layer of management at the assistant manager level.

Decision making

The company, notwithstanding the creation of strategic business units, keeps a tight control on decision taking, which is seen as the prerogative of the corporate team based at the UK head office. Strategic direction for all divisions is decided at this level, while the interpretation of this to suit each strategic business unit is carried out by the appropriate directorate. Amendments to the proposed strategies can be voiced at this stage to allow for appropriate implementation to take place. It is the operation directors who have the responsibility to communicate strategy throughout the business unit, while the delivery of the strategy is left to the unit managers.

Networking

Traditionally, little was made of networking either internally or externally, allowing for the possibility of competition between divisions. However, greater use is now being made of networking, particularly outside the organization. Links with educational establishments are being strengthened with the organization looking toward alternative managerial development techniques.

Management training and development

A management training centre has been operational for a number of years within this company. Management trainees were recruited into a specific division and undertook training for approximately one year before being given a position within the company. Mentoring and coaching were the main development techniques used. Cultural awareness programs have been operating within the company for a number of years, and these have proved successful.

Management is now recruited into a position at either supervisory or managerial level. It is felt that individuals will gain experience in managing while at the same time building up knowledge regarding company procedures and policies.

More attention is being paid to permeating learning throughout the organization by focusing on alternative approaches such as the accreditation of in-company courses and of prior learning, which enables managers to gain academic credit for training and work experience. Some training courses are now being run across all strategic business units and for all levels of management. This should result in managers being closer to the strategic decisions being made.

Support services

Relocation allowances, including the payment of school fees, are offered to internationally mobile managers. Extensive briefing sessions are also given but as yet little support is given to the spouse.

Company B

This organization is much smaller than Company A. It concentrates on its core business of hotel development and operations, and has, relative to its size, extensive holdings outside its home country, although it has to date restricted its operations to Europe.

Organizational structure and communications

There has been a deliberate policy to maintain a small head office which is based in the home country. This has been achieved through devolving much responsibility to unit managers and giving them the power and responsibility to take operating decisions, thus eliminating involvement by area managers. The executive directors have clearly defined spheres of control, such as finance and operations. The size of the company and the length of service of these executives ensures that there is mutuality of trust and respect within their working relationships. This also results in management having clear lines of communication to the top of the organization. The executive team see their role as acting as facilitators within the organization.

The foreign divisions are operated on a devolved basis with each subsidiary responsible for its own operating structure and maintenance of profitability. Each subsidiary is represented on the executive board, and the directors report directly to the managing director.

Decision making

There is an extremely high degree of decentralization within the company, except in the area of financial control. Methods of attaining budgets set for each operating unit are left to the discretion of unit managers. The strategic direction of the company is decided at head office, but this is open to consultation and amendments from subsidiaries. The implementation and interpretation of strategies is then the responsibility of the operating directors within each division.

Networking

Networking is carried out at a local level and is the responsibility of unit managers. There are few company procedures and policies in operation in this context, which results in networking being built up on an *ad hoc* basis, reflecting local needs rather than organizational benefits.

Management training and development

Trainee management selection is coordinated by the operations directors, who act as a 'clearing house'. Candidates are selected by unit managers into a supervisory or managerial position. There is a basic training program covering operational procedures, induction, training techniques, and control systems. The focus is on individualized training for management with responsibility for development and training being placed with individual managers. No career progression promises are given to trainees, the responsibility being devolved to the individual. Guidance will be given, if requested, but otherwise it is up to individuals to negotiate their own training and development opportunities.

Support services

The emphasis on self-development and self-progression ensures that little support is provided to managers by head office. The approach taken to human resource management means that there is little international movement between subsidiaries, and support mechanisms are decentralized on a geographical basis.

Conclusion

Hospitality organizations are increasingly developing into large multisite operations spanning several nations. The management challenge will focus on how strategies allow units to operate effectively at a local level while concurrently the organization achieves maximum global synergy.

This chapter has concentrated on examining the role of human source management within an organization as it grows internationally. International growth, in essence, adds a new measure of complexity to hospitality operations. In order to manage this situation successfully, organizations must address issues on two fronts.

In the first place, the organization must ensure that it allows peripheral units to maximize their local competitiveness. However, this must be done in a manner which is in line with the company's overall strategy. For, if there is too much latitude, the organization runs the risk of allowing regional groupings to evolve which may develop their own strategic aims. If not directly in opposition with those of the parent organization, these may nevertheless pose significant difficulties to the parent in situations where the parent is planning to change fundamental policies and direction.

For example, in the analysis of organizational types based on the work of Perlmutter, it is possible that this type of difficulty could arise particularly as the company changes from a polycentric approach to a geocentric one. Thus the literature identifies a need for an organization to identify both a horizontal and a vertical internationalization strategy. In other words, the organization must plan to harness organizational effort to ensure that energy is released at unit-level operations, in a manner consistent with achieving its corporate goals.

Studies of organizational adaptation to the international management challenge have highlighted many individual factors that need careful attention. In particular, the role of having a cohesive management development pattern has been identified. Managers are, after all, the people who plan and implement organizational strategy, and it is increasingly likely that they will require to work within environments characterized by higher levels of diversity and complexity. To ensure that there is a well of appropriate management expertise to hand, it is essential that the organization provides the type of organizational culture and the appropriate reward packages that will attract and develop people with the requisite interests and potential.

References

Albaum, Gerald, Stransdskov, Jesper, Duerr, Edwin, and Dowd, Laurence (1989) *International Marketing and Export Management*, Wokingham, England: Addison-Wesley.

Barham, K., and Devine, M. (1991) 'The quest for the international manager', *Ashridge Special Report 2098*.

Boella, M. (1992) *Human Resource Management in the Hospitality Industry*, 5th edn, Cheltenham: Stanley Thornes.

Buckley, Peter (1984) 'Multinational operations', in Pickering, J., and Cockerill, T. (eds) *The Economic Theory of the Firm*, Oxford: Philip Allan.

Carlson, J. (1989) *Moments of Truth*, New York: Harper & Row.

Chandler, A. (1962) *Strategy and Structure*, Cambridge, Mass.: MIT Press.

Cullen, P. T. (1981) 'Global gamesmanship', *Cornell Hotel and Restaurant Quarterly*, November pp. 18–25.

Go, F. (1990) 'Tourism and hospitality management: new horizons', *International Journal of Contemporary Hospitality Management*, vol. 2, no. 2, p. 48.

Hedlund, G., and Aman, P. (1986) *Managing Relationships with Foreign Subsidiaries*, Vastervik: Sveriges Mekan Forburd.

Kleinwort Benson (1991) *Quoted Hotel Companies: The world markets*, London: Kleinwort Benson.

Lavin, B. (1991) 'A European perspective to human resource management', unpublished paper presented at IPM meeting, Edinburgh, January.

Lee, J. A. (1966) 'Cultural analysis in overseas operations', *Harvard Business Review*, vol. 44, no. 2, pp. 106–14.

Litteljohn, David, and Roper, Angela (1991) 'Changes in international hotel companies' strategies', in Teare, R., and Boer, A. (eds) *Strategic Hospitality Management*, London: Cassells.

Litteljohn, D., Beattie, R., and Watson, S. (1991) 'Corporate ownership in Europe and its impact on management development', International Association of Hospitality Management Conference, April.

Olsen, M. D. (1989) 'Issues facing multi-unit hospitality organizations in a maturing market', *Journal of Contemporary Hospitality Management*, vol. 1, no. 2, pp. 3–6.

Perlmutter, H. (1969) 'The tortuous evolution of the multinational corporation', *Columbia Journal of World Business*, January/February, p. 12.

Peters, T. (1988) *Thriving on Chaos*, London: Macmillan.

Porter, M. (1980) *Competitive Strategy*, New York: The Free Press.

Robock, Stephan, and Simmonds, Kenneth (1989) *International Management and Multinational Enterprises*, Homewood, Ill.: Irwin.

Scullion, H. (1991) 'Why companies prefer to use expatriates', *Personnel Management*, vol. 23, no. 11, p. 35.

Slattery, P., and Clark, A. (1988) 'Major variables in the corporate structure of hotel groups', *International Journal of Hospitality Management*, vol. 7, no. 2, pp. 117–30.

Thurley, K. (1990) 'Towards a European approach to personnel management', *Personnel Management*, September, p. 57.

Torrington, D., and Hall, L. (1991) *Personnel Management: A new approach*, Hemel Hempstead: Prentice Hall.

Worsfold, S., and Jameson, P. (1991) 'Human resource management: a response to change in the 1990s', in Teare, R., and Boer, A. (eds) *Strategic Hospitality Management*, London: Cassell.

Part 3

Corporate structures and planning

The five chapters in Part 3 are concerned with aspects of the interrelationship between hospitality organizations and their markets. Chapter 10 provides an example of how organizational restructuring has helped Forte PLC to focus on its international development priorities for the 1990s. The complex relationships between international markets and organizational design are examined in Chapter 11. Key themes such as cultural sensitivity, customer-orientation and customization are developed in Chapter 12, and illustrated in Chapter 13 which explains how Hilton International developed their pioneering Japanese service brand. Finally, Chapter 14 explains and illustrates how effective organizational design enables both specialization and integration between corporate and operational levels of strategic planning.

During the 1980s Trusthouse Forte continued to strengthen its UK and overseas market position so that by mid-1991 the group operated some 8,500 outlets in over 30 countries. In anticipation of further international development, a new corporate name (Forte PLC) was announced to coincide with its new hotel brands and collections. The initiative was also designed to communicate the size, diversity and strength of the Forte portfolio. Chapter 10 focuses on the strategy for 'building on strength' which Forte PLC intends to pursue during the 1990s. In particular, it examines how the strategy has been used to focus an extensive hotels portfolio in preparation for further international development.

The process of multinational corporate evolution relating to key issues in structural planning (such as competitive strategy, market development, and cultural sensitivity with respect to both clients and labor forces) is of fundamental importance to international development. In this context, Chapter 11 focuses on the study of corporate design strategies ranging across geographic regions and segments of the hospitality industry. The chapter is divided into three parts, beginning with a review of the basic principles of organizational design and the underlying variables influencing organizational structure. The second part relates topical issues in organizational design to global, societal and cultural factors which are of interest to hospitality firms. The final part evaluates the general manner in which hospitality companies enter the international marketplace and concludes by considering the strategic implications for designing an appropriate and effective corporate structure.

Creating a customer-oriented hospitality organization is a strategic issue – too often customer service is viewed as a tactical problem that can be solved by periodic training courses. To succeed, the firm's culture, structure and reward system must support customer orientation. This viewpoint is endorsed in the industry foreword to Chapter 12 which explores the interactions between the organization, the environment, the employee and the customer to show how a service-oriented culture, flowing from a hospitality company's mission statement, can be implemented and maintained. The chapter presents three strategies for creating customer-oriented organizations based on the extent of uncertainty a firm chooses to resolve and the degree of perceived customization a firm will offer. The implications of the approaches are discussed in relation to organizational structure, communication and customer-service program design.

Cultural sensitivity, customization and service innovation in organizational design are some of the key issues raised in Chapters 11 and 12. Since its acquisition by Ladbroke in 1987, Hilton International has become the most profitable international hotel company in Japan. In October, 1991, Hilton launched 'Wa No Kutsurogi' service, a pioneering Japanese service brand via a network of about 40 participating Hilton hotels around the world. Chapter 13 examines the rationale and the process involved in researching, developing and implementing a customized hotel services package for the worldwide Japanese business and leisure travel market.

If organizations are to respond effectively to their markets, it is essential that they are designed to facilitate both specialization and integration on strategic-planning matters. Chapter 14 begins by outlining and comparing the strategic-planning approaches currently used by a sample of US hotel companies at the corporate (or business) level and at the operational (or unit) hotel level within the same companies. The purpose of this analysis is to show how planning differs at these two levels, how planning at one level relates to the other and how planning at both levels can and should be interrelated. This analysis provides a strong link with Part 4 which is concerned with issues relating to effective organizational performance.

Richard Teare

10

Building on strength at Forte PLC: A structure and strategy for the 1990s

Rocco Forte
with Richard Teare

During the 1980s Trusthouse Forte, the UK's largest hotels and catering company, continued to strengthen its position through expansion in the UK, continental Europe, and North America. By June 1991 the group was operating some 8,500 outlets in over 30 countries, and in anticipation of further international development, adopted a new corporate name, Forte PLC, to coincide with the launch of its new hotel brands and collections. The initiative was also designed to communicate the size, diversity, and strength of the group's portfolio by emphasizing the Forte name in relation to the unique range of choice which it offers. Major business interests include:

- A broad hotels portfolio, from economy to deluxe classifications.
- A range of branded restaurants, spanning the UK popular catering market.
- An international contract food services business.
- A large airport services business supplying meals and other services to airline operators.

The strategy for 'building on strength' which Forte PLC intends to pursue during the 1990s aims, among other priorities, to focus on opportunities for international development Particular emphasis will be on Europe, where the single market offers good prospects for expansion from a UK base. The intention of this chapter is to examine how the strategy has been used to focus the group's extensive hotels portfolio using a series of brands and collections, each embodying a distinct set of characteristics and each appealing to particular customer needs.

The concept of a new brand structure for Forte PLC

The decision to redefine the group's identity arose from a sustained period of development in the 1980s, during which time the nature of the group had been progressively changing too. In reality, this meant that certain parts of the group were much bigger than they had been at the beginning of the 1980s and it had become increasingly apparent that a stronger and clearer corporate identity was needed. Accordingly, research began in order to examine the possibilities for presenting the group's products to the various market segments that they serve in a way which could be easily communicated to customers, which would in turn make the business more efficient to manage, both from the point of view of selling to our customers and in terms of the internal operation of the business. This goal stimulated a range of activities including discussions with customers and broadly based market research which provided certain guidelines for the internal debate which followed, during which the group's structure and strategy for the 1990s was formulated.

As the initial research took place, it became evident that a corporate rebranding initiative was needed so as to consolidate the group's achievements by projecting its strengths and capabilities more effectively. Although numerically Forte PLC has the biggest hotel portfolio in the UK, it had not been optimizing the associated advantages, as rival companies operating better focused hotel brands were succeeding in taking a proportion of market share. It was therefore imperative to react, and the challenge of achieving better product market positioning provided the incentive and the impetus for change.

This posed the question of how best to brand the distinctive hotel products and, at the same time, link them together in an effective way. Among other options, it involved considering whether 'Forte' should be used as an endorsement, or as part of a brand name. Ultimately, the compelling reason for linking 'Forte' with the brand name was that it would unify the separate and distinctive hotel brand types in the portfolio. The concept was reinforced by the international benefits of using 'Forte', which in Latin languages means 'strength'. In practice, the relationship of the hotel brand to the Group has been emphasized by the new signage displayed on all properties. It is essentially bolder and clearer, giving prominence to the corporate logo and the brand type using easily identifiable and memorable color schemes and designs.

Defining the new brand structure

The intention of the rebranding initiative was to define clearly what each brand offered, to communicate the key benefits so that customers fully appreciate the differences, and to assure the consistency of the offer at every establishment throughout the group. The process necessitated a rigorous review of the kind of personality that each hotel brand should portray, and so the services, facilities and amenities common to each brand type had to be prescribed. Having achieved this, the focus on these fundamental issues has been maintained. This involves regularly reviewing the brand framework, which is made up of the cluster of benefits which are on offer, the associated service delivery costs and pricing, and how they relate to the other Forte brand categories and rival brands in the marketplace. Clear definition and focus can be maintained only by imposing the discipline of a regular review of these issues, and in so doing, operating structures and associated expenses can be refined in accordance with what customers are willing to pay for the brand type. This also helps to ensure that a sensible basis for market-led dynamic change is established in every hotel and that complacency in customer service is prevented.

The Forte hotel brands feature purpose-built modern hotels with each brand catering for a different set of customer needs by providing a different level of facilities and service. The three brands are:

- *Fore Travelodge* – roadside budget accommodation brand offering simple modern rooms conveniently situated along major routes.
- *Forte Posthouse* – a UK chain of accessible modern hotels offering comfortable rooms and good restaurant and meeting facilities at competitive prices.
- *Forte Crest* – a chain of high-quality modern business hotels specializing in personal recognition and service.

The Forte hotel collections differ from the brands insofar as they bring together a range of individual properties, each with its own name, style, and character. Like the brands, each collection aims to cater for a particular set of customer needs. The three collections are:

- *Forte Heritage* – a collection of traditional British inns offering a combination of comfort, personal hospitality, and character.
- *Forte Grand* – a collection of first-class international hotels offering traditional European standards of comfort, style, and service.
- *Forte Exclusive* – a collection of internationally renowned hotels offering the finest standards of comfort, style, and service available.

When each of the hotel brand frameworks had been defined in relation to physical design, facilities, amenities, and service standards, it was necessary to identify hotel properties from the prior network which would benefit from repositioning within the newly defined brand structure. In reality, most of the movement related to transferals between the Posthouse and Crest chains.

The new-style Crest brand offers business users enhanced quality and service which is best suited to the most recently constructed Crest hotels and some of the properties which had previously been operated as Posthouses. Differentiation between the two was reinforced by reducing the Posthouse tariff prices to reflect the changes which had been implemented, and adopting the American practice of charging a rate per room rather than per person. In this respect, Forte Posthouse has been instrumental in forging a change in UK pricing policy, as this approach has not been favored in the past.

The research also highlighted that a number of the services which hotels routinely provide are under-utilized, and as part of the process of focusing the hotel products more clearly, careful consideration was given to ways of enhancing the value for money that customers receive. In the case of Forte Posthouse, the lower tariff reflected a reduction in the cost structure of the business, achieved by reducing service levels in some areas and removing room service altogether. This has been replaced by utilizing the revenue-earning capacity of the public areas more fully, in particular the new Posthouse lounge facility which is designed for the service of snacks and refreshments. It is notable that, since implementing the reduced tariff, Posthouse occupancy levels have shown a marked improvement at a time when UK hotel occupancies have been static, suggesting that customers do perceive enhanced value for money.

The process of refining operational guidelines and policies throughout the group has enabled a greater emphasis on replicating consistency in relation to the different types of business and the characteristics which identify every establishment with a given market position. At the present moment, consistency is easiest to achieve in the budget segment of the market because the design concept is standardized and the service element comparatively limited, so it is possible to achieve 100 percent consistency with Forte Travelodge. A prior quality audit of the American Travelodge properties was undertaken at a time when operating standards were known to be variable, arising from the fact that the properties were not owned by the group. The intention of the audit was to promote a quality drive throughout the network in order to motivate franchisees to undertake refurbishment and other work needed to attain a consistent standard and competitive position in a mature marketplace. This initiative was essential to protect the Travelodge brand image at the time, and was successfully completed. The next step is to introduce the new Forte Travelodge signage, during which a further refinement of operating standards will take pace in order to achieve a sharper focus in a market which is characterized by increasing hotel product differentiation.

Although Forte Posthouse properties will not converge from a design viewpoint as there are many existing hotels of varying age, consistency will be achieved by creating a bedroom design with similarities in standards of décor, fixtures, and fittings. The levels of service will be similar throughout the Posthouse chain and the restaurant operation will be the same in menu terms. Overall, this approach will create the same consistency of product and a given level of service. Coupled with this, new operating methods will be explored and the expectation is that this work will facilitate a 95 percent level of consistency across the Forte Posthouse chain.

Appraising the organizational impact of change

Beginning with the announcement of the 'building on strength strategy' in June 1991, completion of the new brand structure was scheduled to take two years, as the work relating to the hotel businesses in particular was extensive. This was reflected in the greater level of awareness and involvement of the top management teams of the respective hotel brands and collections at the planning stage. Consequently, the amount of information available during the early stages of the exercise and the level of understanding of the kinds of change that would take place was greatest among managers and staff working in hotels than elsewhere in the group.

As managers and staff were aware of the reasons for changes, they gave rise to fewer expressed concerns or anxieties at the operational level. Inevitably, day-to-day business continued in much the same way as it did before the exercise began, so the people directly involved in operations were, in that sense, least affected. Ultimately, the rebranding meant that a simpler structure was created for the hotel manager to operate within. This was due to the fact that, in defining each hotel brand, it was necessary to clarify operational policies and procedures. Subsequently, general managers have a better understanding of what they are being asked to do, how they are expected to perform, and how they will be appraised against clearly specified criteria. This means that the general manager's role is actually better defined, and therefore easier, as the ambitious and active manager is more easily identifiable in relation to the critical success factors which have been established for each hotel brand type.

Inevitably, an exercise of this scale and importance can run into difficulties associated with issues such as the approach taken, resistance to change from within, or concerns about the possible impact on the organizational culture. For these and other reasons, it would not have been advisable to implement strategic change of this kind until top management was convinced about the right course of action to take. To some degree, risks can be minimized by attempting to anticipate problems, and in this context it is important to ensure that the right messages about change are communicated throughout the organization. This means ensuring that lines of communication are carefully established so that sources of anxiety and ambiguity are quickly identified and defused, and that signals which might be interpreted as a return to an older, more comfortable, and familiar culture are prevented.

It is therefore important to sell new ideas with consistency and clarity, and to implement them using fresh and innovative methods. If effectively planned, the internal communication process has its own momentum, yet it is important to recognize that there will always be some people who are unable or unwilling to adapt to change. Sadly this is an unfortunate reality which does contribute to labor turnover, an unpleasant side effect for any company which is loyal to its employees and receives loyalty in return.

Implementation

To prepare and plan for implementation in a way which would be easy to monitor, it was first necessary to develop an action program which identified the critical points in relation to completing certain changes by deadline dates. An important aspect of implementation was the refurbishment program, which had been agreed and started some time before the 'building on strength' strategy was announced. Refurbishment of hotel bedrooms was linked to new model standards that had been, or were in the process of being, finalized for each brand and collection type.

The most visible aspect of implementation was the change of signage, which, preceded by a signage audit, was the single biggest task to complete. In effect, this meant examining external and internal signs in order to determine the optimum number of replacement signs needed and the most prominent positions in which to locate them. The signage work was originally scheduled for completion over a twelve-month period, although the majority of the work was completed in ten months. As printed material and literature also has an immediate impact, the planning and coordination of this work had to be undertaken well in advance of the announcement too. Although the critical path for the production of new brochures, stationery, and other material had been carefully considered, the rationalization of print and promotional materials in relation to the planned changes produced an initial cost saving of £1.5 million. This was an unexpected return on investment, which reflects the simpler and more closely integrated structure of the group arising from the overall concept.

Following the June 1991 Annual General Meeting at which the corporate name change had been approved, two conferences were organized to clarify the rationale and explain the implementation plan to all of the group's senior executives. Each division of the group then held its own conference, involving the divisional managing director, directors and senior managers. In addition to this, a 'key communicators' program was established to reach people at all levels of the organization via an information pack which included an audio-tape featuring the chief executive and others explaining the benefits of the strategy.

To assist with the internal communication process, a special pack was developed to facilitate a cascade down to the individual unit level, whereby the unit manager could take staff through a board game designed to highlight the practical impact of the strategy. The pack was also translated into other languages for the benefit of overseas staff, ensuring that all parts of the group had equal exposure to the planned communication from the top through each formal line of the organization. The cascading of informantion about the strategy and its practical implications resulted in positive and constructive feedback as well as an encouraging number of suggestions on ways of improving aspects of the business. These were beneficial outcomes which have demonstrated the value of planned communication on key issues and iniatives, thereby reinforcing the desire to plan and mount similar internal campaigns more regularly in the future.

A structure and strategy for the 1990s

The new brand structure and strategy aims to:

- Enable the group to exploit fully the unique competitive edge provided by the collective strength, diversity, and choice that it provides.
- Help the group to establish a clear position in expanding international markets.
- Help to develop a common purpose by creating a closer association between the group and its core businesses.
- Create opportunities for cross-selling and more effective marketing.
- Make it easier for people at all levels within the organization to understand and to demonstrate the contribution that they can make.
- Ensure the continued success of the business and increased profitability.

The most significant implication of the new brand structure, in operational terms, has arisen from the discipline of defining the operational standards for all types and levels of business activity within the group as clearly and precisely as possible. Previously, the degree of tolerance had been wider, and so variations in operating standards were inevitable. This undesirable source of variety has been removed by defining brand standards for all aspects of product specification and delivery. Accordingly, this makes it much easier to identify and take action against substandard performance, as the organization as a whole is much more focused on achieving performance and quality targets in every division of the business. This inevitably has benefits for the customer, who is able to see the differences which are being achieved in relation to the product specification and the greater consistency of operating standards.

Inevitably, it will be difficult to quantify the specific outcomes of the 'building on strength' strategy until such time as all conversion work has been completed and plans to expand the international presence of the group are fully operational. However, the group as a whole is already benefiting from the impact of greater consistency in all its communications. There is also a better sense of structure and cohesion arising from the perception that the group has taken a dynamic step forward by emphasizing the importance of the developments that lie ahead. Increasingly, these will involve international developments, and the sharper focus of the group portfolio has already proved advantageous in dealing with overseas developers and other agencies.

A priority for the 1990s is to develop the group's overseas presence, which had become too reliant on the UK economy. International expansion had progressed slowly, in part because of the group's preference for freehold hotel property ownership. The lower density of hotels, the availability of suitable sites and properties, and the greater flexibility which is emerging from harmonization in the European Community underline the excellent prospects for firms like Forte PLC with a sound financial base. In conjunction with hotel-led international expansion, rationalization of the group is set to continue, with the possibility of fewer product lines, each with international development potential. A sharper operational focus brought about by fewer, international products will also enable the center to take a more active role in supporting divisional initiatives. The 'building on strength' strategy has signaled a more flexible approach including numerous joint venture initiatives in Europe and elsewhere and a willingness to consider management contracts for hotels that the group does not own. In this context, the hotel brands and collections have an important role to play in the international development which is destined to make Forte PLC a global hospitality company in the 1990s.

11

Comparative corporate structures and design

Bonnie M. Farber
and Preston D. Probasco

The overall goal of this chapter is to describe the process of multinational corporate evolution in the hospitality industry. In the first section of the chapter we set forth the basic principles of organizational design in a generalized discussion of the core variables underlying organizational structure without specific reference to the hospitality industry or cultural context. Next we identify key developments in the area of organizational design that relate to the global, societal, or cultural contexts of interest to hospitality firms. We will employ specific examples to enhance this discussion and to anchor this chapter more tightly to the hospitality industry. Finally, we will evaluate the general manner in which hospitality companies enter the international marketplace and will make recommendations for future strategic implementation as it relates to corporate structure.

Core variables underlying organizational structure

Unique to this chapter is the focus on corporate structure and design. Since these terms are so often used interchangeably, it is crucial to the discussion that we clearly define these terms and the scope of inquiry for understanding the relevant frameworks and analytical tools. For our purposes, and in concert with common usage in the organization theory and organization behavior disciplines, organization design is a major subset of the more inclusive pattern or structure that gives meaning to recurrent activities in an organization, such that design becomes planned structure.

Organization theory then is the most relevant discipline for enabling managers to comprehend their particular organizational situation. And it is precisely that comprehension or perspective that is such a necessary first step toward effective management and control. Moreover, while the levels of analysis relevant to organizations are the individual, department (group), organization, and environment, organization theory concentrates on the organization, group, and organization–environment relations. The hierarchical levels most relevant here are the institutional and managerial levels as opposed to the operational (employee) level. We are therefore interested in the goals and strategies that the top management (institutional level) has for the critical transactions that an organization makes with its environment, as well as the welter of interrelated concerns middle management has with, for example, the specialization, coordination, resource allocation, conflict, power, and technology of major departments within the organization.

Consequently, one can find at least eight structural dimensions for almost any organization. Moreover, there are four additional contextual dimensions which exert a significant effect on the eight structural dimensions, and which are also necessary to understand the organization. The four contextual dimensions that have a major impact on these eight structural dimensions are the goals, technology, and size of the organization plus the relevant environment of the organization. The eight structural dimensions that can be driven by these are complexity, specialization, hierarchy of authority, standardization, formalization, professionalization, centralization, and personnel ratios. Once these have been properly accounted for in an organization, managers must then make explicit their assumptions and inferences (i.e. their model or theory) about what patterns govern all twelve variables. Approximate sequencing of the eight structural dimensions will be one such pattern we will explore. At a more general level, the realization of the potential interrelatedness of all twelve core variables drives managers toward models that will simplify but not trivialize these interaction effects.

Organization theorists who have tried to track these modeling attempts by practitioners and academics usually find at least rough contingency frameworks that capture the essence of these interrelationships. Central to most of these frameworks or meta-theories is the realization that, since there is no one best way to organize in all situations, the best structure and design will be contingent upon the organization's size, technology goals, etc. Thus tight, mechanistic control of various Canadian plants of Continental Can has been appropriately associated with low product differentiation, stable market forces, borrowing from financial institutions which demand no surprises, a routine production technology, internal marketing functions being driven by the priorities of the production function rather than vice versa, a rigid budgeting and planning system along with reliance on a strong production control department to make the trade-offs between quality, delivery, and cost – all supported by a friendly, 'macho' French-Canadian culture. Being able to appreciate the appropriateness of such mechanistic controls when organic, more participative controls are perceived as more normative, is made possible by such a contingency perspective.

Much of the application of the contingency perspective has been guided by a framework that first directs attention to the alignment between the organization and its environment, and then looks at the relative balance internally between formal organizational arrangements, the informal organization (group controls and climate), and the individual as contingent upon the key task technology characteristics. Nadler and Tushman's (1977) version is reproduced in Figure 11.1 to afford us a bird's-eye view of some of the more

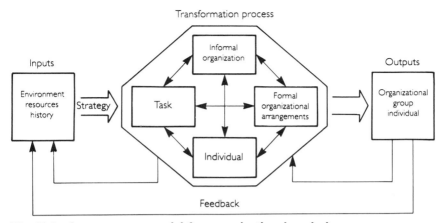

Fig. 11.1   A congruence model for organizational analysis
Source: Nadler, D. A. and Tushman, M. 'A general diagnostic model for organizational behavior: applying a congruence perspective' in Hackman, J. R. and Porter, L. W. (eds) *Perspectives on Behavior in Organizations*, New York, McGraw-Hill. Copyright 1977. Reprinted with permission of McGraw-Hill, Inc.

recurrent contingency/congruency issues that one can expect to encounter. At the same time, this framework implies a more or less natural progression of attention to the twelve core variables from left to right.

Generalizable alignment propositions for structuring organizational life

As we have indicated, there are natural ways of sequencing a firm's attention to the eight structural and four contextual dimensions of organizational life that in turn should prepare the firm for more informed choices between competing forms of departmentalization, varying degrees of decentralization or autonomy and/or participative management, corporate and business-level strategy formulation, and degree of ownership of overseas investments.

The pre-eminence of strategic concerns over competency and implementation concerns

Direct evidence that being relevant and correct in strategic direction is more important for the firm than competency can be seen in the case of the divestiture of non-airline and non-steel businesses by Pan Am and US Steel. Oversold on the 'stick-to-your knitting' advice from Peters and Waterman (1982) – since confirmed to apply mostly to middle management motivations (Leontiades, 1986) – both of these conglomerates experienced greater net losses after their divestiture of unrelated holdings. This also points up the danger of over-generalizing between institutional (top management, strategic) and managerial (major sub-unit, middle management) levels. The prescription first to be effective, then to be efficient is directed primarily to top management, who must absorb the responsibility for the overall success of the firm.

To the extent that being efficient is tantamount to being competent in how resources are utilized, competency is a necessary but insufficient contribution to the firm's overall success or effectiveness. In this sense of competency as doing the thing right, being strategically relevant and correct for the near and far-term market conditions can certainly be furthered by ensuring that the firm's competency matches what the market wants, thus giving rise to a distinctive competency. But as Kimberly and Quinn (1984) and others have shown, there is no guarantee that the market will continue to conform to what the firm is capable of. Thus we end up with such truisms as the need to keep reviewing what the market demands and how the firm can achieve competitive advantage in one or two of the following while being in the ballpark on all five: (1) cost, (2) quality, (3) reliability and dependability, (4) flexibility, and (5) innovativeness.

Pfeffer and Salancik (1978) have alerted us to the danger that the environmental surveillance so necessary for re-identifying the opportunities and threats in the external environment can be severely compromised by the combination of top-level complacency with the 'executive ascendency' pattern (e.g. 'apple polishing') of junior-level managers who give more attention and support to how their superiors view the environment than to what they can discover for themselves.

Functional differentiation and selective standardization

Strategy formulation should certainly include the previous organizational theory concerns relating to the establishment of a firm's overall goals and mission as well as to the development of strategic planning at both the corporate level (i.e. what combination of business units and product lines/services make up a coherent business portfolio) and the business level (i.e. how to compete effectively in any given business unit). Much of this is covered more completely by other authors in Parts 1 and 2 of this book. The remainder of this chapter concerns itself with the use of managerial and organizational tools to direct and allocate resources to *implement* strategic objectives.

Strategy implementation (the overall structuring of organizational life) utilizes the tools of organization technology, design (especially departmentalization), control systems, decision-making processes (with their attendant political processes), corporate culture, and human resource management. Upon review of all of the alignment propositions pertaining to the above in roughly this order, the firm should have a fairly comprehensive perspective for achieving both the internal efficiency (competency) and innovation necessary to support overall corporate effectiveness.

The first such internal alignment proposition deals with the organization's production/service process and pertains mostly to the way tasks are organized to transform organizational inputs into outputs. In the field of organization behavior we call this *organization technology*. Referring to Figure 11.1, after strategy this is the next logical linkage between an organization and its environment. It acts as a constraint in much the same way as strategy does for an organization's internal response to its environment, since it is primarily an internal reflection of whatever it takes strategically to succeed in the environment. Probably the most generalizable reality in organizational technology is the need to reflect internally both the complexity and the instability of the organization's environment. The general systems term 'requisite variety' states that the internal regulatory mechanisms of a system must be as diverse (or somehow accounted for) as the environment with which it is trying to deal. Conversely, any system that insulates itself from diversity in the environment tends to atrophy and lose its complexity and distinctive nature.

The most essential task of the organization at the outset, then, is to differentiate itself internally (specialize by function and work orientation) in order to account for relevant environmental and strategic pressure. As the complexity of the environment increases, we can expect an increase in both internal differentiation and the attendant need to coordinate this increasing internal diversity. The pressure to coordinate activities will be compounded by yet another environmental pressure: namely, increasing instability in how stakeholders such as suppliers, customers, government regulatory agencies, and competitors are acting. In order to cope with both internal variation in the form of increasing differentiation and external variation coming from a complex external domain of stakeholders, an organization must find appropriate forms of standardization (the extent to which similar work activities are performed in a uniform manner) in order to regain some measure of coordination and thus some semblance of control. Formalization usually increases along with standardization as procedures, job descriptions, regulations, and policies all have to be documented. What will then worry the architects of this organization is how to maintain the necessary internal adaptiveness to changing demands from internal and external sources without tripping over the previously installed controls.

Critical interdependencies and appropriate integrative mechanisms

Given that most mediocre companies chronically underestimate coordination costs (Peters and Waterman, 1982), it would be unfeasible and wasteful of managerial energies to try to coordinate work for its own sake. And yet organizations have needlessly and naively signed up for matrix organizational designs and teamwork seminars with the result that they wear themselves out over-managing a situation that was never properly diagnosed in the first place. Thus it helps to first determine the *necessary* nature and extent of the interdependence required by the organizational technology. Pooled, sequential, and reciprocal interdependence require in turn increasingly more involved integrative mechanisms. For low levels of interdependence where departments do not have to interact directly with each other to contribute to the organization (i.e. pooled interdependence), rules and standardization are adequate. For the kind of sequential interdependence where the outputs of one department become the inputs to another, careful planning is needed to assure the suitability of timing, quality, and even transfer pricing between departments.

Finally, mutual adjustment and many more unscheduled face-to-face discussions will be required to resolve joint problems accompanying the exchange of information and resources simultaneously in both directions (i.e. the reciprocal interdependence common in hospitality firms). As a general rule, higher levels of interdependence should receive priority in the resulting design (departmentalization) in order to reduce errors of coordination. At the same time, the exact functions or products/services that require coordination should receive the highest priority. While cross-functional coordination is a critical need for a hospitality organization, the exact functions (and their particular geographical location) that require the most *mutual adjustment* should get the top priority in the final organization design (departmentalization) chosen to relieve bottlenecks and reduce decision-making delays and errors.

The degree of decentralization and the nature of the compartmentalization

Not only must a firm be careful to balance its focus on *internal* concerns regarding the efficiency and well-being of employees with the overall *external* competitiveness of the organization itself with respect to its environment, but its planned structural emphasis must reflect the needs for stability and flexibility (Quinn and Rohrbaugh, 1983; Quinn and Cameron, 1983). If adaptation and growth externally are combined with internal opportunities for employee autonomy and development, the organization is opting more for flexibility and becomes known as a relatively organic system with a more decentralized structure (Burns and Stalker, 1961; Zaltman *et al.*, 1973). In contrast, when an organization's primary emphasis is on productivity, efficiency, and profit achieved in a controlled way, it is said to be more mechanistic and is usually characterized by more centralization. What drives a firm toward either extreme of centralization or decentralization is ideally its corporate strategy and goals, as well as the related contextual variables of environment, technology, and size.

Provided top management's assessment of the environment is strategically relevant and correct, the kind of routine technology (tasks) associated with less complex, stable environments usually benefits from a more mechanistic, centralized system, while the more complex tasks and their coordination deriving from changing, complex environments require a higher degree of interdependence (reciprocal) and the kind of organic, decentralized system that is more capable of the myriad of mutual adjustments needed. More often than not there evolve various blends of centralization and decentralization within any given organization. Adaptive companies use bureaucratic controls in some areas and loose clan control in others. Thus, while informal clan control is helpful in engendering involvement and commitment, tighter controls monitor the bottom-line performance of divisions.

Encouraging people to work together both vertically and horizontally is greatly aided by a tailor-made organization design. Daft's (1989) guidelines, shown in Figure 11.2, reflect most of the conventional wisdom for reducing role ambiguity and linking functions and products or services into a meaningful system.

Political accountability for the effective use of conflict

All of the preceding prescriptions for designing organizational structure carry with them enormous potential for conflict, particularly as they influence the arrangement of power relationships. That this conflict may be necessary more often than not does not make it any easier. Unhealthy corporate cultures tend to avoid the very conflict of ideas and programs that promotes high-quality decisions and innovation. Consequently, one should beware of formal or

Fig. 11.2 Daft's guide for organizational designers

1. Develop organization charts that describe task responsibilities, vertical reporting relationships, and the grouping of individuals into departments. Provide sufficient documentation so that all people within the organization know to whom they report and how they fit into the total organization picture.
2. Provide vertical and horizontal information linkages to integrate diverse departments into a coherent whole. Achieve vertical linkage through hierarchy referral, rules and procedures, planning and scheduling, levels added to the hierarchy, and vertical information systems. Achieve horizontal linkage through paperwork, direct contact, liaison roles, task forces, full-time integrators, and teams.
3. Choose between functional or product (self-contained units) structures when designing overall organization structure. Use a functional structure in a small or medium-sized organization that has a stable environment. Use a product structure in a large organization that has multiple product lines, and when you wish to give priority to product goals and to coordination across functions.
4. Implement hybrid structures, when needed, in large corporations by dividing the organization into self-contained product groups and assigning each function needed for the product line to the product division. If a function serves the entire organization rather than a specific product line, structure that function as a central functional department. Use a hybrid structure to gain the advantages to both functional and product design while eliminating some of the disadvantages.
5. Consider a matrix structure in certain organization settings if neither the product nor the functional structure meets coordination needs. For best results with a matrix structure, use it in a medium-sized organization with a small number of products or outputs that has a changing environment, and which needs to give equal priority to both products and functions because of dual pressures from the environment. Do not use the matrix structure unless there is truly a need for a dual hierarchy and employees are well trained in its purpose and operation.
6. Consider a structural reorganization whenever the symptoms of structural deficiency are observed. Use organization structure to solve the problems of poor-quality decision making, slow response to the external environment, and too much conflict between departments.

Source: Daft, R. L. *Organization Theory and Design*, pp. 249–50 (3rd edn), 1979, St Paul, Minnesota, West Publishing Co. Reprinted with permission of West Publishing Co.

informal organizational arrangements that emphasize autonomous, heavily bounded departments and that deter creative interaction among organizational members.

The preconditions for power or influence all derive from environmental uncertainty and include: (1) heterogeneity of functions and personnel; (2) disagreement over both goals and the means for achieving those goals; (3) increasing decentralization and the resource dependence of sub-units; (4) personnel changes that involve promotions, transfers, and hiring outside expertise; (5) interdepartmental coordination that is not that well defined or definable; and (6) structural change. Basically, to the extent that organizational decisions affect different organizational groups pursuing different sub-goals with different time horizons, attitudes, and environmental constituencies, such political processes as coalition building provide a mechanism to negotiate and reach agreement among several managers whose ideas and cooperation are needed for implementation. Consequently, abdication of influence and conflict avoidance become the major political problem. Since the experience of managers with conflict and power issues may have been negative, conflict avoidance may have become a self-preservation habit and they may be blinded to the necessity of using influence tactics such as internal and external networks, controlling decision premises, persuasion, coalition formation, and legitimate and expert power bases. And for those of us who are just garden variety character disorders looking for ways to avoid unnecessary entanglements with others, the problem of power and politics boils down to the stress accompanying unfulfilled expectations of our position titles or of key players in the organization. Its solution is as varied in style as the personalities and culture of the organization.

Capitalizing on the corporate culture to maintain commitment and focus

Corporate culture represents the evolution of values, beliefs, and understanding that are shared by members of the organization and that give the organization a measure of distinctness in terms of competitiveness and focus. While top management is responsible for the culture, it cannot control the culture according to the easy recipes for solving managerial problems that many management writers offer. While managers can influence the evolution of culture by being aware of the symbolic consequences of their actions and by intentionally fostering desired values through ceremonies and rites and sharing accomplishments, the culture itself is much more a pluralistic result than a solo transformational leadership accomplishment.

Cosier and Schwenk (1990), Eisenhardt (1989), and others have recognized that conflict in the top management team is critical to forging a unifying strategy and vision from a variety of perspectives within the company. Moreover, the unifying properties of the vision derive from the tangible, unifying direction provided by customers. A strong customer relationship in turn was hammered out with full attention to conflicting expectations in one example from a large airline and its large customer (i.e. travel agents and personnel in charge of corporate travel). Here Tjosvald and Wong (1989) found that it was very important to the travel and business people that the sales representatives dealt directly with their problems and concerns. Conversely, customers felt frustrated and lost confidence in being effectively served when the sales representatives dealt with issues in a rigid way or failed to listen. Isadore Sharp, Chairman of Four Seasons Hotels, also seems to be supporting a conflict-positive organizational culture both internally and externally: 'you have to be sincere when dealing with people, and that includes the public and your employees' (Tjosvald, 1991). Finally, ownership and thus the power to define and change the culture extends beyond 'mahogany row'. Employees will not only help shape or refine the corporate vision, but also question its nature and impact upon their own group norms.

This employee involvement will inevitably carry with it more potential for conflict, but it is also essential for organizational commitment and focus in the *process* of exploring and at least partially resolving differing sentiments and viewpoints. As Block (1981) and other organization development practitioners have found, substantial latent energy is available to be shifted away from reactive to more positive norms if these lower-level participants are given the opportunity to identify the nature and significance of the norms to which they have tacitly agreed.

While a strong, environmentally correct corporate culture is a positive force for implementing the strategy of a company, and as such can fill some of the gaps left by the incompleteness of the formal organizational structure (departmentalization), we would be remiss not to call attention to the way the corporate culture can 'enact' its environment. Companies attempt to organize their environment in much the same general way as they organize their internal operations, even though their internal operations are more easily controlled since other organizations are also trying to shape the environment.

Organizational environments therefore become interactive cultural extensions of the organization, since members of the focal organization come to interpret and understand their environment through their beliefs and values. Thus the complexity and instability of an organizational environment is a product of this process of enactment, and consequently should be subject to relatively more control by any given organization. This is important for the purpose of our prior insistence upon adapting strategically to an environment that was somehow formed exclusively by other organizations. This realization can be important in understanding (1) that an organization may have created its own problems by way of the influence it has had on the environment, and (2) that organizational members can play a more important part in the subsequent construction of the environment of customers, suppliers, government regulatory agencies, competition, etc. The effects of multinational hospitality firms on the infrastructure, social institutions, and financial well-being of host countries are a prime example of this phenomenon.

A balance between efficiency and innovation

The age-old dilemma posed by the development of a strong corporate culture that has enjoyed congruence with its environment and may also have become a proactive industry leader is that the organization may not have built in the capacity to change its culture along with its structure and strategy in time for a shifting environment, such as that involved in expansion abroad. In order to deal with the related dilemma of thus needing both the stability to allow efficient production processes and the change required for innovation and adapting to the environment, the *ambidextrous model of change* (Duncan, 1976) distinguishes the initiation of innovation from its implementation. Organic, free-wheeling conditions are used for initiating new ideas, while more rigid, mechanistic characteristics are more suitable for the implementation and operation of the new techniques. Maintaining both conditions requires that some or all of the organization is assigned to the organic, creative process. Then either the organization reverts back to a more mechanistic process (selectively 'freezing' what was a chronically unfrozen organic organization, as Weick (1977) observes) or other parts of the organization take responsibility for using and institutionalizing the innovations.

This may take the form of establishing new venture teams, creating separate innovation departments, encouraging idea champions, and switching structures either from a customarily organic one to an occasionally mechanistic form or vice versa. Encouraging the initiation of change while also maintaining a stable and efficient operation by way of these techniques may still run sufficiently afoul of a very strong culture which only rewards the organic or mechanistic extremes. Then it may be only feasible to subcontract out the missing element. At the very least, then, an organization must distinguish between the *administrative* changes that normally follow a top-down process facilitated by a mechanistic organization structure, and *technical* or *new product* change which follows a bottom-up process enabled by a more organic structure (Damanpour, 1987). Hopefully the administrative changes will facilitate rather than obstruct non-trivial technical and new product innovations.

A final structural perspective for organizations attempting to maintain a balance between efficiency and innovation involves what Lawrence and Dyer (1983) call 'readaptation'. Simply put, the probability of an organization achieving both innovation and efficiency is increased when the organization aligns itself with its environment in such a way as to survive and grow with intermediate levels of both uncertainty and resource scarcity. The complexity and variability of the external elements influence the extent of the information-gathering and processing burden that the organization must carry, while resource scarcity is an assessment of the difficulty the organization has in procuring needed resources. Internally, the organization needs a *balance* of bureaucratic and clan controls to assure an equal emphasis on efficiency and innovativeness.

While clan controls focus on developing a sense of community which hopefully is used to emphasize the value of innovativeness as a norm and thus as a key part of the corporate culture, bureaucratic controls reward the efficiency emphasis. Thus if an organization continues to function in a changed environment as if its old methods and structures were appropriate, the organization acquires too little or too much information (overload) on the variations of all the environmental domains and will then experience either resource scarcity or overabundance with the result being decreased efficiency in addition to the initial lack of innovativeness. The implications of this model of strategic readaptation are varied, but basically the organization must stay nimble or opportunistic enough to move to a new market niche and/or proactively to enact mutually beneficial changes in its relationships with suppliers, customers, government regulatory agencies, and/or competitors. This perspective of readaptation leads us forward into the following discussion of how hospitality corporations engage in alignment activities with the greater global environment.

Organizational design in the global environment

The preceding section of this chapter identified core variables that could be used to describe any organizational structure, regardless of geographic or cultural context. In addition, several principles of organizational design were identified in order to clarify the normative guidelines existing for business firms to plan organizational structures that will maximize their rates of survival and growth. These principles of organizational design were set forth in order of their ideal application sequence to provide the reader with a prescriptive model of organizational learning and design based on adaptation to a continually changing environment. We now concern ourselves with how this general model of organizational design may be used to support a firm's decision to enter the wider international marketplace and to meet the challenges of foreign environments.

Cheng and Ramaswamy (1989) argue that 'firms differ in the extent to which they conduct their system functions across national boundaries' (p. 106). Using Georgopoulos (1970) and Katz and Kahn (1978), they depict a model for organizational systems that assumes organizations (1) acquire resources from the environment, (2) convert these resources into products or services through a work-process subsystem, and (3) export these products back to the environment in exchange for new resources to input into the system. Cheng and Ramaswamy then suggest 'that an organization may find it beneficial to perform some or all of its system activities in one or more foreign countries, either in addition to or in place of those performed in its home nation' (p. 107). To label a hospitality firm as multinational is thus to presume that all or part of its system functions are conducted outside its country of origin. This is the definition of multinational hospitality corporation or firm that we employ in this chapter.

The question of which foreign countries firms select to enter first when internationalizing is directly related to the firms' perceptions of the benefits to accrue through this process of internationalizing. In his 1988 study of the market penetration practices of franchising systems, Welch suggests that early foreign targets are those which exhibit (1) high per capita income, (2) a highly developed retail service sector, (3) cultural similarity (except Japan), and (4) proximity, thus providing to the firm the potential of high market shares and revenues with minimal adaptation headaches. Welch goes on to describe 'second stage countries' as those having greater cultural, income, and political differences from the franchisor's home country. As we will see in later examples, these second stage countries may initially entice firms to enter through an array of tax or political concessions that offset the disadvantages listed above.

The present discussion of multinational corporations and structure assumes a comparative cross-cultural perspective that suggests that multinational corporations from different countries of origin exhibit measurable structural differences. We do not attempt to seek an 'ideal' corporate structure for every hospitality corporation entering foreign markets. Societal contexts of the countries or nations where their operations predominate (Boyacigiller and Adler, 1991) influence corporations too greatly to ignore the effects of societal culture on business firm design. On the basis of evidence from current reports of hospitality industry practices, we argue that multinational corporations exhibit different structure types as they originate from different national sources with different societal norms. Also, when a corporation decides to cross its national borders and to expand outside its country of origin, the resultant organizational structure is influenced additionally by the corporation's need to adapt to its new foreign environments. The objective of this section is to examine how corporations respond to these competing forces from both countries of origin (home countries) and countries into which they expand (host countries).

Alignment with foreign environments

Nadler and Tushman's (1977) congruency model for structuring organizational life identifies four critical inputs that affect organizational design: the environment, prior history, the need for resources or inputs into the work process system, and the strategy of the firm that determines the initial manner in which the firm approaches the environment. As remarked upon in the introductory section of this chapter, being relevant and correct in one's strategic direction is vital to the success of the firm.

Becoming a global player in the international hospitality marketplace may be conceived of as a corporate goal, but it is not exactly a strategic goal. Strategic goals relate to the achievement of survival and growth as measured by market share, and various return on investment measures. To expand internationally, a hospitality company must perceive some benefit that adds to the value of the firm, such as increased profits, increased brand image, or improved customer satisfaction. Upon assessing the advantages of international expansion, and once decided upon entry into one or more foreign destinations, the hospitality firm must then align itself with the new foreign environment in such a manner that it can assure itself of requisite inputs, reasonable work process efficiency, and sources of consumption for its output products and services. The first question of interest after the decision to expand into a particular foreign destination is: what will be the appropriate mode of entry or level of ownership?

Ownership patterns and contractual arrangements

As they expand into foreign destinations, hospitality firms need to decide how much ownership in the foreign operation they desire to retain. This may be a function of the level of investment funds they have to contribute to the equity base of the new foreign enterprise; on the other hand, it may also relate to the firm's history of preferred ownership levels deriving from a specific cultural value system. Multiple ownership forms among hospitality corporations have surfaced; they vary from high ownership/risk to low ownership/risk as follows: (1) one corporation owning several hotels or restaurants; (2) a parent company holding individual subsidiaries owning hotels or restaurants; (3) joint ventures where the division of ownership is agreed upon by the two parties involved; (4) a management company that operates hotels but does not generally own real property; and (5) franchise systems providing methods, technical assistance, and marketing to investors in hotels or restaurant property (Gray and Liguori, 1990). In the USA, domestically based hotel firms are characterized by an increasing movement towards management contracts: that is, the separation of management and ownership roles. This is deduced from a comparison of *Lodging Hospitality*'s 'Chain reports' for December 1990 and August 1991: hotel companies show a trend towards reducing the number of company-owned properties and increasing the number of management contracts.

Although levels of ownership are influenced by the firm's financial resources and specific control goals, other moderating variables come into play when firms move abroad. Gatignon and Anderson (1988) have suggested that firms entering countries with high levels of political risk tend to seek lower levels of ownership control; this could relate to the firms' anticipation that the host governments may suddenly alter national investment rules without providing adequate recourse to foreign investors. Thus we see that host governments greatly impact upon the level of ownership a firm will achieve within the host country. Host government responses can vary from the extreme of nationalizing all hotel or restaurant enterprises to extending open invitations to expatriate firms to set up shop and to enjoy substantial tax advantages and subsidies. Hungary has sought to attract foreign investment by eliminating the need for government approval of foreign investments in Hungarian firms (Benke, 1991). Czechoslovakia has changed its laws to allow 100 percent foreign ownership of local companies in the hope of increasing the presence of multinational hotel companies in those destinations (Delia-Loyle, 1990).

A key concern of hospitality chains moving into foreign destinations is their ability to develop supportive relationships with host country governments which may be suspicious of foreign investors' motives. In order to respond to the control needs of host governments, especially in developing countries, many firms are turning to the joint venture method of doing business abroad. The joint venture provides a flexible and cooperative contractual arrangement that satisfies the host government by providing partial or total ownership and a percentage of profits either to the government itself or to localized national firms.

A sample breakdown of 1991 Soviet versus foreign contributions to joint ventures exemplifies the various roles partners might play in shared ownership ventures:

- 38 percent of Soviet partners invest mostly money;
- 22 percent of Soviet partners provide property (land, buildings) and the rights to use of natural resources;
- 59 percent of foreign investors provide machinery and equipment;
- 20 percent of foreign investors provide money;
- 12 percent of foreign investors provide technologies.

Such agreements enable Soviet firms to import equipment and expertise without raising hard-currency funds or begging for credits. Their foreign counterparts are spared the burden of paying for premises and materials. (*Arguments and Facts International*, 1991, p. 51)

From a lodging perspective, US hotel corporations often agree to some form of reduced ownership contractual relationship with a foreign investor or developer in order to move as quickly as possible into targeted foreign development sites (Bell, 1989). The joint venture method of expanding into destinations such as Asia, Europe and Latin America was preferred by 68 percent of 200 lodging executives representing US companies, whereas direct acquisition strategies were preferred by only 24 percent of the sample (*Lodging Hospitality*, 1991b).

The financial structure of Euro Disneyland is a case in point. Euro Disneyland was developed and financed by two joint venture companies, Euro Disneyland SCA and Euro Disneyland SNC. Euro Disneyland SCA was created to own and operate developments under license from Walt Disney, which will hold 49 percent of the equity, with the remainder distributed on the Paris, Brussels, and London stock exchanges. The other owning company, Euro Disneyland SNC, finances the project, leasing the assets to SCA. French companies own SNC and a small portion (17 percent) is owned by Walt Disney. The SNC partners will borrow heavily from the French government at favorable terms, will take all losses, passing them on to the owners as tax write-offs, and will also depreciate the assets over a ten-year period. In twenty years the fully depreciated assets will be sold to SCA, and SNC will be dissolved (Wrubel, 1989).

Western European firms entering Third World countries also choose the joint venture form of ownership. Travelodge, a division of Forte hotels, for example, has struck an agreement with Asahoteles Ltda. and with Hoteles

Ltda. to create a partnership called Hotels Travelodge de Sudamerica Ltda. to facilitate its expansion into Latin America (*Lodging Hospitality*, 1991b). Austria's IAEG provides finance and management in a Soviet–Austrian joint venture called Intertrust involved in hotel construction using Western methods (*Arguments and Facts International*, 1991, p. 31).

US foodservice corporations also show a marked tendency toward the use of joint venture strategies when exploiting opportunities in exotic hospitality markets. McDonald's unit in Moscow was contracted as part of a joint venture to build at least twenty units, where the Moscow City Council's foodservice division would own 51 percent and McDonald's Restaurants of Canada would operate the units with a minority ownership of 49 percent (Maney and Rinehart, 1990). This willingness to accept reduced ownership status reflects a market penetration strategy focused on structure because investor George Cohon prized entry into the Soviet Union over ownership issues (Foster, 1991).

Many of the examples cited above involve expansion into countries whose governments heavily monitor the ownership forms of firms primarily in order to retain national involvement in local hotel and restaurant properties. In direct contrast, foreign firms find the US government's expectations regarding ownership participation quite minimal. This enables firms from countries such as the United Kingdom, France, and Japan to use creation, mergers, and acquisition strategies with maximum retention of ownership of hospitality enterprises located in the USA. Where host country pressures on ownership participation are low, Western European and Japanese firms seem to prefer higher levels of ownership participation. According to Lehrman (1989), retention of family control and security of the family estate were values in England that caused the large corporation business form to develop more slowly in England than in the USA, with the paramount result that 'ownership often remained private, allowing for business policies designed to achieve a mixture of organizational and kinship oriented goals' (p. 20). The Forte hotel chain is a prime example of the power of the family hotel company in the UK.

Research has been published on the motives of equity investors from Japan who choose to purchase hotel property. According to Hara and Eyster (1990), equity investors are motivated by: (1) strategic objectives, (2) pride of possession, (3) the value of the yen, and (4) the shortage of land in Japan. It is obvious that societal values relating to the possession of real estate affect the decision to retain or relinquish ownership in the hotel firms. Next we will examine the manner in which another societal force, societal authority systems, impacts on the structure of multinational hospitality corporations.

Societal authority systems and organizational design

Referring once again to the Nadler and Tushman (1977) congruency model of organizational life, we note that organizational history is depicted as a critical force shaping the organization as it seeks to manage the information complexity of the environment. Entry into a host country environment often means entry into a society whose basis for formal assignment of authority and power is different from that of the firm's country of origin. In the western hemisphere alone there are significant national differences in patterns of authority relationships among organizational members. Managing the intricacies of new markets and technological adaptations often exceeds the time and resources available during the firm's foreign expansion efforts. This means the structures that emerge in multinational corporations most usually reflect the underlying societal patterns of authority and hierarchy common to the corporations' countries of origin (Maurice *et al.*, 1980). This replication of firms' authority systems in the host country allows firms to move in rapidly, as soon as a foreign destination shows promise of market viability and financial returns agreeable to the interested investors. The expansion of hospitality corporations abroad has often relied on the replication of historical home country authority systems.

It is appropriate at this time to discuss some of the major differences in the formation of authority systems from a cross-cultural perspective. We will limit our comments to a select list of countries that exemplify world regions (North America, Western Europe, and East Asia) where major multinational firms have located hospitality businesses.

The USA and Canada regard organizations as sociocultural systems that need to be flexible in structure. This central concept for the design of business organizations encompasses the 'flexible, organic type of bureaucracy that values a participative humanitarian philosophy over and beyond the industrial-based mechanistic structures advocated by scientific management theorists' (Lammers, 1990, p. 194). US design theorists advocate restructuring organizations as multiple work teams with porous organizational boundaries, where leadership can emerge naturally and change over time as different expertise is needed to solve a variety of environmental challenges. The American concept of leadership is predicated on the assumption that owners and managers (leaders) need not be the same individuals. This basic separation of roles is a byproduct of the act of incorporation whereby the US legal system ratified this new form of business organization in order to reduce the personal risk to operators in the business arena.

Historically, the evolution of organizational structure in Western Europe took a different path. In organizational theory circles of the UK, a popular design focus was the 'pluralism' approach, which stresses a highly bureaucratic organization where authority is tightly held by a central office. Organizational development methods in the UK were heavily biased toward an acceptance of closed-boundary independent sub-units and members, and the need for methods to buffer and control relations between these separate parties.

Hall and Hall (1990) describe French authority as highly centralized, and French society as highly stratified in terms of social class-based networks that provide information-sharing opportunities for network members. French organizational theory concentrates on the actors or interest groups in centralized bureaucracies and their ways of accruing resources and ultimately gaining power from the barter of information. French managers need to be expert boundary spanners in order to move upward in the organization. The use of participative forms of work groups or decentralized decision making was not a focus of French organizational design; in business schools French managers are taught to protect independent thought at the cost of learning to be a team player. Hospitality companies moving into France may need to adapt their concepts of team and consensus decision making until the French managers and employees can be persuaded or motivated to share information instead of bartering it. French companies such as Accor and Meridien tend to retain ownership of their hotel properties as a mode of doing business abroad, and make principal decisions from their French offices.

In Germany, Weber's legacy, the bureaucratic structure, has been stated to be ultimately fair in that its formalized rules presume equitable supervision and treatment of organizational actors. German firms distribute power from the top down in a hierarchy of many layers, with a highly formalized procedural system that is resistant to change (Hall and Hall, 1990). Long-term plans are made by top officials and then passed down the technical authority system. German firms rely on a decentralized phase conducted by appointed department managers who essentially make decisions behind closed doors, as opposed to the decision team and matrix form of decentralization that is increasingly evident in US and Japanese companies. According to Hall and Hall (1990), 'fewer structural means of integrating the various divisions of German firms exist which in turn impedes the flow of information' (p. 41). And as American businesses are quite accustomed to changing their strategies in line with environmental forces, they have a high need for short-term reports to feed them a constant source of information for decision making. German firms are accustomed to less rapid change and provide evaluation reports on a less frequent basis. Companies expanding into Germany may need to devote additional resources to setting up a reporting function within the structure of their normal departments.

These varying positions on authority and hierarchy can be used to explain why multinational corporations originating in the USA and Canada provide for more decentralized decision making than multinational corporations originating from parent countries such as France, Germany, and the United Kingdom. For example, McDonald's corporation permits corporate executives based in Paris to determine the primary strategies for expansion and penetration into the French marketplace, whereas managers of French hotels in the USA receive strategic missives from the French corporate headquarters.

The frequent US reliance on expansion through franchising, contrasted with the French and British merger and acquisition strategies, also demonstrates the underlying commitment of US corporations to highly decentralized organizational formats. Welch (1988) states that 'the business format franchising system was pre-eminently developed in the US and grew rapidly there in the 1950s and 1960s. Although the focus of growth at the outset was domestic, with successful domestic expansion the attraction of foreign markets became more valid' (p. 7). Welch then suggests that since 'the US has long been the home of franchising it is now increasingly viewed as having a receptive environment for foreign franchisors to enter the US market' (p. 10).

Additional insight for the design of multinational hospitality corporations may be gleaned from the results of research on East Asian business systems. According to Richard D. Whitley (1991), 'distinctive forms of business organization have become dominant and successful in Japan, South Korea, Taiwan and Hong Kong; they reflect historical patterns of authority, trust and loyalty in Japan, Korea, and China' (p. 2). In his study, Whitley describes how the issue of authoritative coordination and control may be used to discriminate East Asian business systems.

Japanese society traditionally assigns prestige or status to individual managers more on the managers' expertise in particular business disciplines than on estimations of their personal or political ties. The role of education and academic degrees from recognized Japanese universities is paramount in the selection of managers for Japanese firms; careful selection enables top management to have confidence in decentralizing decision making through delegating functional control to lower-level managers.

In order to provide a convenient backdrop for managers to exhibit their expertise in business functions, Japanese firms tend to be larger with highly differentiated, functionally based subdivisions. Their choice in hotel sites has been primarily that of the upscale large luxury hotel type: they own 6 percent of that market in the USA (*Lodging Hospitality*, 1991c).

Also, Japanese society clearly distinguishes between the investor (owner) whose role is financial lender and controller, and the manager whose role is the efficient allocation of resources in the production of high-quality products or services. As the principal expression of Japanese authority is through functional business acumen, Japanese managers choose to exhibit their mastery of functional operations through extensive formalized policies and procedures that are impersonal in nature. Although US corporations also use manuals of formalized operating procedures, the US practice developed in response to scientific management's call for task specifications to control worker individuality, and has been modified greatly by the behavioral management schools.

Extending the discussion of East Asian business structures, we now turn to firms in China and Korea. Authority in China and Korea derives most often from one's position in family and political party networks: deference to managerial authority figures is extracted from subordinates on the basis of their response to the personal characteristics of family and party leaders. Ownership is not perceived as comfortably separate from management of Chinese or Korean enterprises. Chinese or Korean businesses tend to rely on an interpersonal networking model that restricts the size of firms in these countries and visibly translates into the proliferation of small businesses abundant in countries where Korean and Chinese immigration is high.

Non-Asian hospitality companies have been expanding into Southeast Asia like wildfire. These hotel companies have constructed luxury hotels that sit in stark contrast to the guesthouses typical of those countries. The joint venture properties arising in Beijing have suffered considerable operational difficulties due to conflicting Western and Chinese command philosophies. According to Stross (1990), the generally low productivity of Chinese staff members means that an international hotel in China needs almost 'twice as many employees for a given number of guest rooms as a comparable hotel outside China' (p. 306). Stross also remarks that 'Chinese supervisors are reluctant to use their authority over their colleagues' (p. 310) and 'Chinese who headed board of directors of joint ventures were known to bypass the foreign general manager completely and give orders directly to the shadow structure of Chinese deputies that created a dual management system in the hotels' (p. 327). In this case, the transfer of the classical Western authority structure into the Beijing hotels created as many environmental problems, especially by offending local government officials, as it intended to resolve.

As we have seen in the preceding discussion, the effects of national authority and power systems on multinational hospitality corporation expansion into foreign destinations are considerable, and firms seeking to expand into new countries should isolate the key authority systems that will be interacting with home country authority systems in order to reduce potential bottlenecks in the operation of the firm abroad. At this point, we turn to a discussion of the third force on organizational life described by Nadler and Tushman – resources.

Resource availability as an issue in organizational design

Especially critical is the degree to which sufficient host country infrastructures exist to provide requisite inputs into the task system. As hospitality corporations enter geographic locations that may not have existing suppliers of commodities necessary for the food production goals of those corporations, they increasingly seek linkages with local agencies and national agricultural offices to ensure basic supplies such as the availability of transportation services or locally farmed produce that measure up to the quality standards of the hospitality corporation. Identification of adequate raw material channels judged by the criteria of quality, consistency, availability, and cost has long been a preliminary step in the decision process to take a foodservice chain into a new international market (Go and Christensen, 1989).

The linkages that foodservice corporations form with local agencies range from outright vertical integration through the creation or acquisition of local transportation or agricultural firms to the establishment of joint ventures with local suppliers who service all units in a locale as part of their investment obligation. McDonald's operation of a giant food-processing center outside Moscow allowed it to ensure the pasteurizing of raw milk inside that country (Maney and Rinehart, 1990); this exemplifies the manner in which corporations will integrate vertically to enhance their access to critical resources.

An interesting byproduct of creating sources of raw materials in Eastern Europe is the potential for replacing Common Market beef and other produce with materials from Eastern Europe. The Eastern European countries are more willing to allow McDonald's to export soft commodities than hard currency (Black, 1988).

Comparative modes of compartmentalization

As hospitality organizations grow and expand overseas, the issue of how they compartmentalize their activities becomes increasingly complex. The basic tenet is that environmental uncertainty is reduced by the assignment of scanning tasks to specific departments or organizational members who can keep abreast of subset environmental forces and feed information into the firm's strategic planning process. Firms must differentiate their tasks and products sufficiently, and create subdivisions that can specialize and standardize their operating procedures for increased efficiency. Organizational design theory has provided for several basic formats for grouping organizational activities: (1) by function, (2) by product lines, and (3) by technological process. Functional departmentalization is the norm at the unit level of the typical hotel and restaurant organization. At the corporate level, the operative philosophy seems to be product segmentation. Technological process is not a basis by which hospitality companies compartmentalize.

Most corporations holding hotel or restaurant chains nowadays have multiple subsidiaries, each of which individually represents a distinct product segment of the hospitality or service industry. Holiday Corporation has segments such as Holiday Inn, Holiday Inn Crowne Plaza, and Garden Court Holiday Inn; Forte has Travelodge, Travelodge Hotels, Thriftlodge, and Forte Hotels that meet the needs of different target markets. An interesting note is that many hospitality corporations combine segmented divisions with other types of compartmentalization with no apparent strategic design mission. For example, ITT Sheraton Corporation changed its format from a division based on franchise versus management contract groups to a product segmentation structure based on upscale and midscale segments. Choice Hotels International has redistributed its segmented Economy and Sunburst hotel groups into five geographic regions.

One corporation that made a planned effort to restructure on the basis of product segments is the French-based corporation Accor with no fewer than 38 different product groups hitting almost all possible target hospitality markets. Each product group is led by its own general manager who must conform to the budget and financial expectations of the central office.

To gain increased perspective over the hospitality firm's decision to differentiate its operations within the context of the global environment, we introduce Cheng and Ramaswamy's (1989) systems typology of multinational firms that portrays eight different profiles of international involvement in a firm's operation (p. 107). Firms range in this typology from those whose resources, work process, and outputs are entirely located in one country to those who conduct all of their systems functions across national borders.

Hospitality firms that internationalize can choose several methods of international involvement. Domestic hotel corporations often set up sales offices in foreign countries to market domestic properties to tourists from other countries. Other approaches, common in manufacturing industries, require actual operating facilities to be set up outside the home nation, using domestic raw materials and selling to either domestic or foreign clients. Manufacturing corporations can often place a production factory abroad, while operating other departments, e.g. research and development and marketing, in the home country. This is especially common when the primary consumer markets are still domestic, and the objective of entering the foreign country is to lower material production costs by using cheaper local labor. However, the creation of lodging facilities abroad typically requires inputs from the new country as well as attention to the needs of local clients. The approach of internationalizing all three hotel system components (inputs, process, and outputs) takes into consideration the need to service the locale clientele surrounding the hotel or restaurant unit set up in a foreign destination. Hospitality corporations planning expansion into foreign territories no longer assume that mere replication of the home concept abroad will suffice. Nowadays a focused strategy of defining market segments within the foreign country is being applied.

Regionalization on a geographic basis is an additional design strategy when corporations wish to reduce the span of control over multiple sub-units by assigning regional managers to head regional offices. The corporations may also need to overcome the time costs and logistical difficulties of operating sub-unit hotels or restaurants in locations that are quite distant from each other. Geographic regions are traditionally based on political, economic, and logistical issues, often resulting in a national subsidiary structure. Ronen and Shenkar (1988) identify two advantages of regionalization:

- Products and services are adapted to a region's particular needs and can correspond more readily to consumer demands.
- A regional organization is superior in its response to different customs regulations affecting work and sales patterns, different monetary systems, rates of exchange and tariffs – in short, to many different legal, economic, and social constraints. (p. 34)

The division of corporations into geographic regions will occur most often at levels below the segmented product divisions. For example, the new Formule 1, an economy lodging concept started in France by the Accor chain, has expanded into Belgium, the United Kingdom, and Germany. Regional development managers have been hired to oversee each regional development effort.

At times, as in the acquisition of US economy lodging chains Motel 6 by Accor, and Travelodge by the Forte corporation, a new division may represent both a new product segment and a new region for the corporation. This serves to reinforce the focus strategy of parent corporations seeking acquisitions that provide products appropriate to the market niches existing in the new geographic location, instead of assuming that replication of home concepts into new foreign markets would lead automatically to successful ventures. Accor has made a critical decision not to introduce the Formule 1 economy lodging concept into the US market due to its conclusion that its particular minimal frills modular construction lodging product would not appeal to the US budget traveler.

The structural format of the multinational hospitality firm most in evidence comprises a reasonably identifiable combination of the eight structural dimensions: complexity, specialization, hierarchy of authority, standardization, formalization, professionalization, centralization, and personnel ratios. This format consists of a hierarchically structured organization with subdivisions based on a combination of function, product, and regional specialization (see Figure 11.3). For the most part, each division is heavily standardized with rules and practices being formalized for all operating procedures. The home country has the primary influence on these formal structural dimensions. However, it is the host country that most markedly affects levels of professionalization, centralization of decision making, and personnel ratios of hotel and restaurant sub-units.

Critical internal and external interdependencies

As we have determined previously, multinational hospitality firms exhibit hierarchically based structures that divide into sub-units based on a combination of functional, product, or regional concerns. Given that these divisions exist, we now turn to the issue of how to achieve appropriate levels of integration of these different divisions. When we step back from the limited picture of what a typical multinational hospitality firm's organizational chart looks like, we note a vast network of interdependencies or linkages. These linkages fall primarily into two categories: (1) internal linkages between divisions or actors inside the firm; and (2) linkages between the firm, its divisions, or its actors and external agencies in the environment. A discussion of working relationships becomes paramount at this point.

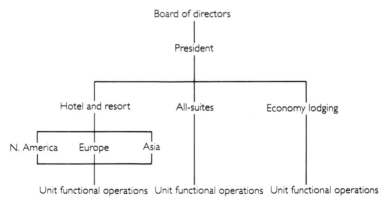

Fig. 11.3 Organizational chart for a multinational hospitality firm

Working relationships exist or should be developed among many subgroups in this picture of the hospitality business and its environment. Externally based linkages are exemplified by the interdependencies existing between:

- the firm and its clients
- the firm and its distributors
- the firm and its suppliers
- the firm and its subcontractors
- the firm and its competitors
- the firm and its owners
- the firm and other agencies in the environment

Internal linkages occur within and across divisions and may be formally designated in the structure, or may arise informally as a natural emanation of human involvement. We need to point out, however, that the principal interest in these linkages relates to their effects on the business system of converting inputs into outputs through a work process system. In this light, we can describe the linkages in terms of sharing (1) system inputs or resources, (2) work technology, or (3) system outputs or rewards. In addition, the sharing can be short term or long term depending upon the cultural forces on the firm and its actors.

As our primary goal here is to examine how hospitality firms may be described in terms of international or cross-cultural variables, we will focus next on the degree to which different countries have formalized social trans-actions that enable members of firms to share resources, technology, or rewards. The USA is a country that exhibits a number of formalized sharing practices with respect to resources. Formal marketing functions have been institutionalized to identify the will of the consumer, and formal personnel departments exist to share the challenges of union–management relations, affirmative action concerns, and benefits package designs that meet employee needs. Information is bought and sold for new business ventures through contracts made with accounting firms that specialize in hospitality market analyses. What so strongly characterizes these formal sharing practices is the tendency in the USA to facilitate the transfer of information between parties on the basis of short-term, low-context, low-trust interactions (Hall and Hall, 1990) and usually for a predetermined price. Another factor that facili-tates the sharing of systems components among US-based agencies is the degree of diversification of US businesses, so that US firms more closely represent the entire business sector, rather than one narrow industry segment.

In contrast, Japanese businesses operate as domain specialists that prefer to grow within industries rather than through diversification into other business domains, which is the more common US entrepreneurial mode of growth. Because Japanese companies tend to focus internally within industries, they require extensive long-term formal linkages with highly trustworthy sub-contractors to gain new technology and supplies (Whitley, 1990). Most often, Japanese firms need to be convinced that a plethora of trustworthy support firms exist to provide supplies and contractors before they will commit to establishing a foothold in a new industry; they prefer to import their own supply firms when a host country permits. Japanese firms expanding into the hospitality arena seek inclusion within well-defined marketplaces (such as the USA) where relationships among the firm and its major supplier or consumer groups can be constructed through traditional social exchange mechanisms.

France is another interesting culture with regard to the sharing of resources. The social class system that underlies the French business hierarchies also provides French businesspeople with critical information networks that are built upon social and friendship ties, rather than business-related transactions. This makes information sharing in France a very politicized activity that requires entry into social circles as a basis for success.

Obviously, these examples are not all-encompassing, but they should serve as a reminder to the hospitality firm doing business abroad that sharing mechanisms differ in each national context, and that design efforts may be required to be successful in accessing or disseminating resources, technologies, or rewards.

Normative design strategies: a cautionary note

In this final section, we examine the potential areas of conflict resulting from inattention to the principles of organizational design outlined at the beginning of this chapter. Our analysis of the expansion of multinational hospitality corporations within the global arena has led to an isolation of several critical design factors that may impact on the effectiveness of the multinational hospitality firm:

1. The degree of careful planning in joint ventures.
2. The level of attention to the cultural forces impinging on regionalization.
3. The firm's ability to coordinate across regions as national subsidiaries mature.
4. The firm's willingness to develop a globally minded workforce.

Point 1 is of interest due to the ever-increasing number of joint ventures emerging as a way to do business in the international hospitality arena. Recommendations to firms considering joint ventures for any of the reasons outlined earlier in this chapter must include the following:

- Clearly define target markets for entry into a locale.
- Establish independent goals for the joint venture firm.
- Define levels of equity participation.
- Define levels of profit sharing.
- Determine the exact period of the joint venture.
- Establish the exact buyout procedure.
- Establish levels of confidentiality and trust.
- Include a break-up clause for unforeseen circumstances.

Successful joint ventures normally require: (1) partners to be complementary, not competitive; (2) a decision process that is simple and fast; (3) high levels of comfort and trust on both sides; and (4) a commitment to excellent products or services (Go and Christensen, 1989).

The second point made above refers to the fact that firms generally regionalize on the basis of factors such as political or economic similarity, or proximity. Ronen and Shenkar (1988) argue that regional formats based on these factors result over time in increasingly divergent national interests and operating procedures. These authors call for firms to 'create a regional distribution that will both maximize the structure's benefits and minimize its disadvantages' (p. 34). They urge firms to 'create regional divisions that share meaningful cultural attributes, e.g. employee attitudes, work-values, languages, and even religions' (p. 34). More work needs to be done in this domain, but hospitality firms can benefit from examining the assumptions they are making when establishing their regional divisions on the basis of economic similarity or proximity.

Point 3 raises the question of how to coordinate regional or national subsidiaries effectively. The head office of a multinational hospitality firm influences new subsidiaries by centralizing decision making; these decisions may involve choice of location, definition of target markets, allocation of resources, etc. Due to the natural process of organizational learning that takes place over time, national subsidiaries become less and less dependent on the head office for expertise in management, especially if the local environments are vastly different culturally from that of the head office. Yet at the same time, head offices must seek to retain strategic control of local units in order to develop strategies for global marketing, global quality management, and global executive development. This requires the head office to gain the cooperation of subsidiaries in different geographic locations in order to meet these global needs.

How then do multinational hospitality firms maintain a portion of strategic control over subsidiaries that are no longer highly dependent on the head office for strategic resources or managerial expertise? Prahalad and Doz (1981) address this phenomenon by calling on the multinational firm to seek influence over subsidiaries by creating a sophisticated organizational context comprising organizational structure, information systems, career planning, and a fostering of common firm culture.

Their conceptualization of this change from substantive control to control through organizational context is depicted in Figure 11.4. Their suggested repertoire of administrative mechanisms to carry out a strategic shift from substantive control over resources to control through organizational context includes:

● Data management mechanisms.
● Managers' management mechanisms.
● Conflict resolution mechanisms (Doz and Prahalad, 1981, p. 16).

The final area where we feel compelled to make observations about the future of the multinational hospitality firm relates to the issue of the

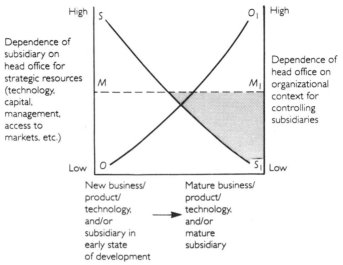

Fig. 11.4 Schematic representation of shifts in the control mechanisms in the head office–subsidiary relationship over time
Source: Reprinted from 'An approach to strategic control in MNCs' by Prahalad, C. K. and Doz, Y. L., *Sloan Management Review*, vol. 22, no. 4, pp. 5–13, by permission of the publisher. Copyright 1981 by the Sloan Management Review Association. All rights reserved.

development of a globally minded workforce. Lo (1990) calls for attention to be paid to the development of managers with a global perspective. They must be sensitive to change and willing to transfer among nations. Often local managers come from geographical and cultural realities quite distinct from those of the major stakeholders in the corporation. This may require that the staffing policy be specified in corporate structures such as joint venture contracts. Host country nationals need to know that positions are reserved for them as well as for expatriate executives (Shenkar and Zeira, 1990).

In summary, we have examined throughout this chapter the subject of organizational theory and its answers for the issue of structural implementation in multinational hospitality corporations. After considerable discussion of the need to seek appropriate designs for hospitality firms operating in the global environment, we conclude that much attention must still be paid to careful scrutiny of the foreign countries which firms choose to enter, and that appropriate structures must be sought that will facilitate both efficiency and innovation.

References

Arguments and Facts International (1991), vol. 2, no. 5.
Bell, D. (1989) 'US chains leave home', *Lodging Hospitality*, vol. 45, no. 7, pp. 46–8.
Benke, G., and Webb, D. E. (1991) 'Foreign investors still welcome in Hungary', *International Financial Law Review*, vol. 10, no. 3, p. 9.
Black, L. (1988) 'Hamburger diplomacy', *Report on Business Magazine*, pp. 30–6.

Block, P. (1981) *Flawless Consulting: A guide to getting your expertise used*, University Associates, San Diego, CA.: Learning Concepts.

Boyacigiller, N. A., and Adler, N. J. (1991) 'The parochial dinosaur: organizational science in a global contex', *Academy of Management Review*, vol. 16, no. 2, pp. 263–90.

Burns, T., and Stalker, G. M. (1961) *The Management of Innovation*, London: Tavistock.

Cheng, J. L. C., and Ramaswamy, K. (1989) 'Toward a systems typology of multinational corporations: some conceptual and research implications', *Academy of Management Best Papers Proceedings*, pp. 106–10.

Cosier, R. A., and Schwenk, C. (1990) 'Agreement and thinking alike: ingredients for poor decisions', *Academy of Management Executive*, vol. 4, pp. 69–74.

Daft, R. L. (1989) *Organization Theory and Design*, 3rd edn, St Paul, Minnesota: West Publishing Co.

Damanpour, F. (1987) 'The adoption of technological, administrative, and ancillary innovations: impact of organizational factors', *Journal of Management*, vol. 13, pp. 675–88.

Delia-Loyle, D. (1990) 'Venturing still uncertain for Soviets and Czechs', *Global Trade*, vol. 110, no. 11, pp. 36–9.

Doz, Y. L., and Prahalad, C. K. (1981) 'Headquarters influence and strategic control in MNCs', *Sloan Management Review*, vol. 23, no. 1, pp. 15–29.

Duncan, R. B. (1976) 'The ambidextrous organization: designing dual structures for innovation', in Killman, R. H., Pondy, L. R., and Slevin, D. (eds) *The Management of Organization*, vol. 1, New York: North-Holland.

Eisenhardt, K. M. (1989) 'Making fast strategic decisions in high-velocity environments', *Academy of Management Journal*, vol. 32, no. 3, pp. 543–76.

Foster, P. (1991) 'McDonald's excellent Soviet venture?', *Canadian Business*, vol. 64, no. 5, pp. 51–65.

Gatignon, H., and Anderson, E. (1988) 'The multinational corporation's degree of control over foreign subsidiaries: an empirical test of transactions cost analysis', *Journal of Law, Economics, and Organization*, vol. 4, pp. 305–36.

Georgopoulos, B. S. (1970) 'An open system theory model for organizational research', in Negandhi, A. R., and Schwitter, J. P. (eds) *Organizational Behaviour Models*, Ohio: Kent State University Press.

Go, F., and Christensen, J. (1989) 'Going global', *Cornell Hotel and Restaurant Administration Quarterly*, vol. 30, no. 3. p. 79.

Gray, W. S., and Liguori, S. C. (1990) *Hotel and Motel Management and Operations*, 2nd edn, New York: Prentice-Hall.

Hall, E. T., and Hall, M. R. (1990) *Understanding Cultural Differences: Germans, French and Americans*, Yarmouth, ME: Intercultural Press.

Hara, T., and Eyster, J. J. (1990) 'Japanese hotel investment: a matter of tradition and reality', *Cornell Hotel and Restaurant Administration Quarterly*, vol. 31, no. 3, pp. 98–104.

Katz, D., and Kahn, R. L. (1978) *The Social Psychology of Organizations*, 2nd edn, New York: John Wiley.

Kimberly, J. R., and Quinn, R. E. (1984) *Managing Organizational Transitions*, Homewood, Ill.: Irwin.

Lammers, C. J. (1990) 'Sociology of organizations around the globe: similarities and differences between American, British, French, German, and Dutch brands', *Organization Studies*, vol. 11, no. 2, pp. 179–205.

Lawrence, P., and Dyer, D. (1983) *Renewing American Industry*, New York: Free Press, p. 13.

Lehrman, W. G. (1989) 'Social organization, institutional environment and the rise of the corporation in the United States and England', *Academy of Management Conference Paper*, 13–16 August, Washington, DC.

Leontiades, M. (1986) *Managing the Unmanageable: Strategies for success within the conglomerate*, Reading, Mass.: Addison-Wesley.

Lo, Gary (1990) Working paper, Purdue University.

Lodging Hospitality (1990) 'Chain report', *Lodging Hospitality*, vol. 46, no. 12, pp. 77–80.

Lodging Hospitality (1991a) 'Lodging today', *Lodging Hospitality*, vol. 47, no. 6, p. 14.

Lodging Hospitality (1991b) 'Lodging today', *Lodging Hospitality*, vol. 47, no. 7, p. 16.

Lodging Hospitality (1991c) 'Investment today', *Lodging Hospitality*, vol. 47, no. 8, p. 24.

Lodging Hospitality (1991d) 'Chain report', *Lodging Hospitality*, vol. 47, no. 8, pp. 69–73.

Maney, K., and Rinehart, D. (1990) 'Here comes the Bolshoi mac', *USA Weekend*, 26–8 January, p. 4.

Maurice, M., Sorge, A., and Warner, M. (1980) 'Societal differences in organising manufacturing units', *Organization Studies*, vol. 1, no. 1, pp. 59–86.

Nadler, D. A., and Tushman, M. L. (1977) 'A general diagnostic model for organizational behavior: applying a congruence perspective', in Hackman, J. R., and Porter, L. W. (eds) *Perspectives on Behavior in Organizations*, New York: McGraw-Hill.

Quinn, R. E., and Cameron, K. (1983) 'Organizational life cycles and shifting criteria of effectiveness: some preliminary evidence', *Management Science*, vol. 29, no. 3, pp. 33–51.

Quinn, R. E., and Rohrbaugh, J. (1983) 'A spatial model of effectiveness criteria: toward a competing values approach to organizational analysis', *Management Science*, vol. 29, no. 1, pp. 363–77.

Peters, T. J., and Waterman, R. H. (1982) *In Search of Excellence*, New York: Harper & Row.

Pfeffer, J., and Salancik, G. R. (1978) *The External Control of Organizations: A resource dependent perspective*, New York: Harper & Row.

Prahalad, C. K., and Doz, Y. L. (1981) 'An approach to strategic control in MNCs', *Sloan Management Review*, vol. 22, no. 4, pp. 5–13.

Ronen, S., and Shenkar, O. (1988) 'Using employee attitudes to establish MNC regional divisions', *Personnel*, vol. 65, no. 8, pp. 32–9.

Shenkar, O., and Zeira, Y. (1990) 'International joint ventures: a tough test for HR', *Personnel*, vol. 67, no. 1, pp. 26–31.

Stross, R. E. (1990) *Bulls in the China shop: and other Sino-american business encounters*, New York: Pantheon.

Tjosvald, D. (1991) *The Conflict Positive Organization: Stimulate diversity and create unity*, Reading, Mass.: Addison-Wesley.

Tjosvald, D., and Wong, C. (1989) 'A study of interdependence in the sales relationship', manuscript, Simon Fraser University.

Tsui, J. F. (1991) 'Investment today', *Lodging Hospitality*, vol. 47, no. 2, pp. 36 & 38.

Weick, K. E. (1977) 'Organization design: organizations as self-designing systems', *Organizational Dynamics*, vol. 6, no. 2, pp. 31–46.

Welch, L. S. (1988) 'Diffusion of franchise system use in international operations', *International Marketing Review*, vol. 6, no. 5, pp. 7–19.

Whitley, R. D. (1990) 'Eastern Asian enterprise structures and the comparative analysis of forms of business organization', *Organization Studies*, vol. 11, no. 1, pp. 47–74.

Whitley, R. D. (1991) 'The social construction of business systems in East Asia', *Organization Studies*, vol. 12, no. 1, pp. 1–28.

Wrubel, R. (1989) 'Le Defi Mickey Mouse', *Financial World*, vol. 158, no. 19, pp. 18–21.

Zaitman, G., Duncan, R., and Holbek, J. (1973) *Innovations and Organizations*, New York: John Wiley.

12

Strategies for creating customer-oriented organizations

John Bowen and John Basch

This chapter presents three strategies for creating customer-oriented organizations. These strategies are based on the extent of uncertainty a firm chooses to resolve and the degree of perceived customization a firm will offer. A customer service matrix is used to illustrate these strategies. The implications of each of the three strategies are discussed in terms of organizational structure, communication, and customer service program design.

Creating customer-oriented organizations is no longer an option; it is a necessity. As Theodore Levitt (1976) states, the purpose of a business is to attract and retain customers. For many years hospitality businesses have been concerned with attracting customers, but the emphasis is changing as organizations realize that it takes four or five times as much money to attract a customer as it does to retain existing ones.

> The importance of customer service as a vital success ingredient for business has never been as great as it is now.
>
> The service expectation levels of the consumer have increased dramatically on a global scale in recent times. Companies have identifed service as the key to differentiation in an increasingly competitive market. It is, therefore, economic suicide for any firm to ignore the demands for service made by its own customers. It's the difference between being in business or not. And the key to any move towards service orientation lies in the firm's culture. Without a 'service culture', the organization can never expect to meet its customers' expectations. Too many other constraints (budgets, for example), and a lack of faith from key people, can all too easily unravel the best intentions of any company.
>
> _Mark Stephenson_

Paul Neilsen, president of a retail chain in Queensland, Australia, says that the main objective of his firm is to satisfy his customers and give them what they need. He states that, 'if we develop a loyal customer base, we can sell anything. People will trust us, and they will trust our name – we can move with the trends and they will follow us.' Paul Neilsen realizes the importance of customer satisfaction; that is the basis for his business. He views customers as an important asset of his company.

Rudi Greiner, Chief Executive Officer of Regent International Hotels and former General Manger of the Regent in Hong Kong, claims that the Hong Kong Regent's total commitment to service is the reason that the Regent houses two of the world's best restaurants, Plume and Lai Ching Heen. To help implement his commitment to service, Greiner has developed a sophisticated training center. Besides the two training rooms, the center also houses a language laboratory, a library, and a reading room where employees can read trade magazines. Greiner's commitment to customer service has benefited the Regent Hotel as well as the customer. In 1990 many hotels in Hong Kong suffered a slump in occupancy, whereas the Regent had an occupancy rate in excess of 80 percent and in October ran a 98.6 percent occupancy rate with the area's second highest average room rate of $260. Another benefit of Greiner's customer service is low staff turnover. Ten years after the hotel's opening, all of the top twenty managers hired before the opening were still with the hotel (Walker, 1991).

The question for hospitality organizations is not so much whether they will become customer oriented, but how they will use customer orientation as a strategic tool. One method of focusing a customer orientation strategy is the management of uncertainty. The unpredictability of consumers, the diversity of their needs, and their interaction with service delivery systems are in themselves sources of uncertainty (Bowen and Jones, 1986). Thus to help gain an understanding of customer service strategies and the choices available to hospitality organizations, it is helpful to review aspects of the evolution of organizational responses to uncertainty.

The evolution of organizational responses to environmental changes

Organizations during the era of the industrial revolution (1820–1930) were mainly managed by a single entrepreneur and management was more or less synonymous with ownership, with the founder and his immediate family being the decision makers. Organizations revolved around production and finding more and better technology to increase production further. The internal consistency of organizations was high and structures were stable. Entrepreneurs had little if any interest in government regulations, trade union demands, or consumers. They concentrated their efforts and energies on producing as much as possible, since they could sell all they had produced.

During the mass production era (1930–50) the organizational focus was on output and finding better technologies to increase output further. All that was produced could be sold, but those producers with the lowest price were the biggest winners. To achieve maximum output at the lowest price there were two important organizational developments: the application of science to find new ways of increasing production efficiency, and the development of budgetary management and financial controls. The former allowed an increase in production efficiency, whereas the latter assisted in pricing strategy. The consumer still mattered little. There was a high volume of demand mainly for basic consumer goods and choice was limited. Standardization of production and more efficient distribution facilitated price reductions. Internally the organization remained highly consistent, and scientific management, applied by engineers, became integrated into the production function. Accounting and financial controls became established at the heart of administration and in many instances became the focus for decision making. This separation of the production from the financial function was the first sign of the creation of functional specialization within organizations.

The mass marketing era (1950–70) gave rise to the rapid development of the marketing function in organizations. Firms realized rapidly that to be successful they not only had to produce more efficiently and at a cheaper price than their competitors, but they also had to market their product. The rapid rise of the marketing function has affected the internal consistency of organizations.

The marketing departments gradually became an influential functional area within the firm and, whereas production and accounting were internally oriented, marketing was externally oriented. Long-range planning helped to deal with the emerging internal conflict and the increasing complexity of the marketplace.

The 1970s saw the advancement of differentiation in the marketplace. Market segmentation and new product development became the new tools of marketers, who were attempting to satisfy the rapidly evolving and diversifying demands of an affluent, international consumer market. The prerequisite of differentiation and the successful delivery of the promised goods and services was information. Information was used to differentiate products and to develop a more precise marketing mix. The need for information created another functional role in the organization, that of the information specialist. This in turn increased the potential for internal conflict with existing functional departments.

Strategic planning evolved as the organization's response to the rapidly changing external environment and was based on anticipating rather than reacting to the changes in the external environment of the firm. Strategic planning added a further specialist function to the existing maze of functional specialists within the organization, thereby increasing the likelihood of organizations entering the 1980s facing not only an uncertain external but also an increasingly turbulent inter-organizational environment (Ansoff, 1984).

The environmental uncertainties and turbulence of the 1980s and 1990s are presenting organizations with the challenge of managing change. The challenges of the 1990s are what Ansoff has called strategic surprises; they are rarely predictable, occur over a short period of time, and require immediate action to produce organizationally desirable results. These are the characteristics of the environmental changes currently facing hospitality firms, and must therefore be considered when designing a service strategy.

Organizational approaches to uncertainty

One method suggested by researchers (Keller *et al.*, 1974; Lorenzi *et al.*, 1981) for dealing with environmental uncertainty is the development of internal structures to absorb or reduce it. These researchers imply that uncertainty is an undesirable characteristic of the environment and that it should be reduced. Other researchers suggest that managers may actively search for change and uncertainty (Miles and Snow, 1978). The prospectors in the Miles and Snow typology are managers who seek change. They are viewed as successful managers who are proactive in managing uncertainty. Some firms choose uncertain environments because they perceive that they offer better opportunities and because managers feel that they have the skills to operate in those uncertain environments.

At first glance these approaches to uncertainty appear very different: one involves avoidance or reduction, while the other takes an aggressive, proactive approach to uncertainty. However, the two options are complementary and often work in tandem. Those firms entering environmentally turbulent markets usually employ strategies which absorb and reduce the uncertainty. And hospitality firms engaged in businesses with uncertain environments often use skilled employees, and empower these employees to enable the firm to react to the uncertainty.

Dimensions of environmental uncertainty

Environmental uncertainty can be analyzed along two dimensions: the extent to which the external domains are simple or unstable, and the extent to which they are stable or complex (Daft, 1983). Environmental complexity refers to the number of external elements that are relevant to an organization's operations. In a complex environment, a large number of diverse external elements will interact with and influence the organization. The number of markets, market segments, and products a firm offers all serve to increase environmental complexity. For example, an international hotel chain such as Hilton Hotels operates in many different countries and tries to gain the custom of many different market segments. It operates hotels focusing on the resort market, the gaming market, the corporate market, and the convention market. Its hotels are located in North America, Europe, Asia, and Australia. The information required to manage such a diverse chain is therefore tremendous, and Hilton cannot predict future events with certainty.

Ahlstrom and Andres (1989) provide an example of how the uncertainty caused by lack of information on cultural differences can cause customer problems. SAS offers an evening flight from Singapore/Bangkok to Scandinavia. It is normal practice for the flight attendants to touch the passengers gently to wake them for breakfast, shortly before landing in Europe. To a Thai Buddhist monk or an Islamic religious leader from Malaysia physical contact by someone of the opposite sex is an affront.

International organizations such as SAS deal with customers representing many cultures. To enable its employees to provide better service through an understanding of cultural differences, SAS developed an intercultural communication department. It is impossible to educate employees about every culture with which they may come into contact, but SAS encourages its flight attendants to act with intercultural sensitivity.

The stable–unstable dimension of an environment refers to whether or not the elements in the environment are dynamic (Daft, 1983). A stable environment is one that experiences little change over a period of months. When change does occur it tends to be incremental and to follow trends, so the firm can predict the future with a fair amount of accuracy. The café or diner in a small town is often operating in a very stable environment. It can predict future events fairly well. An exception would be when the local factory closes down, sending the town into recession.

A nightclub is an example of a firm that operates in an unstable environment. It is difficult to build customer loyalty. The product life cycle of a nightclub is often very sharp and emulates the life cycle of a fad. The customers of clubs are often attracted to the newest club. Thus, as new clubs open, there is often little the owner of an existing club can do to retain its customers. In more rural markets where competition is less likely to occur, the environment for a nightclub may be very stable.

Fluctuation in demand is another source of environmental instability. Fluctuation in demand provides a challenge for management in hospitality operations. Most customer complaints in service firms come when the organization is operating at or close to capacity.

Customer-created uncertainty

The introduction to this chapter noted that strategic management has evolved to become an important part of management planning. One strategic choice for firms is to choose a customer orientation that fits its organization. Since customers are a major source of uncertainty, the choice of the customer service orientation also influences the uncertainty of the organization's environment. Hospitality organizations can choose to operate in an environment where transactions with the customer are either certain or uncertain.

Complexity and divergence of service delivery systems

Shostack (1987) popularized the concept of blueprinting service operations. Blueprinting diagrams process the steps involved in a service operation, showing the complexity and points of divergence of a service organization. Complex service operations have many process steps. Shostack measures complexity by the number and intricacy of the steps involved in the service operation. For example, the registration process at a two-story budget motel with one size of room and only two bed arrangements, double-double or king, is low in complexity. The guest walks up to the front desk, is assigned one of the two room types, fills in the registration form, pays by cash or credit card, receives the key, and goes to the room. In a full-service hotel the process is more complex. The people interfacing with the guest now include a door person and a bell person. The assignment of the room becomes more complicated. There may be several choices for parking, such as valet and self-park – both with an additional charge. The desk clerk will explain the services of the hotel to the first-time guest. Thus the process for the receiving of a guest at a full-service hotel involves more steps than at a limited-service hotel.

Shostack refers to divergence as the amount of latitude the employee has in each step of the transaction. Fast-food operations typically have little divergence in their service production processes. They produce standardized products. They do not want their cooks to be creative. In an upscale restaurant the chef produces daily specials, as well as creating off-the-menu requests for guests. The chef of an upscale restaurant has a great deal of latitude which standardization limits. The complexity of the service is reduced by limiting the number of product choices and involving the customer in the service delivery process.

Fuddrucker's provides an example of reducing complexity. Fuddrucker's is a US gourmet hamburger chain that features a condiment bar allowing customers to create their own hamburger. Customers can pile on lettuce, tomatoes, cheese spread, pickles, and an assortment of other condiments. The customers perceive they are getting good value because they can use as many ingredients as they want. The complexity of the service operation has been reduced enough to offset the cost of the extra condiments.

The interface between the customer contact employee and the customer in a hamburger restaurant without a condiment bar adds many steps to the process, as illustrated below.

Normal process
1. The customer asks for the hamburger.
2. The employee asks what the customer would like on the hamburger.
3. The customer asks what condiments they serve.
4. The employee repeats the list of condiments available.
5. The customer gives the condiments he or she wishes to receive.
6. The order is placed with the cook.
7. The cook cooks the hamburger.
8. The condiments as ordered are placed on the hamburger.
9. The order is placed in the customer pick-up area.

Fuddrucker's process
1. The customer orders the size of hamburger and states how he or she wants it cooked.
2. The order is placed with the cook.
3. The cook cooks the hamburger.
4. The order is placed in the customer pick-up area.

Blueprinting allows a firm to understand its service delivery process and analyze alternative delivery systems. It is an essential process for organizations interested in developing a more effective and customer-oriented service delivery process, and it allows managers to view their customer contact points.

Standardization – a production line approach to service

One approach to services is to industrialize them. Levitt (1976) cites consistency and reduced costs as two reasons for industrializing a service. Low customization and low interaction with the customer are two ways of producing a low-cost service. Hyatt legal services (a standardized legal service in the USA), discount brokerage services, limited-service hotels, and fast-food restaurants are all examples of standardized services that evolved from customized services. The standardization also allows the services to be replicated and is a principal strategy for many chain operations. Langeard and Eiglier (1983) state that firms offering standardized services with limited product assortments have an effective strategy for developing multiple-unit organizations.

One outcome of the increased standardization of restaurants and hotels over the past several decades is that customers are now looking for unique firms that offer personalized services (Schmenner, 1986). Bed and breakfast operations are becoming popular with those travelers wanting personalized service at a moderate price. Boutique hotels are providing an alternative to larger, less personalized hotels. Cafés, bistros, and diners are providing an alternative to chain restaurants. Although the market share of chain operations in the hospitality industry is still growing, small customized businesses present an opportunity for the individual operator or a small chain of unique operations.

Earl Sasser and William Fulmer (1990) cite one danger of standardization. They caution that as services become more standardized they often lose the ability to interact with the customer. This can be a problem in those service organizations, such as hotels, where the guest expects some interaction and personalization of the service. Personnel are often told to respond in a certain manner and follow this script with little emotion or involvement. For example, one guest upon checking into a hotel noticed a band setting up in the lobby. He asked the desk clerk what was going on. The desk clerk replied that he did not know. The guest then asked who would know, to which the desk clerk replied that the assistant probably would. The desk clerk then proceeded to finish the check-in. He handed the guest the key and stated that if there was anything he could do to make the guest's stay more enjoyable, please would the guest let him know. The guest looked at him and stated that there was one thing he could do to make his stay more enjoyable: fulfill a previous request and find out what the band was doing setting up in the lobby. The clerk was taken aback for a moment, and then went to find someone who could answer the guest's question.

The above anecdote illustrates what can happen when we take an assembly-line approach to service. Firms often become more interested in the outcome than the process. This is a characteristic of organizations interested in speed and efficiency and moving bodies through the service delivery process. They forget about the needs of the customer in the process.

Heskett (1986) offers an alternative to low-priced standardized services. He states that do-it-yourself customization is one way of reducing the cost of a service while still offering the customer choice. Fuddrucker's self-serve condiment bar, buffets, and take-away food are examples of services that involve the customer to reduce cost. Little Caesar's grew to become the third largest pizza chain by offering customers a discount for picking up their own pizza. When Little Caesar's entered the pizza business Pizza Hut had the sit-down service market and Domino's had the delivery business, so Little Caesar's created a third market segment, pick-up. They did not need the large physical facilities to accommodate diners, nor did they need a fleet of delivery drivers. They were able to pass the savings of their low-cost operation to customers.

The discussion of complexity, divergence, standardization, and customization has provided some insights into the complexity of building a customer-oriented organization. There are many approaches to building a customer service organization. The Hong Kong Regent, Domino's and Little Caesar's provide some examples of some very different, but effective strategies.

The customer service matrix

The customer service matrix (Figure 12.1) is a tool to help managers form a customer-oriented service strategy that fits their organization. Some organizations may prefer standardization, while others may prefer to offer customized service. The customization may be provided by the service organization or by the customer. There are no universal service strategies. The customer service strategy at the Regent Hotel in Hong Kong is different from the service strategy for McDonald's in Hong Kong. However, it is possible to identify service strategies that will be appropriate for firms sharing similar characteristics. The customer service matrix identifies three effective customer strategies.

The matrix was developed using two attributes: customer-based uncertainty and standardization–customization. It is a modification of the uncertainty matrix developed by Bowen and Bowers (1986). The uncertainty matrix used two attributes, intangibility and customer contact, to identify varying levels of environmental uncertainty. The customer service matrix combines these two attributes into one uncertainty variable, while adding a second variable, customization–standardization. This produces a robust matrix, generalizable to most service organizations.

Three major dimensions of service concepts

Johnston (1989) identified three major dimensions of service concepts. The dimensions were generalist versus specialist, standardized versus customized,

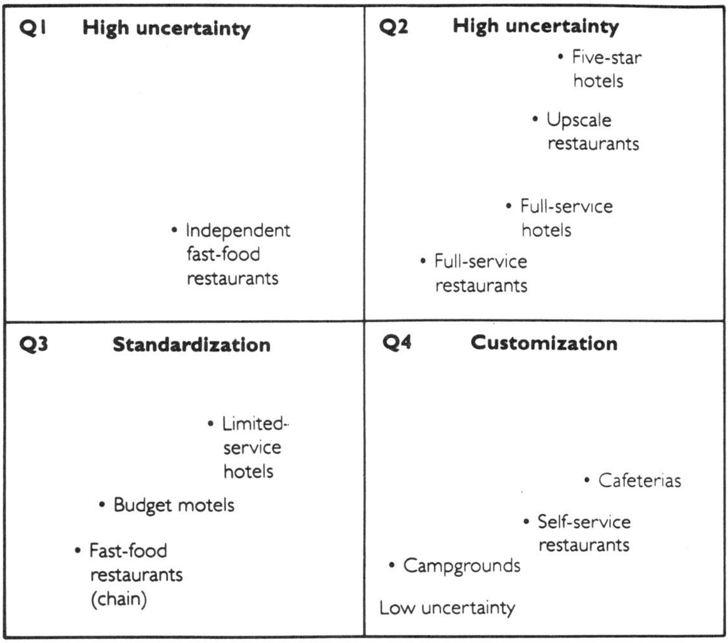

Q1 **High uncertainty**	Q2 **High uncertainty**

• Independent
  fast-food
  restaurants
	• Five-star
	     hotels
	
	   • Upscale
	    restaurants
	
	    • Full-service
	     hotels
	• Full-service
	  restaurants

Q3 **Standardization**	Q4 **Customization**

• Limited-
    service
    hotels
  • Budget motels
 	
• Fast-food
  restaurants
  (chain)
	
	      • Cafeterias
	
	    • Self-service
	     restaurants
	  • Campgrounds
	Low uncertainty

Fig. 12.1   Customer service matrix

and product versus process. A generalist is someone who provides a broad range of service products, as opposed to a firm that specializes in a certain product type. An example of a generalist would be a retail travel agent, while a specialist would be a travel agent selling only cruises.

A product focus takes a production orientation focusing more on the outcome and less on the process or how the product is served. A process orientation places an emphasis more on the delivery of the service and less on the product. Firms taking a product focus reduce uncertainty through reduced customer contact. Typically, they produce a standardized product. As they move from a product orientation to a process orientation, they are creating more uncertainty. The product orientation is concerned with the outcome, while the process orientation is concerned about how that product is delivered. The final dimension is customization versus standardization.

The uncertainty–certainty continuum in the customer service matrix relates to the uncertainty introduced by the customer. This uncertainty includes not keeping reservations or arriving at times other than those reserved, such as a restaurant guest arriving at 9.30 p.m. for an 8.30 reservation (Danet, 1981). Additionally, customers may take longer than expected to complete transactions: for example, the hotel guest who does not understand why he or she cannot get the phone turned on without a deposit and wants a full explanation. Another source of uncertainty arises if some customers are not willing or able to participate in the service delivery process (Langeard *et al.*, 1981).

The greater the amount of uncertainty and customization, the greater the chance that a non-routine transaction will occur. Non-routine transactions can take up extraordinary amounts of time and also test the service operation. Many customers who are completely happy with the basic products a hotel offers become dissatisfied because of how a non-routine transaction was handled. A person planning on paying for a restaurant meal with a check may become irate when told that the restaurant only takes cash or credit cards. Additionally, if the person does not have credit cards or enough cash to pay for the meal, management must come up with a quick solution. Even if the restaurant finally accepts the check, the customer's sense of embarrassment may result in the firm losing the customer's future business.

Customers may have problems interacting with the service delivery system. In a hotel they may request information on how to find various outlets within the hotel. The Travelodge on the Gold Coast (an international resort on Australia's east central coast) is a family-oriented resort hotel. On several occasions they have had families bring their own cooking appliances and try to prepare food in the room, resulting in the fire alarms being activated. Hospitality organizations must communicate with their customers and teach them how to use their services.

Besides the uncertainty caused by individual customers, market segments can be a source of uncertainty. First, the demand in a market fluctuates, putting tremendous pressures on the operation. Additionally, each segment has its own demands and peculiarities. Thus, the more market segments an organization attracts, the higher the potential sources of uncertainty for that organization.

One method of reducing uncertainty is through standardization and an assembly-line approach to service. First, standardization reduces the contact between the employee and the customer. There are fewer choices and few, if any, options for each choice. Communicating the choices through signs minimizes the need for communication between customers and employees. Second, standardization reduces the amount of divergence in the service delivery process – thus employees are faced with less decision making regarding possible outcomes for each customer. The system decides what those outcomes will be, not the customer. Finally, standardization reduces the difference between market segments. A budget chain such as Hampton Inns may attract salespersons, retired persons, and families. Hampton Inns offers one basic product to all segments – it does not try to alter its product to meet the specific needs of each segment.

Customization of the service operation can represent a source of uncertainty as it is characterized by much interaction between the customer and the service organization. The product is modified to meet the individual needs of each guest. For example, a luxury hotel will arrange restaurant and theater reservations for its guests, its restaurants will prepare requests that are not on the menu, and the customer expects the wine steward to explain and suggest wines. The relationship between the guest and the hotel is therefore more intense.

One method of reducing the intensity of the relationship between the customer and the service organization is by involving the customer in the service system. 'Sizzler' is one of the most successful restaurants in Australia and its success lies in the fact that customers perceive they are getting good value for money. Sizzler is a steak and seafood restaurant that features an extensive salad, fruit, pasta, and dessert bar. Customers place their order at the counter and a service person then brings the food to the table. Those customers who have purchased the salad bar then go to the salad bar to select and create their salad plate.

The Sizzler concept provides a good example of an effective customer service strategy. In Australia there is no tip credit system and the effective minimum wage is high. For example, most employees make over $10 an hour and restaurants pass on the high cost of wages to the customer. One result of the high labor cost is a gap between fast-food restaurants and full-service restaurants. The labor-efficient fast-food restaurants are able to provide prices comparable to the United States, but the more labor-intensive full-service restaurants are inevitably more expensive.

Sizzler identified this gap and created a service delivery system to fill it. The restaurant provided table service after the initial placing of the order, and it created an elaborate food bar, enabling the customer to create a customized product.

The strategic and structural implications of each quadrant

The effectiveness of the organization is, in part, determined by the degree to which the organizational structure matches the firm's environment. Two basic types of organizational structure are mechanistic and organic. Table 12.1 summarizes the characteristics of these two structures. Mechanistic structures are effective when work tasks are routine (Perrow, 1983; Pfeffer, 1978). Organic structures are useful when an organization is operating in a complex and dynamic environment (Mintzberg, 1979; Khandwalla, 1977; Duncan, 1979; Burns and Stalker, 1972).

Quadrant one (Q1) is an undesirable quadrant which should be avoided. It offers standardized operations similar to Q3. However, firms operating in Q1 do not have the capacity and systems to isolate themselves from customer uncertainty. Firms in this quadrant are typically one-unit organizations. An example of an organization in Q1 is an individually owned fast-food operation with no chain affiliation. The restaurants in Q1 can operate successfully in stable environments, but they have problems coping with unstable environments. For example, a sudden surge in demand such as a bus load of customers walking into the operation will create considerable stress on the service delivery system.

A US fast-food chain, Jack-In-The-Box, slipped into Q1 during the late 1970s and early 1980s. It tried to be everything to everybody and had an extensive product line. The breadth of its product line increased the uncertainty of its environment. It was unable to keep the buffer inventories of

Table 12.1 Mechanistic and organic structures

Mechanistic structure
- Tasks are broken down into specialized abstract units.
- Rigidly defined tasks.
- Strict hierarchy of control and authority.
- Communication is mainly vertical.
- Content of communication is instructions and commands.
- Loyalty and obedience to organization and superiors is highly valued.
- Knowledge and control rests with formal leader.

Organic structure
- Tasks are broken down into sub-units, but the relation of the task to the total organization is clearer.
- Tasks are flexible and redefined through interaction of organizational members.
- Group involvement in decisions, less hierarchy of control.
- Communication is mainly lateral.
- Content of communication is information and advice.
- Commitment to tasks and process.
- Knowledge and control is located at all levels of the organization.

Source: Based on Zaltman *et al.* (1973), p. 131.

specialized fast-food outlets. The employees had to be more skilled, as they had to be prepared to produce a greater variety of products. Also, the customers had more choice, which increases customer uncertainty. Firms that reduce customer choice can better forecast the demand for individual products. During the 1980s Jack-In-The-Box has headed back toward Q3, a more profitable position.

The only profitable operations in Q1 would be family run limited-service food and accommodation businesses in rural or non-competitive markets. Once these firms grow into multi-unit operations, they usually head toward Q3 or Q2.

Firms operating in Q2 are operating in an uncertain environment. This can be a good strategic choice for those firms having the expertise to provide the high level of service this quadrant demands. Customers frequenting service operations in this segment have high expectations. Those firms that can meet these expectations will thrive; those failing to meet the expectations will have problems. Hospitality operators often associate expensive physical facilities with providing customization through design. However, the physical facilities are only part of the product. The firm must also have an excellent service delivery system.

The lower portion of Q2 is the location of full-service hotels and restaurants. The upper, more uncertain portion is the location of luxury hotels and upscale restaurants. Firms operating in Q2 should have an organic structure. Integration is achieved through mutual adjustment. Decision making should be decentralized among self-contained work units. Lateral communications should dominate.

Those firms operating in Q2 are offering a higher level of customer service than those firms in Q3 and Q4. The level of service is the distinguishing feature between Q2 and Q4, while both the product features and customer service increase when moving from Q3 to Q2. In Q2 firms must deliver good service, since firms failing to deliver good service are at a disadvantage compared to their competition. Firms at the top of Q2 are usually small upscale chains or individual operations. It is difficult to make multi-unit chains out of firms operating in an uncertain environment. The advantage of this position is that it takes considerable operating skills to be successful because customer expectations are high. Firms or individuals who feel they have these skills may remove themselves from the competition of chain operations by choosing this position.

Hospitality organizations in Q3 are characterized by a standardized production process. The employee is an order taker and the customer comes to the operation with predetermined needs. Firms in Q3 usually limit the choice of products and the delivery of these products often involves the customer and technology. In a budget hotel chain the room inventory is readily available to the room clerk on the hotel's computer system. The guest typically takes his or her own baggage to the room. The employees tend to have simple tasks with little divergence.

A mechanistic structure will be the most efficient in this type of organization. Strategic decisions are made centrally, while operating decisions are made by unit management. Communication is usually vertical, flowing down through the operation.

Firms operating in Q3 have several advantages. First, through limited interaction with the customer they have been able to buffer themselves from the environment. The simple delivery system and the involvement of customers in this system allows them to cope with fluctuations in demand. Through careful communication of their product they can teach the customer what to expect and thereby reduce questions.

Q4 uses customer involvement in the service operation to create customization. Here firms have more customer contact than firms in Q3, but they are able to manage this contact through systems that allow customers to create their own products. Sizzler provides an example of a service firm in this quadrant. Those firms operating in Q4 call for a hybrid organizational structure, a mechanistic structure, which is more organic than those of firms in Q3. The employees' work in Q4 is routine and standardized; the customization comes through the involvement of the customer in the service delivery process.

The strategic advantage of firms in Q4 is that they enjoy cost savings by getting the customer involved in the service delivery process. They typically provide the same quality of outcome as those firms in the bottom of Q2, but charge the customer less for equivalent products. Cafeterias provide an example of firms operating in Q4. Two Pesos, a US Mexican restaurant chain, is another example. It provides quality food, similar to that provided in better sit-down service restaurants. Additionally, it provides a condiment bar featuring a variety of Mexican sauces and toppings. Besides lower prices, food and beverage firms in Q4 offer the advantage of quick service and convenient take-out service.

Development of a customer service program for each quadrant

The selection of a service strategy is the first step in the customer orientation process. The second step is developing a customer service system that supports the service strategy. Firms operating in Q3 will require a different system from those operating in Q2. In this section of the chapter we will present a generalized approach to developing a service system and then provide specific recommendations for quadrants 2, 3, and 4. Table 12.2 provides an overview of the steps in the process.

Service culture

A service culture is the first step in developing a customer organization. This means that the ideas, beliefs, and values of the firm influence employees to act in customer-oriented ways. The culture must be developed by top management and flow down through the organization. A mistake of many organizations is that they set up customer service programs without first developing a culture that supports these programs.

Developing a customer-oriented organization requires a commitment from management in terms of both time and financial resources. Often a change to a customer-oriented system requires changes in hiring, training, reward systems, customer complaint resolution, and empowerment of employees. It requires managers to spend time talking to both customers and customer contact employees. Management must be committed to these changes; if they are not, any efforts put into the development of a customer service program will be largely unproductive.

Those firms in Q2 require a more service-oriented culture than those firms operating in Q3 and Q4, although all firms require a service-oriented culture. Firms in Q2 should be prepared to empower employees to resolve customer complaints, this empowerment increasing as one moves towards the top of Q2. For example, one hotel chain gives its front-desk staff up to ten dollars a day to resolve customer problems. Often these problems are not the hotel's fault. Perhaps the guest had an unpleasant trip, in which case the ten dollars might be used to send flowers or a bottle of wine to the room. Perhaps the guest requires an item that is not available in the hotel gift shop, such as pipe cleaners. The ten dollars can be used to purchase these at a local store and send them to the guest with the compliments of the hotel. In luxury hotels

Table 12.2 The process for developing a customer service program

1. Service culture
   - Determine what level of organizational support a customer service program will receive.
   - Develop the structure and systems that support this level of service.
   - Issues:
     hiring
     training
     reward systems
     customer complaint resolution
     empowerment of employees
     MBWA
     debriefing employees
     talking to customers
     uniforms

2. Hiring the right employees

3. Training employees
   - Initial training
   - Continuous training

4. Service delivery system design
   - Layout – signage
   - Educate customer
   - Bottlenecks

5. Employee recognition
   - Customer satisfaction based
   - Awards
   - Praise, inspection, follow-up

6. Customer response system
   - Written
   - Verbal
   - Empowerment of employees

7. Employee response system
   - Debriefing customer contact employees
   - Gain employee input on new products
   - Gain employee input after system changes have been made to identify problem areas

8. Evaluation of customer satisfaction
   - Survey instruments
   - Focus groups
   - Debriefing employees
   - Talking to customers

9. Dynamic system
   - Environmental scanning
   - Adjustment of system based on feedback from customers and employees
   - Employee adjustments

and restaurants the employees should have even more freedom in resolving customer complaints.

Hiring and training

A customer-oriented organization hires employees who will eagerly serve the customer. It uses personnel interviewing, testing, and reference checks to make sure that the employees it hires will fit its customer service organization.

Once it has hired the employees, it spends time training them. The company should first give employees information about the company, its beliefs, and philosophy as well as a history of the organization. Next the company gives information about the unit where the employees will be working. For example, hotel employees are given a tour of the hotel and its outlets. Employees receive information on the services provided by each outlet and the hours of operation. Next the employees are provided with job-specific information. Finally, they are trained in customer service.

Beyond this initial training, employees receive continuous training throughout their career. This includes customer service training, cross training, and communication about promotions. Employees should be made aware of any advertised sales promotions the hotel or restaurant is offering. When a customer asks about a promotion, the employee should be able to provide information. In addition the purpose of the promotion should be understood. The Oakford Hotel recently opened in Melbourne offering half-price rooms, as an introductory appeal. In a customer-oriented organization employees would have been told to treat these customers as full-paying customers who should receive the same level of service. One purpose of a promotion like this is to gain regular customers. If the employees view the promotional customer as cheap and provide inferior service, the promotion will fail.

Firms operating in Q3 and Q4 require employees who will be satisfied doing more routine work, while simultaneously maintaining a customer service orientation. Firms in Q2 require employees who are able to think on their feet and react to events created by the uncertainty of their environment. The screening and hiring process for firms in Q2 will be more complex than for firms in Q3 and Q4. While training is important for all quadrants the training in Q2 will be more extensive. Firms in Q3 and Q4 will be able to make exten- sive use of videos and interactive videos in their training. On-the-job training will be more extensive in Q2.

Service delivery system

Organizations make sure their service delivery system is customer oriented. They educate the customer in the use of the service delivery system through signs, brochures, and trained employees. They eliminate bottlenecks. For example, the Sheraton Mirage on the Gold Coast has eliminated the positions of cashier and receptionist. They cross train all front-desk employees to handle both positions. This allows management to shift employees easily to meet demand, rather than having three people in a queue waiting for the receptionist and the cashier standing doing nothing.

Firms in Q3 try to minimize contact between the service provider and the customer. Signage providing the customer with key information is important in these firms. It reduces the need for the customer to ask questions about the service operation. Limited-service hotels provide maps showing the layout of the facilities as well as the location of the guest's room. Firms in Q4 are faced with the task of training their customers. Firms that require the customer to help deliver the service must make sure the customer understands what to do. Service persons ask customers at restaurants featuring salad bars or buffets if this is their first time at the restaurant. If they say it is, the employee then explains the system to them. Directional signage is also an important feature of Q4 service delivery systems. Queuing systems can be important for both Q3 and Q4 firms if there are times when capacity exceeds demand.

Employee recognition

Developing an employee recognition system based on customer satisfaction is an important part of a customer satisfaction system. This includes both a formal system and an informal system. Formal systems include awards and recognition in the organization's publications. Informal systems include praise, recognition, and follow-up. Managers walking around the operation recognizing employees by name and complimenting them for good work can be a powerful morale builder. People do what is recognized and rewarded. If management appears not to care, how can it expect employees to care? For example, in many hotels managers rarely inspect the hotel rooms with the housekeeper and executive housekeeper. The only time they contact the housekeeping department is when there is a problem. Employee recognition is an important part of the customer service program and applies to all quadrants.

Customer response system

An important part of any customer service program is a response system for customer complaints. Customers who have major complaints quickly resolved to their satisfaction will return around 90 percent of the time; those who have complaints resolved will return around 50 percent of the time; and those whose complaints are not resolved return to purchase around 20 percent of the time (TARP, 1976, 1980). The key to customer complaints is to resolve them quickly as it costs no more to resolve the complaint quickly and there is a much higher return on the firm's investment.

The customer complaint system should seek complaints from the customer. Many customers do not complain; they simply never return. Zeithaml (1981) claims that many people blame poor service on themselves, and therefore do not complain. For example, a guest ordering an exotic restaurant dish does not complain if she does not like it. Instead she blames herself for ordering something different.

Two important tools in customer complaint resolution systems are empowerment of employees and service guarantees (Hart, 1988). Empowerment of employees gives them the authority to resolve customer problems and complaints on the spot. Service guarantees encourage customers to complain since they receive a reward for complaining – the guarantee. Guarantees give the firm a chance to resolve the customer's problem and retain the customer. Another benefit of service guarantees is that they provide a benchmark for employees; they are a way of measuring their performance.

Firms in Q3 and Q4 should use limited empowerment, such as the replacement of unsatisfactory products. Firms in Q2 should give their employees the authority to resolve most customer complaints. Service guarantees are useful for firms in all quadrants. The high level of interaction between the customer and the employee in Q2 makes it effective for firms in this quadrant to train employees to detect customer problems and try to resolve them.

Evaluation of customer satisfaction

Customer-oriented firms stay close to the customer; they find out how they are doing and what needs to be improved. They use formal methods, including surveys and focus groups, and informal methods, debriefing customer contact employees and talking to customers. Some hotel managers have evening cocktail hours or breakfast for selected customers. During these sessions they gain feedback from their customers.

Firms in Q3 use surveys and shoppers (someone hired by the organization to use their services and then to give feedback on how well the organization performed). While firms in Q2 and Q4 have more guest contact and have a greater opportunity to involve guests in focus groups or quasi focus groups, as well as using shoppers and surveys. All firms should use debriefing employees and talking to customers. For example, Sea World, a theme park on the Gold Coast, requires all managers and back-stage employees to talk to customers for thirty minutes every day.

Dynamic system

The organization's needs and those of its customers are constantly changing. To keep up with these changes all customer service programs should receive input from environmental scanning systems. The system should be based on identification of trends and feedback from customers and employees. Employees must be evaluated on their customer service and those who are not effective in dealing with customers should be moved to non-contact positions.

A review of the effectiveness of customer-oriented operations

A survey conducted by Cambridge Reports (Zemke and Schaaf, 1989) asked respondents, 'How well do service companies meet your needs and concerns as a consumer?' Only eight percent of the 1500 sample gave the service firms an excellent rating. More than one-third of the respondents stated that services care less today than they did a few years ago about meeting customer needs. Furthermore, when firms try to implement customer service they often meet with failure. *The Australian*, a major daily paper, reported that companies were spending millions of dollars on customer service programs, but receiving little for the money. The programs seemed to have little effect on the customer service that the firms offered.

There is a tremendous opportunity for those firms which can offer good service, yet many firms seem unable to grasp the opportunity. Schneider (1990) states that becoming a service-oriented operation is difficult because it requires the organization to change. The change process must have management support. In the cases cited in *The Australian* article, the companies asked customer contact personnel to change their habits. The organizations as a whole were not changing, the culture was not changing, middle management was not changing, and nor was upper management changing how it rewarded middle management. The organizations were simply hiring a consultant to come in and 'pump up' the customer contact employees. The existing culture of the organization soon consumed the employee's enthusiasm. Middle management was still concerned with reducing costs and increasing revenue; that is what it was being rewarded for by upper management. Employees spending too much time servicing the customer were reminded that they needed to be more efficient. Management turned down any suggestions to try to retain a customer's goodwill that cost more, or agonized over them for weeks so that when the offer was finally made to the customer it was no longer effective.

A major problem facing organizations that want to become customer oriented is that middle management has traditionally been given the task of controlling the organization. It manages by watching costs, while trying to increase revenues. In short, the culture of middle management in most organizations does not support a customer-oriented organization. Organizations must therefore change from the top down as the focus of most customer-oriented programs is on the lower levels of the organization.

Summary

The customer service matrix coupled with a customer service program provides a framework for creating a customer-oriented operation. However, this takes time and a commitment of resources. For those willing to make the investment, the return is worth the effort. Heskett *et al.* (1990) provide a list of benefits of customer orientation. Employees like to do a good job and they enjoy working for organizations that enable them to do a good job. Thus, a customer orientation increases employee morale and reduces employee turnover. This alone is a powerful benefit. Davidow and Uttal (1989) predict that hotels in the United States will need 25 percent more workers in the year 2000 than they had in 1989. They also state that a prime age group of workers for hotels, the 16 to 24 year olds, will decline by over 25 percent, creating a shortage of skilled employees. Those firms without a customer service orientation are likely to be in a downward spiral: poor service, high staff turnover, low morale, poor service.

Other benefits of a customer orientation include lower rework costs. These costs include the cost of redoing work that is unsatisfactory and the cost of gaining the favor of guests who have been the victims of poor service. Marketing costs also benefit, since satisfied customers make repeat purchases and spread positive word of mouth. Those hotels that have little repeat business have high marketing costs or low occupancy.

The globalization of markets has also created a need for a customer orientation. Those firms operating in Q3 have been able to expand throughout the world. Examples of these firms include McDonald's, Pizza Hut, and Kentucky Fried Chicken. McDonald's has many loyal customers, persons who purchase meals at McDonald's throughout Asia – many of these customers have never been to the United States. McDonald's offers a consistent product at each of its 10,000 units through a customer orientation that reduces uncertainty and uses standardized products.

Food and beverage operations in Q4 provide international travelers with a language-free method of choosing food, at a moderate cost. Food courts are popular in the resort malls on the Gold Coast. They provide international visitors with a method of choosing a variety of food products when they have little or no command of the English language. They can simply point to those items they want. The food courts attract domestic tourists and their families with the variety of foods they offer and their good value.

Firms operating in Q2 cater to international businesspeople and pleasure travelers. Five-star hotels on the Gold Coast of Australia are not judged against other five-star hotels in Australia, but against five-star hotels in Hawaii, Hong Kong, Tokyo, and Singapore. Firms at the top of Q2 are competing against the best in the world. They must deliver excellent service to survive. Furthermore, tourist destinations such as the Gold Coast are competing for tourist business based on service. The visitors' total experience at the hotel, restaurants, and entertainment facilities in the region will affect their decision to return and what they say to others. Consequently, not only should individual organizations be concerned with a customer orientation, but entire tourist destinations must work together to ensure a customer orientation.

References

Ahlstrom, L., and Andres, H. (1989) 'World-class service from a Scandinavian perspective', in Shames, W. S., and Glover, W. G. (eds) *World-Class Service*, Stockholm: Intercultural Press.

Ansoff, H. I. (1984) *Implanting Strategic Management*, Englewood Cliffs, NJ: Prentice Hall.

Bowen, D. E., and Jones, G. R. (1986) 'Transaction cost analysis of service organization–customer exchange', *Academy of Management Review*, vol. 11, no. 2, pp. 428–41.

Bowen, J., and Bowers, M. R. (1986) 'A marketing contingency approach to service organizations', in Venkatesan, M., Schmalensee, D. M., and Marshall, C. (eds) *Creativity in Services Marketing*, Chicago: American Marketing Association.

Burns, T., and Stalker, G. M. (1972) 'Models of mechanistic and organic structure' in Koya Azumi *et al.* (eds) *Organizational Systems*, Lexington, Mass.: D. C. Heath and Co.

Daft, R. L. (1983) *Organizational Theory and Design*, St Paul, Minnesota: West Publishing Co.

Danet, B. (1981) 'Client–organization interfaces', in Nystrom, P. C., and Starbuck, W. H. (eds) *Handbook of Organization Design*, New York: Oxford University Press.

Davidow, W. H., and Uttal, B. (1989) *Total Customer Service*, New York: Harper & Row.

Duncan, R. (1979) 'What is the right organization structure?', *Organizational Dynamics*, vol. 7, no. 3, pp. 59–79.

Hart, C. W. L. (1988) 'The power of unconditional service guarantees', *Harvard Business Review*, vol. 66, no. 4, pp. 54–62.

Heskett, J. L. (1986) *Managing in the Service Economy*, Boston, Mass: Harvard Business School.

Heskett, J. L., Sasser, W. E., and Hart, C. W. L. (1990) *Service Breakthroughs*, New York: The Free Press.

Johnston, J. (1989) 'Developing competitive strategies in service industries', in Jones, P. (ed.) *Management in Service Industries:*, London: Pitman Publishing.

Keller, R. T., Slocum, J. W., and Susman, G. I. (1974) 'Uncertainty and type of process management system in a continuous process organization' *Academy of Management Journal* vol. 17, no. 1, pp. 56–68.

Khandwalla, P. (1977) *The Design of Organizations*, New York: Harcourt, Brace, Jovanovich.

Langeard, E., and Eiglier, P. (1983) 'Strategic management of service development', in Berry, L. L., Shostack, G. L., and Upah, G. D. (eds) *Emerging Perspectives in Services Marketing*, Chicago: American Marketing Association.

Langeard, E., Bateson, J. E. G., Lovelock, C. H., and Eiglier, P. (1981) *Services Marketing: New insights from consumers and managers*, Cambridge, Mass: Marketing Science Institute.

Levitt, T. (1976) 'The industrialization of service', *Harvard Business Review*, vol. 54, no. 5, pp. 63–74.

Lorenzi, P., Sims, H. P., Jr, and Slocum, J. W., Jr (1981) 'Perceived environmental uncertainty: an individual or environmental attribute?', *Journal of Management*, vol. 7, no. 2, pp. 27–41.

Miles, R. E., and Snow, C. C. (1978) *Organizational Strategy, Structure, and Process*, New York: McGraw-Hill.

Mintzberg, H. (1979) *The Structuring of Organizations*, Englewood Cliffs, NJ: Prentice Hall.

Perrow, C. (1983) 'The organizational context of human factors engineering', *Administrative Science Quarterly*, vol. 28, no. 4, pp. 521–41.

Pfeffer, J. (1978) *Organizational Design*, Arlington Heights, Illinois: AHM.

Sasser, W. E., and Fulmer, W. E. (1990) 'Creating personalized service delivery systems', in Bowen, D. E., Chase, R. B., and Cummings, T. G. (eds) *Service Management Effectiveness*, San Francisco: Jossey-Bass.

Schmenner, R. W. (1986) 'How can service businesses survive and prosper?', *Sloan Management Review*, vol. 27, no. 27, pp. 21–32.

Schneider, B. (1990) 'Alternative strategies for creating service-oriented organizations', in Bowen, D. E., Chase R. B., and Cummings, T. G. (eds) *Service Management Effectiveness*, San Francisco: Jossey-Bass.

Shostack, G. L. (1987) 'Service positioning through structural change', *Journal of Marketing*, vol. 51, no. 1, pp. 34–53.

TARP (1976) *A National Survey of the Complaint-Handling Procedures Used by Consumers*, Washington D.C.: White House Office of Consumer Affairs.

TARP (1980) *Consumer Complaint Handling in America: Final report*, Washington D.C.: White House Office of Consumer Affairs.

Walker, R. (1991) 'A salute to the regent', *Asian Hotel and Catering Times*, vol. 13, no. 1, pp. 8–12.

Zaltman, G., Duncan, R., and Holbek, J. (1973) *Innovations and Organizations*, New York: John Wiley.

Zeithaml, V. A. (1981) 'How consumer evaluation processes differ between goods and services', in Donnelly, J. H., and George, W. R (eds) *Marketing of Services*, Chicago: American Marketing Association.

Zemke, R., and Schaaf, D. (1989) *The Service Edge*, New York: New American Library.

13

Culture, customization, and innovation: A Hilton International service brand for the Japanese market

Andrew Bould and Geoffrey Breeze
with Richard Teare

Since its acquisition by Ladbroke Group PLC in 1987, Hilton International has achieved one of the most striking turnarounds in any service industry, becoming the most profitable international hotel company in Japan. Over the three-year period from 1988–90 Hilton's total Japanese sales increased by 112 percent to £273 million. On 21 October 1991 Hilton launched 'Wa No Kutsurogi', a pioneering Japanese service brand, at the Tokyo Hilton hotel with a trade and consumer advertising campaign in Japan and throughout the world via a network of 42 participating Hilton hotels. This chapter examines the rationale and the process involved in researching, developing, and implementing a customized hotel services package for the worldwide Japanese business and leisure travel market.

The development and positioning of Hilton International for the 1990s

In 1991 Hilton International was operating 150 hotels in close to 50 countries around the world, with a further 20 hotels due to open in 1992 or beyond. The company's history dates back to 1949 when it was established as a subsidiary of the Hilton Corporation. In December 1964, having 24 hotels, Hilton International became an independent publicly owned company with its shares traded on the New York Stock Exchange. The agreement governing the spin-off gave Hilton Hotels Corporation the exclusive right to use of the name Hilton for hotels in the USA, and Hilton International the exclusive right to control the use of the Hilton name throughout the rest of the world. The only remaining connection between the two companies is the jointly owned worldwide Hilton Reservations Service. In October 1987 the British-owned Ladbroke Group PLC acquired Hilton International for $1 billion, and alongside interests in property, racing, and retailing, Hilton International has become the group's fourth and largest division.

Following the acquisition, Ladbroke renamed some of its existing hotel properties, thereby augmenting the three established UK Hilton International hotels on London's Park Lane, in Kensington, and at Gatwick Airport by designating Hilton International hotels in seven new locations. The remainder of the existing UK hotel portfolio was reshaped to create a new group of 19 Hilton National hotels. These are lower-priced hotels, situated in regional locations which provide Hilton-style leisure and conference facilities designed primarily with the requirements of UK domestic travelers in mind. Statistically, the differences between customer expectations of Hilton National and International hotels are reflected in the fact that 90 percent of Hilton National customers arrive by car, and represent UK domestic business and leisure trips made by British nationals, whereas an average of 70 percent of Hilton International guests arrive by air and by definition represent a much wider cross-section of nationalities.

Historically, Hilton International's marketing strategy was dependent on Americans traveling abroad. In contrast, the present sales and marketing direction concentrates on providing hotel accommodation to a broader international market. This is reflected in the expansion in the number of sales offices worldwide to 100, with recent openings in Miami, Chicago, Los Angeles, Madrid, and Osaka providing opportunities to gain a much larger share of growth markets. To achieve the objective of a broader global operations base, Hilton is currently engaged in the most extensive and aggressive development program in the company's history. Seven major hotel developments were completed and opened during 1990 and more recent hotel openings have included Bali (Indonesia); Ottawa (Canada); Sharm El Sheikh (Egypt); Berlin (Germany); London (England); Kyongju (Korea) and Izmir (Turkey) among others.

Hilton is the only international hotel company to enter the 1990s with a significant presence in major Japanese cities and currently operates the 808 room Tokyo Hilton, the 527 room Osaka Hilton, the 742 room Tokyo Bay Hilton adjacent to Disneyland, and the 453 room Nagoya Hilton. To secure its competitive edge, Hilton signed an agreement in January 1991 with a newly formed development company jointly owned by The Industrial Bank of Japan, Ltd and The Nippon Fire & Marine Insurance Co. Ltd. Based in Tokyo, Japan Hilton Projects Development Co. Ltd will provide the company with exclusive services aimed at accelerating its expansion both inside and outside Japan.

In recognition of its record of achievement in April 1991 Hilton received the Service Industry Success Award arising from The Opportunity Japan Campaign sponsored jointly by the British Department of Trade and Industry and The British Overseas Trade Board.

In order to replicate its achievements in the Far East, Hilton have developed a customized service package specifically for the Japanese traveling overseas. The stages involved in defining the concept, undertaking the research and implementing an international hotel service brand are related in the following sections.

The strategic role of the Hilton 'masterbrand' audit

In 1988, less than twelve months after Ladbroke acquired Hilton International, a major audit of the masterbrand properties took place. Part of this work involved identifying and appraising the various product features of Hilton hotels, such as 'executive floor' and 'traveler club' provisions. In conjunction with this exercise, an assessment was made of the product segmentation strategies used by competitors, looking closely at the sub-branding developments in the USA and efforts which were being made to introduce sub-brands in Europe. Among other conclusions, it was noted that the sophisticated array of product segmentation types in the USA is atypical, for historical and geographical reasons.

An important objective of the research was to identify what information consumers are able to recall, particularly in relation to the hotel brand names and slogans that were proliferating at the time. As might be expected, there were some significant differences in practice and in consumer reactions to brand developments in the USA compared with the rest of the world. It seemed, however, that comparatively few international hotel companies, including Hilton International, had successfully extended their masterbrand reputation to specific areas of service delivery. This might be due, at least in part, to the perception that some product features had been designed for the convenience of the hotel operator rather than the consumer. If so, this analysis helps to explain why the research highlighted a low level of recall among hotel customers of certain product feature benefits across the range of international hotel brands. To illustrate, the research identified a certain amount of confusion among hotel customers relating to the benefits of being upgraded from a standard to a superior type of guest room.

Defining the Hilton service brand concept

An outcome of the research was a decision to adopt a product development approach which would enable customers to match their needs easily against a specially adapted style or area of hotel service. This initially led to attempts to define the concept of a Hilton service brand which might support the kind of innovations fundamental to Hilton's planned growth. The adopted approach was to consider different service clusters which, when combined, would provide key benefits to customers. At the time, the number of Japanese visitors to Hilton International hotels worldwide had been growing rapidly, doubling since 1988 to reach a figure close to 21 percent of the company's total visitor volume, equalling the number of American guests. The total Japanese outbound market is projected to double again by 1995, but the Japanese are much less used to international travel than most other nationalities, as they have very different cultural expectations from Americans and Europeans, for instance, who are in themselves culturally distinctive groups, but with more similarities than differences.

Hilton's strong presence in Japan, combined with ambitious expansion plans for the region and the size of the Japanese market, provided a firm basis for conducting research and developing a service brand to meet the exacting needs of Japanese business and leisure travelers. To identify the best approach, hotels that were already receiving significant numbers of Japanese guests were identified, as were hotels that were located close to Japanese commercial, industrial, and residential areas. This activity was primarily focused on Hilton hotels in Europe, as the majority of Hilton hotels in the Far East had already incorporated service features and styles suited to the Japanese market.

The role of consumer research

The first stage of the exercise was concerned with identifying 'best practice' within the oganization by finding out how Hilton hotels with an established Japanese clientele were responding to guest requirements. Hilton hotels which, because of their location, should have been receiving a higher proportion of Japanese guests were also examined, and a close correlation was identified between increasing Japanese business share and the successful implementation of customized service features that Japanese guests had requested. On completion of the audit-based comparison, an extensive consumer research program began in Japan, using Hilton hotel database information in order to find out what Japanese customers who regularly travel internationally wanted Hilton hotels to provide.

The culmination of the research was the development of the pioneering Hilton Japanese service brand 'Wa No Kutsurogi' service, meaning 'comfort and service, the Japanese way'. It consists of distinctive service features and special amenities appealing to both Japanese business and leisure travelers. These include Japanese-speaking staff at the participating hotels, safe deposit boxes, hotel information and safety instructions in Japanese, an Oriental food selection, often with authentic Japanese cuisine, and Japanese green tea and items such as slippers, bathrobes and Japanese newspapers. In simple terms, the brand, symbolized by a Japanese crane, the Tsuru, which is the national emblem of Japan and signifies 'freedom, good luck and happiness', aims to attract more Japanese business to more Hilton hotels. The underlying assumption is that, if the majority of visitors feel comfortable with the hotel service environment they experience, the development will have been fully justified in terms of the additional guest satisfaction and new business it will generate.

The program of research was conducted across a wide geographical area and reflected some interesting regional and cultural preferences and differences between northern and southern parts of Japan. It also included discussions with Japanese travel professionals in order to find how the service brand characteristics emerging from the research could be communicated through travel distribution channels. The travel professional network and program of interviews with Japanese business travelers around the world was gradually extended as the global potential of the service brand became apparent. This involved listening to the views of more than one thousand Japanese guests and travel trade representatives. Also crucial during the research was the support given by many Japanese businesses and the commitment of Hilton International Japan, whose knowledge of the market stems from over 30 years of successful operations in Japan.

A strong and consistent feature of the responses received was the value attributed to the provision of Japanese-speaking staff at destination Hilton hotels. Not unnaturally, Japanese travelers wish to feel that they can be understood by someone who knows their culture, needs, and expectations, and who can deal with any problems which arise in an appropriate way. The research indicated that, where a commitment is made by investing in Japanese-speaking staff, Japanese visitors are inclined to feel more confident that other aspects of Japanese service provision in hotel restaurants and guest rooms will be available.

Implementation

Following the research and consultation process, the next stage was to consider how to disseminate the findings throughout the hotel network and how to implement customized Japanese service so that it could be branded and promoted with confidence. Initially this involved identifying Hilton hotels that would benefit from an increased volume of Japanese visitors and, perhaps more critically, those hotels with the capability and determination to implement the brand precisely and without deviation from the established and certified standards. The preparation period for implementation began twelve months prior to the October 1991 launch. The process was to involve as many people as possible at different managerial levels throughout the organization, so that by consultation, discussion, and agreement the participating hotels felt committed to the implementation plan.

In order to validate the authenticity of the brand, implementation involved an inspection by Japanese companies situated in the locality of the hotels. A successful inspection amounted to an endorsement by certification of the local company's confidence in the hotel's ability to deliver authentic Japanese service. The idea emerged from the consumer research, and it offers an effective form of competitive advantage by allowing a selling approach to develop directly from the product itself. Fifteen successful inspections are needed for a hotel to take part, which must then be repeated annually, thereby guaranteeing the maintenance of a network of excellence. Japanese manufacturers are used to working cooperatively with suppliers, and so the idea of building a relationship by asking for their cooperation in defining and designing a product is widely accepted. This approach was particularly helpful during discussions about the possibility of recruiting Japanese-speaking hotel staff from expatriate Japanese communities.

The responses received indicated that it would be less acceptable to recruit an expatriate than a new member of staff direct from Japan, because it was felt that expatriates who had been living away from Japan for five years or more would be less sympathetic to the principles of providing authentic Japanese service. This indicates something of the subtle nuances of relationships and cultural interpretation which separate authentic styles of service which Japanese firms are willing to endorse, from Western interpretations of Japanese service which are less acceptable and by definition likely to be less successful.

Implications for further research and product innovation

The research also highlighted issues with important implications for future product innovation and development. For example, the findings indicated that Japanese visitors do prefer and expect different guest room fixtures and fittings, notably in the bathroom, which should feature separate bath and shower facilities. This has provided the impetus for a more recent consumer research program which focused on guest room design, fixtures, and fittings in order to assess guest needs more precisely.

The research has already highlighted that international business travelers seek security and maximum convenience from product features such as the 'executive floor' concept. This implies providing a totally separate service: meals, meeting and business support facilities, staff empowered to meet requests and make arrangements quickly on behalf of the guest, and other services designed to enable the guest to control his or her environment quickly and conveniently. The array of services needed to achieve this objective on behalf of the guest equates to a specific area of service delivery which can be branded and promoted so that it extends the Hilton name and reputation among brand users. This is achieved by discriminating between guests and implanting a specialized set of service standards specifically for them, above the uniform level of Hilton International service characterized by the masterbrand.

The Japanese service brand provides an example of customization, although with a cultural emphasis rather than with the 'exclusivity' appeal of maximum convenience required by 'executive floor'-type users. A country-based or slightly broader cultural approach to customizing hotel services provides an effective way of identifying more closely with international business and leisure travelers, and in theory new service brands could be developed to achieve competitive advantage in different countries so as to enhance the international appeal of the masterbrand. However, there are a number of longstanding issues which need to be tackled for the benefit of business travelers, who are the largest category of Hilton customers. An example of an area which has recently benefited from product innovation is the Hilton check-in and check-out procedure, which has to be as rapid, flexible, and simple as possible to meet the needs and schedules of international business. Streamlining and efficiency improvements can be made by taking a nonconventional approach and designing a procedure which gives priority to customer needs rather than to administrative ones.

Traditionally, hoteliers have been good at meeting the expressed wishes of their guests, but in the 1990s attention to their non-expressed aspirations will provide a source of competitive edge. In this respect, the Japanese service brand goes further than simply meeting the basic requirements, by providing solutions to potential and often unrecognized problems. A practical aid to the language barrier faced by Japanese visitors is provided in the form of a simple alarm clock. This circumvents the problems of trying to use a guest room wake-up call facility designed primarily for ease of use by American and European guests. However, this relatively simple feature blends into the existing guest room provision, without offending or in any sense alienating other nationalities.

Research conducted specifically to test the reactions of other nationalities to this and other features of the Japanese service brand revealed that Hilton guests generally expect to find a more cosmopolitan mix of people staying in a Hilton hotel than in other international hotels. This is mainly for historical reasons, in that Hilton is among the longest-established international hotel chains and was instrumental in exporting American hotel standards throughout the world. The degree of tolerance among Hilton guests to subtle forms of customization based on cultural and or country characteristics would suggest that there are numerous possibilities for extending, refining, and formulating further service brand variations.

Evidence suggests that economic trading partnerships are growing larger and stronger, and so throughout the 1990s it will be important to monitor closely the dynamics of change affecting the international hotel business. The impetus for change will come from the European and Pacific Rim countries and from the large underdeveloped areas of the world like Latin America and Africa, where in some places newly liberated economies and people will make a difference to global developments. In this context, Hilton has been concentrating on the origin of the guest in order to develop services which meet culturally different needs. This approach has strongly influenced the way in which the organization is structured and the way in which hotel services are delivered.

The key challenge will be to adapt to the ever-increasing mobility of Hilton customers. Currently, some 51 percent of Hilton International guests cross at least one country border to stay in a Hilton, and it is estimated that this figure will be closer to 75 percent by the year 2000. The implication of this is that Hilton will need continually to extend and refine its service branding approach in order to respond to the inevitable cultural transfer which will gather momentum in the years ahead.

14

Hotel strategic planning at the business and unit level in the USA

Eddystone C. Nebel, III,
and Jeffrey D. Schaffer

This chapter addresses strategic planning at two different levels within a hotel company's organizational hierarchy: business-level strategic planning and operational-level strategic planning.

A hotel company is a strategic business unit (SBU). Strategic planning at the SBU level attempts to define the overall approach the business will take in meeting its objectives. In order to do this, a hotel company must (1) identify key success factors within its industry, (2) identify the industry's unique opportunities and threats, (3) identify its own unique resources and skills, and (4) determine the specific strategic gap it will fill.

Most of the strategic planning at the SBU level is intended to impact on the individual hotels within the company. While many decisions have already been made at the SBU level, as hotels increase in size and complexity, so does the amount of strategic planning and decision making at the individual hotel level. The remainder of this chapter illustrates the strategic planning process at the individual hotel level using SWOT analysis. SWOT is an acronym for the process of analyzing internal *S*trengths and *W*eaknesses and external *O*pportunities and *T*hreats in order to arrive at a strategic plan for an individual hotel. Various issues relating to strategic planning at the individual hotel level are discussed and two real-world examples of individual hotel strategic planning are given.

The strategic planning hierarchy

Because most major United States hotels are part of larger organizations, it is important to understand the organizational hierarchy in which they operate and the strategic decisions that are made at different levels within that hierarchy.

Figure 14.1 depicts a typical organization chart for a hotel company and the kinds of strategic decision that are usually made at different levels within the

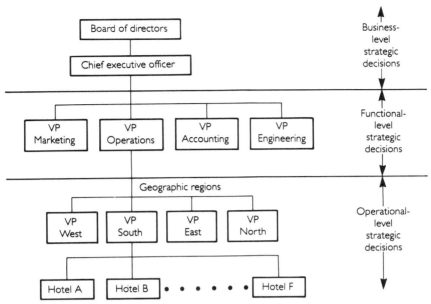

Fig. 14.1 Strategic decisions in a hotel corporation

organization. At the top of the management pyramid is the board of directors and the chief executive officer (CEO), who is responsible to the board for the overall performance of the company. At this level within a hotel company, *business-level strategic* decisions are made.

Directly below the CEO are the functional executives of the hotel company, so named because each is responsible for a particular specialized aspect, or function, of the business such as marketing, finance and accounting, human resources, or food and beverage. Included at this level is a vice-president (VP) of operations who has overall responsibility for the operational activities of the company's hotels. *Functional-level* strategic decisions are made at this level in the management structure.

In a small hotel company, individual hotel managers report directly to the vice-president of hotel operations. In larger companies, regional vice-presidents oversee the operations of individual hotels. They in turn report to the VP of hotel operations. At the regional and individual hotel level, *operational-level* strategic decisions are made.

Corporate-level strategic planning

Strategic planning takes place at each level within a modern business: the corporate level, the business level, and the functional or operational level (Pearce and Robinson, 1988, pp. 8–11). Many corporations are involved in more than one business and sometimes in many separate businesses. For example, International Telephone and Telegraph (ITT) is a giant corporate conglomerate engaged in dozens of different businesses, including the lodging business through its wholly owned subsidiary, Sheraton. Corporate-level strategic plans deal with issues such as the types of business in which ITT should be involved, the overall financial performance and dividend policy of the corporation, the allocation of corporate capital to individual business units, social responsibility, and stockholder relations.

Business-level strategic planning

A second level of strategic planning takes place in individual business units, an example of which would be Sheraton Hotels within ITT. Strategy at this level deals with how best to compete in a particular market area. For example, although Sheraton competes in the lodging industry, it has chosen to limit its activities to only certain market segments within the total lodging market and not to compete in all lodging markets. Examples of strategic decisions on the part of Sheraton would include determining markets in which to compete, geographic expansion plans, and franchising strategy. Business-level strategic managers 'strive to identify and secure the most promising market segment. This market segment is the fairly unique piece of the total market that the business can claim and defend because of competitive advantage' (Pearce and Robinson, 1988, p. 8). Such a business-level strategy, for example, led Holiday Inns, during the 1950s and 1960s, to develop a network of roadside inns catering primarily to individual business travelers and families traveling by automobile. Everything about these motels – their location, architecture, services, amenities, financing, reservation system, and management – was designed with one thought in mind: to capture and defend a significant share of that segment of the lodging market. Each hotel company, by its business-level strategic decisions, tries to do the same thing.

Functional-level strategic planning

The next level of strategic planning is that of function. Functional-level strategic planning is done by the vice-presidents at Sheraton who oversee the operations, marketing, accounting, personnel, food and beverage, and other functions of the company's individual hotels. Functional-level managers implement the business-level strategies of the firm. Business-level strategies often have a multiple-year time frame (for example, it might take three to four years to develop twenty new hotels in major US markets west of the Mississippi). Functional-level strategies are usually characterized by annual objectives and short-term strategies (for example, next year's advertising budget, installation of a new national 800-number reservation system, or development of a quality assurance program).

Strategic planning at the strategic business unit (SBU) level: the lodging firm

Strategic planning attempts to define the overall approach the organizational unit will take in meeting its objectives. The principal purpose of strategic planning and analysis at the SBU level is to identify the major opportunities, threats, and environmental constraints a business or SBU will face in the future. Furthermore, strategic planning for the SBU seeks to identify the key resources and skills around which the business unit can develop a course of action that will exploit these opportunities and address these threats and constraints in a way which will satisfy its goal structure.

The strategy analysis process at the business unit level should consist of four broad steps:

1. Assessment of the current strategic position of the business.
2. Identification of the major strategic opportunities, threats, and environmental constraints that the business is likely to face.
3. Identification of the principal skills and resources that the business can rely upon to build its competitive strategy.
4. Identification of the major gaps that exist between the business's current strategic position and the opportunities, threats, and constraints it is likely to face in the future.

Strategic positioning

Strategic positioning at the business unit level addresses the fundamental question: what type of strategy should the business follow? Strategic positioning can be classified, according to the nature and level of the investment required, into the following categories:

- *Share-increasing strategies*. These aim to increase significantly and permanently the market share of the business. Such strategies require investment levels that are usually substantially greater than industry norms.
- *Growth strategies*. These are strategies designed to maintain position in rapidly expanding markets. Growth strategies generally require high investment levels. However, these are usually no higher than the overall industry average.
- *Profit maximization strategies*. These aim to maximize the utilization of the existing skills and resources of the business unit. Investment under profit maximization strategies is generally at a maintenance level. This generally results in high cash generation from the business.
- *Market concentration and asset reduction strategies*. This type of strategy focuses on realigning the resources and skills of the business unit. This is undertaken to achieve a better position to exploit the new market segments that top management has identified as strategic opportunities. Business units that pursue this type of strategy usually sell or shut down

some of the business's existing asset base while simultaneously making new investments and refocusing business resources.

- *Turnaround strategies*. Strategies that fall into this classification are enacted by the management of business units whose fortunes are in decline. The primary objective here is to reverse declining trends as rapidly as possible. This usually requires the infusion of capital and other resources.
- *Liquidation and divestiture strategies*. This strategic position is taken by the management of firms that wish to withdraw from a particular business. The primary objective here is to generate as much positive cash flow as possible while the termination process takes place.

During the late 1970s and throughout the 1980s, Marriott Hotels, Hyatt Hotels and Holiday Inns pursued share-increasing strategies. These companies expanded rapidly, building new hotels, in some cases at multiple locations, in both primary and secondary markets. Furthermore, these hotel companies sought to exploit the growing segmentation of the lodging market through the development of more specialized hotel units (e.g. Marriott's Courtyard Hotels and Marquis, Hyatt's Regency Hotels, and Holiday's Hamilton Inns and Crown Plazas).

On the other hand, a clear example of a market concentration strategy is American Motor Inns (AMI). One of the largest franchisees in the Holiday Inn system at the beginning of the 1980s, AMI sold off the bulk of their 46 properties in the early 1980s. Resources were then reapplied, 'focusing on secondary markets where large, more powerful competitors would be unlikely opponents', according to Sam Krish, then Senior Vice-President for Corporate Development. The company even changed its name and now operates as Krish Hotels.

An example of a turnaround strategy that failed can be seen in a lodging company that was known as Imperial 400. This company, already in decline in the early 1980s, determined that by locating its motel properties in downtown areas it could maximize year-round occupancy and negate the need for in-house food and beverage facilities. The company sought to expand this format rapidly by developing a form of co-owner management, where unit managers became investor-owners. The strategy did not work because as a result of the co-owner/manager arrangement the company lost control of its quality and consistency standards.

The strategic planning process

As we have seen, at the business level competitive position analysis is used to assess the types of investment strategy a business should follow. The procedures for assessing relative competitive position at the business level are similar to those which are used at all levels of strategic analysis and involve identifying: key success factors; unique opportunities and threats; unique resources and skills; and the strategic gap at the business level.

Key success factors

These are variables which management can influence through its decisions and which can affect significantly the overall competitive positions of the various firms in an industry. They are derived from the economic and technological characteristics of the industry (e.g. segmentation, buying motives, and the degree of product/service differentiation) and the competitive weapons on which the various firms in the industry have built their strategies (e.g. sales and marketing effectiveness, the quality level of facilities and services, the degree of consistency and quality control, and geographic location advantages).

Identifying unique opportunities and threats

This involves an in-depth analysis of the entire industry from four perspectives: analysis of the industry's *market factors*; analysis of the industry's *operational factors*; a comprehensive analysis of *competitors*; and analysis of the factors affecting the industry's *resource supply*.

Market factors include all those elements that relate to the nature of the market(s) that are or have the potential of being served by the business. Market factors include the industry's overall size, its growth rate, the stage of product market evolution, the degree of segmentation or potential segmentation, buyer characteristics, product/service price sensitivity, and seasonality of demand. The primary way that market opportunities and threats evolve is through changes in the basic characteristics of the industry, such as the size and growth rate, buyer needs and tastes, and market segmentation.

Operational factors are those issues that are particular to providing the kinds of products and services produced by the industry. In the lodging industry they include the degree to which product/service differentiation can and is being achieved; the ease or difficulty with which new competitors can enter the industry or existing competitors can expand their market share (i.e. the cost and availability of capital, construction costs, and site availability); industry profitability; and vulnerability to inflation.

Resource supply factors are those related to the availability and cost of the resources that must be brought to bear to operate the business. In the lodging industry a key resource factor is the abundance, quality and cost of the labor supply. Other resource factors include the availability and cost of operating materials, and overall cost trends.

The purpose of a comprehensive *competitor analysis* is first to identify those areas where the firm has advantages over competitors that may be exploited, and second to identify those areas where competitors have advantages that they may exploit. This part of the strategic planning process is crucial because it can lead to the identification of economic and political strategies that may discourage competitors from investing in market segments where the firm desires to focus. Competitor analysis requires identification of major existing and potential competitors, their objectives, strategies, key resources, and major strengths and weaknesses.

Identifying unique resources and skills

Resource analysis at the business level is used to assess the firm's ability to exploit the opportunities and fend off the threats that it faces in its external environment. The process begins by developing a profile of the firm's principal resources and skills. This profile is then compared to the key success requirements of the firm's competitive market environment so as to identify the major strengths upon which it can build its strategy and the critical weaknesses it must overcome to avoid the pitfalls of the environmental conditions which might threaten its viability. Finally, the firm must compare its strengths and weaknesses with those of its major competitors so as to identify areas in which it has competitive advantages or distinctive competencies.

The resource profile of a firm may be thought of as comprehending five broad areas: (1) financial resources, such as cash flow, debt capacity, and the availability of new equity; (2) physical resources, such as hotels and inventories; (3) human resources, such as qualified management personnel in the areas of lodging operations, food and beverage management, sales, marketing, and financial management; (4) organizational resources, such as quality control systems and financial control systems; and (5) technological capabilities, such as efficient low-cost operations, product service developmental skills, and customer brand loyalties. To assess a business's resource profile, it is necessary to identify the major resources and skills it has in each of these areas.

Filling the strategic gap at the business level

Once a business has determined, through the foregoing analytical process, its strategic position, major strategic opportunities, and threats, it is then in a position to forecast the results that will be achieved by continuing with its present strategy. This forecast can be compared with the business objectives developed in the goal formulation process. If major gaps are revealed, the business must adjust its competitive strategy (exploit opportunities, build on competitive advantages, overcome environmental threats, and parry competitive thrusts) so as to achieve its objective. These gaps and the various major strategic issues identified as a result of the strategy analysis process pose the major strategic problems to be solved by the business.

Strategic planning and the individual hotel

Most of the strategic planning done at the business and the functional levels is intended to impact on the individual hotels within a hotel company. Profits are made and losses incurred at the individual hotel level. Individual hotels are the *unique businesses* upon whose collective health the overall health of the company relies. In short, the individual hotel within a hotel company is the critical point of action around which all other activities revolve. Because of this, how they fit into the management and planning hierarchy of their company must be understood.

Reference to Figure 14.1 makes it clear that the individual hotel is at the bottom of both the managerial and the strategic planning hierarchy of a hotel company. Many strategic decisions have already been made at both the business and the functional levels which, in effect, limit the flexibility of strategic decision making at the hotel level. Decisions regarding which market segments the company seeks to serve have already been made at the business level, as have plans for geographic growth. At the functional level, even more decisions affecting individual hotels have already been made. Examples include the exact location, architecture, size, and basic facilities of each hotel. Additionally, functional strategic decisions may have been made concerning specific financial control and reporting procedures, company-wide personnel policies, energy conservation programs, and company-wide advertising and marketing programs.

One might be led to conclude that the managers of individual hotels have little discretion with regard to strategic issues; that the managers of individual hotels are responsible only for efficiently operating their hotel in accordance with strategic plans imposed from above. While this is often true for limited-service budget motels and hotels, as a hotel increases in size and complexity, the amount of strategic planning and decision making that occurs at the individual hotel level increases.

In one sense the general manager (GM) of a hotel is at the bottom of the managerial hierarchy of a hotel company. On the other hand, the GM is at the top of the management hierarchy of a sizable business that could employ over a thousand workers and generate tens of millions of dollars in annual revenues. The GM of a medium-sized to large hotel has reporting to him or her functional specialists in most of the same areas as the functional corporate vice-presidents shown in Figure 14.1. Since an individual hotel is itself a profit center, its GM can be thought of as its CEO. So within the context of the broad business-level and functional-level strategic plans set by the company, individual managers of most medium-sized and larger hotels have ample opportunity to engage in a variety of strategic decisions affecting the profitability of their hotels. Keeping this in mind, we turn our attention to a discussion of the strategic planning process.

A hotel's strategic plan is the specific actions or initiatives it intends to follow in order to compete. The plan will include its strategies regarding pricing, service levels, personnel, renovations, marketing, and a variety of other issues that affect its competitive position. Once developed, a strategic plan may remain in place for some time or, depending on circumstances, may be revised quite often. In either case, a clear distinction must be made between the strategic plan itself and the process a hotel follows to develop a strategic plan. Strategies differ with circumstances, what is good strategy for one hotel may be bad for another. By understanding the process, management will be able to develop a strategic plan to fit whatever circumstances a hotel faces.

Overview of the strategic planning process

The strategic planning process can be divided into four basic steps:

1. Setting organizational goals and objectives.
2. Choosing the proper strategic plan.
3. Implementing the strategic plan.
4. Evaluating the strategic plan.

Figure 14.2 shows the steps involved in the strategic planning process and the manner in which each step relates to the others. Note the left-to-right flow of the dark arrows from goal setting to strategy formulating to implementing and finally to evaluation of results. There is a straightforward and powerful logic involved here. Setting goals is the first step in the strategic planning process. Goals give purpose to activity and define what success is. Setting organizational goals must precede the formulation of specific strategic plans because, to some degree, the choice of strategy depends on a firm's goals and objectives. Note in Figure 14.2 that the goals and strategic options of a hotel are affected by external factors and internal conditions. That is to say, external and internal circumstances limit the range of actions that can practically be taken by a hotel. It can happen that the strategic choices open to a hotel will not allow it to achieve certain goals. For example, a goal to increase room revenues by 10 percent next year may be impossible to achieve in light of new competition and a recession. There may be no strategy the hotel can follow to achieve that goal. Therefore, there exists a two-way interaction between goal setting and the choice of a strategic plan: (1) strategic plans must be chosen in such a way as to meet goals, but (2) the limitations that circum-stances place on strategic options must be taken into consideration when setting goals. This two-way interaction between goal setting and strategy formulation is indicated in Figure 14.2 by the two-headed arrow between the squares representing these steps in the strategic planning process.

Once a hotel decides on its grand strategic plan, it must be implemented. This requires formulating detailed long-term and annual objectives. It also requires operational strategies that follow from the grand strategy. At this point in the strategic planning process, much of the decision making and strategic thinking has been done and the actual work of implementing a

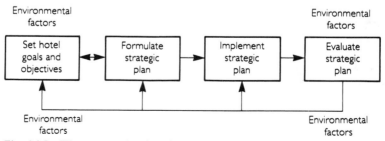

Fig. 14.2 The strategic planning process in hotels

strategic plan begins. It is during this phase that a hotel formulates annual budgets and detailed action plans. Detailed action plans and budgets are the signposts that direct a hotel's activities; action plans are the final result of strategic planning. A hotel's success or failure for the next quarter or year depends on successfully meeting the objectives and budgets it has set for itself through the strategic planning process.

Things do not always go according to plan. Thus, an important part of the strategic planning process is evaluation. Evaluation is an ongoing activity where comparisons are made between anticipated and actual outcomes. An important aspect of evaluation is management's ability to take corrective actions to keep the hotel moving toward its goals and objectives. In Figure 14.2 the arrows from the evaluation step of the strategic planning process return back to each of the other three steps. It is never possible to predict the future with certainty because the conditions upon which basic assumptions are made sometimes change. Thus, a hotel may need to change its operating strategies, sometimes grand strategies need to be rethought, and it can even happen that basic goals must be reviewed as underlying conditions change. The importance of the evaluation step is that it provides feedback to the other parts of the strategic planning process. Feedback gives management the information necessary to take whatever corrective action is appropriate to the circumstances.

Strategic planning is not a management exercise that, once accomplished, remains in place for the life of a hotel. Although plans usually have a specific time frame, strategic planning is best thought of as an ongoing process. As action plans are completed, results are evaluated against objectives and corrective action, if necessary, is taken. As environmental conditions change, basic assumptions and strategies must be reassessed. Although it is possible for certain goals and strategies to remain unchanged for many years, strategies at the individual hotel level often must be reassessed and adjusted more frequently.

Formulating a strategic plan

A strategic plan is based on an internal analysis of the hotel itself and an external analysis of the environment in which it operates. Figure 14.3 illustrates this process. The purpose of an internal analysis is to profile objectively the capabilities of the firm. A hotel's strengths might include its superior location, a particular management capability, or a cost advantage

Fig. 14.3 The process of formulating a strategic plan

over its competitors. Internal weaknesses might include obsolete facilities, high employee turnover, or the lack of a certain management capability.

A hotel might consider the strengths and weaknesses of its major functional departments, such as sales and marketing, accounting, rooms, and food and beverages. It would then develop a company profile of strengths and weaknesses within each of these functions (Tse, 1988).

How does a hotel determine which factors to include as strengths? Are strengths everything a firm does well (that is, its competencies)? A list of competencies would tend to become long and unfocused. Instead, hotels should develop relatively short lists of strengths based on their importance in influencing the competitive environment. A strength should be judged in relation to its ability to improve a hotel's competitive position. A strength gives a business some kind of competitive advantage. For example, a professionally competent executive chef should be listed as a hotel's strength only if his or her presence allows the hotel to gain an advantage over its competitors. On the other hand, a weakness is something that a firm does poorly that could be a competitive disadvantage. It can also be something that a firm is incapable of doing that its competitors can do (Haywood, 1986).

Finally, a list of strengths and weaknesses should be limited to those key factors that determine success or failure in a particular business. All aspects of what a hotel company or an individual hotel does are not equally important in its competitive struggle. Internal strengths and weaknesses should be limited to those areas that are critical to success or failure in the hotel business.

A firm's strategy must be based on external as well as internal factors. Changes in the external environment, such as the development of interstate highways during the 1960s, had a profound effect on the lodging industry. Holiday Inns devised a strategy based in part on this development and became the largest lodging company in the world as a result. At the local level, construction of a new competing hotel is a common example of an external change that might affect the strategy of an existing hotel. The external environment can be divided into two parts: the remote environment and the operating environment.

The remote environment consists of factors that may affect a firm, but over which it has no control. These factors include economic, social, political, and technological developments. Economic expansion or recession, deregulation of the airline industry, increased female business travel, teleconferencing technologies, and higher gasoline prices will, in varying degrees, affect the hotel business and play a role in a firm's ultimate choice of strategies.

The operating environment of a firm relates to factors such as competitive forces in its industry, its customers, suppliers, and creditors, and the labor market in which it operates (Porter, 1980). Factors in the operating environment directly influence how a hotel operates, and changes in these factors have an immediate impact on it. Also, actions of a hotel may impact on its operating environment.

Of particular importance to a hotel's strategic planning are competitive forces, customers, and labor markets. Assessing a hotel's competitive position requires analysis of factors such as location, market share, pricing, age and quality of facilities, competitors' actions, service levels, and marketing strategies. The end result of this exercise is a *competitive profile* of one hotel relative to its competition.

A guest profile is another important part of a hotel's operating environment. A hotel, like any business, needs to know as much as possible about its customers. As a beginning, guests are often classified into market segments based on their travel motives. The advertising and sales methods used to attract each category of guest vary greatly as do the services and facilities required by each. A simple classification by travel motive would be individual transient business; group business; individual transient pleasure; group pleasure; and other. Further subdivision of these broad categories may be useful. For example, the group business market may be further subdivided into conventions and business meetings. In turn, the convention market may be subdivided into business, professional, educational, fraternal, and special interest groups. The object of each further subdivision is to understand better the needs and wants of specific groups of customers so that they can be marketed to and served more efficiently.

Guests are also classified according to geographic, demographic, buying behavior and sometimes even personality and lifestyle characteristics. A geographic classification divides guests in terms of their place of residence. Demographic information includes age, sex, income, family size, education, and occupation. It is most akin to census-type information and is commonly used to differentiate one type of customer from another. Buying behavior includes such factors as frequency of stay, method of making a reservation (that is, through a travel agent, by a direct call to the hotel, through a reservation system, or as part of a package), and whether the guest has responded to a special promotion such as reduced weekend rates. Finally, personality and lifestyle characteristics can be useful in understanding buying behavior. Traits such as leisure-time activities, compulsiveness, gregariousness, and status needs can be important clues to the kinds of services and amenities guests seek while traveling. The importance of these characteristics, especially to resort hotels, is obvious. The trend toward elaborate hotel fitness centers, even in central city transient hotels, is an example of a response to a pervasive health and fitness-oriented lifestyle change in the United States.

The reason for developing a company profile and conducting an external analysis is to put a hotel in a position to:

● Analyze its internal strengths and weaknesses.
● Analyze its external opportunities and threats.

The process of analyzing internal strengths and weaknesses and external opportunities and threats is referred to as SWOT analysis. SWOT analysis allows a hotel to study its options systematically and to clarify the strategic choices open to it. Pearce and Robinson (1988, pp. 292–3) define the four SWOT variables as follows:

- *Strength* – a resource, skill, or other advantage relative to competitors and the needs of the markets a firm serves or anticipates serving.
- *Weakness* – a limitation or deficiency in resources, skills, and capabilities that seriously impedes effective performance.
- *Opportunity* – a major, favorable situation in a firm's environment.
- *Threat* – a major, unfavorable situation in a firm's environment.

SWOT analysis provides a systematic way of focusing on a firm's internal and external situation. Most businesses face both external threats and external opportunities. At the same time, they usually possess internal strengths and have internal weaknesses. The process of classifying each of these four factors and analyzing how they relate to each other helps the strategist to reach conclusions about whether the firm is operating from a position of relative strength or relative weakness and, in consequence, what types of strategy are most appropriate.

A good way to understand SWOT analysis is to depict these four factors in a diagram such as Figure 14.4. The vertical axis of the SWOT diagram portrays major external opportunities at the top and threats at the bottom. Likewise, the horizontal axis depicts internal weaknesses on the left and internal strengths on the right. These two axes divide Figure 14.4 into four quadrants. Quadrant 1 is, of course, ideal. A hotel faces major external opportunities and, at the same time, possesses substantial internal strengths. Such a favorable situation calls for an aggressive expansion strategy oriented toward growth. Consider an established and profitable convention hotel located near a large convention center. If the convention center announces plans for a major expansion, the hotel will likely consider an aggressive strategy that might include a substantial increase in rooms and facilities in anticipation of more convention business. Quadrant 2 depicts a situation where a hotel faces major external opportunities, but is saddled with internal weaknesses that prevent it from capitalizing on them. In this case a hotel must concentrate on overcoming internal deficiencies in order to take

Fig. 14.4 SWOT diagram

advantage of external opportunities. This case warrants an internal turn-around strategy. An example would be a hotel that is missing out on a rapidly growing convention market because of weaknesses in its banquet and catering department. Its strategy must be first to bolster this department and then to pursue aggressively the major market opportunity open to it (Prevette and Giudice, 1989).

In quadrants 3 and 4 a hotel faces major external threats. In quadrant 4, however, it possesses substantial internal strengths with which to meet its challenge. For example, a hotel may lose a major part of its transient business market to a new competitor with a better location. If this hotel's strength includes a strong and innovative sales and marketing department, it might decide to pursue an aggressive strategy of developing new markets to replace the one it has lost. Quadrant 3 confronts the hotel with a difficult set of circumstances. It not only faces a severe external threat but, at the same time, possesses internal weaknesses that make the external problem all the more serious. A hotel must adopt a defensive strategy in such circumstances. One such strategy, known as retrenchment, often results in belt tightening and cost reduction. Management feels the firm can survive (or else a strategy to sell the business, or its liquidation, would be appropriate), but only if costs are cut. At the same time, most firms also initiate a strategy intended to overcome the critical internal weaknesses that contributed to its predicament. Desperate times often call for desperate measures; retrenchment and turn-around strategies usually result in drastic cost cutting, employee layoffs, and replacement of key executives as the business struggles to survive. An older hotel, whose physical and service standards have slipped over time, may face a crisis situation when new hotels are built that compete directly for the same market segments. The strategic response is often to bring in a new GM and department heads who cut costs drastically in an attempt to keep the hotel afloat financially until turnaround strategies can be implemented.

The scope of hotel strategic planning

There is considerable latitude for strategic planning and decision making for medium-sized and larger hotels. Local conditions surrounding individual hotels will often vary widely, even within a small geographic area (Dev, 1989). Some of the factors that vary from one hotel to another within the same hotel company include the hotel's size, age, physical condition, types of market served, location relative to competitors, unionization, local economic conditions, ownership structure, and local labor market.

Another reason why certain strategic decisions must be made at the individual hotel level relates to the organizational and operational complexity found among medium-sized and larger hotels. As hotels grow in size, they become more complex. As a hotel's size and complexity increases, standardization becomes less possible (or desirable). Thus, local managers of complex hotels are responsible for developing and implementing many of the strategies and plans necessary for their business's success. Whereas managers of fast-food stores need only concern themselves with 'doing things right' (that is, being efficient), managers of complex hotels must be concerned also with 'doing the right things' (that is, being effective). We can put this into perspective by noting that a successful McDonald's will have annual sales of about $900,000 and that a 100 unit budget motel will have sales of about $750,000. According to *Lodging Hospitality* (Anon., 1988), the Four Seasons Hotel in Washington, DC, a medium-sized hotel with 197 rooms and suites, had revenues of $22.5 million in 1987; the Ritz-Carlton Hotel in Chicago, with 437 rooms, had revenues of $40 million; and the New York Hilton and Towers, with 2,100 rooms, had revenues of $120 million.

The hotel planning time horizon

A certain amount of planning must take place simply to maintain a hotel's long-term viability. This constitutes one obvious type of strategic planning. With the exception of decisions to maintain building and equipment, the time horizon of most hotel-level strategic decisions is determined by factors in the markets in which it competes. The planning horizon could be as short as a few months if a hotel is revising its advertising and pricing strategies during its slow season. The planning horizon could be as long as a couple of years if the decision concerns building new meeting facilities to compete in the business meetings market. A six- to twelve-month time horizon might be required to perfect a new restaurant concept. Generally speaking, most strategic planning at the individual hotel level seldom exceeds a time horizon of more than a few years. This is not to say that GMs do not think about the long-term future of their hotels. They do indeed. What it does mean is that most of the *strategic decisions* that an individual hotel must make (that is, those that affect its competitive position) will seldom have time horizons of more than two to three years.

Research into hotel general manager effectiveness (Nebel, 1991) has formed the basis for much of our discussion about strategic planning at the individual hotel level. The following quotes and the two hotel-level strategic planning examples that follow are based on that research.

Here is what excellent GMs feel about their hotel's planning horizon. One described his time horizon as 'ninety-day decision making.' He did, of course, make many strategic decisions that affected his hotel's longer-term future. Nevertheless, an important point was being made. As an *operations manager*, this GM expects to begin seeing the results of his decisions rather quickly. A similar sentiment was expressed by another GM. When asked about his planning horizon, he said he liked to stay three to six months ahead of his staff. Another describes his job as being 'visionary'. To him, a visionary is one who plans six months to two years into the future. In this GM's opinion, changing market conditions make it impossible to plan any more than two years into the future. One GM, whose company is noted for its systematic planning, considered the 'long run' for a hotel to be a vision that looks three to five years down the road. These managers all expect their hotels to be viable businesses for many years to come. Still, most of the strategic decisions they make have fairly short-run time horizons.

The GM's role in strategic planning

A hotel GM plays a crucial role in strategic planning. Figure 14.5 shows the organizational structure above and below the GM in a hotel company. When a hotel is owned by a group of investors but managed by a hotel company, a GM has two bosses: his or her immediate hotel-company superior (often a regional VP) and the investor group that owns the hotel. It is not uncommon for a regional VP to be an experienced GM who, in addition to having responsibility for a number of hotels in the region, also manages a hotel. Regional VPs are, without a doubt, busy people. They do not have time to gain in-depth knowledge about each hotel reporting to them, or each hotel's local environment. Regional VPs must certainly approve major strategic initiatives initiated by the GMs they supervise, but it is unlikely that regional VPs can initiate strategic plans for the hotels under them.

Hotel owners are often real-estate developers, successful businesspeople, or large institutional investors such as insurance companies and pension funds. These groups usually have diverse business interests and often little detailed knowledge of hotel operations. For this reason, hotel companies contract with owners to manage their hotels. Investor groups cannot be expected to be the sole initiators of strategic plans. They are certainly intimately involved in the strategic decision-making process, but often in a ratifying role rather than an initiating one.

Therefore the individual hotel's GM plays a central role in evaluating a hotel's strategic options. The GM must understand and rationalize the goals of both the hotel company and the hotel's owners. The GM has responsibility for the total business success of the hotel. Of all the hotel's executive staff, the GM brings the most hotel experience to the job of formulating a strategic plan. Strategic planning involves input from all of a hotel's key executives. A hotel's department heads, and especially its executive

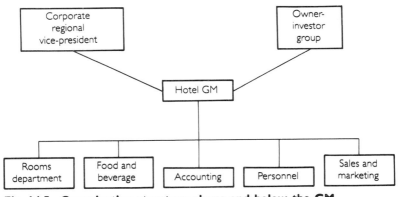

Fig. 14.5 Organization structure above and below the GM

committee members, play a vital role in this process. These executives, however, are fully engaged with the day-to-day management of their departments. To be effective, a GM should take a leadership role in developing a hotel's strategic plan. Such a role, of course, includes full consultation with and concurrence from upper management, owners, and key hotel department heads. A GM must be convincing and persistent when presenting ideas up the line. Regional VPs and owners will naturally question any and all plans, especially if ill-conceived. Effective strategic planning also requires input and agreement from department heads. They must be part of the process if they are truly to 'buy into' a hotel's plans.

Setting a hotel's strategic service vision

Heskett (1986) believes that all successful service firms have developed a *strategic service vision*. Such firms have: (1) a targeted market, (2) a well-defined service concept, (3) a focused operating strategy, and (4) a well-designed service delivery system. A targeted market means a clear identification of the group(s) of customers a company intends to serve. Knowledge of one's customers means not only knowing who they are but also their needs. A well-defined service concept refers to how a business's services are perceived by its customers and its employees. Since many hotel services are intangible, guests' perceptions are important. A service concept is concerned with the way guests view the services a hotel provides and also with the way in which employees view the kinds of service they are providing. To be effective, a hotel must be sure that both groups are in correspondence with regard to this vital question. A focused operating strategy sets forth the service elements that are of strategic importance for carrying out the service concept. Hotels, like people, cannot usually be good at everything. They therefore need to focus on the things that they must do well. Finally, a well-designed service delivery system brings together all of the management procedures, systems, and physical facilities necessary to deliver key services to a specific target market. The service delivery system puts together people, facilities, and technology to carry out the hotel's strategic service vision.

Determining markets to serve

One outstanding GM sounded like he was quoting from a textbook when he said 'Choosing target markets is an essential element of planning.' He also echoed Heskett by pointing out that a hotel must decide on a proper 'service level' for each market segment it chooses to target. Another GM felt that good hotel planning results in 'a product well positioned in the marketplace and a good service delivery system.'

For many reasons, the lodging market is far from static, and competition is usually keen. Effective hotel managers keep a close eye on market conditions and often begin their strategic planning with a thorough review of the markets their hotel is currently serving and those it may wish to serve in the future (Haywood, 1986).

Setting service and quality standards

When one outstanding GM took over management of a major hotel, his review of the markets it was then serving revealed a startling possibility. It appeared to him that the hotel was targeting the right markets, but that it might be charging too little. With some service upgrades and a selective renovation program, the hotel could move up a quality notch relative to its competition. The GM felt that current guests would be willing to pay higher room rates for improved services and upgraded quality. It turned out that he was right. With improved services and freshly renovated guest rooms he raised room rates and, lo and behold, occupancy increased! This was all the more remarkable because it was accomplished during a period of falling city-wide occupancies. This GM had not changed the hotel's target markets; he just understood that his guests were willing and able to pay more for an enhanced level of service and quality.

Two important variables that affect service levels and quality goals in hotels are (1) staffing levels and (2) capital expenditure decisions. There is a relation-ship, though not a direct one, between a hotel's level of guest service and its number of employees. Higher service levels often mean more employees (and, of course, higher labor costs). For example, the Ritz-Carlton Hotel in downtown Chicago is reported to have 630 employees for its 437 guest rooms. On the other hand, the Roosevelt Hotel in New York City employs 500 people for its 1,070 rooms (*Lodging Hospitality*, 1988). Both hotels are quite successful. Both hotels are quite different. They cater, of course, to different market segments, provide different levels of service, and employ vastly different staffing levels in relation to the number of guests they serve.

Certain hotel capital expenditures are dictated solely by physical consider-ations. When heating systems fail they must be replaced, when roofs leak they must be repaired. But capital expenditures are also driven by the types of market a hotel wishes to serve. Hotels 'wear out' quickly from intensive use. It is easy, in pursuit of short-run profits, to put off replacing carpets, repainting a ballroom, or modernizing guest bathrooms. Such decisions, however, may be inconsistent with a hotel's long-term goal of catering to certain market segments. Thus, unless a hotel makes a conscious decision to refocus its attention on a less demanding or less quality-conscious type of guest, capital expenditure levels must be maintained, sometimes even in the face of falling short-term profits.

The remainder of this chapter will demonstrate the use of SWOT analysis in hotels. The examples are actual situations drawn from two hotels that took part in the GM research conducted by one of the authors (Nebel, 1991). The hotels' internal strengths and weaknesses, and external opportunities and threats, were determined from conversations and meetings with the GMs and other senior executives. What follows are real situations as well as the actual strategies each hotel formulated.

Two examples of hotel-level strategic planning

In the real world, hotels usually possess internal strengths and weaknesses and face external opportunities and threats. The practical question that must be answered is whether, on balance, a hotel is operating from a position of internal strength in an environment that offers opportunities, or whether it is operating from a position of internal weakness in an environment that offers threats.

An aggressive strategic plan

When Ben Franklin took over as GM of the Stars and Stripes Hotel, it might at first glance have appeared that his hotel's operating environment was one of numerous external threats and few opportunities. To begin with, the local hotel market was overbuilt. Over the past four years, eight new hotels had added 4,500 new hotel rooms to the city's inventory. All except one of these hotels competed directly with Ben's hotel. There had been a serious downturn in one of the area's major industries, thus causing a substantial drop in business travel. In consequence, city-wide hotel occupancy had fallen by 20 percent. Other external factors looked like threats. Although the city was a major tourist destination, there were no funds available to promote tourism that might offset the fall in business travel. The city's convention center, while large, was currently operating close to capacity and could not be counted on to boost business further. Finally, the hotel's major competitor had a better location, was larger, and had superior facilities. Although the Stars and Stripes was not losing money, both occupancy and average room rate had fallen from previous levels, as had profits.

A pessimist would have cause to view this external environment with some alarm. Ben Franklin is an optimist, so he chose to look at other factors and also to interpret existing conditions differently. Although the city was overbuilt, things had stabilized; there were no new hotels planned, and a few older, less competitive properties were in financial difficulties. So, it was possible that the city's hotel inventory might fall slightly over the next few years. While not growing rapidly, the city's convention business was quite large and healthy. It represented a stable core business for Franklin's hotel. Although far from a certainty, it seemed likely that the city's convention center would be doubled in size within the next five years. While the city had little money to advertise, it was a nationally recognized tourist destination with considerable appeal and potential.

Being new to the city, Ben wondered if business travel had really fallen as much as most locals thought. Could the expansion of hotel rooms have spread the existing business around and made it appear to have decreased? These were his preliminary thoughts about the operating environment facing his hotel. The only major remote environmental factor of note was the fact that the US economy was expanding briskly and inflation was low, an encouraging sign for pleasure travel. On the international scene the dollar had fallen in value, thus stimulating foreign travel to the United States. The remote environment looked favorable for the next few years.

Franklin felt that his hotel possessed considerable internal strengths. To start with, it had a very good location: it was within walking distance of the convention center, the central business district, major shopping areas, and the city's entertainment and dining district. It could therefore effectively serve the business, convention, and pleasure travel markets. The hotel's design and maintenance were also quite good. The hotel was basically well managed, was operating smoothly, and was delivering quality guest services. Finally, the parent hotel company was well managed and highly regarded in the markets in which it competed.

Franklin's internal analysis did reveal one rather substantial weakness. Although only about a decade old, the hotel had already begun to look a little worn and dated. Physical upkeep had been neglected during the past three years of declining revenues and profits. The hotel needed a general refurbishing to bring its 'look' up to the standards of the eight new competing hotels. Money needed to be spent to make the hotel look fresh again.

These were his preliminary findings concerning external opportunities and threats, and internal strengths and weaknesses. Franklin discovered that his sales staff felt that the individual transient market, whether the pleasure or business traveler, had dried up for the hotel. His sales staff did feel that the group pleasure market held promise, and they were devoting resources to it.

This left conventions and meetings as the hotel's primary market. The facts bore this out. In 1985, 82 percent of the hotel's total room-nights had come from group business, and 90 percent of that was convention and business meetings. This was not unusual. After all, the Stars and Stripes is a large convention hotel. In order to protect its dominant market, the hotel had a policy of not accepting individual transient reservations through its corporate reservation system more than two weeks in advance. By so doing it felt it was guarding against overbooking transient guests at the expense of its dominant convention business. Since transient reservations had not been accepted more than two weeks in advance, there was the possibility of a substantial number of reservation turndowns of people who tried to book more than two weeks ahead. Franklin analyzed transient turndowns in the reservation system in some detail and concluded that there was a small but consistent base of transient business travelers of which his hotel was not taking full advantage.

He also studied the results of an aggressive advertising campaign the hotel had conducted a few years earlier. The campaign, conducted during a major city festival, was aimed at pleasure travelers. High occupancies had occurred during the normally slow summer months of that year, but management had attributed this increase more to the appeal of the one-time festival than to the appeal of the city. Were the same results possible based only on the city's appeal, if low, off-season room rates were offered? In analyzing the hotel's group business over the past few years, it became apparent that there was significant business in some geographic markets that had simply never been solicited. Summing up the positives, Ben concluded that his hotel faced a variety of interesting external market opportunities, which included:

- A small but consistent transient business base.
- A possibly large, but price-sensitive, off-season pleasure market.
- A number of neglected geographic markets for group business.
- A large and stable convention and group base.
- A possible doubling of the city's convention center.
- A modestly growing group pleasure segment.

Franklin felt that most of his external threats were behind him. Problems in the external environment had already occurred and his hotel's position was unlikely to erode further over the next few years. On the other hand, it appeared that most of his external opportunities were still in the future. He judged the opportunities to be significant, if not unlimited, so his outlook could be described as optimistic if not wildly enthusiastic. Still, when coupled with his assessment of the hotel's strength, he placed himself within quadrant 1 of the SWOT diagram. Point *a* of Figure 14.6 would be a good representation of his assessment. If the market opportunities he identified were to materialize, if the convention center expansion became a reality, and the local economy rebounded somewhat, his situation would improve dramatically. If, at the same time, he could overcome his one major internal weakness through an aggressive renovation program, then the future might indeed look bright. This condition could be depicted as point *b* in Figure 14.6, which calls for an aggressive strategy.

Based on this kind of thinking, Franklin formulated an aggressive strategic plan. The major elements of this plan were as follows:

- The hotel embarked on an aggressive $49 per room summer rate advertising campaign. Ads were placed in major metropolitan markets within

Fig. 14.6 SWOT analysis

a 500 mile radius and were intended to appeal to the transient pleasure market.

- Transient rooms were made available through the company's national reservation system six months in advance, but without any price discount. This was a move to increase transient business travel but only at favorable room rates.
- Rooms were discounted through the reservation system only when the hotel had fewer than 950 group-rooms booked. In this way he was able to keep the average room rate for transient business high when the hotel had few individual rooms available because of heavy convention bookings.
- He canceled most of the hotel's $40 per room contacts with airline crews in anticipation of increased occupancy and higher room rates.
- He assigned sales representatives to New York City and Washington, DC, to develop new group business that had never before been solicited.
- He won approval from corporate for an $11 million renovation and refurbishing program for the hotel to bring it up to the standards of its newer competitors.

These were aggressive, bold moves on Ben Franklin's part which were instituted during a period of depressed city-wide occupancies and room rates. As it turned out, his assessment of conditions was quite accurate and the aggressive strategy proved to be successful. The advertising campaign added 36,000 room-nights during the next summer, saving the hotel from a disastrous period. Transient business travel did increase when the reservation system was opened six months in advance, and these bookings were predominantly at high rates. Group business increased from the New York and Washington, DC markets. Finally, the renovations kept the hotel at a quality level comparable to its competitors, thus making unnecessary the discounting of room rates in order to compete. Over the first two years of this strategy, occupancies increased by more than 15 percent and average room rates rose by over 10 percent. The resulting revenues and profits were sufficient to justify the $11 million renovation as well as the other expenditures related to the hotel's new strategic plan. As a final footnote, the city's convention center was, in fact, doubled in size. By pursuing an aggressive strategy, Franklin had a newly renovated, profitable hotel ideally positioned to benefit from additional convention business.

Because the Stars and Stripes Hotel was basically internally strong, we have focused mostly on the strategic moves that related to its external environment. Different external and internal circumstances will call for a hotel to fashion different strategies. The second example is a hotel that had to fashion a very different strategy to survive.

A plan of retrenchment and turnaround

When Napoleon Bonaparte became GM of the Hotel Parie' it faced major external threats. It also had a number of internal weaknesses, which made the situation quite precarious. The hotel was losing a lot of money and its owners were seriously considering filing for bankruptcy. Here is the situation Bonaparte faced. The 500 room Hotel Parie' was a four-year-old luxury property built to cater to affluent business travelers and to small, upscale business meetings and conventions. Its preconstruction feasibility study envisioned about 50 percent of its occupancy from individual transient business guests, 40 percent from small, upscale group business, and 10 percent from individual pleasure travel. From the day of its opening, radical changes in local business conditions resulted in most of the transient business travel market being lost, with little likelihood of its return. For the first three years of its operation this hotel suffered low occupancies and heavy losses.

Compounding these threatening external conditions were severe internal weaknesses. As losses mounted, the GM who had opened the hotel seemed unable to cope with the situation. More and more, the hotel was allowed just to run itself with little direction from above. Management and staff turnover was high, morale was non-existent, and the hotel was suffering operating losses of half a million dollars each month. When Bonaparte took over as GM, occupancy the previous year was 30 percent and a 'realistic' occupancy goal for the next year had been set at 40 percent. If this hotel was not dead, it was certainly crippled. Its situation corresponded to something like point c in quadrant 3 of Figure 14.6. The Hotel Parie' had serious internal weaknesses and faced ominous external threats.

The strategy Napoleon chose to follow was a combination of both retrenchment and turnaround. He needed to cut costs quickly. Previous management had done little in this regard, even in the face of low revenues and huge losses. Bonaparte's first move to forestall bankruptcy was to slash the hotel's staff by 120 people and then to economize in every other way possible. These were extremely difficult decisions, but in desperate circumstances extreme measures are often required. This is a classic example of a retrenchment strategy designed to keep a business alive while a turnaround strategy can be devised.

Because of the many internal problems his hotel faced, Bonaparte's turnaround strategy had to focus on internal issues. Although many things had to be done, the most important, he felt, was to rekindle a winning feeling among his management and staff. While it was understandable that after three years of heavy losses attitudes had turned negative, a continuation of a negative mindset would prevent a turnaround from ever occurring. Napoleon first turned to goal setting. The hotel's previous occupancy goal for the next year had been 40 percent. At this occupancy the hotel would continue to lose large sums of money and, in all likelihood, would be thrown into bankruptcy before the end of the year. Working toward a 40 percent occupancy goal was a futile effort since, even if reached, it would not avert bankruptcy. However, a 60 percent occupancy, coupled with labor cost saving already accomplished, would result in a positive cash flow that would keep the hotel going. Thus, in the fall he announced to his executive staff that the hotel's occupancy goal for the coming year had been raised from 40 percent to 60 percent and that he had every intention of meeting that goal. This was a stunning statement for the hotel's executives. They knew that the hotel would probably finish the current year with an average occupancy of only 25 percent! Napoleon did not give them much time to think about this. At the same time as announcing the new occupancy goal, he initiated a series of changes which included:

- Spending $60,000 on guest room rehabilitation.
- Adding $60,000 to the hotel's employee training budget.
- Relocating the catering department so that its offices were adjacent to the sales department. He also began an extensive upgrade of both departments' physical appearance.
- Constructing a VIP lounge adjacent to the main lobby.
- Initiating a number of ambitious civic projects requiring the active participation of most key executives.
- Embarking upon a complete reorganization of the hotel to make it more responsive to the guests' needs.
- Increasing the number and quality of the hotel's sales managers in order to concentrate on the small convention and business-meetings market.
- Increasing the secretarial and support services of the sales department.

In addition to these initiatives, his management style consisted of an aggressive, hands-on involvement in every aspect of the hotel's operation. He also exerted constant pressure on executives to produce results. To his way of thinking, he had 'eliminated the excuses and then demanded results.' Some thought of him as a tyrant; others as a genius. He was trusted by some of the staff and not by others. No matter what their individual feelings, after one year there was a unanimous feeling that his strategies and personal involvement in the hotel's management had saved the hotel from bankruptcy. As it turned out, the hotel did meet its 60 percent occupancy goal, a result thought completely unattainable just fifteen months earlier. The hotel also accomplished most of the other initiatives Napoleon had forced on it.

Napoleon Bonaparte's first year at the Hotel Parie' had been one of long hours, hard work, and constant agitation. It was also one during which things started to get done, victories were won, and people accustomed to failure began to experience success. Through all the hardships there was, as his staff called him, this 'little bulldog of a GM' constantly prodding, pushing, and challenging them to reach goals and to achieve results they had previously considered unattainable. His turnaround strategy transformed a losing team into a winner. Internal weaknesses were overcome, and the hotel was repositioned into the small convention and business-meetings markets. The hotel was saved from the brink of bankruptcy and is now a viable business with a future. A strategy of retrenchment and turnaround, born out of desperation, worked.

References

Anon. (1988) 'Lodging hospitality's top 400 performers', *Lodging Hospitality*, vol. 44, no. 9, pp. 50–3.

Dev, Chekitan, S. (1989) 'Operating environment and strategy: the profitable connection', *Cornell Hotel and Restaurant Administration Quarterly*, vol. 30, no. 2, pp. 8–13.

Haywood, K. Michael (1986) 'Scouting the competition for survival and success', *Cornell Hotel and Management Administration Quarterly*, vol. 27, no. 3, pp. 80–7.

Heskett, James, L. (1986) *Managing in the Service Economy*, Boston, Mass.: Harvard Business School Press.

Nebel, Eddystone, C., III (1991) *Managing Hotels Effectively: Lessons for outstanding general managers*, New York: Van Nostrand Reinhold.

Pearce, J. A., II and Robinson, B. R. Jr (1988) *Strategic Management*, Homewood, Ill.: Richard D. Irwin, Inc.

Porter, M. E. (1980) *Competitive Strategy: Techniques for Analyzing Industries and Competitors*, New York: Free Press.

Prevette, L.K., and Giudice, J. (1989) 'Anatomy of a turnaround: the Los Angeles Biltmore', *Cornell Hotel and Restaurant Administration Quarterly*, vol. 30, no. 3, pp. 30–5.

Tse, Eliza Ching-Yick (1988) 'Defining corporate strengths and weaknesses: is it essential for successful strategy implementation?', *Hospitality Education and Research Journal*, vol. 12, no. 2, pp. 57–72.

Part 4

Corporate systems
and analysis

The five chapters in Part 4 are concerned with some of the key functional and operational issues relating to effective organizational performance. Chapters 15 and 16 both address the critical role of information in managing and appraising multinational hospitality operations. Increasingly, operational concerns are focusing on productivity and service quality requirements, which, if considered separately, provide sources of conflict. Chapter 17 examines the relationship between labor strategy and productivity and concludes that future developments will be driven by the need for greater productivity. In achieving this, it is necessary to maintain a clear understanding of customer needs and expectations of hospitality services. Chapter 18 examines the strategic role of service quality in achieving business objectives, which is illustrated by Hyatt's approach to developing flexible and responsive corporate and regional organizations in Chapter 19.

On both sides of the Atlantic significant demographic changes have been occurring in recent years and the hospitality industry, which has traditionally depended on a supply of young, low-cost workers, is having to cope with the consequences of a diminishing labor supply. The international hospitality industry provides comparatively few examples of effective strategies for achieving high productivity or the innovative use of technology. Chapter 15 argues that, if managed strategically, information technology may offer some of the solutions to the problems faced by multinational-hospitality firms as they seek to improve service quality in an increasingly competitive arena.

Chapter 16 seeks to examine how information, both financial and non-financial, can be used to monitor the progress of a business in order to predict the likelihood of success or failure. Central to this analysis is the potential use of failure-prediction models to assess corporate financial positions. Where appropriate, such models are applied to financial data from the hospitality industry using examples of successes and failures in financial terms. The concluding section of the chapter considers the effectiveness of general prediction models and their potential range of applications.

As neither the workforce nor the organization change every time business strategy changes, it can be assumed that labor strategy operates independently. However, the relationship between organizational behavior and labor markets critically depends on productivity targets and the degree of workforce stability. Set in the context of hotels, Chapter 17 highlights how organizational behavior relates to the economics of hotels, and argues that productivity incentives must be set within a coherent policy framework if they are to be effective.

Ultimately, maintaining quality is concerned with how the operation is managed in order to ensure that service is right first time, every time. The authors of Chapter 18 argue that if management intervention in service interaction is to be effective, it is necessary to identify how the competencies associated with the management of quality can be developed in the context of total quality management. This perspective provides the basis of a framework for identifying quality as a strategic issue and for developing and maintaining a strategy of service quality excellence in multinational hospitality firms.

The final chapter is set in the context of predicted two billion global business and tourism-related travel movements by the year 2000. Specifically, Chapter 19 aims to highlight Hyatt International Corporation's entrepreneurial approach to development and to examine some of the organizational implications of developing a global network of hotels and resorts which is responsive to regional needs and opportunities.

Richard Teare

15

The strategic role of information technology systems

Paul R. Gamble

It seems almost tautological to consider the strategic role of information technology (IT) systems. Most writers appear to assume automatically that there is a link between strategic management and IT. Yet the empirical evidence to support such a view is very hard to find in almost any industry. It might be suggested that the role of computerized reservation services (CRS) in the airline industry and to a lesser extent automated teller machines in banking have been in some way strategic. Undoubtedly, such developments have had a major impact on the distribution channels for some services with a corresponding impact in marketing and sales. And viewed in the context of the financial difficulties of the world's major airlines and the repeated expressions of consumer dissatisfaction with banking services, the short-term advantage of such systems becomes apparent. However, it is difficult to sustain an argument that a true strategic repositioning has been achieved through IT.

Perhaps the best example of strategic influence is available anecdotally. It has been suggested that IT, particularly in the form of personal computers (of which there were a paltry half million or so in the Soviet Union of 1991) were partly responsible for defeating the coup attempt against Gorbachev. It was PCs, acting as word processors and communications devices, that enabled the forces of democracy to keep people informed throughout the crisis (Abrahams, 1991). The technology involved here was not especially advanced in Western terms. In 1991, due to trade embargoes, the Soviet Union possessed very few computers, and was even using 80286 microprocessors. The equivalent of an IBM PC AT cost 80 times its Western counterpart.

The strategic influence of technology

The potential strategic influence lay not so much in the hardware of the devices but in the way that they were used. This is actually a key point. When considering the effect of IT, the technology as hardware often receives the greatest emphasis and yet frequently the hardware is of the least importance strategically. Frederick Winslow Taylor (1911) would have been unlikely to regard his scientific management as a technology which affected the behavior of an organization. Yet the impact of scientific management on the work groups exposed to it was so strong that in 1914 the method was banned by the US Congress from use in American defense industries.

Conceptually, it is useful to understand what is really involved when the role of technology is examined. Winner (1977) separates technology usefully into three broad but distinct elements.

- Technology as apparatus is intended to refer to tools, gadgets, or physical devices (probably the most common conception of technology).
- Technology as technique includes skills, procedures, or routines to achieve a purpose related to specific goals.
- Technology as organization describes social structures which are created to achieve technical, rational productive ends.

Thus Winner offers technology as machines, technology as expertise, and technology as politics. In practice, information technology spans all three facets of this definition. The effect of technology on various characteristics of organizational behavior has been studied for many years principally from two perspectives. Quantitative approaches using comparative analysis have attempted to identify purported relationships between technology and some aspect of the size or structure of an organization. Systems approaches have tended to favor a more descriptive but perhaps more holistic overview. This work has often been based on definitions which seek to bring the elements of technology together. Thus Perrow (1973) defines technology as 'the actions that an individual performs on an object with or without the assistance of mechanical devices, in order to make some change in that object' (p. 194). Pugh and Hickson (1976) present a definition at a higher and possibly more strategic level which seeks to encompass all three elements. To them, technology is 'the sequence of physical techniques used upon the workflow of the organization ... the concept covers both the pattern of operations and the equipment used' (p. 93).

In essence many studies have attempted to plot the impact of what Fox (1974, p. 1) calls 'material technology' on what he calls 'social technology.' Material technology can be seen, touched, and heard, while social technology seeks to order behavior and relationships in purposive ways. Given the extent to which technology straddles these two areas and the differing levels of meaning which the word acquires, it is unsurprising that research findings are sometimes contradictory.

At the beginning of the 1980s, Keen (1981) observed that this blurring of effects was impeding the development of a clear theoretical basis for studying the impact of IT. Keen noted that, in considering the effects of such potentially strategic issues as office automation, teleconferencing and electronic banking the literature had not yet reached the point of articulating the interconnection between IT and strategic management. There was no finite set of concepts, no analytical framework, nor even a reasonably coherent set of normative prescriptions. A predominantly tactical orientation of little apparent relevance to the formulation of objectives or organizational goals characterizes the approach and this has advanced little in the intervening decade.

The diffusion of IT as an innovation

This lack of a theoretical framework and the failure to distinguish properly between the relative importance of material technology and social technology seems to mislead both managers and researchers. In particular, both groups often appear to be surprised by the stage which the hospitality industry has reached, or failed to reach, in the continuum from invention, through innovation to the diffusion of best practice. Three examples at the extreme ends of the technological spectrum might serve to illustrate the point.

In a monograph on the progress of office automation, Webster (1991) suggests that information technology in the office may *still* have very radical consequences for the way that office work is organized. However, she goes on to note that its impact to date has been negligible in terms of work organization and the design of office jobs. Essentially one artefact, the word processor, has replaced another, the typewriter. The modern word processor is a microcomputer with a much broader range of functions than a typewriter. As a device it has been available for more than twenty years but it does not seem to have had any strategic impacts as yet. From a tactical perspective it is even possible that some deskilling has taken place at lower organizational levels and that, at higher levels, managers now undertake for themselves tasks which were formerly delegated.

Another strategic advance that has been waiting in the wings for a decade or more is the convergence of both voice and computer technologies. In the early 1980s, IBM even bought a telephone equipment manufacturing company called Rolm so as to position itself strategically for this developing market. It is clearly a market of major strategic potential, especially in the global hospitality industry. A telephone reservation confirmed instantly over the same line by fax offers significant customer benefits. The major technology involved here is that of integrated services digital networks (ISDN) which will permit voice, graphic, and data signals to be encoded and transmitted digitally over the same lines. However, during the decade little real commercial progress was made. IBM subsequently sold its share in Rolm and the world's major network operators such as British Telecom and France Telecom announced BISDN in 1991 (broadband ISDN). This has a higher capacity than ISDN and will be better for linking into the local area networks of PCs, but progress has been very slow and it may be ten more years before widespread end-user services actually arrive.

A third example might be drawn from the related technology of artificial intelligence (AI) and expert systems. In the mid 1980s much was forecast for this type of software development and indeed, some applications using an AI methodology have been incorporated into software used by the hospitality industry. Yield management systems developed by one of the leading companies in the computerized property management system (PMS) market, Computerized Lodging Systems Inc., incorporated these techniques into a rule-based system written in list processing language (LISP) to interface with their PMS. It was developed and tested at the Sonesta Hotel in Cambridge, Massachusetts, and incorporated some 2,000 rules (Berkus, 1988). Burger King Corporation bought a version of Mrs Field's Cookies AI-based retail operations intelligence (ROI) software (Newquist, 1991a). British brewers Inde Coope installed a prize-winning expert manufacturing intelligence system (Flood, 1991).

Yet none of these examples is really of strategic import; none of them has changed the business process involved. Yield management is a tactical pricing system, ROI is a work scheduling, tactical marketing, and personnel management system, and the brewery system monitors electricity usage in manufacturing. AI Corp, one of the world's largest specialist companies in the artificial intelligence field had a turnover in 1990 of only $23 million and its nearest two rivals could manage only $5 million.

Both theoretically and practically, therefore, it can be argued that the role of IT in strategic management is still emerging. The 1970s were characterized by formal, analytical approaches to strategic planning exemplified by writers such as Mumford and Pettigrew (1975). In the 1980s this changed to a pronounced emphasis on competitor analysis and the search for competitive advantage, best exemplified by Porter (1985). If these theoretical foundations are developed, the 1990s could see an emerging recognition that IT is an enabling mechanism which facilitates organizational change. Such a change could support the redefinition of business scope and the implementation of business structures which will improve competitive actions in the marketplace. In order to achieve this movement, the perception of IT as a predominantly machine-based technology obsessed with processor speeds, transfer rates and disk capacities must change. Strategically, the role of IT in terms of expertise (management know-how) and politics (networks of decision makers) must come to the fore.

Pressures for change: technology push versus knowledge pull

The rate at which innovations are adopted and the way in which they affect the behavior of an organization depend on a number of factors. Essentially, these may be categorized as the importance of influences within, balanced against the strength of forces without. These two approaches are sometimes categorized as technology push and knowledge pull. Technology push refers to industries in which changing technology fundamentally affects the nature of goods and services. Thus an automobile factory seeking to compete with a robot-driven production line is being pushed by technological change. On the other hand, a dynamic company which is actively seeking to improve its competitive position might be keen to obtain technology. Thus a hospitality company might decide that a daily analysis of a city's business travelers would offer a significant competitive advantage. It might then seek a technology which would allow it to collect and model large volumes of data conveniently and rapidly.

A recognition of the need for change must come largely from existing managers within the prevailing organizational culture. The rate of change is therefore governed by this constraint. In the adoption of innovation, the attitudes of key administrators have been widely hypothesized to correlate positively with rates of adoption. Many of the studies conducted to test this idea were carried out in the public sector. However, in a study of innovation in the shoe-manufacturing industry, Cohn (1980) set out to determine whether the results could be generalized to firms in the commercial sector. Overall his findings confirmed earlier work but with two important codicils.

The first of these is the absence of a consistent relationship between presidential (chief executive) attitudes and adoption. Cohn accounts for this in terms of the consensual management style employed in the shoe industry and suggests, therefore, that the chief executive's influence may depend on the decision-making structure of the firm. The second codicil relates to adoption behavior and the attitudes of the total management staff, not fully examined in earlier studies. Cohn found a link between the behavior of senior middle managers and the rate of adoption of innovations. He argues that the risk and uncertainty of planning for change may be borne by a few managers who bring an innovation to trial. Favorable attitudes (and results) amongst these managers may then foster the necessary cooperation and support from other managers. On the other hand, unfavorable attitudes to innovation by the total managerial staff do not seem to impede the innovation if it is supported by a senior manager. The risks of adoption are borne by those who decide to support the trial.

In a hierarchical industry like hospitality, organizations could respond to knowledge pull or to technology push particularly if senior managers are inclined to do so. Thus the strategic stance that these firms habitually adopt may give a clue to their future behavior. In this respect, Nystrom (1979) distinguishes between positional and innovative companies. Innovative companies take the view that the future is uncertain and changing, and they assume a posture accordingly. Positional companies operate in what they perceive as stable environments; they eschew change and adopt innovation reactively in response to their operating environment. Most crucially, Nystrom overlays these categories with a notion of latency, related to organization size and innovative orientation. A small organization with an unclear innovative orientation is classified most centrally as positional. Basic orientation may be changed and innovative potential increased following a change in top management.

Clearly, a company involved with microelectronics would be foolhardy to take any but the innovative stance. Hospitality companies are difficult to categorize as anything other than positional. If a more strategic orientation is to be adopted in the 1990s, some examination of the external forces for change must be identified.

Technology push

Since information is central to the management of all types of organization, the cost of handling and processing it is an important criterion for deployment. In the last decade, the economics of IT have changed both absolutely and relatively. At an absolute level, it is expected that these changes will continue at the rate of 20 to 30 percent per year. Table 15.1 illustrates what effect this might have.

These data are derived from a study by MIT, taking 4.5 million instructions per second (MIPs) as a measure of processing power. It will be noticed that the cost of a computer of this type was considered equivalent to 210 workers of a certain skill level in 1980, but that this is equivalent to only one-eighth of the cost of one worker by the year 2000. Organizations and managers therefore face quite different trade-offs in the next decade.

During the 'competitive' era of the 1970s, it was argued (Porter and Millar, 1985) that information technology would not only transform the nature of products, but would change the nature of competition itself. Organizations would therefore need to be connected to this type of technology and their managers would need to understand how to exploit it if strategic shifts were to be achieved. A recent report (Craver, 1990) on the implementation of strategic IT projects called for companies to achieve a ratio of one to three within the next five years. This refers to one manager in four who can combine business understanding with a direct competence in the use and application of information technology. Such demands for the so-called hybrid manager whose functional competence is counterpointed by computer literacy are a more complete recognition of the nature of technology in both its material and its social sense. It argues for a manager with the ability to deploy IT effectively, at least for tactical purposes.

Changing demographic structures

Technological substitution of labor in service industries becomes even more critical if demographic issues are considered. Predicting population changes is not particularly onerous since it usually takes sixteen years or so for those born in a certain year to enter the labor force. The more difficult aspect to

Table 15.1 Computing cost performance trends for obtaining 4.5 MIPs

	1980	1990	2000
Cost			
1981 projection	$4.5m	$0.3m	
1988 projection		$0.1m	$0.01m
Number of people equivalent			
1981 projection	210	6	
1988 projection		2	0.125

the problem is that of predicting participation rates and the net balance of migration.

During the period 1975 to 1985, the size of the European Community (EC) labor force increased by about 12 percent to just over 140 million. This was caused partly by population growth and partly by increasing participation rates of women. Based on Eurostat estimates (de Jouvenal, 1989) the 1990 labor force of 145 million will rise to around 147 million by 1995, remain at about that level to the year 2000 and then decline fairly rapidly to 132 million by 2025. This may well be a rather pessimistic estimate since it assumes that participation rates of women will remain at their 1985 levels. OECD forecasts predict that participation rates will increase by some 5 to 10 per cent which would mean that the size of the labor force would be more or less constant. However, both bodies assume a reduction in the size of the male workforce. There will inevitably be changes in the age composition also. These changes relate primarily to the reduction in the 16 to 24 age group, which will fall from just under 20 percent of the European workforce today, to slightly over 14 percent by the turn of the century. This is quite important because it is through the 16 to 24 age group that new skills are traditionally transmitted into the labor market.

In the USA, a changing demographic composition can also be observed. Thus in the period 1985 to 2000 the workforce will increase by a net 25 million workers. Of these 20 percent will be non-white, 40 percent will be white women and 20 percent will be immigrants. The average age of the workforce will rise and such traditionally disadvantaged groups will represent the largest share of the workforce since 1918 (Hudson Institute, 1987). Simply absorbing additional labor into the tertiary sector without the use of productivity-enhancing working methods or new technology will lead to a decline in productivity. The record of the service industries, and especially the hospitality industry, in this respect is not encouraging. Over the period 1979 to 1985, productivity in UK hotels, measured by output per employee, actually declined by 0.7 percent per year (Medlik, 1989). In the USA, over the period 1970 to 1985, productivity in services declined by 0.2 percent (Hudson Institute, 1987).

Labor market changes

To exacerbate the situation, there is an underlying trend by which many information-based occupations in other service sectors will increase in terms of both quantity and quality. Thus, to name some examples, information technology specialists, health service technicians, engineers, and even finance specialists are growing occupational groups. It might be expected that these occupations will become more attractive to younger people who are better equipped and have reached a higher educational level. Service industries may therefore become increasingly dependent on an older age group, the 45 to 64 year olds. This group, the second largest numerically, received minimal schooling during their formative years. They received minimal training at work. They have also suffered the greatest skills obsolescence due to structural changes in the economy (the shift from manufacturing) and, in the case of women, due to child rearing.

During the next 25 years it is quite possible that Europe will move into the same situation as the United States, where women are the dominant component of the labor force. Under such a scenario, the skills gap might well worsen. However, the changing skill content of service jobs means that many women seeking employment in the 1990s may require considerable retraining. It is unrealistic to assume that such women are going to be content to occupy the relatively low-paid occupations of unskilled manual work.

At the same time, an aging labor force will exert increasingly severe fiscal pressure on social security systems. Between 1965 and 1986, compulsory social security contributions across the whole of the EC increased from 27.1 to 40 percent (OECD, 1988). This is roughly a 50 percent increase over a 25-year period and is due in part to increasing standards of health care for the elderly. By 2025 the proportion of those aged 60 and above in relation to the active population will be over 70 percent in Germany and Holland, over 60 percent in Belgium and Italy and over 50 percent in France and Spain. In the UK it will be 46 percent. Based on current trends in health care and social security, it is estimated (Rajan, 1990) that social security contributions will have to increase in Europe alone by between 15 and 40 percent.

Bearing in mind that older members of the population will have greater political influence, two possible options seem to present themselves. The first is for employers to accept a decline in relative competitiveness by absorbing the cost increases of additional taxes. The second is to restructure work in some way so as both to raise productivity and to reduce employment. In particular, this might mean greater technological substitution for labor, which the service industries have been especially poor at achieving in the 1980s.

The changing demographics of the labor market will therefore require a technological response in terms of both workers and consumers. In some countries the dilemma is more acute than in others. For example, in Germany persons under 25 represent one-third of all employees in the hotel industry and the proportion of young people is declining rapidly (Castan et al., 1990). In the late 1980s, American hospitality companies operating in the northeastern states took to recruiting drives in northern Europe to attract students prepared to work in hotels and restaurants during their summer vacations. By the end of the decade, the American fast-food industry in particular was beginning to recognize the extent of the crisis (Davids, 1988).

It may be possible to address the problem if disadvantaged groups can somehow be retrained to make a more effective contribution to employment. Disadvantaged groups refers mainly to women, ethnic minorities, and the unemployed. In some cases it might involve the redeployment of redundant older workers. Perhaps the best known of these schemes is the McMasters program used by the McDonald's hamburger chain (deMicco and Reid, 1988). A scenario in which cheap young people are substituted by cheap old people or minority groups is not an attractive vision for the turn of the century. Even when women constitute the majority of the workforce, there are still many issues of equality of opportunity to resolve (McRae, 1990). At present women returners and minority groups run the risk of being sidelined through the rapid obsolescence of existing skills. If the hospitality industry were to lean increasingly on an older workforce, issues of training and capital investment would assume greater strategic importance, especially in relation to IT.

Towards a strategic perspective

So far, service industries have not done especially well either in terms of repositioning or in terms of technological substitution. A number of possible explanations might be proposed. Some benefits from IT are hard to measure, such as the convenience of being able to link into your bank account from a PC. Some benefits may simply increase the severity of competition and are passed on to the consumer in the form of lower prices or better service. Financial and travel services spring to mind here. These might be linked to a third reason: namely, that consumers are actually demanding more by way of quality-of-life improvements. All three are relevant and important explanations. The most worrying possibility, however, is that some organizations have applied IT to areas of low payoff where there is little bottom-line impact. The literature is full of examples of refinements to accounting systems which produce no real economic gain. There are also examples of cost displacement where people costs are replaced by system costs. Most alarming of all are situations where no one took the opportunity to rethink the management of change associated with IT. The result is a superficial alteration in procedures. The example of word processing given earlier is telling in this context.

Venkatraman (1991) suggests that there are five levels of progression by which the move towards a strategic business reconfiguration based on IT might be achieved. Each of these is meant to be viewed as a distinct level with its own specific focus.

1. Localized exploitation
At this level, IT applications are deployed which improve the efficiency of isolated operations. Such applications are relatively discrete and do not necessarily benefit related areas of operations. Inventory control applications for either materials or reservations are good examples of localized exploitation.

2. Internal integration
Some integration is achieved at the second level for both the technical (machine) and organizational (expertise and political) aspects of the technology. Thus, in technical terms, common hardware platforms are used and common software standards are defined. A cursory inspection of most hospitality organizations in the early 1990s will reveal that much of the industry is still inclined to utilize a variety of hardware and software solutions. Although some relatively well-integrated PMS applications are beginning to

be deployed, there is as yet little sign that the roles and responsibilities of the managers who should exploit these systems is being developed in parallel. Thus the fundamental gain associated with integrating the business process is not being achieved.

3. Business process redesign

Business process redesign is regarded as a revolutionary rather than an evolutionary step. Thus instead of allowing the current business processes to constrain the type of IT infrastructure that is developed, the business process itself is redesigned around the available IT capabilities. Such a major departure from conventional approaches is justified in terms of the additional and different facilities that IT can provide for managers. In hospitality terms, the move from conventional food and beverage control procedures as devised by Hilton in the mid-1960s (which is ingredient based) to the catering information system of the 1980s (which is market driven and recipe based) represents such a revolutionary change.

4. Business network redesign

A new information environment then permits the business scope to be redefined at level 4. Here we might see the emergence of what has been termed the 'virtual corporation.' A virtual corporation is a kind of meta-organization which is not bounded by geographical, political, or financial structures. It is an extension of what marketeers have referred to as vertical integration. A hotel company which moves towards the guest by taking over an airline or a travel agent, or moves towards its suppliers by taking over a wholesaler is integrating vertically. The links in a virtual corporation are different. Here shared networks of information drive and support the various stages in the value chain, coordinating them as if they were a single corporation even if they are in fact independent of each other. The beginnings of business network redesign can be perceived in an airline computerized reservation system which is linked to travel agent, hotel and car rental computer systems.

5. Business scope redefinition

As the information network extends, so it becomes possible to redefine the objectives or mission of the organization. New products and services might be added either conventionally or through being enabled by IT. An expert system designed to plan itineraries, minimize time and cost for the customer, and maximize leverage for the organization could be an example of such a new service.

To underpin a progression of this sort, IT must be able to provide a more effective decision support environment. The evolution of information systems in the direction of more intelligent functioning was set out over twenty years ago by Zannetos (1968). Writing before the significant emergence of work in human problem solving and knowledge-based programming,

Zannetos set out a prescient scheme for the implementation of intelligent information systems. Categorized in eight levels, these began with the simple storage of raw data and progressed through classification and aggregation of data, automatic comparisons, simple manipulation to transform data, and management by exception. At level 6, the system would begin to examine and change its own decision models so that by level 7 it could begin to derive new, abstract functional relationships. In other words, at level 7 an inductive reasoning process would be employed analogous to the inference engine of a knowledge-based system of the 1980s. Finally, level 8 postulated the development of metasystems capable of generalizing problems by class and beginning a search for cause on that basis.

Inhibitors of the strategic process

For IT to exercise a strategic role, it must be perceived as a strategic option by the managers who employ it. If this perception is to be accepted, managers in the hospitality industry must begin to recognize that Venkatraman's level 1, localized exploitation, is not the extent of what the technology has to offer. At the same time, the industry will need to value managers trained to deploy IT in a different way. It is interesting to ponder why, when the consumer electronics industry is incorporating fuzzy logic into the latest generation of camcorders, it is almost impossible to cite an example of an information system in the hospitality industry that has reached Zannetos' level 5, automated management by exception reporting. Even in 1991, variance analysis or opportunity cost evaluation are carried out manually if at all in most hotel information systems.

Despite this, the technology itself has now reached a stage where level 6 intelligence (examination and change of the decision model) is certainly possible and this would permit a revolutionary change in business process design. Thus an intelligent forecasting system, based on both internal and external data, might be used to predict the individual demand for food and beverage products at a given meal period. Integrated with a catering information system, computer programs would then control inventory, schedule production, and provide advice on merchandizing. The supporting process changes that would be required in terms of food production and service systems based on cook-chill or sous-vide have been available for some time.

It might be argued that such a scenario is open to the challenge posed at the beginning of this chapter. A charge could fairly be laid that these changes are more tactical than strategic. The answer would have to lie in the redefinition of objectives that would necessarily underpin changes of that type. To some extent, strategy depends on where and, perhaps equally, when you sit (Rumelt, 1979). After all, there are many types of strategy. Not all strategies are associated with a grand design, fully developed and widely communicated in advance of any activity. While a planned strategy of this sort is what most people might think of when the word 'strategy' is used, other types of strategy are equally possible and maybe even more probable.

The main obstacle to the implementation of an effective strategic role for IT is largely managerial. A lack of strategic vision, an inability to view IT in strategic terms, inexperience with IT and IT-based applications, organizational inertia, low economies of scale for integration, and a perceived mismatch with market needs might all be cited as factors which inhibit strategic applications of IT in the hospitality industry. It is therefore necessary to examine where the seeds of positive change for the future might lie.

The identification of strategic opportunity

In this context it is useful to consider some of the findings of the *Management in the 90s* research program from the Sloan School of Management at MIT (Scott-Morton, 1991). The MIT 90s project is interesting partly because of its sheer scale (it included some 32 different research projects, cost $6m, and extended over five years) and partly because it was sponsored by a dozen of the world's leading companies in search of strategic direction. Four of its main findings are of key interest at this point.

- The project concluded that there is no evidence that IT provides organizations with long-term sustainable competitive advantage. Temporary advantage may be gained, but IT systems are easily copied by competitors. The real benefits of IT derive from the constructive combination of IT with organization structure, supporting the trend towards new, more flexible forms of organization. Benefits also derive from people who are capable of exploiting the information and the new functionality that IT can provide. Significantly, when faced with difficult trading conditions at the end of the 1980s, American Airlines put the software for the oft-cited Sabre system on the market. Clearly the algorithms applied to the database were being copied and the competitive advantages associated with this application of IT had been reaped.
- The nature of work is changing as the economics of IT change. Pens are being replaced by workstations (sophisticated microcomputers). In order to respond effectively, organizations will need to pay considerable attention to education, training, and work design. The rate at which managers and workers can learn new skills will determine the rate at which an organization can respond to change.
- Managers must be the agents of change. This is rather old hat perhaps, but what is being advocated is a more proactive role for managers. In particular, the research program highlighted the role of managers in predicting and intercepting change before outside pressure from customers, suppliers, competitors, and regulatory authorities becomes irresistible. The project emphasized especially the role of senior managers in providing what was called *disconfirmation*, starting to alter established beliefs and values in advance of generally recognized requirements for change. Basically, this means making people uncomfortable with an unworkable present and preparing them to act quickly to influence the future.

- There are therefore new rules for organization leadership. An innovative and responsive organization requires more the style of a missionary who encourages and persuades, than that of a corporate general who decides and gives orders. Leadership, especially of large organizations, is too big a task for one person. IT can be used to empower managers and workers down the line. At the same time, lower-level managers must accept responsibility for their new roles and must seek to protect the values of the organization as a whole rather than just to preserve their own narrow parochial interests. The traditional hospitality problem relating to the indifferent treatment of discounted customer groups by staff in full-service hotels illustrates this problem.

Some of these findings require a radical rethinking of how organizations might be structured and how people will work within them. IT will be an important facilitator in this process. For example, a matrix structure based on team working and a flexible approach to tasks could be expedited technologically by electronic integration. The need for local area networks (LANs) can be justified in terms of the tasks to be performed, not simply in terms of the number of computers. If even three or four machines in an office are linked by a LAN to provide for file sharing, the performance capability of the work group based on shared access to common information is altered. Computer communication networks which link hotels to powerful databases such as Sabre are merely the same exercise on a global scale. However, the technological link based on cabling and software is only the first step. A matrix structure for a hotel or a restaurant operation requires an entirely different approach to the organization of work, the definition of roles and responsibilities, and the basis by which performance is appraised.

The need for strategic repositioning

If disconfirmation is to be an accepted stance, the application of current IT-related advances and the convergence of others presents the prospect of a strategic reconsideration of the manner in which hospitality services are provided. Some current industry practices are overdue for reconsideration. Anecdotally, it might be suggested that in 1990 a hotel employs roughly the same number of people to produce a banquet of a certain size as was used in the time of the Romans. Today's hotel kitchen is not the technological cockpit of a modern food production and service system that an outsider to the industry might reasonably expect. More formally, Shamir (1978) has observed that the demarcation of work in some service situations is neither rational nor functional. To have separate waiters serve food and wine, or even food and coffee, to the same customer cannot be justified on efficiency grounds.

At this point, to engender a strategic repositioning, it is a question not so much of looking forwards as of looking to the past. In his seminal marketing paper, Levitt (1960) urged companies to try to think in terms not of products but of customer satisfactions. Too often it is possible to lay the charge of product orientation at the feet of many so-called management information systems. The obsession with technology rather than information results in situations in which systems deliver a great deal of operational data but little by way of management information. It is therefore necessary to plough through pages of data or to rework the presentation of a report in order to develop an interpretation of what has been produced. Even in areas such as finance, where the performance of IT is sometimes regarded as integral to corporate performance, there is concern as to whether IT is contributing to management or whether it is merely contributing to operations (Collins, 1991).

Perhaps the classic example of an absence of information is the daily rooms report produced by almost every PMS on the market. In large systems the report can run to several pages of printout covered in numbers, with the expectation, presumably, that someone will read and respond to such an output each day. Research shows that managers adopt a variety of techniques for reducing these numbers to manageable proportions and for quickly restructuring the reports to provide real information. Sometimes this even involves transposing computer printouts by hand onto another form (Gamble, 1986).

The techniques employed by these managers are susceptible to adoption by another computer program. Indeed, rule-based programming was considered to be a major advance in computer science in the 1970s and underpinned the work in artificial intelligence and expert systems in the 1980s. Yet managers have failed to recognize that the rules which they apply every day to the interpretation of some reports are amenable to the workings of an expert system. A change in application of this sort can be considered strategic because it will shift the orientation of managerial work from an essentially clerical perspective to a higher level of decision making.

Speculation and application

Although expert systems suffered from being oversold in the 1980s, so that the reality fell somewhat short of the expectation, there have been a number of significant applications which hold promise for the hospitality industry. Many opportunities for innovation based on IT-related advance currently exist. Some of these are confined, more or less, to a level of technology that has been available for decades. Others combine old ideas with new capabilities.

Thus Brooklyn Union Gas, a utility company, has developed an expert system written in BASIC to prompt its customer service agents through the process of issuing credit agreements in the field. This makes available to the agent the calculations necessary to determine financial arrangements, but ensures that they stay within the bounds of company policy. A parallel is easily drawn with a hotel sales force seeking to negotiate convention or function deals with prospective guests. Such negotiations are complex and require not only a calculation of the trade-offs between food and beverage, room hire, and room rate revenues, but a consideration of hotel policy and market positioning. The Union Gas system runs on a computer costing $300. An expert system running on a notebook computer could enable either a single hotel or a group of hotels to develop and manage its sales force from a more strategic perspective.

At the same sort of technological level, the US Internal Revenue service has developed an expert system called Correspondex. Written in C and running on commercially available PCs, the system composes letters based on an evaluation of a taxpayer's situation. Using a knowledge base of standardized paragraphs, the system composes an appropriate letter and then monitors any customized paragraphs that may have been added by a human clerk. Correspondex not only provides for a certain grammatical accuracy, but also ensures that contradictory or confusing information is not despatched (Newquist, 1991b).

The parallel to hospitality systems is obvious, as is a possible link to what is known as a smart form. A smart form is simply a form developed by an expert system. It guides the clerk through a data collection process, offering advice and prompting for responses interactively. While a completely standard pre-printed form is most efficient for room reservations, other types of sale require a more variable range of responses. The convention sales deal negotiated out in the field can be processed back in the office by another expert system application. As the data are being transferred from the sales computer and analyzed to generate a written response, other information systems can be updated.

At a higher level of integration, it is possible to address a more complete range of production problems through the convergence of process control and rule-based programming. Mrs Baird's Bakery, the largest independent bakery in the USA, opened a fully automated bakery in Fort Worth, Texas, in 1991 that was controlled by an expert system. Written in Gensym's language G2, the expert system schedules and monitors all aspects of production. The design provides for an integration of process control and decision support functions that enable the bakery to meet production schedules at a specified level of quality and a controlled level of cost. Such a production system is rather more advanced than that available to the Romans. Although the example given is drawn from the food manufacturing industry, the translation into some types of limited menu or high-volume foodservice environments could well be feasible. The concept being used would be that of a flexible production process responding to the automated interpretations of an intelligent market information system.

The convergence of image recognition and expert systems has already found applications in other hospitality-related fields. Sabre, the American Airlines CRS, has deployed a videodisk application which enables reservation clerks and travel agents to display images of hotels, rooms, and background information to prospective customers. Another airline, Northwest, has used the same technology to match ticket images with ticket records, cutting retrieval time for documents by an order of magnitude, from hours to seconds (Thompson, 1991). Image recognition systems raise to a higher level the extent to which document- and file-processing procedures may be automated, and they are used extensively by banks. The potential for the application of the technique to processing vouchers and other documents in hotels is obvious.

The convergence of voice recognition with expert systems has also made a successful commercial debut. The Audi Quattro car introduced in 1991 includes an in-car telephone which works on voice recognition. The system, programmed to recognize two users, enables a driver to select up to 40 telephone numbers which can be activated by short phrases, giving complete hands-free operation. In terms of product enhancement this technology may have some applications for the control of in-room services. It might also be seen as an extension of the marketing technique used by the budget hotel chain Climat de France. Reservations confirmed by credit card for a Climat hotel allow the guest to obtain a vended key against a credit card swipe at the point of arrival. Here the convergence would bring together pulse tone telephones, voice recognition, and expert system techniques to provide a completely automated reservation system capable of servicing a chain of standardized, limited-service hotels.

Problems of implementation

From a strategic perspective, there are two key issues in the implementation of new forms of service delivery managed and operated through new technological processes. The first is that solutions to hospitality industry problems are to be found not only in the material technology of computers and communication systems, but also in developing the potential of the managers who must make them work. The second involves the problems of organization culture which prevent large companies from exploiting the synergy which is available to them.

The UK drinks distribution and hotels group, Greenall Whitley, provides an example of what can be done. Starting with a clear statement of goals, an improved method of corporate control was introduced in 1989 with the aim of overhauling the group's information and reporting processes (Harvey, 1991). At this time, senior managers were obliged to puzzle their way through 60 pages of computer printout and miscellaneous other data to understand the group's position.

Following a systems study, it was determined that 80 percent of the critical success factors which acted as the basis for high-level decision making were financial. In turn this allowed the system developers to sidestep issues of standardization across the many computer systems used by the company and to develop an information system which took as its source data the accounting systems of its subsidiaries. Over a period of two years, the proportion of accounting data was reduced to about half of the system's input as market measures such as market share and product performance assumed an increasingly important role. By 1991 the group was obtaining about 20 percent of its strategic information from external measures, including competitor performance. The directors were then able to focus on key issues in such a way that both revenues and occupancies within the hotel group were substantially improved. The information system thus led to improved financial and operational control, enabling managers to identify areas of comparatively poor performance more rapidly. More importantly, it resulted in qualitative improvements in information. Quality in this context refers to aspects such as timeliness, consistency, and intelligibility, which allow managers to form better mental models of the markets in which the company is trading.

The virtual hospitality company

There is emerging in the 1990s a potential coincidence of business forces and developments in information technology. In the business world there have been major efforts to establish more efficient, tightly coupled business relations, partly in response to the recession of 1990/91. These take a variety of forms but are usually associated with attempts to increase productivity, reduce costs, and improve service. Information technology can be used to a growing extent to facilitate such developments through improved connectivity. In an idealized form, this could involve electronic interaction with the customer, possibly at home or in the office and result in the organization and delivery of a service from airline tickets through hotels to car hire and itinerary scheduling. What is beginning to emerge is the so-called virtual corporation. A virtual corporation is really a network of different companies which cooperate through electronic links to provide a total product or service. Essentially they involve a conscious attempt to redesign business networks. Computerized reservation systems operated by the airlines might be seen as the heart of such networks in the hospitality industry.

In these situations it is necessary to set up the sort of efficient management structure and information flow which would be expected of a single, large, mature organization. Even within some large companies, no real advantage has been sought as yet from the increased connectivity that information technology can support. Very often, international hospitality companies operate as a group of loosely linked mini-companies, hindered in their attempts to establish closer links by corporate culture or by the past limitations of IT.

The analogy used in the MIT 90s study is that of a power saw. When it is a given to a lumberjack for the first time, the worker labors to pick up the cumbersome tool and, with great effort, begins to move it backwards and forwards through a log. It is clumsy and hard to use, the teeth on the chain keep moving. The problem is that no one thought to explain that there was an on switch so that the machine would do the cutting by itself.

Assuming a strategic role for information technology systems

In a major study completed in 1989, the American Hotel Motel Association identified three major challenges which have to be addressed in the 1990s if a more managerial perspective of technology is to be adopted (AHMA, 1989). First, there must be a commitment to bridging the gap between business needs and technological solutions. This requires close cooperation between IT managers and operating managers or, better, the training and development of hybrid managers. Second, the industry must adopt a more innovative and positive stance to the introduction of change. Finding new versions of old solutions does not meet this criterion. Third, given the apparent fragmentation of product structures, hospitality executives must develop precise service strategies to meet ever more rigorous customer demands. If the virtual corporation is extant, survival requires that each element in the network understand its precise contribution.

To assume a strategic role in the hospitality industry, information technology must be perceived as possessing a strategic capability. It is a question of recognizing that there is an on switch and then pressing it. Such recognition must come from management. It is possible to envisage a spectrum of benefits from IT, each of which is more difficult to achieve than the last. At the simplest level lies improved operational control, which, by and large, the industry is beginning to exploit. Beyond that are benefits in terms of the quality of information of the type achieved by Greenall Whitley. At a higher level still lies the prospect of business process redesign. Leaner forms of organization with fewer management levels and increased spans of control backed by empowerment down the line may be foreseen. Finally, there is the prospect of a truly strategic role in which the information system focuses on defining the function of the business within a virtual corporation. Comprehensive decision support systems then provide for improved corporate models, identifying the options open to managers within the network of providers. When that choice has been made, more highly automated and 'intelligent' production and service systems facilitate the delivery of customer satisfactions.

Fanciful as it may seem, the seeds of this future can be seen in many hospitality businesses which have chosen to offer only a part of the total service and openly depend on other hospitality providers. A La Quinta Inn in the USA will depend for its foodservice on a nearby restaurant owned by another operator. A Forte Travelodge in the UK may link to a nearby Happy Eater.

The question to be put is not so much whether the hospitality industry might respond to technological innovation, but whether it is capable of doing so managerially. Technological innovations are a great deal easier to manage than innovations in social processes. The industry constantly demonstrates that it is capable of buying technology in the form of computers or even satellites. However, that is only the beginning of the story. A parallel step has to be made by the people who choose to deploy that technology in one form or another. If the choice involves the daily copying of printouts onto other papers, there is no real advance. The relationship between an organization and its technology, strategic or otherwise, is a reflection of the choices made by managers. The challenge for the future, therefore, is not the technology but the managers. If information technology is to have a strategic role, that role must be created by informed managers.

References

Abrahams, P. (1991) 'Eastern Europe', *Financial Times*, 17 September, p. 11.

AHMA (1989) *Looking Forward: A management perspective of technology in the lodging industry*, Washington, DC: American Hotel Motel Association.

Berkus, D. (1988) 'The yield management revolution', *IAHA The Bottomline*.

Castan, A., *et al.* (1990) *1993 and Beyond: The impact of EC legislation on the hotel, catering and tourism industries*, Paris: Cornell-ESSEC.

Cohn, S. F. (1980) 'Industrial product adoption in a technology push industry', *Industrial Marketing Management*, vol. 9, pp. 89–95

Collins, T. , (1991) 'Finance managers attack IT record on cost-cutting', *Computer Weekly*, 14 November, p. 4.

Craver, D. (1990) 'Training the hybrids in their own image', *Computer Weekly*, 5 April, p. 16.

Davids, M. (1988) 'Labor shortage woes', *Public Relations Journal*, vol. 44, pp. 24–9, 59.

de Jouvenal, H. (1989) *Europe's Aging Population: Trends and challenges to 2025*, Paris: Butterworth.

deMicco, F., and Reid, R. (1988) 'Older workers: a hiring resource for the hospitality industry', *Cornell Hotel and Restaurant Administration*, vol. 28, pp. 56–61.

Flood, G. (1991) 'Brewers tap into a winning system', *Computer Weekly*, 26 September, p. 4.

Fox, A. (1974) *Man Mismanagement*, London: Hutchinson.

Gamble, P. R. (1986) 'Computers and innovation in the hospitality industry: a study of some factors affecting management behaviour', Ph.D. thesis, University of Surrey.

Harvey, D. (1991) 'Ups and downs of executive information systems', *Computer Weekly*, 16 May, pp. 32–3.

Hudson Institute (1987) *Workforce 2000*, New York: Hudson Institute.

Keen, P. G. W. (1981) 'Communications in the 21st century: telecommunications and business policy', *Organizational Dynamics*.

Levitt, T. (1960) 'Marketing Myopia', *Harvard Business Review*, July/August, pp. 45–60.

McRae, S. (ed.) (1990) *Keeping Women In*, London: PSI.

Medlik, R. (1989) 'Profit from productivity in tourism', *Tourism*, vol. 61, p. 14.

Mumford, E., and Pettigrew, A. M. (1975) *Implementing Strategic Decisions*, London: Longman.

Newquist, H. P. (1991a) 'In unexpected places', *AI Expert*, vol. 6, no. 8, 59–61.

Newquist, H. P. (1991b) 'Where you least expect AI', *AI Expert*, vol. 6, no. 9, pp. 59–61.

Nystrom, H. (1979) *Creativity and Innovation*, Chichester: John Wiley.

OECD (1988) *Statistiques des Recettes Publiques des Pays Membres de l'OCED*, Paris: OECD.

Perrow, C. (1973) 'A framework for the comparative analysis of organizations', *American Sociological Review*, vol. 32, no. 2, p. 194.

Porter, M., and Millar, V. E. (1985) 'How information gives you competitive advantage', *Harvard Business Review*, July/August, pp. 149–60.

Porter, M. E. (1985) *Competitive Advantage: Creating and sustaining superior performance*, New York: The Free Press.

Pugh, D. S., and Hickson, D. J. (1976) *Organization Structure in its Context: The Aston Programme 1*, Aldershot: Saxon House.

Rajan, A. (1990) *1992: A zero sum game*, London: The Industrial Society.

Rumelt, R. P. (1979) 'Evaluation of strategy: theory and models', in Schendel, D. E., and Hofer, C. W. (eds) *Strategic Management: A new view of business policy and planning*, Boston, Mass.: Little Brown.

Scott-Morton, M. S. (1991) *The Corporation of the 1990s*, Oxford: Oxford University Press.

Shamir, B. (1978) 'Between bureaucracy and hospitality: some organizational characteristics of hotels', *Journal of Management Studies*, October, pp. 285–307.

Taylor, F. W. (1911) *Principles of Scientific Management*, New York: Harper.

Thompson, D. (1991) 'Imaging meets expert systems', *AI Expert*, vol. 6, no. 11, pp. 24–32.

Venkatraman, N. (1991) 'IT induced business reconfiguration', in Scott-Morton, M. S. (ed.) *the Corporation of the 1990s*, Oxford: Oxford University Press.

Webster, J. (1991) 'Revolution in the office? Information technology and work organization', *PICT Policy Research Papers No. 14*, London: ESRC.

Winner, L. (1977) *Autonomous Technology: Technics-out-of-control as a theme in political thought*, Cambridge, Mass.: MIT Press.

Zannetos, Z. S. (1968) 'Towards intelligent management information systems', *Industrial Management Review*, vol. 9, no. 3, pp. 21–38.

16

Corporate performance appraisal in the international hospitality industry

Debra J. Adams
and Francis Kwansa

Few would argue that the growth of the hospitality industry on a worldwide basis has been less than phenomenal. In the widest sense, the term 'hospitality' is taken to include not only hotels, motels, restaurants, and institutional catering, but also leisure activities such as sporting facilities, clubs, theatres, and concert halls. This growth has partly been due to the substantial increase in the demand for tourism in many areas of the world, and it has been supported by the expansion of the major multinational hotel and leisure groups into new markets which have become more readily accessible for trade.

As with any other business, the hospitality industry is not without its failures, and the factors which are often cited as the cause of failure are the very characteristics by which the industry is typified. In many sectors of the industry considerable levels of investment are required, resulting in high fixed costs and a high break-even point. Profits are significant once the break-even point has been cleared, although costs can escalate rapidly if uncontrolled. The most significant factors to affect profitability are material, wage, and site costs.

This chapter seeks to examine how information, both financial and non-financial can be used to monitor the progress of a business in an attempt to predict the likelihood of business success or failure.

Types of early warning system

Techniques for predicting corporate collapse may be classified into those which are based on financial information and those which are based on operational details and observation. Financial techniques may be separated into two approaches. The most commonly used financial technique is that of ratio analysis, sometimes referred to as univariate analysis. This technique is based on the calculation of individual ratios using data from the trading accounts and balance sheet. In the last two decades a technique known as multi-discriminant analysis (MDA) has attracted much attention in accounting circles. Broadly speaking, this technique utilizes a series of traditional ratios and combines them to produce a single weighted statistic. This statistic may then be used within specific guidelines to assess the potential for success or failure of individual companies. There are, however, several non-financial factors that are important contributors to business failure, and consequently techniques that rely solely upon financial ratios fail to capture the role of these other factors in the failure phenomenon.

There are a variety of non-financial models available, but that produced by Argenti is one of the most prominent. He developed the model from a wide review of actual cases and literature, and discussions with bankers, receivers, accountants, and business operators. The model focuses on factors such as management problems (e.g. an autocratic chief executive, non-expert board members, a weak financial director) along with weaknesses in the accounting systems, operating environment, and financial results. The factors included in the model are weighted using a score system by which an organization can be assessed. The value of the score determines whether a company is in danger of failing or not. The effectiveness of any technique for predicting failure, whether it is based on financial or non-financial methods, should be measured in terms of the following:

- The accuracy of the method over a large sample.
- The size of the 'grey area': that is, the area in which both success and failure are likely.
- The size of the lead time: that is, the time between predicting failure and failure actually occurring. Obviously the longer the length of time, the more useful the technique.

Many analysts believe that the signs of possible failure can be detected much earlier, even during the growth years, and that if indications are dealt with, disaster may be averted. The purpose of this chapter is to look at recent corporate failures to consider whether any warning signs were visible. To do this, techniques based on financial and non-financial methods are considered, using examples drawn from the international hospitality industry. Such prediction models, if proved to be effective, provide the manager with a much-needed additional technique for monitoring business performance. The demand for effective methods is ever increasing as companies seek to maintain and extend their markets. For many this has meant expansion overseas and a move away from a highly centralized management structure. Decentralization can raise the level of risk if the traditional role of the corporate head office is not adapted accordingly. The manager who successfully heads these more diverse types of operation is heavily reliant on the effective use of internal company reporting mechanisms.

The UK perspective

Rapid expansion has taken place in the hospitality industry during the 1980s, throughout all sectors. Within the hotel sector, room stocks have increased by some 40 percent. This period of growth has been fueled by the need for the large chains to maintain competitive advantage and by the provision of a suitable environment for growth. However, the key feature of the UK hospitality industry is the extent of the fragmentation of ownership. The hotel sector is predominantly independently owned with 90 percent of all hotels individually owned, and these commanding 70 percent of all hotel rooms.

The number of units classified as 'catering' by the Central Statistical Office, which includes the hotel sector, has consistently grown year on year with an overall growth from 1980 to 1990 of approximately 10 percent. The majority of these units, some 90 percent of them, have annual turnovers of less than $450,000. In the UK the industry sector to show the highest failure rates during the 1980s, after the construction industry, is the hotel and catering industry (Business Monitor definitions). The number of insolvencies and bankruptcies in the UK is monitored by the Department of Trade and Industry, and figures clearly indicate that in the hotel and catering sector there has been a dramatic increase in failures in the early 1990s.

The tide now appears to have turned and many companies are seeking to consolidate and rationalize their operations. For some, this change in policy has come too late, so that extensive restructuring or even suspension of trading has already taken place, with both small and large companies being affected. When any industry is faced with difficult trading conditions, alternative strategies must be implemented to ensure survival. Instead of planning for growth, managers must now plan for survival. This requires monitoring the business carefully in order to identify those businesses or divisions which may be candidates for failure in the future.

The American perspective

Corporate failure in the lodging industry

The company Dun and Bradstreet tracks the number of business failures annually according to the Standard Industrial Classifications (SIC) codes of industry in the United States. The lodging industry is classified under 'services', while the restaurant and food service industry is classified under 'retail trade'. Table 16.1 shows that, within the services industry, the number of business failures in the lodging segment was relatively small in 1987 and 1988. However, the dollar amounts of liabilities involved in the failures were $554 million in 1987 and $400 million in 1988. In terms of the liabilities involved, the lodging industry represents one of the most significant segments in the services industry. The restaurant and food service segment of the retail trade industry (represented by the eating and drinking places'

Table 16.1 Failure report for the lodging and foodservice industries

	1987		1988	
	Number	%	Number	%
Total services	23,802	100	21,929	100
Hotels and other lodging places	334	1.4	307	1.4
Total retail trade	12,240	100	11,488	100
Eating and drinking places	2,807	22.9	2,655	23.1

classification) shows the highest number of business failures of any single segment. In terms of dollar value of liabilities involved, there were $552 million in 1987 and $526 million in 1988, which makes this segment the leader. In the context of all other industries in the American economy, the most business failures occurred in the retail trade industry between 1984 and 1988. Thus, this distinction between the restaurant and foodservice segment in terms of business failures is dubious, yet significant.

Data from Dun and Bradstreet show further that, when business failures are broken down into failures by age of business, the retail trade industry leads all other industries. Some 42 percent of businesses that failed in the retail trade in 1988 had existed for three years or less before they failed. Close to 60 percent did not survive beyond five years. With the collapse of the real-estate market in 1991 and the prolonged recession in the American economy, many believe that more failures will occur in the lodging industry. The American Council of Life Insurance estimated that 8.1 percent of an estimated $11.8 billion of outstanding hotel loans held by insurance companies were delinquent. This represented the fifth consecutive year that the delinquency rate of hotel loans had exceeded that of loans to other types of commercial property. Many analysts seem to agree that, because of the weakening performance of the lodging industry, loan default rates will continue to rise.

Factors in lodging business failures

Many of the lodging businesses that have failed or are distressed are unable to generate enough operating income to cover:

- operating costs
- debt service
- adequate return on equity

These businesses also typically experience some combination of higher construction, operating, and interest charges, lower-than-average room and occupancy rates, and less efficient management than was anticipated when the business started. Generally, major infusions of capital are required just to keep these lodging businesses operating. To the equity holder, the significance of these symptoms is felt not only in the lack of cash flow, but also in the decline in the market value of the business compared to the book value. Several signs may indicate that a lodging business is experiencing cash-flow problems and may possibly fail. These include neglected maintenance and housekeeping, which usually occurs when management tries to 'cut corners' by holding down expenses. In addition, promotions that involve significant discounting and giveaways such as free meals or rooms may indicate management's desperate need for cash. Another sign is changes in trade credit arrangements: that is, when suppliers abandon their customary credit facilities and begin to demand cash on delivery. This represents a strong sign that suppliers doubt the business will survive. Finally, an unusual exodus of employees and management from the company is indicative of imminent disaster.

Economic factors

These are often the cited causes of business failures in the lodging industry. The factors include insufficient profits, high interest rates, loss of market share, lack of consumer spending, and no future. Saturation of hotel rooms combined with decreased economic activity and increased competition in all segments of the lodging industry today has contributed significantly to lower occupancy rates and diminishing profits. The saturation problem is blamed generally on two tax laws of the 1980s. The first provided tax incentives for real-estate financing, thus encouraging the construction of many more hotels than were necessary. The second tax law simply removed many of the tax shelters provided by the first tax law, and since hotel construction tends to lag behind demand for hotel rooms, the emergence of a glut on the market was almost inevitable.

The lodging industry is notorious for relatively high debt levels. High-debt financing arises from the need to cover up front initial construction costs, cost overruns during construction, and deficits from the first few years of operation. Additionally, the financing terms of hotel loans are typically established during the construction phase of the project, and this may not reflect the abilities of the operating management to generate higher operating margins. Invariably, the high debt levels with their interest obligations become a recipe for failure if projected performance does not materialize. During the economic expansion of the 1980s, some lodging companies obtained debt capital from the sale of junk bonds with significantly higher interest rates. In the current recessionary environment, it continues to be difficult for these lodging companies to manage their debt burden.

A study of solvency ratios of the hospitality industry from COMPUSTAT data files confirms the extent of leverage in the industry. Whereas the food-service industry exhibits similarity in leverage use with the Dow Jones Industrial Companies, the lodging industry's average leverage ratios are almost twice as high as the Dow Jones group (see Table 16.2). With such a high level of leverage, the large interest expense would tend to have a dampening effect

Table 16.2 Average solvency ratios: food-service and lodging industries vs. Dow Jones industrials, 1984–1988

	Debt/equity ratio	Debt ratio
Foodservice		
1984	0.377	0.252
1985	0.509	0.296
1986	0.558	0.302
1987	0.522	0.286
1988	0.513	0.288
Lodging		
1984	2.106	0.526
1985	1.728	0.535
1986	2.051	0.507
1987	1.989	0.465
1988	2.369	0.527
DJI		
1984	0.451	0.221
1985	0.468	0.228
1986	0.545	0.251
1987	0.684	0.244
1988	0.718	0.284

on profitability. Using samples of 14 lodging firms, 38 foodservice firms, and 30 Dow Jones industrial companies, all publicly traded, the profitability of the highly leveraged lodging firms is significantly lower than that of the industrial companies.

Internal factors
The factors reviewed here concern experience, sales and expenses.

Experience factors include incompetence, lack of product line and managerial experience, and lack of balanced experience in the functional areas. The lodging business is very management intensive in that it requires professional managers with requisite skills in service, marketing, control, and food and beverage management. Indeed, the value of a lodging investment depends to some extent on the quality of management operating the business. Therefore, lack of experience and competence is a recipe for failure in the lodging business. Lack of managerial expertise is reflected in higher operating costs, lower occupancy, higher employee turnover, and less overall profit potential from sales. Furthermore, misdirected or inadequate ability in marketing and promotional efforts can destroy a marginal or successful property.

Sales factors include general economic decline, inadequate sales, competitive weaknesses, inventory difficulties, and poor location. Some observers of lodging industry failures blame the feasibility studies which prompted the construction of the properties. In other cases, the target markets upon which the business depended were misread by the feasibility study, did not materialize as anticipated, or weakened. Therefore, incorrect feasibility studies led to sales problems which in turn led to business failure.

Expense factors include burdensome institutional debt and heavy operating expenses. The impact of interest charges is obvious when considering that typical debt ratios in the lodging industry range from 0.60–0.90. An operational expense such as utility expense can be burdensome, especially when inefficient property management systems exist in the property.

Other factors that are less important but contribute to business failure, as identified by Dun and Bradstreet, include neglect, disaster, fraud, customer, asset and capital causes. The components of each of these causes are as follows:

- Neglect: bad habits, marital and family problems, poor health.
- Disaster: act of God, fire, strike, employee fraud, death of owner.
- Fraud: embezzlement, premeditated overbuy, false agreement.
- Customer: too few customers, receivables difficulties.
- Assets: excessive fixed assets, overexpansion.
- Capital: burdensome contracts, excessive withdrawals, inadequate start capacity.

Corporate failure in the American retail trade and service industries

Dun and Bradstreet annually track the number of business failures by industry and provide a breakdown of the causes of failure. Table 16.3 shows the causes of failure in the American retail trade and service industries (in which restaurants and other eating and drinking places are included). The percentages represent the proportion of total failures attributable to each of the causes (since some failures are attributed to a combination of causes, the total exceeds 100 percent).

Table 16.3   Causes of business failure: American retail trade and service industries

Causes	% failures (retail)	% failures (services)
Neglect	2.0	1.1
Disaster	0.6	0.2
Fraud	0.4	0.1
Economic factors	71.2	71.4
Experience	20.1	23.0
Sales	13.0	11.6
Expenses	5.8	10.6
Customer	0.3	0.4
Assets	0.3	0.1
Capital	0.7	0.2

Source: Dun and Bradstreet Business Failure Reports (1987).

Factors in service and retail trade industry failures

Several factors have been offered to explain why restaurants fail. Some of these factors have been determined empirically, while others are the result of post-mortem observations of restaurant businesses that have failed.

Economic factors

This is the most important cause of failure in restaurant businesses. In this category, insufficient profits and no consumer spending are major contributors. When Wendy's International, Inc., was experiencing financial distress in 1985 and 1986 (net losses of $4.9 million and a negative return on equity (ROE) for the first time in the company's history), management attributed these conditions to softness in the economy and to low discretionary spending by customers. Similarly, Victoria Station, a medium-sized, limited-menu restaurant, suffered financial difficulties between 1980 and 1983. When the company suffered an $8 million loss and a negative ROE in 1983, these circumstances were attributed to poor economic conditions.

Other factors

Asset causes of restaurant business failures frequently include overexpansion of units. In addition to poor economic conditions, Victoria Station additionally suffered from an expansion program that was too rapid and very costly. The concept was also very inflexible. It consisted of railroad boxcars filled with railroad memorabilia that served as the dining rooms. These boxcars were expensive to renovate and maintain, and difficult to adapt for alternative concepts. Therefore when customer count began to decline, it became difficult for management to reposition the concept. Taco Viva was a regional Mexican restaurant concept that went public in 1982 and initially experienced much success. However, the glamor and pressures of being listed on the stock exchange led to a rapid expansion into several different states at a time when the Mexican food segment was saturated. High start-up expenses along with rapid decline in customer count eventually led to the company being bought out by the Vista Group of London.

A Mexican-American restaurant chain named Naugles was in financial distress in 1986. Similar to Taco Viva, this regional chain went public and

Table 16.4 Average profitability ratios: foodservice and lodging industries vs. Dow Jones industrials, 1984–1988

	Foodservice ROE (%)	Lodging ROE (%)	DJI ROE (%)
1984	16.35	9.37	13.84
1985	10.46	5.20	9.46
1986	2.17	10.35	9.76
1987	10.56	10.97	14.32
1988	1.8	7.26	8.57

immediately began to expand rapidly. In a rush to expand, the company lost focus of the fundamentals that had earned them their trademark and continued to make them successful. Customer loyalty had developed as a result of generous portions of food available at relatively low prices. In an attempt to trim expenses and increase profitability, portion sizes were reduced drastically, and this contributed to customer disenchantment.

Some restaurant businesses that failed were victims of their *franchise arrangements*. For example, D'Lites of America was established as a healthy fast-food concept that provided an alternative to the very successful and larger chains such as McDonald's and Burger King. As a policy, the company obligated itself to buy back non-performing franchises. As competition with the larger chains grew and customers became dissatisfied with D'Lites' product delivery, franchises began to fail. The buyback of the failing franchises became a drain on cash flows, eventually leading to D'Lites filing for bankruptcy.

In some of the failed restaurant businesses, *the loss of key management personnel* contributed significantly to the companies' demise. Sambo's was a low-priced pancake and coffee house that targeted blue-collar workers. Started in 1957, its success with customers was derived from the perceived value the concept provided. In addition, another unique feature which attracted and retained many of its unit managers was a profit-sharing program that allowed managers to own stock in the company and receive a percentage of the restaurant profits. Management abandoned the profit-sharing plan in 1977 following an ultimatum by the Securities and Exchange Commission. Many managers were required to refund portions of the profits paid to them and as a result they filed lawsuits against the company. Because of disenchantment, high management turnover in the following years (100 percent in 1978) eventually led to Sambo's filing bankruptcy liquidation in 1985.

There were instances where unit managers and other top management *lacked requisite skills to manage* effectively and successfully. In spite of such deficiencies the companies failed to provide adequate training to management. This was cited as a factor during the period of Naugles' financial distress.

The importance of the factors for failure prediction

Tavlin *et al.* (1989) examined some hospitality business failures and concluded in their study that there was a common theme throughout all the companies investigated. The theme was the lack of execution of the companies' mission and goals, and this was shown through the lack of responsiveness to change, inadequate manager and employee training, and failure to execute the company's concept properly. Other common factors included undercapitalization, overexpansion, failure to diversify, abandonment of a successful concept, and lack of adequate internal controls.

It is obvious at this point that there are several non-financial factors that are important contributors to business failure. Techniques that depend solely upon financial ratios to predict or explain business failure (Altman's Z-scores and other MDAs) fail to capture the role of these non-financial factors in the failure phenomenon. The events approach to studying business failure provides an alternative yet complementary method of gaining a more complete understanding of why businesses fail.

The events approach

This approach views business failure as a process beginning with the firm in financial distress and ending with the cessation of business or bankruptcy. As a result, the focus is on bankruptcy-related events that occur during this process rather than on financial ratios. The events approach offers a framework for assessing the likelihood of failure of a firm given the occurrence of one or more specific events, such as debt restructuring, loan default, or a quarterly or annual net loss (Giroux and Wiggins, 1984).

As financial distress sets in, there are reactions by the firm's management intended to stave off this misfortune, while creditors and other equity holders take similar actions to protect their interests. From the firm's point of view, policy and organizational changes will typically be enacted in order to revitalize and turn around the agency's operation and maintain liquidity.

Some of the turnaround actions may include the repositioning of an old concept, such as an old hotel, for a new market. In the case of Wendy's International, Inc., this involved the creation of the Super Bar concept. The Super Bar was designed as a self-service food bar and was expected to remove Wendy's from head-on competition with other large hamburger chains. In the case of Naugles, the actions intended to combat the deteriorating conditions involved the creation of new menu items, the redesign of the interior and exterior of existing and new restaurant units, the development of a new market campaign, and the implementation of cost controls.

At other times the specific action may involve management reorganization intended eventually to restore profitability. This occurred in the case of Wendy's International, Naugles, Sambos, and Burger King under Pillsbury. In addition, unprofitable units are usually closed or sold, debt accommodation or loan workout is also arranged with creditors, and sometimes a merger is chosen. Sometimes these actions are the necessary tonic that nurses the sick firm back to health (e.g. Wendy's). For other firms which may be beyond salvaging or which opt for the wrong strategies, the failure process ultimately leads to liquidation. What the events methodology does is to identify several events that are significant failure events and test empirically (using statistical techniques such as chi-square) to see if they are unique to firms that have failed.

Using this technique, Kwansa and Parsa (1990) selected twelve restaurant firms that had filed for bankruptcy between 1970 and 1985 and twelve non-bankrupt restaurant firms. These firms were compared along fourteen failure events. The events were pending lawsuits, auditor's opinion, default in franchise royalties, renegotiation of franchise contract, couponing and discounting expense, decline in unit gross sales, net losses, dividend reduction/elimination, bond rating downgrading, discontinued operations, management reorganization, debt accommodation, loan default, and bankruptcy filing. Results of the study showed that seven of the fourteen events investigated were unique to all the firms that failed and not to the non-failed firms. These events were net losses, management turnover, loan default, franchise royalty default, credit accommodation, decline in unit sales, and renegotiation of franchise contracts. All these events which were observed in the firms that failed occurred within two years of bankruptcy filing.

The events approach offers another valuable dimension to the study of business failure which the traditional multiple discriminant analyses are not effective in tapping.

Financial techniques for predicting failure

The univariate approach – that is, the calculation of a series of individual ratios using data taken from the company accounts – was first used in the 1930s. More recently, Beaver (1968), in a general study, determined that the ratio measuring cashflow to total debt correctly classified firms as failed or non-failed at least 76 percent of the time. In each of the cases the predictions were for 1–5 years prior to failure. In a study on restaurant failure in America, Olsen *et al.* (1983) found the ratios given in Table 16.5 to be the best indicators of impending failure over the time spans indicated.

To use this technique effectively as a monitoring device, a variety of ratios should be calculated regularly, taking care to ensure that a standard formula is always used. The predictive power is derived by comparison: comparing ratios over time for the same business to establish whether the situation is improving or declining, and comparing ratios between similar businesses to see whether the company in question is performing better or worse than the average industry result. Intra-firm comparison, although useful to potential investors, industry observers, and participants, does have several inherent dangers. The most significant concerns the validity of using averages calculated by leading industry consultants from a diverse sample of companies in the hospitality industry. Key accounting ratios are given in Table 16.6.

Table 16.5 Individual ratios as indication of restaurant failure

Ratio	Months prior
Current assets/current liabilities	5–9 months
Working capital/total assets	6–9 months
Earnings before interest and taxes/total assets	16–18 months
Earnings before interest and taxes/revenue	12–18 months
Total assets/revenue	11–19 months
Working capital/revenue	7–11 months

Source: Olsen *et al.* (1983).

Table 16.6 Financial ratios for measuring performance

- **Profitability and operating ratios**
  Return on assets
  Number of times interest earned
  Net return on assets
  Net income to revenue
- **Debt and gearing ratios**
  Debt ratio: total debts in relation to total assets
  Interest cover
- **Liquidity ratios**
  Current ratio
  Acid test ratio
  Accounts receivable/payable ratios
  Stock turn
  Working capital cycles
- **Shareholders' investment ratios**
  Return on shareholders' capital
  Earnings per share
  Price/earnings ratio
  Dividend yield

Broadly speaking, ratios can be grouped into four categories:

- Profitability and operating ratios.
- Debt and gearing.
- Liquidity: control of cash and other working capital items.
- Shareholders' investment ratios.

Many of these are standard ratios and used with specific operating statistics for the hospitality industry (Table 16.7), they provide an array of management information.

Benchmarks and guidelines for ratios are commonly cited. However, care should be taken as the magnitude of ratios can vary considerably from one industry to another. For example, a standard for the current ratio for the measurement of liquidity is often quoted as 1.5 to 2 – that is, ensuring that current liabilities are covered at least 1.5 times by current assets. However, many successful industries in the retail sector, for example, regularly exhibit values as low as 0.8. Consequently, the needs of the particular industry sector should be considered.

Multi-discriminant analysis

It is possibly the volume of information provided from traditional ratio analysis which has led many writers to be critical of accounting ratios as a sound monitoring device. Various writers argue that traditional ratios do not work as they have failed to change with and adapt to changes in the business

Table 16.7 Operating ratios for the hospitality industry

- Accommodation operations
  Average room rate (£/room)
  Average guest rate (£/guest)
  Room occupancy (%)
  Guest occupancy (%)

- Food and beverage operations
  Average spend (£/meal)
  Gross profit (£ or % to sales)
  Gross margin (£ or % to sales)
  Gross operating profit (£ or % to sales)
  Net operating profit (£ or % to sales)
  Wages (£ or % to sales)
  Stock turnover (times)
  Stock days
  Seat turnover

Source: HMSO (1969) A Standard System of Hotel Accounting, reproduced with permission of the Controller of Her Majesty's Stationery Office.

environment, and in reality businesses have continued to fail despite the use of the technique as a monitoring device.

The questioning of the application of univariate models is not new. In 1968 Altman proposed that the prediction of corporate solvency or failure could be measured by a single value or Z-score. The Z-score model was refined by Altman, and subsequent predictive models in use in the UK and USA are all based on the resulting statistical technique, called multi-discriminant analysis (MDA). Generally, MDA models contain a number of predetermined ratios (five in Altman's version), each with its own weighting, such that the sum of the products of the individual ratios and individual weights yields a Z-score. Guidelines are then provided from research for the interpretation of the score. Two well-known models based on the technique are those of Altman (US based) and of Taffler (UK based), and these have been widely used as the basis for research on the use of Z-scores for failure prediction.

The models of Altman and Taffler

Altman's original model, developed in 1968, was derived from discriminant analysis and is shown in Table 16.8. The model postulates a score whereby, if the answer is 1.8, the failure is certain, and if 2.7 (originally 2.9) the failure is highly unlikely. The two limits are described as follows:

- An upper limit, where no failed companies are misclassified.
- A lower limit, where no on-going companies are misclassified.

Lying between these limits is what Altman describes as the 'zone of ignorance' or the 'grey area' where a small number of failed and a small number of on-going companies are misclassified. Altman's own research using broadly

Table 16.8 Z-score model developed by Altman

Altman's model (1968):

$$Z = 1.2 \; X1 + 1.4 \; X2 + 3.3 \; X3 + 0.6 \; X4 + 1.0 \; X5$$

where:

X1 = working capital/total assets
X2 = retained earning since inception/total assets
X3 = earnings before taxes and interest/total assets
X4 = market value of equity/book value of debt
X5 = sales/total assets

Altman's revised model (1983):

$$Z = 0.717 \; X1 + 0.847 \; X2 + 3.107 \; X3 + 0.420 \; X4 + 0.998 \; X5$$

where:

X4 = book value of equity/book value of debt

manufacturing companies found that the model correctly classified 95 percent of the firms, one year prior to failure. Using data from the two years prior to bankruptcy, the correct classification fell to 72 percent. Earlier data did not provide a reliable classification. Altman has since recalculated his model (1983) using the book value rather than the market value of equity, and analyzing the same group of companies used to develop the 1968 model. Changing the ratio X4 to the book value of debt produced a change in the weightings used in the model. It can be observed that a small change to the specification of an individual ratio does produce substantial changes in the weights of the other ratios in the model. As a result the cut-off point in the 1968 model is amended to 1.23 from 1.81.

Taffler has published a formula (1977) for the UK industries and the final model is shown in Table 16.9. Taffler (1982) indicated that a score in excess of 0.2 and certainly 0.3 is characteristic of a company with good long-term survival prospects, while below 0.2 and certainly below 0.0 the company is likely to fail.

Table 16.9 Z-score model developed by Taffler

Taffler's model (1977):

$$Z = 0.53 \; X1 + 0.13 \; X2 + 0.18 \; X3 + 0.16 \; X4$$

where:

X1 = profit before taxation/current liabilities
X2 = current assets/total liabilities, i.e. total debt
X3 = current liabilities/total assets
X4 = the 'no-credit interval'

The 'no-credit interval' is defined as:

$$\frac{\text{Immediate assets} - \text{Current liabilities}}{\text{Operating costs} - \text{Depreciation}}$$

Problems in the usage of multi-discriminant models

Controversy has surrounded the use of the models since their conception. Leading writers in the field of accounting fail to agree on the effectiveness of the models as a means for predicting corporate failure. The authors themselves have issued different and conflicting guidelines for the use of these models over the period since their initial release. However, the following points are commonly raised on the appropriateness of these models.

- *Recognition of industry types.* When using discriminant analysis, the final model developed is for a specific industry group. The difficulty is in establishing whether the model may be used to transcend industry groups, particularly whether a model developed for manufacturing industries may be legitimately used for service industries. Inman (1982) used the model for a hotel and catering company, and for an overseas trader. He stated that the hotel and catering company 'appears to require some serious attention if collapse is to be avoided.' Although there is no clear evidence about the importance of industry type, common sense would suggest that specific industries have specific requirements in terms of prediction models and that the ideal solution would be for each industry type to have its own model.
- *Meeting the mathematical standards.* The methodology in developing the original model is complex, and consequently the model cannot be arbitrarily altered in terms of its constituents or cut-off points to meet different needs. For example, Altman's original model included a ratio based on the market value of equity, and many researchers, including Altman himself, assumed that the book value could be substituted. This proved to be invalid and Altman has since revised the model.

Case-study: Failure prediction in the UK leisure industries

During the 1980s the increase in the number of companies entering the leisure sector has been well documented. These companies provide a range of recreational activities and services such as sporting facilities, clubs, licensed and unlicensed eating facilities, short-stay accommodation, theaters, and concert halls. Such companies thrived under conditions of low interest rates, high consumer demand, and ample supplies of credit available for expansion. However, in recent months the demise of a number of these companies has been widely reported in the financial press. In many cases the key features of the recession – high interest rates, increasing inflation, and rising unemployment – have been blamed as the cause of failure. Are these the real reasons for the growing numbers of business closures and liquidations? Could failure have been predicted earlier?

To analyze this, the financial technique using Z-scores will be applied to the financial statements of several leisure companies selected on the basis of their varying fortunes. The success of the technique is then assessed in terms of the reliability of the results and, where failure has already occurred, the effective lead time for correct prediction.

The definition of failure

Before an analysis of the success of MDA techniques can take place, it is necessary to define what is meant by the term 'corporate failure'. Lev (1974) states that the definition of failure can be rather ambiguous: to some it means a situation known as technical insolvency, where a firm is unable to meet its maturing obligations such as long-term loans and other deferred liabilities; others restrict the term to the condition where the total value of the firm's assets is smaller than that of its liabilities. However, a firm can be temporarily insolvent yet continue to operate for a limited period, during which time it may recover. Alternatively, business failure may be interpreted in the legal sense of bankruptcy or liquidation, where the firm is forced to cease trading by its bankers or creditors. In this sense the broad definition provided by Lev is helpful: failure is interpreted as constituting severe financial difficulties which have become obvious through forced liquidation or lack of stock market confidence followed by a takeover or forced acquisition.

Testing the model

In order to assess the effectiveness of the two MDA models chosen, financial data from eight companies from the leisure sector has been gathered from computerized databases and the companies' own accounts. This data has been analyzed using spreadsheet models containing the MDA formula. A profile of the principal activities of those companies is shown in Table 16.10.

Notes for users

Altman's model

In the application of the data to the 1968 model, the following interpretations of the model have been made: market value of equity = book value of the reserves and ordinary shares from the balance sheet as recommended by Altman in his early research; book value of total debt = the total of long- and short-term debt; earnings before taxes and interest = operating profit before other income.

Taffler's model

In this model the 'no-credit interval' component has been included as follows: immediate assets = current assets; operating costs = sales minus operating profit; depreciation is not available, but the effect of including a value will be to decrease the Z-score further.

Table 16.10 Principal trading activities of companies analyzed

Company name	Principal activities
Allied Leisure PLC	Unlicensed eating places; sporting facilities and sports players; nightclubs and licensed clubs.
Edencorp Leisure PLC	Theaters, concert halls, etc.; sporting facilities and sports players; other recreational services; unlicensed eating places.
European Leisure PLC	Recreational services; public houses and bars; nightclubs and licensed clubs; licensed eating places; sports goods, sporting facilities, and sports players.
First Leisure Corporation PLC	Holiday camps; other tourist or short-stay accommodation; licensed eating places; other recreational services; sporting facilities and sports players; theaters, concert halls, etc.; camping and caravan sites.
Leading Leisure PLC	Licensed hotels; unlicensed hotels; building and construction; owning and dealing in real estate.
Mecca Leisure Group PLC	Central office of mixed-activity enterprises; nightclubs and licensed clubs; holiday camps; other tourist or short-stay accommodation; licensed eating places; licensed hotels; betting and gambling; owning and dealing in real estate.
Stanley Leisure Organisation PLC	Central office of mixed-activity enterprises; betting and gambling; sporting facilities and sports players.
Whitegate Leisure PLC	Other tourist or short-stay accommodation; hospitals, nursing homes, etc.; other recreational services; sporting facilities and sports players.

What the models tell us

Table 16.11 lists the Z-scores for the eight companies.

Allied Leisure (year of incorporation 1982)

In May 1991 this company was granted a stock exchange listing. Previously it had traded on the Unlisted Securities Market. The trading results over the period show a consistent increase in both sales and earnings before tax. Expansion has been funded from both equity and long-term loan sources. The leverage ratio has fallen dramatically over the last five years as the equity

Table 16.11   Z-score performances of selected companies

	1986	1987	1988	1989	1990
Model: Altman (1968)					
Allied Leisure		1.62	1.01	1.23	1.44
Edencorp Leisure				1.55*	
European Leisure	5.34	−0.78	4.11	1.46	1.15
First Leisure	2.21	2.87	2.69	2.36	3.48
Leading Leisure	1.10	0.79	1.06	0.96*	
Mecca Leisure Group	1.72	2.41	0.96	1.44*	
Stanley Leisure	8.25	6.13	5.56	4.24	3.62
Whitegate Leisure			8.58	1.91	0.51
Model: Altman (1983)					
Allied Leisure		1.61	1.05	1.22	1.25
Edencorp Leisure				1.17*	
European Leisure	4.04	0.09	3.10	1.16	0.88
First Leisure	1.88	2.25	2.11	1.87	2.55
Leading Leisure	1.07	0.81	1.11	0.99*	
Mecca Leisure Group	1.62	2.09	0.80	1.31*	
Stanley Leisure	7.85	5.77	4.57	3.41	2.93
Whitegate Leisure			6.00	1.41	0.51
Model: Taffler					
Allied Leisure		0.18	0.12	0.11	0.21
Edencorp Leisure				0.44*	
European Leisure	0.73	0.10	0.53	0.34	0.10
First Leisure	0.27	0.35	0.38	0.35	0.53
Leading Leisure	0.15	0.11	0.16	0.13*	
Mecca Leisure Group	0.23	0.32	0.03	0.17*	
Stanley Leisure	0.53	0.47	0.38	0.23	0.44
Whitegate Leisure			0.69	0.00	−0.61

* Indicates the last year of accounting information available.

and reserves held have increased. The current ratio has also significantly improved over this period. The market reports show an increase in share prices up to 1990 with a small downturn at the start of 1991. Altman's model places the company in 1990 in the region for failure, although the 1983 model is less damning; Taffler's model is more confident.

Edencorp Leisure PLC (year of incorporation 1989, suspended from trading December 1989)

This company briefly traded in the late 1980s before being suspended. In the latter stages of its life, the use of loan capital was substantially increased, raising the gearing of the company. Altman's model clearly indicates failure; however, Taffler provides a positive result. This is due to the reliance of the latter model on the relationship between assets and liabilities. An analysis of the accounts for 1990 would provide more conclusive results.

European Leisure PLC (year of incorporation 1935)
This company traded well during the 1980s with a rapid growth in sales supported by a growth in earnings before tax. The interim results announced in March 1991 indicate that the company is experiencing a problematic period. The Chairman states that 'tight consumer spending and high interest rates led to very difficult trading conditions.' Market reports indicate a lack of shareholder confidence in the company with share prices reaching a low in June 1991. Both Altman's and Taffler's model provide positive results up to 1988, although the trend is downward. The year 1987 is significantly highlighted by both models and this corresponds to a restructuring of the finances of the company. However, Altman indicates failure from 1989 with a score of 1.46 and Taffler confirms this in 1990 with a score of 0.1.

First Leisure Corporation PLC (year of incorporation 1981)
This company had expanded rapidly in the 1980s, achieving consistent sales and profit growth. Expansion was funded from increases in both equity and long-term loans. The market confidence continues to increase with share prices increasing virtually without restraint. Both Altman and Taffler provide very positive results for this company with the Z-score increasing over the period considered.

Leading Leisure PLC (year of incorporation 1983, dealings in company's securities cancelled December 1990)
This company expanded rapidly in the 1980s with the majority of funding coming from short-term loans. At the time of suspension the gearing was particularly weak and share prices were virtually at zero. Altman and Taffler both provide clear failure predictions from as early as 1986.

Mecca Leisure Group PLC (year of incorporation 1985, shareholders accept offer for share capital from the Rank Organization, August 1990)
This company expanded rapidly in 1988 using both long- and short-term loans. Market reports indicate a loss of shareholder confidence during 1989 with the share price plummeting in the period before the acquisition of shares by the Rank Organization. The Z-scores from both models are fairly erratic due to the restructuring of the equity and debt provisions, but both provide an overall view of failure from 1988 onwards.

Stanley Leisure Organization PLC (year of incorporation 1980)
This company has expanded its asset base during the late 1980s. This has been funded from a combination of equity and reserves. The market reports indicate confidence with share prices remaining buoyant. However, in 1991 the share price shows a slow downturn. Both Altman and Taffler provide a very positive result for this company, although a downturn in the Z-score can clearly be seen.

Whitegate Leisure PLC (year of incorporation 1987)

Despite a substantial increase in sales, the retained earnings have been small with a substantial extraordinary loss in 1990. The market reports show that the share price has plummeted since the start of 1990. Both Taffler and Altman provide a very positive score for 1988, but this is replaced in 1989 and 1990 with predictions of failure.

The value of the Z-score

These results would appear to indicate that a Z-score can be used successfully as a warning device. However, the debate continues as to how soon before failure the outcome can be predicted. In the examples demonstrated, clear prediction of failure is limited in the majority of cases to two years prior to failure. This lead time is obviously important to the manager in order to provide sufficient time to reverse the course to failure. Altman suggests that there are six courses of action available if a manager gets a poor Z-reading.

- Change the product or management personnel.
- Sell off unprofitable equipment, operations, or entire divisions.
- Solicit a takeover from a healthy company.
- Alter the financial structure (debt or equity).
- A bankruptcy reorganization.
- Liquidation.

However, in many cases two years is considered too short a time to achieve a reversal in the fortunes of a company.

Conclusions

In order to recommend Z-score analysis as a technique for predicting failure in the leisure sector, the reliability of the method must be tested further using a larger sample. However, this preliminary investigation clearly suggests that Z-score analysis is an effective monitoring device, particularly when there is a dramatic change in the value from year to year. The next step must be to determine the effective lead time for the prediction of failure, the key to success if the model is to be used effectively by firms operating in international markets, where time is required to implement a strategic change in direction. Another important consideration, if this model is to be used on an international scale, is the difference in accounting conventions from country to country. Standardization of the definitions used in the model is a prerequisite of success. Consequently, the alternative approaches to items such as the revaluation of assets, the capitalization of interest, and the misuse of extraordinary items can seriously undermine the effectiveness of the use of financial techniques for monitoring performance.

Current research indicates that the most effective use of the Z-score process is to develop the model for specific industry types to take account of differing asset structures, financing needs, and operating conditions. However, this preliminary research indicates that MDA may be used effectively as part of an overall approach to corporate failure prediction. The earlier part of this chapter highlights the significance of non-financial factors in failure prediction, and therefore, in conclusion, an approach which utilizes a combination of these methods is to be recommended.

References

Altman, E. I. (1968) 'Financial ratios, discriminant analysis and the prediction of corporate bankruptcy', *Journal of Finance*, vol. 23, pp. 589–609.

Altman, E. I. (1983) *Corporate Financial Distress: a complete guide to predicting and avoiding bankruptcy*, New York: John Wiley.

Beaver, W. H. (1968) 'Alternative accounting measures as predictors of failure', *Accounting Review*, vol. 43, pp. 113–22.

Dept. of Trade and Industry (1991) *Business Monitor*, May 1991, Department of Trade and Industry.

Dept. of Trade and Industry (1991) *Business Trends*, London: Dept of Trade and Industry.

Dun and Bradstreet (1987) *Business Failure Reports*, New York: Dun and Bradstreet.

Giroux, G. A., and Wiggins, C. E. (1984) 'An events approach to corporate bankruptcy', *Journal of Banking Research*, vol. 15, no. 3, pp. 179–87.

HMSO (1969) *A Standard System of Hotel Accounting*, London: HMSO.

Inman, M. L. (1982) 'Appraising Altman's two-formula prediction', *Management Accounting*, June, pp. 11–14.

Kwansa, F., and Parsa, H. G. (1990) 'Business failure analysis: an events approach', *Hospitality Education and Research Journal*, vol. 14, no. 2, pp. 23–34.

Lev, B. (1974) *Financial Statement Analysis: A new approach*, Englewood Cliffs, NJ: Prentice Hall.

Olsen, M., Bellas, C., and Kish, L. V. (1983) 'Improving the prediction of restaurant failure through ratio analysis', *International Journal of Hospitality Management*, vol. 2, no. 4, pp. 187–93.

Taffler, R. (1982) 'Forecasting company failure in the UK using discriminant analysis and financial ratio data', *Journal of the Royal Statistical Society*.

Taffler, R., and Tisshaw, H. (1977) 'Going, going, gone: four factors which predict', *Accountancy*, vol. 88, pp. 50–4.

Tavlin, E. M., Moncarz, E., and Dumont, D. (1989) 'Financial failure in the hospitality industry', *FIU Review*, vol. 7, no. 1, pp. 55–75.

17
Labor strategy in international hotel management

Michael Riley
and Peter A. Jones

While it is undeniably true that labor strategies follow directly from business strategies, inasmuch as it is business objectives that determine the quantity and quality of the workforce, it is also true that you do not change your workforce every time you change your business strategy. There is always an element of continuity and stability in organizational behavior. It follows, therefore, that the scope and purpose of labor strategy must embrace both the implications of change that stem from business strategies and economics, and the sustaining function of organizational design that comes from the need for stability. These two aspects invariably represent conflicting pressures on strategists, who must maintain a balance. The hotel industry is no exception and provides a very clear example of the conflicting pressures of having to cope with economics on the one hand, and the need for continuity of staffing on the other.

The degree of difficulty of this balancing act depends upon the nature of the business itself, the character of its labor markets, and the rate of technological change: in other words, its environment. The environment of the hotel industry has often been described as volatile. If that is true then it is predictably volatile in that, almost universally, the product market is highly competitive, the labor market dynamic, and the rate of technological change slow and incremental.

Strategic thinking in labor matters always begins with two key questions: on what does productivity depend? and how stable do I want the organization to be? These questions represent the interests of business and continuity respectively. However, at the sharp end, different questions are being asked by busy operations managers. They are asking: what sort of people do I want? and who do I want to retain? Here is the inherent problem for strategy, in that the volatile environment of the hotel industry, with a heightened sense of the immediate, encourages managers to think only in terms of staffing questions and not about the broader issues of productivity and organizational stability.

This chapter will suggest that there are two forms of labor strategy. These are, first, a broad framework which moderates the impact of the environment, and second, a problem-centered approach which works within the broad framework.

This discussion begins with a brief description of a framework for understanding the relationship between a hotel organization and its environment. The aim here is to give an integrated portrait of the context of labor strategy. This is then applied to the hotel environment. This, in turn, is followed by a suggested scheme by which policies and strategies can be developed. Attention then turns to the development of problem-solving strategies supported by hotel examples. The discussion concludes with some criteria by which we might judge labor strategy and some of the problems for devising such strategies that are inherent in the structure of hotel companies.

The framework of labor strategy

The purpose here is simply to describe how the environment and the organization interact, without, at this stage, referring specifically to the hotel industry.

If labor strategy is about managing the relationship between the organization and its environment then there are two requirements here. First, we must identify those dimensions of organization that are both under the control of management and which come under pressure from the environment. Second, we must have a clear view of that environment to know what pressures it can exert.

In response to the first requirement, a way into this relationship is to conceive of an organization in seven dimensions, all of which represent some form of stability, order, and continuity (see Table 17.1). These dimensions form what we might call the constituency of labor strategy. Strategic decisions will impact across these dimensions and it is through them that management becomes aware of environment pressures.

Before describing the environment it is worth repudiating the impression which may have been given that managers simply respond to environmental pressures. This, of course, is not true: managers are active market players and therefore influence their environment. In response to the second requirement – that is, getting a clear view of the environment – the environment of an organization can be conceived in four distinct but highly interdependent areas: economics, technology, the qualitative nature of consumer demand and what the competition's strategy is.

Taking economics first, three aspects of the *economic environment* are immediately relevant to labor management. These are the necessary rate of productivity, the pattern of customer demand and its impact on the labor force size, and the conditions of supply and demand in the labor market. It is not difficult to see that pressure here impacts on the stability of the organization, its training capacity, and its reward system. Some of the solutions to

Table 17.1 Seven organizational dimensions

● Stability	The rate of labor turnover and the rate of variation in workforce size
● Occupational value differentials	The relative value placed on occupations represented by pay differentials
● Training capacity	The capacity of the organization to train newcomers and develop the skills it needs
● Rewards	The level and form of rewards; their capacity to attract labor and induce increased performance
● Knowledge base	The human capital of the workforce; the sum of its knowledge
● Intergroup relations	The state of cooperation, competition, and status hierarchy between groups within the workforce
● Morale	The level of motivation at the individual and group level

economic pressures may come from the technological environment. Problems of productivity may be solved by technological substitution.

A closer look at the *technological environment* reveals an important relationship between changes in technology and certain dimensions of the organization. In understanding technological advances it is not just the rate of change that counts, but the type of impact it makes on the organization. This can be envisaged by the following typology:

A. Steady state (i.e. no change).
B. Gradual change built on existing knowledge and skills.
C. Gradual change based on new knowledge and skills.
D. Incremental change built on existing knowledge and skills.
E. Incremental change built on new knowledge and skills.
F. Revolutionary change.

Note the obvious importance of existing skills and knowledge. New knowledge of any sort brings changes in training capacity, reward systems, occupational values, and intergroup relations. Furthermore, by altering jobs, technology alters labor markets, making them bigger or smaller, or creating entirely new ones. There are obvious implications for recruitment policies here.

The way in which the third element of the environment, *the qualitative nature of demand*, influences the organization is through the processes of 'trading down', 'trading up', and 'following fashion'. The first two are linked to the economic environment; the latter not so. Where customers move between quality bands they alter or create a hierarchical structure of quality. The key point here is that in industries where labor is demanded for what it can directly produce (without intervening machines) then a movement in 'taste' dictates a movement in skill levels. This creates two problems for strategy: how to make the acquisition of skills fit the fluctuating pattern of demand, and whether to hold onto skill in conditions of trading down – the skill-hoarding phenomenon.

In the foreground of management's perspective is what the *competition are doing*. There are two types of currency here: action that might worsen my position (e.g. increasing pay) and new ideas. Managers copy each other and search for ideas which 'work'. In other words, managers' perception of other organizations includes a large element of comparing relative success.

What is being argued here is simply that changes in the environment bring pressure for change in each of the seven dimensions of the organization. Management, either proactively or reactively, uses strategy to control these dimensions (Simms *et al.*, 1988).

The hotel industry environment: a review

The purpose here is to bring together key features of the environment of a hotel industry in such a way as to point up the perennial dilemmas facing strategists.

Three aspects of the *hotel economic environment* exert strong pressure. These are, first, that consumer demand fluctuates universally in the very short term as well as seasonally; second, that the majority of jobs in hotels are unskilled; and third, that productivity is essentially individual productivity, and there-fore good selection and motivation are always paramount. As we will see, these three pressures are related and work in tandem (Riley, 1991a).

Short-term fluctuations mean that in some way the organization must have a flexible workforce if losses are to be avoided. This involves pay flexibility, numerical flexibility, and sometimes, but rarely, functional flexibility. Numerical flexibility implies that a part of the workforce must have weak tenure on their jobs. From an organizational perspective, hotel managers are always presiding over organizations which have skilled and unskilled ele-ments. Most of the need for flexibility falls on the unskilled. It would be wrong, however, to think that these peripheral workers with weak job tenure were somehow not as important to the hotel as, say, some skilled permanent employees. In economic terms, the reverse is true. The contribution to marginal revenue product is greater for the unskilled than for the skilled. Think of how many expensive meals a skilled chef would have to produce to match the marginal revenue of a cheaper room cleaner!

The fact that a high proportion of hotel jobs are unskilled is of enormous significance to the labor market. With high labor turnover, it might not seem so, but the fact that most jobs are unskilled places jobs in a large labor market and thus likely to be in surplus. This surplus obviously exerts a downward pressure on the rate of pay. The surplus in the market and the necessity of a peripheral element in the workforce help the hotelier to control costs. This process is aided further by the *technological environment*.

In terms of our typology of technological change, the hotel industry tends to behave in the manner of incremental change (D or E). Changes are usually in the form of substitution of work through some technology or method revision, or by fabrication, the buying in of the produce of labor. The character of change is almost universally deskilling. What is more the motive for technological change is invariably cost reduction. Here it can be seen that two forces work together as it is easier to make numerical micro-adjustments in the unskilled workforce than in the skilled, so it is always in the interest of managers to deskill! However, there are some exceptions to this rule: for example, the introduction of information technology has been a process of reskilling rather than deskilling.

From what has been said so far, a pattern is emerging in the way that the unskilled element in the workforce, the surplus in the labor market, and the deskilling process all point to one happy cost-reducing scenario. Alas, this convenient picture breaks down when the question of 'quality' is introduced. *Quality* speaks of skill, of continuity, of a stable workforce, the very opposite of the economic and technological cost-cutting pressures. Here then is the dilemma for the strategist. If the economics are at odds with the qualitative needs for skill development and continuity, how is skill to be maintained and how stable should the organization be? One obvious implication of this dilemma is whether to maintain skill by training, or by buying it in from the labor market. A less obvious but more curious implication is that hotels have two workforces with some people having strong tenure and others very loose job tenure.

The problem with 'two workforces' is: how do you motivate them? People on loose tenure and strong tenure working side by side present a particular motivational problem, especially when the employees are unaware of their tenure status but are aware of the nature of the business. The acceptance of a degree of employment uncertainty is probably a cultural norm in the occupational community of hotel workers. The criterion of merit used so often in judgment requires a good deal of management vigilance to maintain consistency in the face of constant personnel changes. Wanting to keep certain people while at the same time needing a peripheral workforce presents management with a complicated motivational obligation: for the most part, managers have to get the best out of people with loose job tenure. Let it be clear that, as productivity is individual productivity, the need to motivate is an unrelenting task.

The question of skill relates directly to *change in customer taste*. Going down the road of growing your own skilled people can be expensive, but leaving it to the labor market runs the risk of market dysfunction. If, for example, customers begin trading down, managers may after a time decide to deskill their skilled occupations and employ cheaper people. In time, this restructures the whole labor market so that, when an upturn in quality is demanded, the market cannot provide. In such circumstances, hotels chase the residue of skilled workers with ever-increasing rewards or are forced to spend money on training.

In summary, the hotel environment provides the strategist with a number of conflicts which have to be resolved through strategic policies across the seven dimensions. The broad conflicts are:

- The need for stability and the need for numerical fluctuations.
- Cost-cutting pressures and skill development.
- Motivation in the context of uncertain employment tenure.
- A hidden structure of 'two workforces', making motivation more complex.
- The pressure to deskill versus motivation.

Strategy as a policy framework: the process of development

What is strategy?

Usually the word 'strategy' is associated with the word 'planning'. This is correct, but strategy means more than designing a program of action for the future. Such programs require objectives, but where do these objectives come from? In the case of business strategy, the objectives come from alternatives derived from market information: in other words, strategy comes from the pursuit of identified targets. This is not the case with labor strategy, where the concern is with continuity and change. In this respect, labor strategy is more architectural in tone. The central element to all strategy, which precedes the planning process, is the creating of a vision. Put simply, 'what do I want my organization to look like in the future?' Anyone who has ever sat down to write a mission statement or vision statement knows just how hard this is.

The creation of a vision is never easy. Common sense and the daily 'reality' get in the way. However, we move towards what we can see, and therefore all planning processes require a model to head towards. Only when the model is in place can you see what must change. In the case of labor strategy, we are thinking about people, skills, motivation, knowledge, how work should be organized, control, and authority. These are the bricks that make up any organization. As in any building, the quality and quantity of these bricks are interrelated and interdependent, so any vision and consequent design must examine the interconnections between all these parts of the organization – in itself, a complicated process. What is more, organizations live in labor markets, and therefore the vision should embrace the relationship between the organization and its labor markets. The vision is a framework.

To come down to earth for a moment, strategy is not only about a vision of the organization. It has a more focused perspective. While the broad strategy acts as a framework, specific problems may arise which are handled within the framework by specific actions. The purpose of the framework is to ensure that, whatever problem-centered strategy is needed, its consequences throughout the organization are understood. In other words, strategy is both a framework and a problem-solving technique.

Ask the right questions

To pick your way through this maze requires a particular *questioning technique*, which at its simplest argues that the objectives of your labor strategy come from asking:

- What do I want?
- Why do I want it?
- What does this assume about technology, labor markets, and the behavior of people?
- What would need to change from the present position?

These questions need to be addressed across the range of organizational

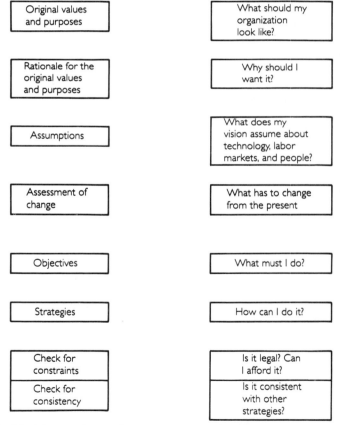

Original values and purposes	What should my organization look like?
Rationale for the original values and purposes	Why should I want it?
Assumptions	What does my vision assume about technology, labor markets, and people?
Assessment of change	What has to change from the present
Objectives	What must I do?
Strategies	How can I do it?
Check for constraints	Is it legal? Can I afford it?
Check for consistency	Is it consistent with other strategies?

Fig. 17.1 Model question and answer progression
Source: Riley, M. (1991), Human Resource Management: A guide to personnel practice in the hotel and catering industry, published by Butterworth-Heinemann.

dimensions and issues. Questioning can give you a headache, so it always needs to be set in a procedural format. This format has three stages, the first of which is not really labor strategy at all, but business strategy. The stages are as follows:

- Review the business strategy.
- Make a technological assessment.
- Apply the questioning technique.

Only from this process will actual concrete strategies emerge. At the heart of this approach to developing strategies is a questioning framework. The assumption of this framework is that strategies begin with the question: what do I want? This emphasizes the importance of managerial will in strategy. It also argues that the starting point is a vision of what the organization ought to be like in the future. The emphasis is on values and primary purposes, what the company stands for and its principal goals.

Figure 17.1 is a model which shows the progression of the question and answer. Note that the planning process in the conventional sense begins at the fifth point, and that 'means' enter at the next stages. The means can be, for example, structures, systems, specific appointments, or policies.

Remember that this framework is simply a sequence of questions, but what are these questions about? Where do you start? The questions start with an examination of each of the seven dimensions of the organization and a look at the values associated with these. Table 17.2 illustrates the type of basic question associated with each dimension. All that is being suggested here is

Table 17.2 Asking the right questions

• Stability	How stable do I want my organization to be? Which occupations require stability?
• Occupational value differential	On what basis are occupations different: supply conditions, level of skill, level of responsibility?
• Training capacity	On what does the continuity of skill depend?
• Rewards	How much incentive do I need to get the level of performance I want?
• Knowledge base	How much of the knowledge of staff is actually necessary? How far can knowledge be substituted by information? Does this knowledge form a basis for technological change?
• Intergroup relations	How far should the relationship between departments be governed by cooperation or competition?
• Morale	Is morale related to goals achieved or to standards maintained, or both?

that managers review strategy by carefully questioning each of the dimensions of the organization. For each dimension there could be different starting questions representing the values associated with that dimension. At this point it would be useful to give an example using the dimension of stability.

Original purpose and values
I want a stable organization with a constant workforce and minimal labor wastage. This requires a strategy to produce job security for the workforce.

Rationale for the original purpose and values
Why do I want stability?

- I do not anticipate fluctuations in demand.
- I anticipate regular technological change.
- I need to increase the value of human capital because the new technology develops from existing knowledge.
- Existing skills are very specific to the organization.
- I want to avoid a difficult labor market and heavy recruitment costs.
- I want to avoid high training costs.
- I want loyalty and commitment.
- I think that I will get an emphasis on quality if I offer security.
- I want flexibility and adaptability in my workforce.

Assumptions
What does the desire for stability and its policy arm – job security – assume?

About people
- The investment already made in skill is not a barrier to learning, or, if it is, then a job security policy will overcome it.
- People will be prepared to pass on their skills to others willingly. Again, the relationship between their own investment and job security policy is crucial.
- By taking the sacrifice out of learning, people will be prepared to abandon old skills for new.
- By feeling secure, people will show more commitment to their work and to the firm. In other words, security motivates.
- In the long term, people will find their own ways of doing things. Therefore, detailed specification of ends (quality and quantity) is probably better than tight control of means.
- There is a danger of dependency which matters if technology grants workers a degree of autonomy.
- People will value long-term personal relationships with co-workers.
- The culture and values of the workplace will be continuously reinforced and will therefore be stronger.
- People will either consciously or unconsciously forgo their labor market power – weaken it in return for security.

About the labor market
- You will not be able to find the skills you need at a price you are prepared to pay.
- The jobs you have are not easily substitutable by people with different skills.
- After a while your firm will not be 'visible' in the marketplace.
- You do not want or need new blood.
- You can attract sufficient people at your prescribed port of entry. If the port of entry is subject to fierce market competition, it might endanger the strong internal labor market you need to construct.
- Internal training produces better skills than the open market.

About technology
- The type and rate of change can be handled by the workforce.
- No revolutionary change is on the way.

On the basis that the answers to these questions convince you that you actually do want a stable workforce, clear objectives come into view.

Objectives
What must I do?

- Ensure I have a retraining capacity.
- Ensure that productivity improves consistently.
- Apply pay levels that will prevent temptation to leave. (Do I want to become a market leader?)
- Offer a package which is unconditional on performance.
- Ensure managerial control over the deployment of skills.
- Promote from within.
- Reduce ports of entry to the necessary minimum.
- Negotiate a flexible union agreement.
- Lower manning levels.
- Possibly build a buffer of non-secure part-time employment to account for fluctuation in demand.
- Grant a degree of autonomy as to methods while keeping control of the quality of the final product.
- Develop a style of supervision suitable for long-term relationships.
- Have a communication policy that assumes that people are interested and involved.

Clearly the objectives follow from the answers you give to your own questions, but what follows from the objectives is some form of action. The whole purpose of this question sequence is to make thinking easier, more logical, and more long term.

Forms of strategic action

After the thinking comes the action. By its very nature, strategic action impacts upon the status quo, so it is always a form of intervention.

Types of intervention

- Restructuring, e.g. organizational change.
- Technological, e.g. technological substitution.
- Procedural, e.g. a change in systems and procedures.
- Substantive: a change of content of a policy, e.g. pay level.
- Behavioral, e.g. an attempt to change employee behavior by some form of training.
- Appointments, e.g. introducing new people to get a fresh approach.
- Research, e.g. investigation of problems.

Used in any combination these are the means by which the objectives of the strategy are implemented. With each form of action comes a form of monitoring to measure the impact of the change.

Strategy as problem solving: alternatives or consequences

So far strategy has been conceived in its broadest perspective, where the concern has been with the environment and with a policy framework. If now the perspective is lowered from the big picture to the more immediate and focused, it becomes possible to address specific problems.

Does the same questioning technique apply? Yes, but only in part. If it is assumed that there exists a policy framework then the technique for specific problems requires a different but related question sequence. Figure 17.2 illustrates the sequence.

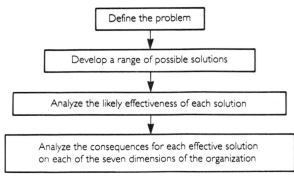

Fig. 17.2 The problem-solving sequence

The underlying assumption here is that any solution impacts not just on the problem but on the organization as a whole. An example from the hotel industry would be appropriate at this juncture.

Example: a shortage of skilled kitchen staff

Definition of the problem
There is a demand for quality food in the consumer market. The hotel is finding it hard to maintain quality because of insufficient skills in the kitchen. Possible causes are as follows:

- Labor market not producing applicants at any reasonable price.
- Poor in-house training capacity.
- Hiring standard too high.
- Labor turnover.
- Poor supervision.
- Poor morale.
- Restrictions on labor market mobility.
- A combination of some or all of the above.

Range of solutions

- Increase pay.
- Retrain supervisors.
- Replace supervisors.
- Lower hiring standards.
- Deskill occupations by technological substitution or product buy-in.
- Change conditions of employment.

Each of these solutions should now be examined, first in terms of probable effectiveness, then in terms of the impact on the seven dimensions of the organization. To take the example of deskilling by technological substitution or product buy-in: if this policy is adopted, what are the possible consequences in the medium term?

- *Stability*. May make the kitchen more unstable as unskilled workers tend to change jobs more often than skilled.
- *Occupational value differentials*. The differentials within the kitchen will be increased.
- *Training capacity*. New but lesser skills will be required by the skilled supervisor. The training activity will increase as labor turnover increases. Eventually the organization will lose the capacity to teach the 'old skills', making deskilling permanent.
- *Rewards*. It may be possible to lower the hiring standard and lower the pay accordingly. Kitchen supervisors may demand more pay for extra training and supervision of unskilled staff. Lower morale may require an incentive. More interest in unionism.

- *Knowledge base*. The knowledge will be altered. Initially the skills of chef will be redundant and replaced by new and lesser skills.
- *Intergroup relations*. The status of the kitchen may be eroded in the eyes of other departments and other kitchens.
- *Morale*. Deskilling always demotivates.

The point being made here is that any form of action changes more than just the problem at which it was aimed. This is why the framework of strategy and the problem-solving aspect are umbilically linked. Problem-solving strategies are like drugs: they have side-effects which should be known beforehand.

Criteria for judging strategies

The obvious criterion for judging any strategy is if it works. If it meets the objectives, it is successful. To this should be added the codicil: with the minimum of adverse consequences. It is possible, however, to go further in judging labor strategy if we reverse our perspective and look at it from the employee's point of view. Motivation is always an issue in the hotel industry because productivity is essentially individual productivity. It would be easy to enter a debate as to what motivates, but that debate can be circumnavigated by simply saying that everything does – as long as it tells the same story.

The individual is more likely to 'sense' what you are doing if your labor strategies are coherent than if he or she is being pulled in two different directions at the same time. If, for example, an individual is given close supervision and is expected to show initiative, or has insecure tenure of employment and is expected to be committed to the organization, then motivational efforts are handicapped. Such contradictions are often only apparent to the individuals concerned, but they undercut management's efforts to motivate. The case for coherence in labor strategies is that eventually employees will sense it and will be able to 'make sense' of what is expected of them. In other words, whatever you do is more likely to work if all the messages tell the same story. This gives another criterion by which we might judge labor strategy: coherence. The questioning framework is a method of achieving such coherence.

If the question is asked: on what does the success of any management action depend?, the bottom line answer is: on their authority. Here, then, is another criterion for judging strategy: it must always enhance the authority of managers. Obvious contradictions in policy can make managers at the sharp end look ridiculous. This is another argument for coherence.

Some problems

Who should devise strategy?

For many hotel companies the development of coherent labor strategies is problematic for two reasons: the structure of the organization, and the nature of the business itself. In fact, who develops labor strategy is itself the subject of a strategic decision.

The structure of hotel companies normally displays a wide geographical spread consisting of single units linked to a small head office. This places strategic considerations in the center–unit debate: that is, in the debate as to how much autonomy the units have and how much power lies at the center. The problem this creates is: who should develop the strategy and how should it be communicated? The 'local conditions' argument pushes the debate towards the unit management, but the message from the hotel environment suggests that units alone cannot solve problems such as shortage of skill, and this pushes the argument back towards the center.

For international hotel companies, the common policy is to allow 'local conditions' to predominate because of labor laws. This is often accompanied by a policy manual laying down policies and procedures. The problem here is that the need for uniformity may make such policies ineffective. Looking at the pressures from the environment, it becomes clear that qualitative aspects of labor require control from the center as the units are immersed in the economics of the business where the pressure is against quality. This aspect carries its own problems in that executives at the center have to persuade unit management of the need to tackle a problem that is not, to the unit, immediately pressing or obvious.

While strategic policy must be made at corporate level, there is a role for unit management in its development. The opinions of hotel managers should feed back into policy-making bodies within the company. This way the center–unit debate will not get in the way of good strategy development.

The problem of time

Perhaps the more understandable difficulty comes from the 'immediacy' of hotel life itself. Perspective tends to the short term because of the volatility of the environment and the perishable nature of the product. But neither of these two considerations represents an excuse for leaving labor affairs to the caprice of the local labor market. Experience shows that the strongest environmental influences are competition from other hotel companies and an upward pressure from the consumer to increase quality. When they arrive together hoteliers are reminded that increasing skills requires a long-term perspective.

The problem of development

All hotel companies share the same problem in terms of the costs of developing employees to become supervisors and managers. The problem is that they are valued in their early employment for their technical skills rather than for managerial skills. Although technical knowledge is a prerequisite of managing, it is still technical knowledge. It may well be that an employee would piece together a knowledge of systems and procedures through a technical perspective to the extent that he or she would 'know where trouble was coming from'. But that skill can be only a foundation for management skills. As people rise, their contextual knowledge has to go beyond technical systems. It is possible to graft on managerial skills, with difficulty, but the ability to grow in perspective – to see the ever-bigger context – is a matter of development which may be achieved only through being given ever increasing responsibility and risk. A common problem in the development of hotel managers is that they often see their self-identity in the original technological terms. This is a barrier.

The role of strategy here is to ensure that career management knows the career path, but also to ensure that the 'store and grow' stages of the career path actually do let the people 'grow' and not leave them marking time. If senior executives do not know what they want or expect from their managers then career management becomes a random exercise. The questions: what do you want? and why do you want it? were never more salient than in this area.

These problems exist for international companies as well as for purely national-based organizations. The international dimension adds further problems. There are three problems here. The first is that management has a different value and style in different cultures. Second, rates of learning vary from country to country. What is unskilled work in some countries can be regarded as skilled in another. Third, the culture of international hotels is basically Western European, so training takes on the additional burden of culture transfer as well as teaching skills and knowledge.

These three elements must form part of any training strategy because the easy route of imposing, without thought, American–European management style and definitions of skill and quality will lead to frustration.

Summary

In a volatile environment management exert their will only if they know what they want. This requires forethought, questions, and a vision. What has been proposed here is not any particular strategy but a rational questioning approach designed to bolster management's will by making them realize what they want but above all making them sure of why they want it.

One of the underestimated side-benefits of having a public strategic vision about labor matters is that management's authority is enhanced, which makes it easier to implement the policies themselves. Taking an overview of human resource development in hotels, it is possible to suggest that companies need to be more curious as to the skills needed by hotel management. The variety of career channels almost certainly produces a variation of skills in both type and level. This inconsistency makes strategic policy more difficult to implement.

It is predicted here that future development in labor strategy will be driven by the need for greater productivity, which will shift the emphasis away from 'the sort of people we want' to 'what do we really want them to do?': an emphasis on roles and jobs as well as the people who will have them.

References

Riley, M. (1991a) 'An analysis of hotel labour markets', in Cooper, C. (ed.) *Progress in Tourism, Recreation and Hospitality Management*, vol. 3, Belhaven.

Riley, M. (1991b) *Human Resource Management: A guide to personnel practice in the hotel and catering industry*, Oxford: Butterworth-Heinemann.

Simms, J., Hales, M., and Riley, M. (1988) 'An examination of the concept of internal labour markets in UK hotels', *Tourism Management*, vol. 9, no. 1, pp. 3–12.

18

Developing and maintaining a strategy for service quality

Andrew Lockwood, Evert Gummesson,
Jan Hubrecht, and Martin Senior

The hospitality industry has always had a fascination with quality, typified by the grandest of hotels and the finest in dining. The growth of interest in manufactured product quality through the late 1970s and early 1980s was followed by the development of approaches to service quality in the late 1980s. Into the 1990s, the hospitality industry seems increasingly to be taking on board the message that quality is really about satisfying the needs and expectations of the customer. There can be as much quality in a Burger King or a Motel 6 as in a three-star Michelin restaurant or a five-star luxury hotel.

If the term 'quality' is to be of use to hospitality managers, it must take account of the predominance of customer requirements. There are many definitions of quality which emphasize the role of the customer. Juran (1974) described quality as 'fitness for purpose or use ... judged by the user, not manufacturer.' The British Standards (1987) definition of quality is 'the totality of features and characteristics of a product or service that bear on its ability to satisfy a stated or implied need.' For the hospitality industry, managing quality is a particularly difficult and complex problem, combining, as it does, features of both a product and a service. Not only does the hospitality industry face the manufacturing problems of providing a high quality of food or accommodation, but it also needs to counter the problems of service delivery through the high level of interaction between staff and guests.

The need to deal with these issues, however, is ever more important to the success of individual units or companies and to the industry as a whole. Lewis (1989) identified three environmental factors that are encouraging the development of providers' awareness of service quality:

- *Consumer expectations and awareness.* Customers are becoming increasingly demanding of the products and services they buy, as well as the way in which those products and services are delivered.

- *Technology*. The development of more sophisticated technology allows managers to provide a wealth of additional and convenience services, but there is no doubt that customers still value personal contact.
- *Competitive environment*. The recent trend is to view quality service as the critical factor in determining a competitive edge in an increasingly competitive and international marketplace.

This chapter will explore how service quality can be developed and maintained in hospitality operations as a key strategy for business success. The development of service quality must be founded on building quality into the operation – the quality of design. This must be based on a clear understanding of the needs and expectations that customers bring to hospitality operations. Maintaining quality is concerned with how the operation is managed to ensure the quality of conformance and the reliability of the operation to provide that level of service, right first time, every time.

Quality of design and service delivery strategies

Any service, just as any physical product, needs to be properly designed. In a small 'mom and pop' type operation, the design may be based on the professional skills of the owner or owners, as they are likely to be personally involved in the service delivery. The design need not necessarily be documented. This mode of operation, however, places limits on the size and growth of the service organization.

When service firms grow, and when specialization, as well as decentralization, becomes necessary, managements need to establish a clear service delivery strategy with a documented service system design. Otherwise the service will lack direction and the quality of performance will vary considerably both between units and between employees within units.

Services are produced and delivered, partly, in interaction between the customer and the service provider. Gummesson (1992) identifies four different interactions that can occur when a customer enters a service operation:

- Between the customer and the service provider's employees.
- Between the customers themselves.
- Between the customer and the physical products and the physical environment.
- Between the customer and the service delivery system.

Service delivery, however, does not only consist of customer interactions but also involves the interactions and other work going on inside the service organization to produce the service. A service organization can be seen to consist of the following participants, although one person, such as a hotel manager attending to a guest at the front desk, may take more than one role:

- Customers.
- Contact staff (front-of-house personnel).

- Support staff (back-of-house personnel).
- Management.

The four types of interaction described above can also take place within the organization where the customer is not present. These complementary interactions would include contact as follows:

- Between personnel in the same functional area.
- Between functional areas.
- Between personnel and the physical product and the physical environment.
- Between personnel and the service delivery system.

With these interactions and participants identified, a full picture of the interactions within the service delivery system can be drawn. Figure 18.1 illustrates the complexity of the interactions occurring within a service business, but even so does not tell the whole story. For example, only two customers are drawn and in reality there will be many more. Similarly, only one manager, one customer contact employee, and one back-of-house employee are shown. Only one interaction with the physical product, the physical environment, and the service delivery system is shown, but a customer may well interact with the organization more than once during the same service event and on many occasions over time.

Increasingly, the complexity of the service encounter is being recognized and planned for, such as in the emerging field of service design (see, for example, Hollins and Hollins, 1991). The complexities and dynamics of service delivery described above can best be established by flowcharting, a well-known technique for graphically showing activities and their connections. The best-known approach to creating a general flowchart format for services has been developed by Shostack (1981, 1987) under the label of 'service blueprinting'.

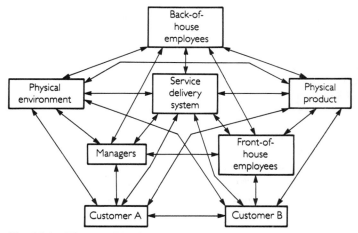

Fig. 18.1 The complexity of service interaction

A service blueprint integrates the elements and interactions described above. It is built inside a matrix where the horizontal upper line shows the customer's path while vertical lines illustrate activities within the service provider's organization. The distinguishing feature of a service flowchart as compared to an ordinary flowchart is that customer logic – the way the customer thinks, feels, and behaves – is used as the starting point. The customer's path, moving from left to right on the chart, can then be matched with the service provider's organization. Where there is interaction between the customer and the service system, provider logic is confronted by customer logic. It is also necessary to show the internal interaction between the front-line staff, the support staff, and management. The service flowcharts described so far only include human interactions, while interactions with physical products and between customers should also be systematically included.

Shostack's service blueprint approach also defines the 'line of visibility'. This line divides the service process into two, where one part is visible to the customer and one part is not. It is important to determine what the customer should and should not see. At Stew Leonard's huge fresh-food store in Connecticut, USA, the shopper sees right into the dairy, bakery, and butchery. This creates a sense of participation and also provides direct evidence that the food is fresh. It forces management and employees to observe strict discipline – very little can be hidden from the customer. By this and other means, such as entertainment for children, Stew Leonard's has become more than a store; it has become a goal for combining leisure with weekly shopping.

The blueprint method also introduces the idea of failpoints. Failpoints are the weak links in the chain of service activities. No chain is stronger than its weakest link, especially in the service process. The failpoints are where the risk of failure is greatest, and they are therefore identified to remove them and so prevent quality problems.

There are significant strategic benefits in using service flowcharts:

- They are helpful in the development of a corporate strategy. A flowchart provides an overview. Everyone can see which elements constitute the service, how these are connected and how they relate to the customer. Those who participate in strategy formulation can tend to exaggerate the significance of their special function. This may distort their view unless the basis for a holistic view of the service is provided.
- The flowchart can be helpful in determining the standards required in each element of the service, as well as for the total service, and suggesting how these quality dimensions could be measured. It thus helps in establishing a quality strategy for the service company. This quality strategy, where quality is defined as customer-perceived quality linking customer needs and customer satisfaction, is the basis for the firm's marketing strategy.
- The flowchart provides a basis for identifying and assessing cost, revenue, and capital invested in each element of the service. It simplifies the establishment of a financial strategy.

- The flowchart identifies the points at which customers interact with employees and with the service delivery system, thus allowing a labor strategy to be developed.

The service design forms the basis for determining the strategies for the functional areas of the service firm. These strategies, identified above, include marketing/competitive strategies, financial strategies, and labor/human resource strategies.

Marketing and competitive strategies

A basic tenet in services marketing holds that improved quality will strengthen a company's competitiveness. This is supported both by research, most notably the PIMS studies (Buzzell and Gale, 1987), and by practical experience. The significance of this statement is only fully evident when service quality is defined in terms of customer-perceived quality. Quality in this sense is a mixture of objective knowledge and subjective perceptions through experience, emotions, word of mouth, promotion campaigns, rumors, and so on. The service design constitutes a rational basis for both the external and the internal marketing strategies. Three particularly significant marketing strategies will be considered.

The customer as focus
The customer's path is the starting point in service design. Thus customer needs and behavior – the customer logic – will guide the development of the service design. Flowcharts have long been used in the development of computer programs. Computer programming, however, does not inherently regard the customer's path; it tends to be oriented to available computer software and hardware. Similarly, in service firms, internal technicalities such as financial report systems or routines for salary payments are often given priority at the expense of the customer.

Every employee affects customer relations
This is reflected in the concepts of interactive marketing, part-time marketers, and moments of truth. The front-line employees are in constant and direct contact with the customer. This personal contact, although focused mainly on producing the service, also becomes interactive marketing, which it is suggested has more impact than mass marketing (Grönroos, 1990). These staff are hired primarily for other tasks, but in the event become part-time marketers (Gummesson, 1990). In services marketing we talk about the service encounter or moments of truth (Carlzon, 1987). Each contact becomes a moment of truth. In each moment of truth, the customers decide whether they liked the service or not and whether they will be patrons of this service provider in the future.

Differentiation of the service offering

In a competitive market, it is essential to differentiate a service to fit a specified group of customers – a market segment – and to stand out as in some respect unique in comparison with competitors. Grönroos (1990) makes a distinction between core service, facilitating services, and supporting services. If the core service is the same among all competitors – which is quite common in mature industries – the creation of a competitive advantage must be found in the other two. Facilitating services are those necessary to consume the core service. Swedish Rail until recently had an information, ticketing, and payment system that made it difficult for passengers to travel by train. Instead people chose their own car or airlines which gave much more friendly access. Supporting services are not necessary for the consumption of the core service, but they add to the value for the customer or at least differentiate one provider from another. The way the customer is treated – with courtesy, even compassion – particularly in the hospitality industry can be a decisive differentiating factor to support the core service.

Financial strategies and resource effectiveness

The service design determines what elements and interactions should be included in the service, which in turn determine the three key financial factors of an operation: namely, revenue, cost, and capital employed. Table 18.1 describes the relationship between these financial factors and the linked ideas of productivity, quality, and profitability.

Quality, productivity, and profitability are inextricably linked. Managing one will affect the others. Jones (1988) introduces a model of how they are related. A crucial question must be: what is the cause and what is the effect? The traditional view is that quality costs money and has to be held back in bad times. Quality is only produced when you can afford it. At these times, the focus is on productivity: that is, getting more out of the same resources or getting the same from fewer resources. In practice this means cost reduction or a reduction in capital employed, usually making staff redundant, cancelling promotional campaigns or new building programs, and so on.

Table 18.1 Productivity, quality, and profitability and their connection with the three financial factors

Productivity	Emphasis on resource effectiveness; in practice and especially in times of economic malaise, usually means reduction of cost and capital employed
Quality	Emphasis on customer satisfaction, value to the customer, and revenue
Profitability	Emphasis on the combined effects of revenue, cost and capital employed

It is, of course, true that aiming for a higher standard of physical product costs money. For example, the Jury's Hotel in Dublin has some luxurious suites that for many reasons are more expensive. They are more spacious and more lavishly furnished, and they even have a jacuzzi with a built in television set and telephone. However, the idea that higher quality is more expensive is challenged by Crosby's (1979) slogan 'Quality is free!' Crosby suggests that if you do it right first time, you will avoid rework and irritation among your customers. This means a cheaper product or service in the end. You lower the need for personnel, space, goods in stock, and administration, thus reducing cost and capital. At the same time you enhance your image among customers, encouraging repeat custom and increasing revenue. This zero-defects strategy for quality has been supplemented by the zero-defection strategy: 'keep every customer the company can profitably serve!' (Reichold and Sasser, 1990). Gummesson (1991) shows that there is no general relationship between cost and quality, and that each case must be examined in relation to its own specific conditions.

The costs of quality are usually divided into three types:

- *Costs of failure*. These are the costs of having made mistakes. They can be split into internal and external failure costs. Internal costs are those incurred where mistakes are found before they reach the customer or cross the line of visibility. They include scrap, rework, downgrading, and excess inventory. External failure costs are those incurred when mistakes are not found before they reach the customer. They include such things as repair and warranty claims, providing replacement goods or services, and the potential loss of future business.
- *Costs of appraisal*. These are the costs of inspection to make sure that the number of mistakes is kept down and to ensure that any mistakes that are made are identified before reaching the customer.
- *Costs of prevention*. These are the costs of avoiding mistakes through such activities as training staff and establishing a well-designed service delivery system in the first instance.

Crosby suggests that a service firm can waste as much as 35 percent of its costs on producing 'non-quality'. He estimates that appraisal and failure costs account for approximately 95 percent of this total, whereas prevention costs account for the other 5 percent. Turning this ratio around by allocating a much higher percentage to prevention costs should provide a massive potential for reducing total cost in any service business.

Returning to the causal relationships, Gummesson (1992) suggests that quality provides the key to both productivity and profitability. These relationships are shown in Figure 18.2.

Human resource strategies

The use of blueprinting as part of the service design process highlights the importance of employee involvement in the delivery of product and service

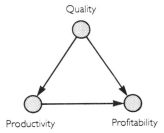

Fig. 18.2 The golden triangle of success
Source: Gummesson, (1992).

quality. It also highlights the difficulty of ensuring consistent quality when production necessitates such a high human input. This employee input cannot be controlled and directed in the same way as the systems and technology of production or service delivery.

Human resource strategies need to be developed that will reinforce the drive toward quality. These strategies will start with recruitment and selection, but must also include conditions of service, communications, training, and reward strategies. The aim must be to build a workforce motivated to provide excellent service. In this way not only will the organization ensure the quality delivered to the customer, but also it will be able to attract and retain the highest-quality employees. Poor service is not only bad for customers; it is also dissatisfying for the employees who deliver it.

The organization needs to provide a caring and supportive environment, but in order to make the best use of its employees' potential, it also needs to provide an environment that will encourage participation in the quality improvement process and empower employees to make these improvements for themselves. The hospitality industry is not noted for the foresight of its human resource strategies, and this could provide the major stumbling block for companies in making major quality improvements.

Understanding customers' needs and expectations

Service quality as a business concept is new compared to the concept of product quality, and this is reflected in the way in which the service quality literature has been developing. The literature is unanimous in recognizing the value of providing good service quality to the customer, but shows that the nature of service quality is still in an early stage of conceptualization and understanding. Many writers on this subject come from the USA, the UK, and Scandinavia, with many having marketing-related or service industry backgrounds as practitioners, consultants, or academics. The diverse nature of the literature and its contributors emphasizes the wide interest in this subject.

Despite the amount of interest being shown in service quality, however, the actual concept still appears to elude a clear definition (Shams and Hales, 1989). Much of the problem is due to the word 'service', which is ambiguous in its meaning (Middleton, 1983). A service may refer solely to the encounter between a service provider and a customer. It may refer to the products of service industries. Or it may refer to all transactions that are in essence a 'service' to the customer (Foxall, 1984).

The hypothesis that service quality can refer to all transactions in the marketplace is supported by the theories of many marketing and service industry authors. Grönroos (1984) has identified two key aspects of a service: the 'functional' aspects of the service, which are about how the service is delivered; and the 'technical' aspects, which are about what is delivered. Lehtinen and Lehtinen (1985) present two models showing that service quality can be divided into 'physical quality', 'interactive quality', and 'corporate quality', or separately as 'process quality' and 'output quality'. A substantial research study by Parasuraman *et al.* (1985) identified five key dimensions which customers employ when evaluating services. These dimensions were: tangibles; reliability; responsiveness; assurance; and empathy. Nightingale (1986) in his study of the hospitality industry identified that customers perceive both 'physical' and 'psychological' aspects as important to service quality. The psychological aspects are frequently more decisive in choosing between alternative service offerings.

In the view of these authors, service quality appears to encapsulate several key features, but although the wording and descriptions differ, many of these features are similar in content. Essentially, service quality appears to include 'tangible' elements, which are represented by references to technical quality, physical quality, output quality, the tangible dimension, and physical aspects; and also appears to include 'intangible' elements, which are represented by references to functional quality, interactive quality, corporate quality, process quality, the dimensions of reliability, responsiveness, assurance and empathy, and psychological aspects. If service quality is considered to include both tangible and intangible elements then the hypothesis that service quality refers to all transactions in the marketplace can easily be accommodated.

Although the general composition of service quality has been identified, for practical purposes it is still necessary to identify the specific elements of service that contribute to perceptions of quality. However, this cannot be done without knowledge of the context in which the concept is being considered, since all purchases will involve different permutations of the critical elements. The next section considers service quality in the hospitality industry and will identify the key elements of service in the hotel industry.

Quality in hospitality operations

Identifying key elements of quality common to the whole of the hospitality industry is problematic because the industry is made up of a very large and diverse range of hotel, catering, and leisure organizations. However, it is possible to identify a broad range of key elements within particular sectors, such as the hotel sector. Many studies have been carried out in the hotel industry to identify the attributes that contribute to both customer satisfaction and customer dissatisfaction. However, the findings from these studies are not always comprehensive or rigorous enough to be adopted as definitive guides to service quality elements. Furthermore, since the researchers who carry out the surveys often have different objectives and different approaches to the collection of the data, many of the studies are not sufficiently compatible to enable their results to be directly compared. The results from five such studies are briefly summarized here to present an indication of the elements that may be critical to service quality in the hotel industry. These studies are Atkinson (1988), Institute of Sales and Marketing Management (1986), Knutson (1988), Oberoi and Hales (1990), and Wilenksy and Buttle (1988).

The four most important attribute categories derived from the studies were as follows:

- Bedroom and bathroom cleanliness.
- Bedroom facilities and comfort.
- Friendly, courteous, prompt, and professional service from staff.
- Safety and security.

These findings suggest that, to maintain customer satisfaction in a hotel, the facilities must be clean, comfortable, sufficiently equipped, and safe and secure. The service provided by the staff must be friendly, efficient, and professional. These findings also support the model suggested by Jones and Lockwood (1989) that customer satisfaction (and service quality) is dependent upon the quality of both the tangible and the intangible elements of contact with the hotel's facilities and staff (see Figure 18.3).

Even though the results presented have come from a disparate range of hotel studies, these findings are not particularly surprising. It is likely that good housekeeping, good facilities, and good service will always be key elements of quality in any hotel experience. It is therefore necessary to consider

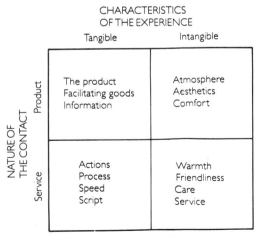

Fig. 18.3 Hotel quality matrix

service quality elements in more detail and for each of the subsectors of the hotel industry. The next section will describe a study that was carried out by one of the authors in a subsector of the UK hospitality industry – the roadside lodge sector.

Quality in budget hotels: a case study

Over a period of two years a qualitative and quantitative study was used to identify the key elements that were considered important by guests staying overnight in a chain of low-tariff roadside lodges or budget hotels. Thirteen separate lodges were used in the study for carrying out in-depth interviews and questionnaire surveys. Since the study was carried out with guests using roadside lodges operated by one organization only, it is not possible to assume that the results represent all guests staying in all types of overnight accommodation.

The qualitative study was primarily conducted to identify the criteria that could be incorporated later into a structured questionnaire. The method was an in-depth interview approach using Kelly's repertory grid technique (Kelly, 1955) to identify the most salient constructs for discriminating between various hotels that the respondents had used in the past. From the 47 guests interviewed, 564 separate constructs were elicited and then content analyzed to produce a small number of construct categories. These construct categories were then considered to represent the quality criteria that may be important to overnight guests. Table 18.2 shows the first 25 construct categories, which represent 92 percent of the responses provided.

The most frequent construct category elicited was 'value for money'. This may not be surprising since the respondents staying in a roadside lodge are likely to be price sensitive. They therefore consider that value for money is an important consideration during any overnight stay. The second most frequent category elicited was 'overall standard', which reflects the respondents' concern for 'total' quality. The quality of a hotel or lodge visit is likely to be dependent on the quality of many factors, and not just a few isolated ones. The next two most frequently mentioned construct categories were 'cleanliness' followed by 'friendliness of staff'. As documented in many other hotel studies, these two constructs of quality criteria do appear to be important attributes. Table 18.2 also shows that both tangible and intangible elements were considered important in hotel stays.

Due to their relative placing in the list, the first two-thirds of the construct categories were considered the most valuable attributes for being included in a larger survey using structured questionnaires. Since the study was interested in identifying both the most important attributes to lodge guests and the best performing attributes in the lodges, the questionnaire design closely followed the format developed by Parasuraman et al. (1985). Each attribute was assessed separately against customers' expectations and against customers' perceptions on a seven-point Likert scale. As the service provided by this company for lodge guests includes the actual lodge and the associated

Table 18.2 Construct categories

Category	Percent	Cumulative percent
Value for money	13.6	13.6
Overall standard	7.1	20.7
Cleanliness	6.9	27.6
Friendliness	6.7	34.3
Food quality	5.8	40.1
Style of hotel	5.4	45.5
Service quality	4.4	49.9
Decorations/maintenance	3.5	53.4
Lodge concept	3.5	56.9
Comfort	3.3	60.2
Location	3.1	63.3
Restaurant style	3.1	66.4
Leisure facilities	3.0	69.4
In-room facilities	3.0	72.4
Market level	2.4	74.8
Telephone	2.0	76.8
Temperature	2.0	78.8
Management	2.0	80.8
Children's facilities	1.8	82.6
Consistency/assurance	1.8	84.4
Bar	1.8	86.2
Bathroom	1.6	87.8
Noise	1.6	89.4
Social interaction	1.5	90.9
Security	1.1	92.0

restaurant facilities, some of the attributes were included twice. Table 18.3 shows the results from the 365 questionnaires that were returned correctly completed.

The figures in Table 18.3 show that, overall, the respondents had higher expectations (E) of the attributes than their perceived performance (P). This is reflected in the difference (D) scores, which highlight how much each attribute has either over- or underperformed against guests' expectations.

The original list of construct categories displayed in Table 18.2 did not include the construct category 'children's facilities' because of its low rating. However, this was included in the questionnaire at the request of the client organization. Table 18.3 shows that this attribute also scored low in the questionnaire survey. This provides some evidence of the validity of the methods chosen. Furthermore, the four construct categories that scored the highest in the original interviews closely match the four highest attributes on the 'expectation' dimension for both lodges and restaurants in the questionnaires (see Table 18.4), and show some similarities with the findings from the hotel studies reported earlier.

The emphasis of the interviews and questionnaires was slightly different. The first focused on salient attributes from past hotel experiences and the

Table 18.3 Questionnaire results

	Attributes	E	P	D
Q1	Location of lodges	6.28	5.69	−0.59
Q2	Cleanliness of lodges	6.80	6.50	−0.30
Q3	Comfort of lodges	6.57	6.22	−0.35
Q4	Decorations and maintenance of lodges	6.65	6.44	−0.21
Q5	Children's facilities in lodges	4.23	4.24	+0.01
Q6	Staff friendliness in lodges	6.74	6.42	−0.22
Q7	Service in lodges	6.71	6.35	−0.36
Q8	Overall standard in lodges	6.78	6.43	−0.35
Q9	Value for money in lodges	6.74	6.29	−0.45
Q10	Suitability of restaurants	6.52	4.43	−2.09
Q11	Location of restaurants	6.60	5.84	−0.76
Q12	Cleanliness in restaurants	6.87	5.46	−1.41
Q13	Comfort of restaurants	6.58	4.96	−1.62
Q14	Decorations and maintenance of restaurants	6.39	5.25	−1.14
Q15	Food quality in restaurants	6.73	4.66	−2.07
Q16	Staff friendliness in restaurants	6.71	5.23	−1.48
Q17	Service in restaurants	6.77	5.28	−1.49
Q18	Overall standard in restaurants	6.77	5.22	−1.55
Q19	Value for money in restaurants	6.71	4.73	−1.98
		6.53	5.57	−0.96

Key: E = expectation score, P = perception score, D = difference score, + indicates perceptions exceed expectations, − indicates expectations exceed perceptions.

Table 18.4 Comparison of most salient construct categories with important attributes

Interviews	Questionnaires
Value for money	Cleanliness
Overall standard	Overall standard
Cleanliness	Service
Friendliness	Value for money and Friendliness[*]
Food quality	Food quality

[*] Same lodge and restaurant aggregate scoring in Table 18.3.

second on important attributes for current lodge experiences. It might, therefore, be expected that the order of attributes would vary. However, they do in fact show many similarities with each other and with the other hotel study results. It may be assumed, therefore, that these findings provide a general indication of which elements contribute most to quality in hotels and similar lodging establishments.

A second stage of this survey was carried out to identify employees' level of empathy for their guests: that is, how well employees identified what their customers expected from the service, and how well employees correctly identified what their guests thought of the service once it was delivered. This was done by asking the roadside lodge staff to complete similar questionnaires. In this case the questions were oriented toward the employees. They were asked to comment on what they thought their customers would expect from the service and what they thought their customers thought of the service provided. Table 18.5 shows the difference between customers' expectations and perceptions in one column (customer dissatisfaction), and the difference between customers' combined scores and employees' combined scores in the second column (employees' empathy).

The value of showing these two columns together in Table 18.5 is that it is possible to identify the courses of action that may be effective in improving customer satisfaction. For example, the worst-performing attribute was 'suitability of restaurants' at −2.09, but this was also one of the best empathy scores showing a small difference between customer experiences and employee perceptions of those experiences. This indicates that the customers' dissatisfaction with the restaurants was well known to (or well guessed by) the employees. Employees may therefore be holders of valuable information which organizations could tap into through quality assurance programs, such as quality circles. Conversely, where employees have scored low on empathy,

Table 18.5 Customer dissatisfaction levels and employee empathy levels

	Attributes	Customer dissatisfaction	Employee empathy
Q10	Suitability of restaurants	−2.09	0.49
Q15	Food quality in restaurants	−2.07	1.29
Q19	Value for money in restaurants	−1.98	1.86
Q13	Comfort of restaurants	−1.62	1.06
Q18	Overall standard in restaurants	−1.55	0.81
Q17	Service in restaurants	−1.49	0.82
Q16	Staff friendliness in restaurants	−1.48	0.76
Q12	Cleanliness in restaurants	−1.41	0.75
Q14	Decorations and maintenance of restaurants	−1.14	0.99
Q11	Location of restaurants	−0.76	2.21
Q1	Location of lodges	−0.59	0.37
Q9	Value for money in lodges	−0.45	1.28
Q7	Service in lodges	−0.36	0.66
Q8	Overall standard in lodges	−0.35	0.63
Q3	Comfort of lodges	−0.35	0.58
Q2	Cleanliness of lodges	−0.30	0.34
Q6	Staff friendliness in lodges	−0.22	1.10
Q4	Decorations and maintenance of lodges	−0.21	2.03
Q5	Children's facilities in lodges	+0.01	1.17

such as with food quality, employees may benefit from increased awareness of customers' dissatisfaction and from increased training in delivering quality food. It is possible, though, that the physical facilities in the restaurant or the food production system itself may be responsible for the poor food quality.

Table 18.5 shows other attributes that have scored poorly for customer satisfaction, particularly those that are one point or more. Where these attributes are related to poor empathy scores, such as food quality, restaurant service levels, restaurant friendliness and restaurant cleanliness, improvements may be made through increased education and training of employees. Where the attributes are related to physical aspects, such as restaurant suitability, restaurant comfort, and restaurant decorations/maintenance, improvements may be made through some form of redesign and refurbishment. Where the attributes are related to systems or processes, such as food production and cleaning activities, improvements may be made through systems redesign.

Furthermore, if some of these improvements were carried out then it is likely that they would have a positive knock-on effect on some of the other attributes, such as value for money and overall standards.

In summary, the key elements of quality identified in the case study for hotel and lodge guests appear to be broadly related to: good housekeeping (cleanliness), professional service (service friendliness), value for money (relative prices for standards), and standard of food (food quality). These with other attributes translate into the perceptions of overall quality that were also considered a key element. As illustrated earlier, these attributes can be divided into tangibles and intangibles, but of these it appears that the most critical attributes are often the intangibles.

The case study also considered a range of possible actions that might lead to increased customer satisfaction across a range of attributes by using feedback from both customers and employees. The particular recommended actions identified in this study are closely related to the principles of 'total quality management' (TQM).

Maintaining quality through total quality management

According to Oakland (1989), total quality management is 'an approach to improving the effectiveness and flexibility of businesses as a whole. It is essentially a way of organizing and involving the whole organization: every department, every activity, every single person at every level.'

TQM assumes that the whole organization is committed to delivering quality not just to the obvious external customers, but also to the less obvious internal customers. The production or service delivery system is seen as a series of links in a quality chain with each employee acting as a supplier to the next employee until the product or service is finally delivered to the customer. All departments, all processes, all systems, and all individuals in the organization need to be involved in the quality effort. Any single element of the chain that is not involved will cause quality problems that will eventually affect the final customer. This chain also extends backwards to the organization's suppliers, and a lot of attention must be given to assuring the quality of initial inputs.

The process of product or service delivery at the customer–supplier interface is the core of total quality management. Finding ways of improving the quality of this process at each stage in the organization offers a way of improving the overall quality of the product or service finally delivered to the external customer. For these improvements to be made, the organization must provide a commitment to quality at all levels of the organization, starting at the very top. It must improve communications, both lateral and vertical, throughout the organization. It must provide a culture where quality matters, and where errors and defects are not tolerated.

Moreover, these 'soft' measures alone are not sufficient. The organization must also introduce some 'hard' procedures and systems to support the quality endeavour. A good quality system, perhaps based on ISO 9000 or BS 5750, must be developed. The organization needs a network of quality teams, such as quality councils, quality circles, or corrective action teams, to drive the quality improvement effort. Finally, the organization needs the right tools for measuring and monitoring the standards achieved.

Developing an approach

Dotchin and Oakland (1991) suggest six key elements of the total quality management approach:

- Recognizing customers and discovering their needs.
- Setting standards that are consistent with those requirements.
- Controlling the production and service processes and improving their capability.
- Establishing systems for quality.
- Management taking responsibility for setting quality policy, providing motivation through leadership, and equipping people to achieve quality.
- Empowering people at all levels in the organization to act for quality improvement.

The simple description above hides the complexity of introducing these ideas and systems into an existing organization. There are not, as yet, any proven guidelines for the steps that need to be taken to introduce TQM into an organization. It seems that each organization needs to take an incremental approach, moving at a pace and direction that best suits its existing culture and management style. The case study that follows shows how one hospitality organization has started down this path and illustrates the practical implementation of the concepts introduced above.

Total quality management at Scott's Hotels Limited (CHIC)

This section charts how a major hotel company embarked on a quality program, identifies its successes and failures, and gives some practical advice on where to begin. It also explains the problems and solutions to be found along the route of continuous improvement. The company discussed here is Scott's Hotels Limited. This company started life in Canada as CHIC, Commonwealth Holiday Inns of Canada Ltd, back in the late 1950s. It opened its first Holiday Inn in the UK in 1970. In the late 1970s the company's assets were acquired by Scott's Hospitality, Inc., a Canadian-based company with a billion dollar turnover. Today its United Kingdom umbrella organization is called Scott's Hospitality Ltd, which, apart from a hotel division, has interests in food retailing and related companies.

As early as 1984 the executive group determined that the issues that would set the company apart from the competition were to be service and quality. At that time Sir Colin Marshall was attempting the turnaround of British Airways, his example having been preceded by Jan Carlsson at SAS.

Having entered the hotel scene in 1970 with a new product far superior to the competition, Scott's Hotels' competitive advantage was clearly in the product. Throughout the 1980s, however, the hotel industry underwent dramatic change. Not only did ownership of just about every hotel group change, but major reinvestment took place to bring hotels generally up to a more acceptable level, for the ever more discerning and knowledgeable business and leisure traveler.

So in 1985, with the franchisor who also operates hotels in the UK, the company embarked on a joint retraining program for all staff with the prime aim of getting people more involved in running the business, more aware of customer needs, and more able to react to those needs. The ultimate aim was to provide a superior service. The vehicle used was called a 'service chain', an adaptation of the quality circle.

It was not much more than 24 months later that the cracks appeared. The program was called 'Together We Care', but the company realized that, whereas together they might have cared, individually nobody gave a damn! It was a well-designed program. Although it was full of slogans, hype and exhortations, it was backed by training and other video-based learning. But what had been designed was in reality no more than a customer care program.

Today, with the benefit of hindsight and experience, it is possible to stand up and admit that mistakes were made. But then most companies do make mistakes. Recently, at the annual Perkins Awards one of the finalists made its presentation by way of a road map. Road signs indicated the milestones the company had reached, the dead ends and wrong turns indicated errors, and the junctions represented decisions needing to be made. The presenter said, 'If you look back from here all the way to the start you can see a pretty smooth surface. However, it is not until you closely examine the last few miles that you see the uneven surface, the pot-holes that resemble the mistakes one makes in this continuous journey.' The ability to learn from mistakes and to acknowledge at the outset that there is no clear formula for success is obviously important. What there is, is no more than a list of ingredients and a recipe, but the cake will be different in shape, size, taste, and content every time. In dealing with people's hearts, minds, emotions, and feelings, it is not possible to be sure what may be around the next corner. It is this conceptual thinking that most data-rational people have problems in coming to terms with.

At about the time when the cracks started to appear in the 'Together We Care' program, Jan Hubrecht, the Managing Director, went 'back to school'. During two years of part-time studies, he was able to crystallize many of his thoughts and experiences, which was an essential part of the relaunch of total quality management in the company in 1989.

The company decided to stick with 'Together We Care' as the sign-off line. The most compelling reason was simply that they were quite willing to stand up in front of their staff and admit that they had got it wrong the first time. But they did not want people saying things like 'Whatever will they dream up next time' or 'It's only flavor of the month – if we don't get involved, we won't be wasting any of our time.'

It is important to make the distinction between customer care and total quality. As an example, picture an apple the way it used to look in Apple Marketing Board advertisements – highly polished and shining, presented with a little leaf and sprayed with a fine mist of water – highly appealing. This is only the outside. This is customer care. Now if we cut it open and look inside at the core and the pips, can we be sure that these seeds will produce future strains of quality apples, or do they need recultivating? Total quality would mean having absolute confidence in the continued consistent quality of our apple.

Introducing TQM into an organization is not easy, however. Consider a heart transplant. When a heart is transplanted, complications sometimes arise. When they do, it is often the existing organs in the body that reject the new heart. So for a heart transplant to work well, the patient needs to have a healthy body. Similarly, with TQM the organization needs to be healthy. The Scott's Hotels' health checklist is described over the next few pages.

A new formula: top management commitment

Where the company had gone wrong last time was a clear case of 'Do as I say, not as I do'. The evidence was, as always, that actions speak louder than words. For years, the company had practiced knowing what was best for the customer. Hoteliers must be among the most arrogant people in the world. For almost two thousand years they have been practitioners of 'knowing what's best for the customer'. Scott's Hotels were no different, for when the customer comment cards indicated that their customers could not sleep because of noise, or mentioned the absence of tea and coffee facilities in the bedrooms, the hotel discounted their views. So not only was there a lack of action, but there was also a more deep-rooted problem of not wanting to listen.

Commitment is vital, but so too are consistency and involvement. The slightest waiver or perceived disbelief from top management will send operating people running back to the levels of control comfort with which they are so familiar. Indeed, people will, for a while at least, just sit on the sidelines observing the behavior of others to determine whether or not this is for real. After all, why should they jump in, get involved, and spend energy, if top management does not? So if the message is quality and yet management continues to measure the things that it used to measure, like food cost or labor cost percent, you might as well forget it. These and similar control measures should not be dropped totally, but the manager lives by the rules that are laid down. What gets measured gets done!

Then, of course, there is the willingness to stand up and be counted, to spend hours spreading the gospel. The message is clear, top management commitment is a vital ingredient to change, and quality programs driven by non-line functions are doomed to failure. Additionally, a quality drive must be based on a hard-headed strategy or cracks will rapidly emerge. The setting, monitoring, and adjustment of quality goals, which are top management's primary tasks, are in Scott's Hotels' case carried out by a Total Quality Steering Group that the Managing Director chairs, and which publishes the Annual Quality Plan.

The business focus

This is the second ingredient. What are the products or services we produce or sell, and who is our customer? With those simple decisions made, at least it is possible to design products and services with the target audience in mind and to determine the core competencies that in the long term will determine the selection and training focus. Indeed, one might decide that this focus changes somewhat from hotel to hotel. Although the focus in Scott's Hotels' case is the business traveler, the dependency on, for example, conferences, the corporate sector, or the long-stay guest must be an influencing factor in the design of products or services.

Research

Two years before the relaunch, Scott's Hotels started to research and they have not stopped since. The art of listening is slowly being developed and now takes place at director level as well as at hotel management level with 'focus groups'. Postal and telephone questionnaires are additional techniques now being used by the hotel management, and these involve members of staff. In addition, Scott's Hotels use professional market research companies to complete the picture.

The aim is to deliver what the customer actually wants, as opposed to trying to sell what is produced. Although, at times, the removal of well-hardened ear wax has resulted in minor surgery, it does highlight repeatedly how hard it is to change from a product- to a market-led focus. Having meetings with customers, not to sell but to listen, is slowly becoming a routine that is practiced at every level in the organization.

New products and services are now introduced with greater knowledge of customer requirements, and unlimited service guarantees are often attached. For example, in the company's restaurants and in room service there is a promise to deliver within a set time frame, or 'it's on the house'. These unconditional service guarantees tell both the staff and the customers that the commitment to quality is serious. There is also a concentration on rectifying key issues that were, or are, a source of annoyance to clients, and an endeavor to link quality to suppliers, thus increasing the ability to deliver 'right, first time every time'.

Internal research is equally vital. It is critical to understand what and how the 'troops' feel. A professionally produced and executed employee research program will give important clues as to the chances of the quality plan succeeding, especially where hygiene factors are concerned. Additionally, it gives the organization a good picture of how staff view management and their own efforts in the search for excellence. In Scott's Hotels, senior management repeat this exercise every 18–24 months.

Standards

The standards-setting process can then begin, with the aim of at least matching, and hopefully exceeding customers' expectations. This is easier said than done! Amenity creep and personal standards, interpretations, and demands may all undermine the objectivity with which standards setting must be achieved. The recent story of a well-known international airline serves as a useful reminder. Someone in the organization had decided that all call buttons should be responded to within such a short time frame that it caused a major rethink in staffing. Not only could the target not be met, but after some research it was found that the standard was of no consequence to the customer and had also interfered with the delivery of other important service requirements.

Scott's Hotels' standards, although never perfect, were reintroduced, and all employees in the organization were retrained over a period of twelve months and 'signed off' by their general manager.

Compliance

Successful quality programs are those where people are responsible for checking their own performance, and this principle formed the basis of the plan. Admittedly, it was backed up by management checks and occasionally mystery guest checks. Registration for BSI 5750/ISO 9000 is part of the formal process. Checking one's own performance, however, is not the only element in the process. If it is understood that the program is about striving for continuous improvement, then it is equally important to set targets. So each hotel and each department within each hotel agrees achievement targets with its employees every quarter.

Self-checking was first tested in one of the company's housekeeping departments some five years ago. They successfully moved away from the system where a supervisor checked some 60 rooms per day to the situation where each chambermaid/guest room assistant checks his or her work and is empowered either to hand a room direct to reception for letting or to put the room 'out of order'. What management found was that rooms were returned with no loss of standards, and that morale and job satisfaction improved significantly. It is not until you start debating the issues with your staff, in a culture where people do not feel threatened about giving and receiving feedback, that you realize how pathetic and daft the old system was.

'You've got to remember that I am married, have two children, both of whom go to school. We own a house, have a mortgage, we take our holidays abroad ... and you don't trust me to clean a bedroom!' This was the feedback received at one such interview. To build up a trust with staff, where they know that their mistakes will be treated with understanding and guidance, is as important as getting managers and supervisors to know and practice a different management style.

Reward and recognition

There is nothing more motivating than to be part of a winning team and whereas the first 'Together We Care' program concentrated on material reward – with a huge supply of gifts for staff – the concentration is now on the non-financial and non-material methods of recognizing and rewarding people. There are hundreds of ways of doing this, and when it is done sincerely and genuinely, when it is based on guest feedback and improvement, it has greater impact and is better received than material reward.

Nevertheless, in order to complement the non-material program of recognition, the company is now working on a new system of financial reward. This has become possible because of the progress made with quality concepts, which has begun to improve flexibility and profitability. The principle is that people are rewarded for additional skills and for their flexibility in working in more than one department.

The group also changed the criteria for employees of the quarter or year, hotel and departmental managers of the year, and performance bonuses to reflect achievements in quality. The reporting system has also changed dramatically, and whether general managers produce monthly, quarterly, or annual reports, quality measures are reported consistently and improvement targets are agreed and measured by each unit. 'Zero defects' does have a role in the service sector and has forced hotel managers to address the huge waste factor in the industry.

Employee participation

Training and education processes and employee involvement are areas where an investment of a six-figure sum per annum is made by the company. The specific training programs embarked on include: quality awareness roadshows, quality circles and associated techniques training, quality circle facilitator workshops, attendances at national conferences, and lastly training directed specifically at departmental managers and supervisors. The spread of units and sites across the country has a large impact on both costs and logistics. In addition, the company has produced a six-module quality awareness training program of some twelve hours' duration which every new employee is to undergo during the first thirteen weeks of employment.

To summarize, there is general awareness training for all employees, specific circle techniques training for all circle volunteers, and most importantly training directed at managers with the aim of helping them understand how to manage differently, or to begin the process of organizing, not supervising. This latter middle management group must not be ignored, as rightly or wrongly they often feel left out of the process. Although the reduction in layers of supervisors and managers goes hand in hand with employee participation, managers are essential to effect change.

However, managers and supervisors do feel threatened. This is really quite simple to understand and there is a need to deal with the questions that get asked consistently: 'how is this going to affect me?', 'how do I have to do things differently?', 'how is it going to be measured?', and most importantly, 'how is it going to be rewarded?' To manage this process, the company has devised a $2\frac{1}{2}$-day training program aimed specifically at this group, which is followed up by one-day training sessions for more junior supervisors. As part of the training an informal dinner is held, attended by the Managing Director, which is meant to 'loosen up participants' so that they feel less inhibited to ask questions. After the training the aim is to have the management group see quality as a joint effort. Training must be a non-stop process. As Tom Peters explains, 'You train and you train and you train, and then you start all over again.'

The educational process is then enhanced by a series of communication strategies. Apart from the company newspapers, one of which is totally dedicated to quality, quarterly staff meetings are run where all staff get together. 'Head of department' meetings are also being changed to 'quality improvement team' meetings – the principle being that each departmental manager, and all of them as a team, directs, manages, and monitors the quality drive in each business unit and ensures that the seven key quality measures cascade down into each department. The Managing Director's involvement, 'to talk quality' at quarterly staff meetings, is a critical part of the whole process. The favored method is to get employees to prepare questions in advance, which are then written on flip chart paper and posted around the room to be dealt with in an informal style.

Employee involvement is a key element in Scott's Hotels' total quality approach, and to date the company has some 400 employees who spend an hour a week in company time to solve problems. Each group meets in a dedicated quality circle room that, in high pressure business times, may be requisitioned by the General Manager for letting to clients. Circles are supported by a permanent circle facilitator, again a volunteer, who as a rule is a more senior member of the operational team. A commitment of up to 75 percent of facilitators' time is not uncommon. Facilitators provide moral and training support and are the communications link between the circles and hotel management. The facilitators' ability to influence and ensure that circles choose appropriate projects, meaning ones that are within their control, is critical. The support structure is completed by the quality circle support team, made up of senior members of the management team. These groups meet monthly to hear progress reports from the circles via the facilitator and act to support the circles. Their other task is to receive and approve the circles' recommendations.

It is not uncommon for circles to take up to nine months or even a year to establish themselves, during which time they are taught all the necessary skills and techniques. Progress to date has been excellent. Circles have resolved problems large and small with the most amazing solutions. At the outset a combination of things, like the ability to improve efficiency or guest services, was used to justify the expenditure. Today the belief is that, even if circles do not meet these criteria, factors like recognition, self-esteem, and personal growth make working with circles extremely worthwhile.

With involvement comes empowerment, and after lengthy debate with unit management it was agreed not to restrict or limit staff in how much they could do to rectify a problem. The objective in this respect is to empower, indeed oblige, staff to do anything to ensure that customers will return to the hotel and not buy empty bedrooms in the hotel down the road. One of the many measures used is the level of complaints that are received by head office. These are down in number for the second successive year: a 24 percent fall in year 1, and a further 12 percent drop in year 2. The Managing Director believes that this is because people are more caring and more attentive and because they recognize that a customer will stay with you either until his death or until someone seriously upsets him, whichever comes the sooner.

Shaping expectations

The final ingredient is shaping customer expectations. Whether one is or is not the 'World's Favourite Airline' is really immaterial. The timing of such a message is critical, and it is imperative that the quality infrastructure is in place and that progress is being made. There are many horror stories of PR exercises that have backfired on unsuspecting companies. For Scott's Hotels, it is still too early to embark on a major public relations/awareness strategy.

Yet the company is getting known for its TQM approach. Its sales people do spread the gospel and get very encouraging feedback from clients. One of the things Scott's Hotels did early on in the project was to publish the 'obsession with quality' formula. Although it was aimed at the company's own staff, management made the decision to put one of the posters in each hotel's front lobby, and the requests for copies keep coming in. This is a very rewarding and strong signal to hotel people that quality is something customers demand.

TQM planning: the process of continuous improvement

The previous section outlined the thrust of how Scott's Hotels reorganized for quality and gave some idea of the company's actions and progress. This section outlines some of the future plans.

Total quality management has three broad angles. 'Total' means that everybody is involved, everyone has a role to play. By 'quality' is meant simply delighting the customer. 'Management' means organizing, not supervising.

The objectives are simple; the process of continuous improvement has three aims: people retention (i.e. company employees); attracting and retaining customers; and profit improvement. The activities aimed at employees fall under the four headings of: empowerment; recognition and reward; training; and communication. The company will be working on how to communicate its seven performance measures effectively to all staff both verbally and pictorially, and how to make everybody understand how their individual contributions make up the whole.

As far as training is concerned, the concentration will be on assertiveness skills. 'Telling in an asking sort of way' is how the company refers to the process of explaining to your boss that maybe your idea is better. The greatest benefit that people in quality circles received from their training involved the learning of problem-solving techniques; this has been added to the list for the years ahead. With creativity comes risk taking, and part of the necessary cultural change is to run courses that help people to use their creative talents and to start taking acceptable risks. Non-vocational training opportunities complete the picture. There is little doubt that everyone works more and more in a team-driven environment. The other courses that the company will be running should help people understand what makes teams successful, what the individual characteristics of team members are, and how to recognize and use those individual talents.

Empowerment has really shown that there is a huge reservoir of untapped potential in all employees. QATs and QITs (quality action teams and quality improvement teams) will complement quality circles so that more and more people get involved in both the prevention and cure aspects of problem solving. This will lead to greater and greater involvement, with everybody correcting guest issues and making sure that guests will return.

For Scott's Hotels, delighting the customer comes from honing employees' listening skills and having a plan to rectify guest issues that cannot be solved on the spot. The same principle applies to solving staff problems, and introducing new products and services is not a matter reserved solely for guests, but also extends to staff. TQM planning means that relationships will improve at all levels in the organization.

Management issues involve leading by example, making the tools of the job available, and removing obstacles. It is too often forgotten that work should be *fun*! Quality improvement is also a learning process. Whereas consultants can and often are an invaluable source of information and references, for the hard work and talking there really is no substitute for running the quality program 'in house'.

A fascinating issue is how people react. There is always a large group of people to whom it makes great sense – give them the education, the guidance, and the tools, and they will get on with it. The doubters, however, require a great deal more time. What one has to do is to take the time to listen and provide answers to the many legitimate questions they have, but once this group is convinced they will turn out to be the most loyal allies. In this constant world of change, it requires time and effort to deal with that section of the workforce, the managers and supervisors, who have most to fear and who have to change their management styles most dramatically.

Summary

The recession of the early 1990s hit the hotel industry hard, following close on the upset of war and the threat of terrorism brought by the Gulf crisis. However, Scott's Hotels' resolve and commitment to quality did not falter.

When the recession did come and the business travel market collapsed in January 1991, there were enough people 'on board' to ride out the storm. The company made four pledges. These were: not to make people redundant, to increase the effort and investment in sales, not to postpone any refurbishment or reduce capital allocations, and lastly to continue the efforts to improve quality.

The recession has indeed provided a chance for management to demonstrate that it is very serious about quality. It has also provided an opportunity to demonstrate that quality is not about cutting costs, but about managing waste. A target saving of £350,000 for the year was set; after six months, the quality improvement team had saved in excess of £400,000. Prior to the involvement with total quality management, the company did just like everyone else and simply cut costs indiscriminately. The QIT has scored some impressive results and both staff and customers are pleased with the outcome so far. The shareholders, who must not be forgotten, are delighted that the company has built such a springboard for adding value.

The way forward

The challenge to improve the quality of hospitality products and services faces all organizations in the industry. The case studies discussed in this chapter show that it is possible to identify the key customer expectations that form the basis of a quality service design and that implementing total quality management offers the opportunity to improve the quality of conformity to those customer expectations.

Every organization needs to assess its own capability for delivering quality and the stage it has reached in developing a quality strategy. Teboul (1991) has identified three stages in the development of a quality strategy: the corrective and defensive strategy, the assurance strategy, and the offensive strategy. At the corrective and defensive stage, quality is seen as a problem that requires control to filter out poor performance before it reaches the customer. Quality remains as a defensive weapon. If we stop doing things wrong, then our customers will not complain as much! At the assurance stage, quality is seen as a broader issue and attempts are made to help everyone in the organization deliver good service that conforms to the customers' expectations. At the final stage, quality becomes an offensive strategy. The organization can rely on the commitment of every employee and the reliability of every process to such an extent that it uses quality as a differentiating factor to build competitive advantage.

There would seem to be, as yet, very few hospitality organizations that are approaching the final stage. The rewards for those companies that reach this stage first must be enormous.

References

Atkinson, A. (1988) 'Answering the eternal question: what does the customer want?', *Cornell Hotel and Restaurant Administration Quarterly*, vol. 9, no. 2, pp. 12–14.

BS 4778 (1987) *Quality Vocabulary: Part 1 International Terms, Part 2 National Terms (ISO 8402, 1986)*, London: British Standards Institution.

Buzzell, R. D., and Gale, B. T. (1987) *The PIMS Principles: Linking strategy to performance*, New York: The Free Press.

Carlzon, J. (1987) *Moments of Truth*, Cambridge, Mass.: Ballinger.

Crosby, P. (1979) *Quality is Free*, New York: McGraw-Hill.

Dotchin, J. A., and Oakland, J. S. (1991) 'Theories and concepts in total quality management (TQM)', *Proceedings of the 2nd European Quality Conference for Education, Training and Research*, European Foundation for Quality Management, Oxford, 18–19 April.

Foxall, G. (1984) 'Marketing is service marketing', *Service Industries Journal*, vol. 4, no. 3, pp. 1–6.

Grönroos, C. (1984) 'A service quality model and its marketing implications', *European Journal of Marketing*, vol. 18, no. 4, pp. 36–44.

Grönroos, C. (1990) *Service Management and Marketing*, Lexington, Mass.: Lexington Books.

Gummesson, E. (1990) 'Marketing organization in service businesses: the role of the part-time marketer', in Teare, R., Moutinho, L., and Morgan, N. (eds) *Managing and Marketing Services in the 1990s*, London: Cassell.

Gummesson, E. (1991) 'Truths and myths in service quality', *International Journal of Service Industry Management*, vol. 2, no. 3, pp. 7–16.

Gummesson, E. (1992) *Quality Management in Service Organizations*, New York: SQA.

Hollins, G., and Hollins, B. (1991) *Total Design: Managing the design process in the service sector*, London: Pitman.

Institute of Sales and Marketing Management (1986) *Hotel Survey*, London: ISMM.

Jones, P. (1988) 'Quality, capacity and productivity in service firms', *International Journal of Hospitality Management*, vol. 7, no. 2, pp. 104–12.

Jones, P., and Lockwood, A. J. (1989) *The Management of Hotel Operations*, London: Cassell.

Juran, J. M. (1974) *The Quality Control Handbook*, 3rd edn, New York: McGraw-Hill.

Kelly, G. (1955) *The Psychology of Personal Constructs*, New York: Norton.

Knutson, B. J. (1988) 'Hotel services and room amenities in the economy, mid-price and luxury segments: what do travelers expect?', *Hospitality Education and Research Journal*, vol. 12, no. 2, pp. 259–64.

Lehtinen, U., and Lehtinen, J. R. (1985) 'Service quality: a study of quality dimensions', *Second World Marketing Congress Proceedings*, vol. 1, University of Stirling, 28–31 August.

Lewis, B. R. (1989) 'Quality in the service sector: a review', *International Journal of Bank Marketing*, vol. 7, no. 5, pp. 4–12.

Middleton, V. T. C. (1983) 'Product marketing: goods and services compared', *Quarterly Review of Marketing*, vol. 8, no. 4, pp. 1–10.

Nightingale, M. (1986) 'Defining quality for a quality assurance programme', in *The Management Hospitality II*, Connecticut: AVI.

Oakland, J. S. (1989) *Total Quality Management*, Oxford: Heinemann.

Oberoi, V., and Hales, C. P. (1990) 'Assessing the quality of conference service product: towards an empirically based model', *Service Industries Journal*, vol. 10, no. 4, pp. 700–21.

Parasuraman, A., Zeithaml, V. A., and Berry, L. L. (1985) 'A conceptual model of service quality and its implications for future research', *Journal of Marketing*, vol. 49, no. 1, pp. 41–50.

Reichold, F. F., and Sasser, E. W. (1990) 'Zero defections: quality comes to services', *Harvard Business Review*, vol. 68, no. 5, pp. 105–11.

Shams, H., and Hales, C. P. (1989) 'Once more on goods and services: a way out of the conceptual jungle', *Quarterly Review of Marketing*, vol. 14, no. 3, pp. 1–5.

Shostack, L. G. (1981) 'How to design a service', in Donelly, J. H., and George, W. R. (eds) *The Marketing of Services*, Chicago, Ill.: American Marketing Association.

Shostack, L. G. (1987) 'Service positioning through structural change', *Journal of Marketing*, vol. 51, no. 1, pp. 27–43.

Teboul, J. (1991) *Managing Quality Dynamics*, Hemel Hempstead: Prentice Hall.

Wilensky, L., and Buttle, F. (1988) 'A multivariate analysis of hotel benefit bundles and choice trade-offs', *International Journal of Hospitality Management*, vol. 7, no. 1, pp. 29–41.

19

Developing a responsive global network of Hyatt hotels and resorts

Bernd Chorengel
with Richard Teare

Set in the context of predicted two billion global business- and tourism-related travel movements by the year 2000, this chapter aims to highlight Hyatt International Corporation's entrepreneurial approach to development and to examine some of the organizational implications of developing a global network of hotels and resorts which is responsive to regional needs and opportunities.

Expanding the global network of Hyatt hotels and resorts

With deregulation of airfares post-1992 and the lowering of trade barriers in Europe, Hyatt predicts that the 1990s will see a dramatic increase in business travel within Europe. In response to this trend, Hyatt is developing a network of hotels in major cities throughout Europe and its other regional organizations in Asia-Pacific and the Americas. Initially targeting those which have intercontinental airports, the company's five-year development plan for the region focuses on the major cities across the whole of Europe, thereby expanding on the existing base of hotels in six European countries.

In mid-1991, there were 159 Hyatt hotels and resorts around the world. Hyatt International Corporation and its subsidiaries operate 37 hotels and 16 resorts in 27 countries, and Hyatt Hotels Corporation, a sister company, operates 89 hotels and 17 resorts in the United States, Canada and the Caribbean. Hyatt's business objectives are reviewed internally every year in relation to the long-term goal, which is to attain Hyatt representation in every intercontinental city. The most recent internal survey identified 150 intercontinental destinations worldwide which are suitable for a Hyatt development. This represents the potential, and the number of intercontinental destinations is growing, so that by the year 2000 there are likely to be a further 20 destinations with the potential to sustain a Hyatt property.

Hyatt hotels and resorts are deluxe properties, renowned for their dramatic architectural atrium lobby designs featured at Hyatt Regency and Grand locations. Hyatt also operates the smaller 'European-style' Park Hyatt hotels, which are mainly situated in international business destinations. Although the three hotel categories represent differences in size and design, they offer the same deluxe standards of comfort and service.

This approach contrasts with a growing number of the company's competitors who are proliferating hotel brands for the economy, mid-priced, and deluxe sectors of the lodging market. Hyatt defends its position by concentrating on what the organization is best placed to deliver. This is reflected in Hyatt's experienced and highly professional inventory of managers, many of whom have spent most or all of their career with Hyatt. Consequently, the organizational culture is well defined and would conflict with any decision to introduce hotel brands designed for a different sector of the market.

Hyatt currently has 17 hotels and resorts under construction and around 25 new development projects in preparation. The program of expansion is set to continue throughout the 1990s, with Hyatt adopting the roles of co-developer and hotel and resort manager. In newer markets, such as Eastern Europe, the pace of development is often dictated by the local political climate. In most cases, Hyatt initiates the development process by investing in the real estate in partnership with a joint venture company. After developing the property, Hyatt may 'trade on' the real estate, retain the hotel management contract, and use the profits generated from the real-estate transaction to invest in the next development project. In order to illustrate this approach, two examples are provided of recent development projects in Eastern and Western Europe respectively:

- In Eastern Europe, Hyatt Regency Belgrade was the first project in Yugoslavia to have a foreign company as a majority shareholder. Five Yugoslavian state-owned companies hold a 49 percent stake in the joint venture with the remaining 51 percent held by the First National Bank of Chicago and HIC. The hotel was also the country's first project to use a debt/equity swap arrangement as part of its financing. This followed a dramatic change in Yugoslavian legislation relating to joint venture regulation in order to encourage foreign investment as part of the process of rebuilding the country's economic infrastructure.
- In Western Europe, Hyatt Regency Birmingham is a good example of Hyatt's European development activity. Construction of the £34 million hotel was orchestrated by a joint venture partnership comprising HIC, Birmingham City Council, and Trafalgar House Building and Civil Engineering Holdings Ltd. The project was supported by a £6 million Urban Development Grant, the largest grant ever approved by the UK Government's Department of the Environment for a project of this kind.

By using joint venture and management contract arrangements of this kind, Hyatt plans to double its present portfolio by the end of the decade.

Changing travel patterns are also affecting demand for luxury resort hotels. Prosperity in the Pacific Rim has lead to an upswing in tourism, especially in Korea, Taiwan, and Japan. In Thailand, tourism generates more revenue than any other industry, and Indonesia's tourism revenues have tripled over the past few years. Increasing numbers of visitors are going to Malaysia and the South Pacific islands, and in Australia and New Zealand (visited by more than 300,000 Japanese alone in 1988) tourism is the leading producer of foreign currency.

Hyatt's resort business is currently growing at a rate of 10 to 15 percent a year, and growth is expected to continue as the resort developments provide facilities designed to satisfy leisure, business, and conference travelers. New Hyatt resorts currently cost an average of US$ 200,000–400,000 per room to build, about 50 percent more than a typical city center hotel. In part, this is because Hyatt tailors its resorts to the local location rather than imposing a standard format regardless of local needs. This involves incorporating natural landscaping, local architectural elements, and native stonework into the structure. A good example of this philosophy is the Grand Hyatt Bali, which opened in April 1991. Conceived as a Balinese 'water village', the resort is constructed on a series of islands surrounding an existing ancient temple. The resort's restaurants specialize in Indonesian and Asian cuisine and a central pavilion features traditional handicrafts and Balinese dancing.

Planned or entrepreneurial development?

Although formalized strategic planning offers certain advantages, it can also promote a centralized bureaucratic approach, stifling initiatives from the regional organization which is best placed to respond to local market opportunities which arise. Hyatt therefore favors a more entrepreneurial style of development which draws heavily on one-year business plans produced at hotel or unit level. This exercise involves unit managers from all departments in a comprehensive examination of local and regional market trading conditions. The exercise is also designed to integrate with a review of operational factors ranging from 'quality' issues such as refurbishment needs to an appraisal of performance targets, both in terms of occupancy levels and financial results on a month-by-month basis for the year ahead.

In producing their plan, unit managers are also required to make assumptions about what is likely to happen in the general business environment and what may happen in the near future. From a corporate perspective, the aim is to identify and assess all of the opportunities which are likely to occur within each region as quickly as possible, and, to a large extent, the unit-level plans facilitate this. Corporate staff at head office in Chicago then look at the plans and the assumptions that have been made on a regional basis in order to see how politics and economics have been interpreted. In Southeast Asia, for instance, the stability and vitality of business in Malaysia, Singapore, and

Thailand are closely interlinked, so regional assessments are essential. Ultimately, the Chief Executive's role is to go through the assumptions and predictions noting scenarios which need to be monitored carefully, particularly if it is felt that the impact of uncontrollable factors may be critical. By reviewing the prospects for the year ahead from a global perspective and before unit business plans are fully developed, it is possible to provide the regions and individual units with a strategic overview of key global trends and developments in the Americas, Europe, and Asia-Pacific. This provides a macro perspective from which regional and unit managers can draw as they prepare their detailed action plans.

The whole approach to data gathering, evaluation, and planning is therefore entrepreneurial, involving the regional organizations as much as possible so that managers throughout the global network are encouraged to identify and respond to opportunities via a streamlined planning process, with the center providing coordination and control support. As planning responsibility is shared throughout the global organization, changes in local market conditions can be identified rapidly. When, for example, the complex process of change began to gain momentum in Eastern Europe, details of development opportunities began to emerge instinctively from all parts of the global organization. The information came from managers at all levels in the organization who were either witnessing change or gathering market information from talking to business travelers and others with experiential knowledge of what was actually happening. The sensitivity, involvement, and sense of collective responsibility which characterizes Hyatt's entrepreneurial approach to the market thereby provides a rich and well-informed source of data for planning purposes, enabling the center to identify and prioritize development possibilities and potential.

Networking corporate and regional organizations

A secondary but nonetheless important factor which facilitates effective relations between the corporate and regional organizations is the high degree of stability which exists within the organization as a whole. The four most senior executives of Hyatt have service records ranging from fourteen to twenty-one years, and there are many other managers who have been with Hyatt for ten years or more. This produces a stabilizing influence on the culture of the company, because many of the general managers were food and beverage or other line managers when the present senior executive team were managing hotels. Consequently, the views and personalities of senior managers throughout the company are familiar, which is an advantage during detailed planning discussions as the managers know and understand how others will be thinking and feeling. This in turn encourages more junior managers to exchange views and to communicate new ideas more freely. To encourage the generation of new ideas, it is essential to have regionally based planning, and Hyatt's decentralized approach supports this rather than frustrating it. In fact, Hyatt has consciously tried to maintain a very informal structure and way of handling information and ideas, by emphasizing personal communication and the two-way flow of ideas. This fosters a sense of commitment through accessibility so that the relationships between Hyatt's corporate and regional organizations might accurately be described as an extended family arrangement.

Although lines of communication are generally relaxed and informal, it is necessary to work at maintaining mutually supportive networks within the overall organization. To maintain a sense of vitality and unity of purpose, managers are encouraged to ask questions whenever they meet guests or other business representatives, or travel. In this way the organization is exposed to different kinds of thinking and varied opinions from which it can learn. The process of interaction can be stimulated in a variety of different ways. For example, all of the general managers are invited to attend conferences at approximately eighteen-month intervals. The conference is a low-key event with varied sporting and social activities, enabling the business agenda to be conducted in an informal and interesting way, and enabling managers to interact in a relaxed atmosphere. The company puts people together, guides them, and pairs weak and strong individuals during discussion sessions. The objective of all of this is that people learn from each other. Wherever possible the company tries to broaden the agenda to stimulate wider discussion of important business issues. If the general manager can set the tone by talking economics, understand what the customer wants and the market needs, and then communicate these things to line managers, it is an important and significant achievement.

The current degree of responsiveness within the organization as a whole is also related to a deliberate attempt to shift the emphasis from the center to the regions. At one time Hyatt was a highly centralized organization, with twenty vice-president positions in the Chicago office. Today, Hyatt has five vice-presidents and a much stronger regional focus. However, as Hyatt expands and the world changes, the current structure of the organization may need to change. In order to remain responsive it is vital to observe, to talk to people, to look at the company's strengths and weaknesses and, if necessary, to be prepared to change any part of the company that might prevent Hyatt from staying close to its customers.

Maintaining service quality

Given Hyatt's market positioning, it is of fundamental importance that the organizational network is responsive to customer requirements. The company is very aware that guest needs and expectations are becoming more sophisticated all the time, and so to stay ahead it has to appraise continually the range of services and technology that it provides. In practice this means developing a worldwide customer orientation, as the only alternative would be to commission consumer research on a global basis. Hyatt's aim is to develop a service culture which closely mirrors certain Hyatt standards and customer expectations, but at the same time draws on aspects of local culture so that the service is as natural and authentic as possible. In this way it promotes localization and preserves the charm of individual customs and traditions. They should be reflected in every Hyatt hotel so that the guest is aware of the unique features of the host country.

To achieve this Hyatt deliberately seeks to avoid replicating design and service concepts in a standardized way by ensuring that all of its services and amenities assume national characteristics. In Japan, for example, it provides Japanese slippers for the guests to use in their bedroom, and there are variations in the layout of the bathroom to reflect a Japanese style. This helps to ensure that Hyatt guests find interesting variations in amenities and services and that Hyatt is recognized in Japan and in every other country in which it operates as a company that uses a familiar cultural framework as the basis for planning and providing a high-quality product. The company's ability to sustain this approach to customization is helped by the multinational composition of the Hyatt management team. For example at the corporate office in Chicago senior staff represent eight different nationalities from Europe, Asia-Pacific, and the Americas. A similar degree of diversity can be found throughout the organization, both in specialist support functions and within the individual hotel operations.

Hyatt managers are constantly exposed to a variety of cultural perspectives in discussions spanning a wide range of issues. Consequently, new policies and procedures are tested against multinational views to identify the possible implications arising from implementation in different places. As a result, hotel staff around the world can relate more easily to the instructions which are given. The danger is that if policy documents are written by an American living in New York, or by an Englishman living in London, then the author may communicate what he thinks is right from a relatively narrow perspective. However, to a Balinese person it may make no sense at all, because the instruction does not fit into the relevant culture and way of life. Therefore, the instructions which come out of Chicago are based on what the company would like to achieve. As the corporate staff number around 40 people, which in comparison with other multinational hotel firms is a relatively small team, it is possible to devise policy which is flexible enough to fit with different cultures. Hyatt then requires each hotel to interpret the objectives in an appropriate style which is sympathetic to customs, traditions, and values.

The general manager of each hotel is expected to ensure that Hyatt policies on quality standards are fully implemented, as the company prefers not to use quality-audit specialists. This is because most of its general managers are very experienced Hyatt personnel and the company trusts their business sense. They understand the key quality points and if any of them are not consistently achieved, the situation is soon revealed. Information is transferred quickly because the decentralized approach prevents management organization and reporting structures from becoming too bureaucratic. This has enabled the company to develop a responsive organization that reacts quickly to customer and employee needs and priorities. In this sense, Hyatt policies and procedures encourage individualism and flair in planning, implementing, and controlling guest services. By investing in managers who are encouraged to interpret quality standards in a cultural context, the company is also investing in a commitment to quality in Hyatt hotels around the world.

Global networking implications for the future

Throughout the 1990s it will be necessary for Hyatt as for other multi-national hospitality companies to examine continuously the organizational implications of the changes taking place in Europe and elsewhere. The company currently has a strong presence in Asia-Pacific and is confident that Japan will continue to prosper. China is changing quite rapidly, despite recent setbacks, and the outcome of internal change will become clearer during the next three to five years. Latin America has to change rapidly, and this will be facilitated by the USA because America's economy is declining. We are likely to see the forging of some very large and powerful trading relationships consisting of the USA and Latin America, Japan and China, and Europe. To create a stronger relationship with Latin America, the USA may need to waive debt repayments and see that the Brazilian, Chilian, and Argentinian economies grow. By the end of this decade, at most ten to fifteen years from now, Europe will be dealing with the Americas and a similar kind of trading alliance in Asia. Europe's locomotive will be Germany, perhaps with the UK; in Asia it will be Japan and Korea, and Australia will need to ensure that it has an established role within the Asian trading alliance; the USA will be driving the North/South American trading alliance.

If these three large and powerful trading blocs do develop, they will dominate global business transactions. As a result of this, it is possible to foresee much greater cross-cultural exposure of personnel taking place – Asians working in Europe and vice versa at hotel management level. Consequently, the more that Hyatt managers interact by cross-exposure to different geographical operating environments the better, because they will become more knowledgeable managers and it will benefit the company in the long run.

Endword

Expectations of the future given events in the past

Michael Olsen

Introduction

The hospitality industry has emerged as a major global industry in the last decade. Travel, lodging, and foodservice sectors combined are being increasingly referred to in all forms of literature as one of the world's largest industries in terms of employment and aggregated gross domestic product. With this new role on the world's business stage has come a new hospitality organization. One that is leaner, more decentralized and poised for the future.

As can be seen by a review of the contributions to this text, the future holds considerable challenges and excitement for the hospitality executive of tomorrow. It is our purpose here to try to synthesize these thoughts in order to identify potential patterns of change likely to influence the industry over the next decade. In the following sections some of these patterns will be highlighted in order to draw attention to their possible impact upon hospitality firms.

Changing industry structure

It is clear that the first pattern of change is in the structure of the industry. It is no longer an industry that is dominated by independent owners and operators. Large multinational chains continue to grow and expand to all parts of the globe and they continue to threaten the independent operator. Expansion is often the result of strategic alliances which bring together many elements of the travel chain. These alliances are also based upon technological advantages such as computerized reservation systems. The alliances have served the industry well in bringing together all those organizations which provide travel services to the public.

The buyers of travel services have contributed to this restructuring by consolidating purchasing power in order to bring about more control to the purchase transaction. For example, corporate travel managers are beginning to take more control over the travel purchase decision by using fewer travel intermediaries such as travel agents. By using fewer members of the travel distribution network they are able to use purchasing power to extract better prices from airlines, car rental agencies and lodging firms.

This reduction in the number of intermediaries used has forced many small firms out of business and resulted in the growth of large firms with regional, national and international marketing power. Because they have control over larger volumes of business this gives them more influence over how the industries' overall inventory of airline seats, hotel rooms, etc. are utilized.

These major structural changes will demand approaches to the management of hospitality firms that will require management to balance the traditional need to maintain high standards of operation with the increasingly more important ability to analyze the events which are occurring in their business environments. The expectation for all levels of management will be to enhance their perception of the environment and to expand their thinking to a higher plane. This will allow them to observe the potential short-term and long-term threats and opportunities that could have some impact upon the firm.

Investment capital influences organization expectations

In the late 1970s and throughout the 1980s, the hospitality industry, in particular the lodging sector, became an attractive investment for both primary and secondary sources of capital. The allure resulted from the attractive real-estate markets worldwide which encouraged banks and other sources of capital to loan funds for developments in the industry. Institutional investors, such as pension funds and insurance companies, also jumped into the equity offerings of hospitality firms.

This motivation to invest was driven by inflationary forces which benefitted the balance sheets of international firms holding real estate in the industry. This brought a new set of expectations for financial performance. Hotels were no longer looked at as just places for travelers to stay and in the process generate profits. They became assets that required high returns in order to satisfy the investment community. Managers had to become as concerned about shareholders' feelings as they were about customers' feelings.

This pattern of change shaped the strategic alliances that developed rapidly in the late 1980s. Global market penetration and market share became important objectives. Consolidation became crucial as firms needed new partners to help finance and market a worldwide presence. This resulted in the need for fresh thinking about how to manage hotels. Return on assets became just as important as percentage return on profit. Every square foot of a hotel was carefully scrutinized to be sure that it had the potential to generate the maximum amount of revenue. This way of doing business is now the industry norm and will continue to shape the way the hospitality firm is managed in the years to come.

This approach does not come without its problems. The pressure for growth resulted in over capacity (particularly in North America), brand and product proliferation and declining occupancies. This occurred at the same time that there was a global level of inflation that brought the cost of building a new hotel room to new heights. The inability to maintain growth and the increasing pressure from the capital market community forced hospitality firms to sell off assets and in return take back management contracts to manage these assets. Firms shifted from being asset holders to being asset managers.

In general, most publicly traded hotel companies have followed this trend. Only those firms that have considerable internal resources of their own can think about asset acquisition. Similarly, those firms that are not publicly traded and thus have no need to respond to the earnings and growth demands of the shareholder can think about investing in hotels. For those who have the funds to invest, the 1990s have so far been ideal times since many hotels have gone into foreclosure and are being purchased at amounts of 40 to 60 percent below the original costs. This is serving to further consolidate the industry and shape the way business is done.

Technology

Now that consolidation is occurring the major challenge facing the multi-national hospitality firm is utilizing its capacity to the fullest. Seats and beds must be filled and to accomplish this firms must invest heavily in technology. Technology in this case refers to the way rooms, meals, etc. are reserved and sold around the world. While it is still unclear how many 'global reservation' systems exist, or are evolving, and to what extent they will represent the total industry capacity, they will have significant impact on where customers stay and how they will get there. What will determine that impact will be how rapidly both the customer and the hospitality firm can adapt to and apply changing technology in this field. It is without a doubt that this evolution in technology will continue to shape the forces that drive customers, competitors and suppliers.

Technology is not only being used to build and sustain demand for sales. It is also being used to increase security in hotels and transportation systems, to improve decision making and to instantly connect managers and corporate headquarters no matter where they are in the world. Since communication about customers, performance and environmental events is essential in a firm operating globally, this form of technology will do much to improve the management of multinational hospitality organizations.

One way of reducing the cost of technology development, but still remaining competitive, has been through the use of strategic alliances. The latter portion of the 1980s saw an almost feverish pitch of activity in this area. Those firms that pursued alliances in order to obtain assistance or an advantage in technology appear to be satisfied with their efforts but those that did so later in time or for other, less clear reasons may not be quite so pleased. The reason for this displeasure may be the result of their decision to enter an alliance that was available out of a fear that they would be left out of some new world order of hospitality firms if they did not. Many of these types of alliances did not offer any technological gain. These firms are at a clear disadvantage and will continue in this way until they either develop their own technological advancements or join late (if they can) one of the already established alliances.

Pricing

As firms continue to consolidate and enhance global marketing efforts, and the buyer continues to concentrate purchasing power, and technology facilitates this process, price becomes a key issue. More broadly, the price structure of the entire industry is affected. This in turn will shape the types of product available to the traveling public.

Evidence of this new pattern of pricing can be found in several events currently observed within the industry. First, sophisticated management decision support methods, such as yield management software programs, are helping managers to price and utilize available capacity properly. Secondly, the mix of new development in the lodging sector has been in favor of low-price or limited-service hotel properties. This has put pressure on all levels of the industry to lower prices to compete. While this is not yet a universal pattern around the globe, it is one that is occurring and will continue to spread. The aforementioned consolidation of buying power is the third event which is serving to change pricing structure. This too has been a force for pushing prices lower and it is not likely to subside in the near future.

Increasing activity in the political environment

Government intervention in business is not new. There are many ways that the political environment can impact upon business. Laws affecting development, repatriation of profits, regulations regarding employment mix of nationals versus foreign labor, requirements for purchasing supplies from local firms and taxes, are just a few examples of the direct way the political environment of nations can impact on the investment in firms and how they are managed. As firms continue to grow it will be important for them to pay more attention to the local, national, and international political environments if they expect to survive in the long run.

One example of the influence of the political environment is the increasing public awareness of issues reflecting concern over the health of the environment. The fact that many developers throughout the world have ignored the possible damage to the environment caused by the development of hospitality projects has left the public and their governments angry. These concerns have resulted in public policy directives which are impacting on the hospitality industry. Thus, hospitality firms must face new constraints on development that have the potential of negatively impacting on the environment. Waste water and solid waste are two major areas of concern that the industry is required to address in order to become a responsible member of any community. It can be expected that there will be many more examples of this type of government influence upon the industry in the future.

Firms are downsizing and decentralizing

The competitive environment of the past several years is now affecting the design of multinational hospitality firms. Whereas the model of organizational design prior to this time was a rather centralized structure with several layers of management between the unit level manager and the chief executive officer, the current model reflects the removal of these layers of middle management. The traditional organization chart has become flatter. Unit managers are now expected to be expert operators as well as accomplished strategic managers.

This downsizing has removed a great deal of the headquarters' support that unit managers in the field at one time relied upon to assist them with marketing, finance and human resources management. The unit manager is now expected to develop skills that extend beyond operations management and into these other functional areas of management. This has changed the profile of the qualification and responsibilities of the unit manager and will continue to do so as events in the business environment become even more competitive and decentralization continues.

Because of these new demands upon managers at all levels of the organization, multinational firms have been turning to professionally trained top level managers to run these businesses. It is felt that this type of manager better understands the complexities of doing business in a dynamic international environment. Thus, increasingly the heads of international hospitality firms have come from other industries and have utilized basic financial and marketing concepts to put the firms on course for the future.

Strategic directions

Multinational hospitality firms appear to be developing two types of generic strategies as they face these patterns of change in the environment. The first is a focus strategy which implies that they are developing only one main core brand. The second is the multi-brand or multi-concept approach. While neither strategy can be found in its purest form, it is likely that these will be the two major directions firms are headed in the near future.

Firms following the focus approach are trying to concentrate on one product and create a unique concept that will give a desired market niche. Meridian, the Paris-based luxury hotel chain, suggests that they are doing things the 'French Way' and Swissotel, the international hotel chain and unit of Swissair, suggests that they are providing a Swiss experience. McDonald's continues to grow internationally with its famous golden arches. Firms such as these are betting their future on their marketable attributes.

Multi-brand firms stress the continued development of new products. Accor, the French hospitality conglomerate, is an excellent example of a firm following this strategy. They now have over five hotel brands which have allowed them to dominate the French lodging market with estimates suggesting that they control as much as 15 percent of the total room night market. No estimates have been provided regarding their foodservice market share. In these cases, while this has proved to be a successful strategy until now, it is too premature to tell if they will run into the problems experienced by the old Holiday Corporation and Marriott. While they were successful in developing many new concepts, it appeared that each new brand that entered the marketplace contributed to the shortening life cycle of their other brands. The result of this type of approach is that eventually the core brand can get old and has to be discarded. Holiday Corporation experienced this problem and managed to deal with it successfully by selling the Holiday Inn brand to Bass PLC, who must now revitalize an aging product. With the world's supply of tired hotel rooms increasing, this multi-brand strategy could prove to backfire on firms pursuing this approach.

The alternative to developing new brands is to participate in strategic alliances which offer complementary brands. The recent contract by Forte with the American quick-service Italian theme restaurant chain called Sbarro is such an example. This type of alliance allows firms to add brands to their portfolios without the high risk and cost associated with new-product development. It can be expected that this type of activity will continue to be part of most multi-based, multinational firms.

Summary

What is clear is that change is certain in the hospitality industry over the next decade. Strategic alliances by customers, suppliers and competitors will continue to affect the way multinational hospitality firms are managed. An industry this large will continue to be noticed by governments and affected by the political forces directed at business. Competition will become more intense and be based upon strategic marketing programs that will increasingly have to rely upon a price/value relationship. This will all have to be accomplished by management that is more versatile, professionally trained and able to think strategically in a more hostile environment.

Index